USING PROJECTIVE METHODS WITH CHILDREN

Using Projective Methods with Children is an enhanced synthesis of Steve Tuber's previously published research on the study of projective methods to assess the representations of self and others, as well as the actual interpersonal experiences children internalize in the form of these representations. Integrating conceptual and empirical work, with an emphasis on the Rorschach Inkblot Method (RIM), the book offers unique, evidence-based information on the importance of assessing particular aspects of a child's inner self. The studies cover a broad range of topics such as dreams, anxiety disorders, political oppression, homelessness, and multiculturalism, and each is supplemented with an analytical introduction. A section that discusses future areas of research is also included.

Steve Tuber, PhD, is the author or editor of six critically acclaimed books and more than one hundred papers on the intertwining of assessment and treatment in children, adolescents, and adults. He is a professor of psychology, program head, and director of training at the doctoral program in clinical psychology at the City College of New York, CUNY.

USING PROJECTIVE METHODS WITH CHILDREN

The Selected Works of Steve Tuber

Steve Tuber

NEW YORK AND LONDON

First published 2018
by Routledge
711 Third Avenue, New York, NY 10017

and by Routledge
2 Park Square, Milton Park, Abingdon, Oxon, OX14 4RN

Routledge is an imprint of the Taylor & Francis Group, an informa business

© 2018 Steven Tuber

The right of Steven Tuber to be identified as the author of this work has been asserted by him in accordance with sections 77 and 78 of the Copyright, Designs and Patents Act 1988.

All rights reserved. No part of this book may be reprinted or reproduced or utilised in any form or by any electronic, mechanical, or other means, now known or hereafter invented, including photocopying and recording, or in any information storage or retrieval system, without permission in writing from the publishers.

Trademark notice: Product or corporate names may be trademarks or registered trademarks, and are used only for identification and explanation without intent to infringe.

Library of Congress Cataloging-in-Publication Data
A catalog record for this book has been requested

ISBN: 978-0-815-37181-6 (hbk)
ISBN: 978-0-815-37182-3 (pbk)
ISBN: 978-1-351-21678-4 (ebk)

Typeset in Bembo
by Out of House Publishing

CONTENTS

Acknowledgments	*x*
Introduction	*xi*
About This Book	*xii*

SECTION ONE
The Conceptual Links Between an Object Relational Approach to Normal and Pathological Development and Projective Methods   **1**

1   A Conceptual Framework for Projective Assessment:
The Domains of Negative and Positive Object Relations   3

Paper used: Tuber, S. (2012). A conceptual framework for projective assessment: The domains of negative and positive object relations. In *Understanding Personality Through Projective Testing* (pp. 7–28). New York: Jason Aronson

SECTION TWO
The Projective Tasks Used in This Book   **25**

2   Measures Employed to Assess Object Representations: The
MOA Scale   27

Paper used: Tuber, S. (1992). Empirical and clinical assessments of children's object relations and object representations. *Journal of Personality Assessment*, 58, 179–197

vi Contents

3   Using the MOA Scale With a Nonclinical Population   32
    Paper used: Tuber, S. (1989). Children's Rorschach
    object representations: Findings for a nonclinical sample.
    *Psychological Assessment: Journal of Consulting and Clinical
    Psychology*, 1, 146–149

4   Using the MOA Scale With a Slightly Older Population   38
    Paper used: Blatt, S., Tuber, S., & Auerbach, J. (1990).
    Representation of interpersonal interactions on the Rorschach
    and level of psychopathology. *Journal of Personality Assessment*, 54,
    711–728

5   The Object Representation Scale for Dreams (Krohn)   52
    Paper used: Gluckman, E., & Tuber, S. (1996). Object
    representations, interpersonal behavior and their relation to
    the dream reports of latency-aged girls. *Bulletin of the Menninger
    Clinic*, 60, 102–118

6   The Animal Preference Test   66
    Paper used: Rojas, E., & Tuber, S. (1991). The Animal Preference
    Test and its relationship to behavioral problems in young
    children. *Journal of Personality Assessment*, 57, 141–148

SECTION THREE
**Assessing the Object Relations of Varying Child
Populations**   **73**

7   The Object Relations of Children With ADHD   75
    Paper used: Meehan, K., Reynoso, J., Ueng-McHale, J., Harris,
    B., Wolfson, V., Gomes, H., & Tuber, S. (2009). Self-regulation
    and internal resources in school-aged children with ADHD.
    Bulletin of the Menninger Clinic, 72(4), 237–261

8   Assessing Narcissistic Pathology in Children Using the RIM   89
    Paper used: Weise, K., & Tuber, S. (2004). The self and
    object representations of narcissistically disturbed children:
    An empirical investigation. *Psychoanalytic Psychology*,
    21, 244–258

Contents **vii**

9 Assessing the Object Relational World of Preschoolers With
Imaginary Companions 104

Paper used: Meyer, J., & Tuber, S. (1989). Intrapsychic and
behavioral correlates to the phenomenon of imaginary
companions in young children. *Psychoanalytic Psychology*,
6, 151–168

10 Assessing the Object Relations of Boys With Separation
Anxiety Disorder 117

Paper used: Goddard, R., & Tuber, S. (1989). Boyhood separation
anxiety disorder: Thought disorder and object relations
psychopathology as manifested in Rorschach imagery. *Journal
of Personality Assessment*, 53, 239–252

SECTION FOUR
Assessing Object Relations With Child Populations
Under Extreme Duress 127

11 Using the MOA Scale With a Child Inpatient Population 129

Primary paper: Tuber, S. (1983). Children's Rorschach scores as
predictors of later adjustment. *Journal of Consulting and Clinical
Psychology*, 51, 379–385

12 Rorschach Assessments of Homeless Children 138

Primary paper: Donahue, P., & Tuber, S. (1993). Rorschach
adaptive fantasy images and coping in children under severe
environmental stress. *Journal of Personality Assessment*, 60,
421–434

13 Another Study of Homeless Children 149

Paper used: Donahue, P., & Tuber, S. (1995). The impact of
homelessness on children's levels of aspiration. *Bulletin of the
Menninger Clinic*, 59, 249–255

14 Rorschach Assessments of Children About to
Undergo Surgery 155

Paper used: Tuber, S., Frank, M., & Santostefano, S. (1989).
Children's anticipation of impending surgery: Shifts in
object-representational paradigms. *Bulletin of the Menninger
Clinic*, 53, 501–511

viii Contents

15 Children's MOA Responses Under Extreme Political
Oppression 161

Primary paper. Munczek, D., & Tuber, S. (1998). Political
repression and its psychological effects on Honduran children.
Social Science & Medicine, 47, 1699–1713

SECTION FIVE
Using Projective Methods in N of 1 Case Studies 173

16 Using the Children's Apperception Task as an Idiographic
Indicator of Treatment Themes Over Time 175

Primary paper. Tuber, S. (2004). Projective testing as a heuristic
"snapshot" of themes in child and adult psychoanalysis:
The Case of Lisa. *Journal of Infant, Child and Adolescent
Psychotherapy*, 3, 486–508

17 Using the Rorschach as a Predictor of Change 193

Primary paper. Tuber, S. (2000). Projective testing as a post
hoc predictor of change in psychoanalysis: The case of Jim.
In *Psychoanalytic Study of Lives Over Time*. Eds. J. Cohen &
B. Cohler. New York: Academic Press, 283–308

18 Two Case Studies of Children With ADHD 211

Paper used: Tuber, S., Harris, B., Meehan, K., Reynoso, J., &
Ueng-McHale, J. (2006). Rorschach configurations of children
with ADHD. In *The Clinical Assessment of Children and
Adolescents: A Practitioner's Guide*. Eds. S. Smith & L. Handler.
New Jersey: Erlbaum, 451–468

19 Briefer Vignettes Linking MOA Scale Scores to
Child Treatment 223

Primary paper. Tuber, S. (1989). Assessment of children's object
representations with the Rorschach. *Bulletin of the Menninger
Clinic*, 53, 432–441

Contents **ix**

SECTION SIX
More Recent Research, Including Future Possibilities   **233**

20   Ongoing Research Linking the Rorschach Task With
     Clinical Work With Children   235

References   *241*
Index   *261*

ACKNOWLEDGMENTS

I am deeply grateful to the colleagues over these many years that co-authored the papers used in this volume. For each and every one of the papers, I enjoyed our camaraderie and scholarly interaction and you have all made my professional life richer and fuller. Thus thanks go to: Sid Blatt, John Auerbach, Evelyn Baez Rojas, Elaine Gluckman, Kevin Meehan, Joseph Reynoso, Ben Harris, Jasmine Ueng-McHale, Karen Weise, Jodie Meyer, Rodger Goddard, Paul Donahue, Sebastiano Santostefano and Debra Munczek.

I also so appreciate the editorial efforts of Nina Guttapalle at Routledge Press and the now decade-long support of an editor at Routledge, Anna Moore. Finally, I have a deep debt of gratitude to Karen Tocatly for her many levels of help in preparing and editing this manuscript.

INTRODUCTION

For nearly 40 years, my academic interests have revolved around a single theme: how are our internalized representations of ourselves and others affected by who we are, where we are from and what we do? This interest no doubt is linked, in part, to my own very personal needs and wishes. But it is also a function of the training I received in psychodynamic theory in the mid 1970s while at the University of Michigan's clinical psychology program. Trained by such great clinical scholars as Marty Mayman and Irene Fast, I couldn't help but thrive on the clarity with which they integrated the thinking of David Rapaport and Jean Piaget into a holistic and heuristic theory of personality. This clear depiction that our earliest relationships and interactions create templates through which we can begin to make micro- and macro-level predictions about how others will perform and about what we need to say and do to optimize our standing with others and with ourselves was both vital and inspiring. Graduate school also engendered a love and investment in the study of projective techniques, most notably the Rorschach Inkblot Method (RIM). Thus a link between a methodology (the use of projective methods to assess the representations of self and others) and an arena of personality (the actual interpersonal experiences we internalize in the form of these representations) was forged that has remained alive and well in my professional life to the present day. While many theorists have made wonderful contributions to the clinical literature (Rapaport, Schafer, Lerner, Blatt among many others) on the use of projective testing, and many more empiricists have used projective methods in their research (Exner, Weiner, Meyer, etc.), relatively few have linked psychodynamic theorizing with an ongoing attempt to empirically validate these theories. The present work collects many of my efforts in this regard, bridging the conceptual and the empirical in a way that I hope will be useful to you.

ABOUT THIS BOOK

The book will be divided into six sections. In Section One, a conceptual depiction of normal and pathological child development will be provided, as presented previously in my first book on psychological testing (2012). Section Two will outline the methodologies employed in the various empirical studies described in the remainder of the book. Section Three will focus on clinical syndromes I have studied using these methods, including separation anxiety disorder (with Goddard); narcissistic pathology (with Weise); the use of imaginary companions (with Meyer); and Attention Deficit Disorder (with Meehan et al.). Section Four will describe a series of studies in which exceptional environmental phenomena imposed specific difficulties on the subjects undergoing an assessment using projective methods. This section will include works on impending surgery; inpatient hospitalization; the impact of homelessness on projective method performance; and political oppression and its sequelae in children. Section Five will describe a series of works that used N of 1 case histories as their primary means of linking projective methods with individual psychopathology. Section Six will discuss future areas of research using the methods I will describe, including descriptions of several projects currently under way.

SECTION ONE

The Conceptual Links Between an Object Relational Approach to Normal and Pathological Development and Projective Methods

1

A CONCEPTUAL FRAMEWORK FOR PROJECTIVE ASSESSMENT

The Domains of Negative and Positive Object Relations

Paper used: Tuber, S. (2012). A conceptual framework for projective assessment: The domains of negative and positive object relations. In *Understanding Personality Through Projective Testing* (pp. 7–28). New York: Jason Aronson.

Prelude: A Story

As I did in my book on the clinical foundations of psychological testing, I'd like to begin by telling you a story. It's a story about a five-year-old girl I assessed many years ago without any projective tests used at all. The two interviews I had with this girl, I'll call her Patty, and a single interview with her mom, forever changed my thinking about personality development, psychopathology and assessment and in that sense are directly related to how and why this book came about.

My first job as a newly minted Ph.D. was at a community mental health center in New England. One of my duties was to do liaison work with the county's foster care agency, providing assessments and consultations as needed.

One day I was asked to do an assessment of a five-year-old girl because her mother was about to be discharged from an inpatient facility. This intermittently chronically, severely and sometimes psychotically depressed woman was a single mom and the foster care agency had concerns as to whether the child was robust enough to be able to go back and live with her. I was told that the woman clearly was very attached to the girl but had had multiple hospitalizations and hence multiple separations from her daughter throughout the girl's life. I was also told that this little girl was born with a significant neurological/developmental delay affecting her myelin sheaths. These sheaths were not fully functional, so that most of her skin was quite raw to the touch. It was as if her skin housed a collection of live wires without insulation, so that touching this girl, even in a gentle caress, would be experienced as a violent pummeling.

4 Conceptual Links

I was 27 years old then, and, as Bob Dylan once put it, "I was so much older then, I'm younger than that now." In that spirit of linear cockiness I immediately thought: "Oh, she has a severely depressed mother, this is a dyad with multiple separations, and she herself is a neurologically delayed child, so this has to be a massively troubled child." Patty comes to see me, and she's an adorable-looking, blonde-haired, blue-eyed little person. She's appropriately shy when I greet her. She makes eye contact regularly and comes into the room with me faithfully and easily. She warms up appropriately, and slowly and easily allows herself to begin to play with the toys at the table. Her play is robust and alive and complex and coherent and interesting. She has a meaningful range of affect and as she warms up to me, we're definitely playing together, indeed we're having a great time. She leaves at the end of the session with a strong "Good-bye, Dr. T."

As she walks down the hall with her foster mother, I stand and watch her leave, stunned. How could she be this sane, this healthy, given what I know of her background? It made no sense. She "must" be another one of those kids who has made a kind of precocious false attachment. "I'm sure it's that," I soothingly tell myself, but I'll see her a second time, "just to make sure."

So she comes in a second time and sure enough she's every bit as lovely as she was before. She can get frustrated at points in her play when things don't fit exactly right and she doesn't feel fake in any way. She's even become a little attached to me. It's the second time she's seen me and she wonders if we are going to meet "more times," as she really likes the toys I have. She's just completely a delight and I'm now completely baffled. I have no clue.

So I resort to what people always do when they're completely baffled, which is that they grab another theory. And the theory I grabbed was, well, her foster parents must have somehow made up for all the other difficulties in her life. She had indeed returned to the same foster parents each time her mother had to be hospitalized and they were terrific people from what I was told. So that certainly played a part in it.

But I was still confused. Having such viable foster parents just didn't feel like it was enough to me, because most of the first two years of Patty's life were with this mom who was not doing very well. The mother had had a significant postpartum depression, but hung in there with the baby for the first 11 months of life, and then shortly thereafter began her series of separations, but they grew in duration only late in her third year. My knowledge of the primacy of the first years of life couldn't account for Patty's significant mental health. So I called up the head of the foster care service and I said: "I don't know what's going on. I don't get it. She seems much healthier than I would have ever imagined and I'm delighted, but I don't understand it. Would it be okay if I met the mother?"

As it happened, Patty's mother was to be discharged the next day, so I called her up and made an appointment. Ms. X walked in and this woman in her mid 20s looked like a caricature of what a severely depressed person looks like. Her face looked 25 years older than she was. It was lined. She had a gray pallor to her. Her shoulders were stooped over. She kind of slumped when she walked. She seemed lethargic. And it wasn't just that she was over-medicated, she was not. She seemed deadened, really just hanging on by a thread. It was very poignant and moving just to have her walk in the room.

A Conceptual Framework for Assessment   5

She sat down tentatively and I said to her, "You know I've met your daughter and she's really terrific. I would like to ask you some questions just to get a better sense of what it's like being a mom to Patty and what your experience was raising her." As soon as I asked what was it like being a mom to Patty she started to cry and talked about how profoundly guilt-ridden she was that she was never the mother that she really wanted to be, and how she had tried so hard all these years to hang in there and to be there for her, but at times she just got overwhelmed by her experience, to the point where she had to go away. She knew when she became that depressed that it was better for her daughter to be in foster care, but she was just so upset about that, and felt like she had failed at the most important job there is in life. I said, "Would you mind telling me something about what it was like to have her as a baby?" She became especially tearful at that and said, "Oh I remember that as vividly as if it happened yesterday." "Well what was it like? Can you give me an idea?"

"Well, you know, I feel really bad about that because I was so sad after Patty was born. I loved the fact that I had a baby. I wanted this baby, but I didn't have anyone. I'm really an outsider in my family. I was really on my own, and I was just so beat and so exhausted all the time that I really could not do much." "Well what did you do? What was it actually like to be with Patty?" She said, "There's really one thing that I do well." "What's that?" I asked. And she said, "I actually have a really nice singing voice." "So tell me about you and Patty." She replied, "I would lay on the couch and I had one of those things that you can put a baby in and they can be propped up at an angle, and I put her in that seat really, really close to me so she was like this close, about 8 inches or so from my face, and I would sing to her all day."

Now you, the reader, should know that I tell this story to begin my semester of teaching about testing each year, and every time I tell this story, every time, it makes me well up with tears. In part I grow tearful because I'm reminded of how when I heard Patty's mom tell me of her singing to her daughter, tears began coming down both my cheeks and hers. But really I grow emotional because at that very moment I knew that I had had the first true "light bulb" moment of my professional life. It became suddenly clear to me, and my guess is it's already clear to you, that given this child's significant neurological delay, she had received exactly the type of parenting early on that was ideally suited to her. If she had had the kind of parent who had tried to hold and physically caress her, as almost every other parent would have done, Patty's experience of the first six months of her life would have been excruciatingly painful, with all the emotional sequelae such physical pain would likely have caused. But instead she received an experience of caretaking that was conveyed in the exact modality that she most needed; a modality that didn't involve touch, that involved a most loving, vivid connection through voice and eye contact. This child's actual experience, therefore, the phenomenology of her infancy, was in fact that of having a mother who was, in Winnicott's (1960) apt phrasing, surely "good enough."

That suddenly explained things to me in a way that I've never forgotten. It taught me so profoundly that it is the child's "actual experience," to use Escalona's (1968) phrase, that has predictive value. Even truly and potentially toxic variables as neurological impairments or severe maternal depression have a specific meaning that is expressed differently when in interaction with each and every person. It is our mandate to make our best attempt to get at

6 Conceptual Links

our patient's actual experience, the phenomenology of their lives as they experienced it, if we are going to be able to be of use to them.

This eye-opening clinical experience with Patty occurred in the context of my finishing my work on my dissertation, a dissertation that used an object relations perspective with the Rorschach (from now on I will be using the acronym RIM for Rorschach Inkblot Method, following Weiner (1994)) to assess whether object relations paradigms in young children could have some value in predicting their long-term outcome. As will be discussed later on in this volume, the positive correlations found between these object relational assessments and later psychiatric outcome were marked and more robust than a large number of other potential predictors. The "perfect storm" of an eye-opening clinical experience with Patty and a confirming empirical experience with my dissertation subjects provided the impetus for me to begin studying and writing about the heuristic power of object representations in understanding personality. This volume is a compendium of this "storm" of interplay between the clinical and the empirical.

I must present a strong caveat to begin this book. I am not a major researcher. Although the empirical works below were all published in refereed journals, my sample sizes were very small, there was rarely a clinical control group and thus the findings presented are illustrative and hopefully generative but they are not definitive in any rigorous psychometric sense. I have no pretense about that. I do think the empirical findings I will present shed light on the conceptualizations at the heart of psychodynamically informed theorizing and that they thus have a useful place in the recent push to provide a basis in empirical evidence for psychodynamic hypotheses about the nature of personality and the clinical modalities that may be of help to our patients.

As I also stated in my first book on testing, from a purely psychometric view, I can sympathize with those researchers who cast a doubtful eye on projective methods. I, too, am not sure that they're tests. The RIM, for example, is really not a great "psychometrically proper" test. It doesn't have the kind of validity that certain psychometricians would demand of it, even though I think a reasonably objective person reviewing the literature would agree that in certain important contexts, it has meaningful construct validity. But the RIM is not the Minnesota MultiPhasic Inventory (MMPI) in this regard. Nor is it an IQ test that's been standardized for degree of difficulty in the ways you can't standardize a projective measure. As Weiner (1994) has written, the RIM is not a test. It, like the Thematic Apperception Test (TAT), Animal Preference and Sentence Completion tasks, is a method. They are all tools that I believe give us a vibrant other means of assessing phenomenology. Just as importantly, the ability to get at a person's actual, visceral experience is also a window into the meanings they attach to their behaviors, ideas and affects. If we are capturing salient parts of their experience from their point of view (from the inside) we can derive a more veridical sense of the meanings they attach to who they are and what they do. If we then link this quest for meaning to the fundamental assumption that a person's behaviors/thoughts/feelings, no matter how maladaptive or bizarre or self-defeating they might appear to others, are their best attempt at adaptation, we derive an approach to assessment that links symptomatology to a patient's best attempts at meaning-making. This in turn enhances the chances that we will assess our patients with a humble balance between full respect for their attempts at

A Conceptual Framework for Assessment **7**

adaptation and yet a focused appreciation for the ways in which these attempts have gone awry. The empirical studies described in subsequent chapters have always tried to keep this "inside" focus as much as possible.

As much as this book reviews and thus values empirical attempts to validate theory, it would be remarkably over-simplifying the work of any skilled "depth" clinician to view clinical work as solely a matter of capturing the full aliveness of their patient's experience from the patient's point of view. The exclusive focus on capturing phenomenology is limiting the clinician solely to his or her intuitive capacities, their clinical "feel" for their patients. This intuition is a necessary but hardly sufficient condition for a deep understanding of our patients. It must be imbued with a conceptual framework that places idiographic meaning in a developmental/dynamic context, a theory of personality, if you will, that links individual experience to the wider contexts of human adaptation. Thus before I move to methodological concerns and empirical validation, I need to provide the conceptual framework and scaffolding upon which we can place projective test data. The present chapter, taken from my previous testing book (Tuber, 2012) provides this scaffolding.

When someone comes to you seeking help, whether for a consultative interview or for a testing, the odds are overwhelmingly good that they're going to come to you with a series of symptoms. These symptoms can be "external" in their initial presentation: school is boring; my boss is demeaning; my spouse is hurtful. They can be internalizing: I'm feeling anxious or depressed, I can't sleep or eat or pay attention. As simplistic as this appears, these "complaints" are the basis of our initial mandate for our work as diagnosticians. Our mandate becomes more complex because we must link those symptoms to a complicated, whole human being. We must begin by asking ourselves if it is possible to convert the patient's symptomatology into a narrative that can eventually make sense both to us and to the patient. We begin this process by placing the symptom picture into a dynamic context. That is, we understand symptoms as maladaptive attempts to make meaning out of experience. In other words, we link symptoms to conflicts, to tensions of both a conscious and unconscious nature, that have led the patient to behave in a manner that they believe is both necessary and the most adaptive stance they can muster given the limits of their awareness of their experience. We then assess the nature of the breadth and depth of the person's symptoms: Is this a person where the symptoms run deeply, but within a very narrow vein of their being? Such a person could, for example, reveal a profound paranoid hyper-vigilance, but only in a sexual context. Symptomatology can also spread across almost every domain of personality, leaving in its wake a significant vulnerability in relatedness, thought, play and defense. Is this more pervasive vulnerability a shallow series of limitations or is the patient profoundly affected across almost each and every domain we assess? To get a true measure of how pervasive the impact of the patient's conflicts are, we must now describe those domains of personality we feel are necessary to measure. These domains serve both to articulate what we feel are the central components of personality and provide a rationale for using projective testing as an especially adept means of assessing these domains.

8 Conceptual Links

I am now going to walk us through an "organizational chart" of personality. This chart is obviously idiosyncratic in that I am only including those domains I have found of greatest heuristic value to students in their process of internalizing a theory of personality development that places their patient's symptoms in a dynamic context. It is important to stress that what I mean in this instance by "dynamic" is the multi-directionality of the forces that bring each of these domains to life. A domain such as "object relations," for example, never stands alone, but is always in an active interplay with each and every other domain of personality. (It is also why I have strived in recent years to include measures of affect and defenses in my assessments of object relations; please see Section Six for more work in this area.) This is true both in the moment that the patient first steps into your consulting room and historically for the patient throughout their life. The process of creating a viable working model of personality is thus an initial depiction of its various elements and then, often much later in our training, feeling fully comfortable with having each of these domains, and each of the various subsets within a domain, "speak" to all the other domains in an interactive matrix we then call "experience." It should be clear from the start that adhering to this notion of dynamic interaction makes personality development a remarkably complex, "messy" way of being. Thinking of personality in this dynamic way is not for the faint of heart, nor is it for those who need or desire to tie up loose ends into neat packages. Once I've gotten to know someone, whether personally or professionally, I've never had the experience of their being "neat" and packaged, and so we must have a great tolerance for the ambiguities inherent in what it is to be human, even though we face the necessary and thus daunting task of trying to clearly make sense out of their "messiness."

The organizational chart begins with the patient's particular set of symptoms at the top. Just beneath this set of symptoms would be a box labeled "conflicts" with arrows pointing in both directions from these two boxes. Placing a "conflicts" box directly linked to symptomatology is my way of stating that symptoms have meanings and a narrative created by the patient that "explains" this meaning to them. Even if this "meaning" is attributed solely to others (as in very young children), it still exists in the minds of our patients. There are also degrees of awareness involved in this meaning-making process, as both conscious and unconscious elements of meaning making are always in play. This emphasis on the inevitability of meaning and the roles of conscious and unconscious processes is what makes this organizational chart an inherently psychodynamic depiction of how personalities proceed. I do want to acknowledge here as a crucial caveat that although I am convinced of the heuristic value of such an approach to understanding and teaching personality development, I am not suggesting that it is only through the revelation of such processes that symptoms are ameliorated. This chapter is about framing personality development, but the linking of this framework to treatment approaches is both more complex and beyond the scope of this book. I have worked with many children and adults over the years where a short-term (if not

A Conceptual Framework for Assessment **9**

one session) consultation addressed symptoms without getting at their *full* meaning, yet still remain convinced that linking symptoms to conflicts/dilemmas is of great benefit to the patient in their capacity to create new meanings for their behaviors and feelings.

Directly beneath the box labeled conflicts is a box that asks the fundamental question for which projective testing is best equipped to answer. It's entitled: "how pervasive are its effects?" As interesting and valuable as the "conflicts" box may be, it essentially asks the "why?" question about a symptom. Projective testing is not nearly as useful and is inherently more speculative in this "why?" domain. While testing provides, at its best, a vibrant, three-dimensional image of where a patient is at the moment, an attempt to link the present to its historical origins is always sketchy. It is dependent almost entirely on the depth, quality and veracity of the history taking that should be part and parcel of every thorough assessment process. For our purposes, that is, for the purposes of placing the projective testing process in a conceptual context, we are less interested in the "why?" of the symptoms than we are in the "what?" and the "how?" of them. Asking how pervasive are the effects of the patient's conflicts is essentially a what/how question. It seeks to get beyond the "phenotype" of the symptom picture and to assess to what degree the conflicted experience of the patient has affected various components of their personality. The clearer we are about what and how deeply the components of personality have been affected, the better position we are in to discuss the strengths the patient brings to their difficulties as well as their limitations. When this information is then dynamically linked to the patient's history, the "what" and "how" of the present can be illuminated by the "why" of the past in a manner that brings the patient most alive to themselves and to those that wish to be of help.

At this point the organizational chart we are creating begins to most fully mimic that of a true organizational chart. Underneath the box labeled how pervasive are the effects of the conflict(s) are six boxes, which are the domains of personality I have been alluding to. Before I proceed to articulate each of the boxes and what they consist of, it is crucial to remind you again that we are thinking about these boxes in a dynamic way, meaning that every one of these boxes has a "force" of its own. Every one of these boxes contains a construct that is inherently active and shifting depending on the situation. Each domain also typically has a modal experience and a range of functioning, from most to least adaptive, depending upon the contexts in which it is evoked. Every one of these boxes, moreover, interacts with every other one, so that the "messiness" I described earlier, which I should more favorably call "complexities" of personality, is given full credence. I will discuss how each of these boxes "dances" with the others as we describe them. If a visual image is helpful to you, think of a drawing by Escher in which each of these domains or boxes is like a stairway, constantly interweaving with the others. It becomes impossible to tease apart completely where one stairway ends and another begins, but rather they intertwine in ways that create one another and enhance or diminish one another as

10 Conceptual Links

we follow them. More precisely, rather than stairways, which imply a certain static quality, think of the domains as intertwining Escher-like escalators, so that you get a more vivid sense of the aliveness and mobility of each of the domains. These escalators, moreover, may change direction up or down on a moment's notice, depending upon whether a situation causes the patient to "regress" or "progress" in the face of a difficult or easily mastered context. If the image that you're now forming in your mind seems remarkably complex and dynamic, then you're taking on a most useful mindset with which to begin to make sense both of personality and of the projective methods we will be using to assess personality. In simpler terms, I will be arguing that a battery of projective methods (in conjunction with intelligence and other measures outside the purview of this book) provides a particularly coherent and interactive way to assess each of these domains that I think is somewhat different from and independent of doing clinical interviews. It thus can provide a meaningful broadening of the way in which you come to understand personality.

Let's return to the six domains that lie at the core of the organizational chart we're creating. I begin with a domain central to psychodynamic thinking in the United States since the 1970s and in Europe since the 1940s that I split into two separate domains. The domain is entitled "object relations" and I have two boxes as a means of speaking to what Bowlby (1983) has beautifully depicted as the going towards/fear dichotomy underlying this crucial component of personality. Within the "anxiety" box, I have labeled: annihilation, stranger, separation, castration, loss of love and loss of meaning anxieties. In the "going towards" box, I've labeled: trust, the capacity to be alone, autonomy, curiosity, competence, the capacity for empathy and reflective functioning as the sequelae to relatively secure attachments. It is these two domains that have been at the very core of all my empirical efforts to be described below.

No reference to object relations development can begin without a brief discussion of its milieu, the "Holy Trinity," so to speak, of Self-Affect-Other. Experiences of self and others occur in the bath of affect: from birth, we feel hunger viscerally but soon it becomes linked to how others help assuage it and thus change our felt experience; we feel curious and make eye contact with an other who mirrors (hopefully) our interest; we feel unsettled/discomfort and soon someone comes to hold us, etc. Each and every action quickly takes on an affective valence and our near utter dependency as newborns requires an "other" to mediate these feeling states, leading to feelings about one's self as the central collection point of these affective experiences.

At first we start out with a very limited number of others: perhaps a mom, a dad, a sibling, a grandparent, a caretaker, all in all a relatively small number. Over a period of time these "others" increase, in quality and quantity. We similarly start off with a very global, undifferentiated self, that over time becomes much more sophisticated and complex and differentiated. Last, we start off with very powerful but markedly global affects, and over time those affects become much more nuanced. Each of these constructs of self, other and affect begin to become internalized over time; that is, they shift from solely external "events" to sources of memory, association and representation. Eventually these representations can be called up at will by the baby/toddler and as they develop a "past," these interpersonal/affective representations guide and shift their expectations of the present and future. We develop templates of who we are, who others are and how we feel in those interpersonal contexts. If we are very fortunate, these templates are predominantly benign or benevolent and thus remain flexible enough to accommodate to new experiences that enrich and differentiate our prior representations.

My detailing this process toward increasing differentiation of each leg of the "trinity" implies a developmental perspective as the engine fueling this differentiation process. We must go at this unfolding of personality from the beginning. So in the beginning there – as Winnicott famously stated (1960) – is no such thing as a baby; there is the unit of baby and caregiver. This unit differentiates in large part at first through the power of monotony. That is, it is the predictability and reliability of the caretaker that are the key determinants as to whether a baby can start to make sense out of the chaos of its initially undifferentiated experience.

Crucially, there are a number of resources that the baby brings to the table to foster this developmental unfolding. The first is that it can see most clearly at about eight inches, and eight inches is almost exactly the distance between the eyes of the baby and the face of the caretaker when the baby is being cradled in the feeding position. Thus, the "thing" that babies can see most clearly is whoever is feeding them. The rest of the world is experienced as if the baby was quite nearsighted. This provides a built-in focal point to what the baby takes in visually, a sort of "tunnel vision" that is marvelously present to help accentuate the baby's focus on what is most important – her eventual internalization of her caretaker.

The second vital skill a baby brings to the caregiver is his relatively advanced capacity for sucking, a skill so primed it renders the baby an "expert" within the first 48 hours of his existence. Not only is this biological adaptation crucial to his literal survival, when combined with his visual acuity in the 8–11-inch focal length, it provides the baby with a running start toward negotiating a relationship with the caretaker that, even with a first-time parent, provides some opportunities for mutual connection and competence. This connection and competence will hopefully prove to be the basis for a mutually rewarding relationship over time.

The last essential item that the baby typically brings to her caregiver is the worst cry you can imagine. A newborn's cry is different from any other being at any other time in development. It's much sharper, more piercing and thus almost intolerable. This provides a most useful negative reinforcement paradigm: caretakers will want to do almost anything to get the baby to quiet down, which in all likelihood means that they will quicken their reaction time to comfort and/or feed the baby. They will be further moved to do this caretaking predictably and reliably, creating the very monotony I described earlier as the key to enhancing the baby's

12 Conceptual Links

beginning feelings that the world can be made sensible. It is provocative to speculate about the psychological etiology of that newborn cry. Perhaps that cry is so frantic and piercing in large part because it is the cry of someone who has no reason yet to believe there's an "other" out there, who doesn't believe that this other will care, who thus has no conception that they're capable of being loved. What makes this psychogenic speculation most powerful for most new babies who are lucky enough to have "good enough" care is that by about two to three months of age that cry is gone. A three-month-old cries at a very different frequency, a very different pitch than a newborn. And why is that? Perhaps it's because they've been humanized. They've gotten enough predictable care so that they know that when they start to feel hungry or uncomfortable a familiar caretaker will come along. Indeed, one of the great miracles of human development is that by three months of age most babies are well along in the process of becoming humanized.

How do we know this? Well, we know that around this age comes perhaps the first and therefore most important initiative taken by the infant to enhance its development, namely the "social smile." Parents are nearly universal in their depiction of the great relief and enhanced connection they feel toward their child when she begins to smile in direct response to their ministrations. In layman's terms, the baby's social smile is "pay back." You talk to parents before their baby has a social smile and their dedication is strong but exhausting, the child care relentless and tinged with a certain mystery and even alienation. But once they say their baby smiled at them, their sense of purpose as a parent changes, because suddenly they feel like this "person" recognizes them and has somehow derived a distinct connection to them. This takes parenting into the mutual world of meaning making, and neither parent nor child are ever the same again.

Now think about what it's like for the poor baby who doesn't have a monotonous mother, who doesn't have a predictable, reliable caretaker. From the baby's point of view, their experience, if they could verbalize it, might be: "as much as I'm being taken care of right now and it's all good, I never know for sure that when I look away, she might not be there when I look back." Think about the terror involved if the baby turns her head and the parent is not there when she returns to look. We have a jargon term for this terrifying moment that is the first stage in the box I've labeled "negative object relations" and it's called annihilation anxiety. If the baby can't count, in this first, primal way, on you as her parent to actually be there when she comes back to you, it's as if the world has been blown up. It is as if an atomic bomb has gone off in the baby's life, because the child in the first roughly six months of life has a markedly limited capacity to make sense out of the world. It is your reliability and your consistency as a parent that creates the milieu for predictability. As the brilliant work of infant researchers such as Beebe (2005), Stern (1985) and Tronick (1989) have shown, if the mother is too intrusive or too disorganized or too depressed to stay with the baby in its emotional and behavioral shifts, at first you'll see the baby trying to do whatever it takes to recapture a rhythm with its parent that will ensure their nascent continuity: "Maybe

A Conceptual Framework for Assessment **13**

if I turn away, will that work? Well, maybe if I start to cry, will that work? Maybe if I smile, will that work?" As the child's attempts to restore connection get more and more frantic, he becomes at greater risk for internalizing the visceral sense that being fundamentally wiped out could happen at any moment. This is why the word annihilation is so appropriate at this early stage of life. There is no stable platform on which the baby can count.

Think about this very rough analogy to everyday adult life. You're driving in your car at night and you're lost. You're far away from anywhere that you know, and you have very little gas left in the tank. You're driving on a curvy road that's utterly foreign to you. Your anxiety is rising with each passing mile. And each time you go around a curve you're hoping, hoping to see a house or something familiar you can turn to for help. Your cell phone doesn't work. You're rapidly losing your sense of competence and safety. As awful as this predicament sounds, it's nowhere near the depth of panic initiated by annihilation anxiety because as an adult there is at least the possibility of an alternative plan. You as an adult have a temporal context to rally behind. You can pull off the highway and wait, knowing that with the daylight comes a better chance for a plan of action to present itself. A young baby of this age, without the monotony of reliable care, has no sense of time, no reliable past to hold on to, no sense of faith in a future. Their panic is endless, timeless and therefore annihilating.

Perhaps more than any other author, Winnicott (1945) spoke to the nature of annihilation anxiety and perhaps spoke to it most eloquently in his discussion of what he called X plus Y plus Z time. When a baby feels hungry, we can call that moment Time X. If you had a totally attuned caretaker, the moment the baby felt hunger, it would "magically," that is, immediately, get satisfied. Most of the time, however, there's a certain temporal gap between need and fulfillment. Winnicott called this gap X plus Y time, with the plus Y indicating a gap in time with which the baby can still cope. Now if the caregiver comes along in X plus Y time, she attends to the baby before he is not so unraveled. Now the extraordinary point about X plus Y time is that it teaches the infant an amazing lesson. What it teaches the child is that Mommy's not an extension of baby, there's actually the beginning of separation and difference that inexorably begins to be felt by the existence of this gap of time. Now the younger the baby, the less amount of time she can stand before she has to have the gap closed. Newborns have a very, very small gap. We again can think of the evolutionary advantages to their piercing cry: it is "nature's way" of saying that the caretaker doesn't have the time to move at their own pace, they must accommodate to the baby's harsh, piercing sense of time.

By six months the baby has much more X plus Y time available. If the caretaking has been consistent and reliable, the baby has learned that you, the caretaker, may be different from them but can, in fact, be counted upon. The baby can more or less easily be distracted for a moment or two, or held instead of fed while the food is getting prepared. The bottle that used to take *forever* to warm now merely takes a long time so that the baby survives that X plus Y time.

14 Conceptual Links

But if X plus Y time goes into plus Z time, and there's still nobody available to take care of the baby, that's when the baby starts to fall apart, because the baby doesn't have the ability to hang in there and cope on its own. This is where annihilation anxiety lives. It lives in the Z time. Time has outstripped the baby's capacity to contain its affect or regulate itself. This state of being calls to mind the "failure to thrive" babies described by Spitz in the 1940s, babies whose lack of care led to their losing their responsiveness, then their weight and ultimately to their deaths. Annihilation anxiety starves the child of the expectation of care, eventually leading to either complete dread and/or total lethargy. It is why this anxiety is so traumatizing, why infants will do almost anything to stave it off and why its existence in older children and adults can induce what we call "psychotic" behaviors to ward off this depth of aloneness, despair and pervasive angst.

Let us assume, to move our passage though this domain along, that Z time was never reached and now the baby's about 6 months old. The baby is sufficiently robust. He can look a bit like a Buddha, often "chubby" and beatific, and can be propped up or sit on his own and explore the world capably and happily in his radius of eighteen inches or so around him. And then you, the caregiver, make a "mistake." You invite over Uncle Sid. Uncle Sid is not the kind of guy who really knows babies but he thinks he does. So what do you do when you are Uncle Sid and you think you know babies but you really don't? You unthinkingly reach quickly to pick up the baby without recognizing your intrusiveness. And what does the little baby do? The baby has stranger anxiety. The baby is terrified because Uncle Sid doesn't act like their mommy or their daddy. Uncle Sid has a very different style, a very intrusive pace, and he violates the child's rudimentary sense of what is to be expected from the world. The child, who up to that point could often thrive within the predictability of the people around her, can't generalize yet to the fact that people can be quite different from those they are used to and still be benevolent. In Piagetian language, they cannot accommodate to new schema nearly as well as they can assimilate new information into old schema. If the impinging new adult is too dramatically different from their existing schema of interaction, the baby can only cope by avoidance, withdrawal or distress. It is this distress that we call stranger anxiety. To go back to my Uncle Sid example, the baby will immediately signal to her comforting caretaker that Uncle Sid has to go and only when back in her caretaker's arms would she be inclined to even look back at Uncle Sid. If Uncle Sid gets the message, he may shift his approach to a more careful pacing that the child can tolerate, and perhaps down the road, Uncle Sid may even become accommodating enough to the child that he may get to hold her after all. The stranger anxiety has abated.

But think about how different stranger anxiety is from annihilation anxiety. In annihilation anxiety there's no one to turn to, there is nowhere to go. The world has suddenly become this awful cliff you've fallen off. Winnicott (1945) talks about the experience as if you're falling forever and ever; there's no safety net. That is very different from stranger anxiety. The visceral belief that there is a home base

A Conceptual Framework for Assessment **15**

provides an entirely new level of comfort than the previous, "base-less" experience of annihilation. While an anxiety that provides no base upon which to land evokes in its adult forms a psychotic level of despair (depression) or a schizophrenic retreat into a madness that is broken from reality constraints, the adult analogue to stranger anxiety is perhaps most akin to a profoundly phobic orientation to the world. Here a safe place may exist (one's house, for example, in an agoraphobic state) but any thing or person or place outside of that comfort zone could prompt the same visceral dread, if not the same pervasiveness of scope as someone in the throes of an annihilating anxiety.

Let's move the child further along this "negative object relations" domain. The child is now a bit older, typically towards a year, maybe a year and a half, old, and now the world has fundamentally changed in its orientation, for now the child can walk. The world is now experienced vertically and at a relatively dizzying speed; the child's capacity for exploration and her immersion into a world of novelty and startle is a marked advance over a world explored horizontally (crawling) or statically (sitting). With this newfound freedom comes the potential for disruption, as novelty can quickly change to hurt (the child falls down, for example), confusion (the child feels lost in a foreign room or place) or intimidation (a barking dog or a loud, "menacing" peer arrives). The child loses his feeling that the world is at his pace and looks, sometimes quite frantically, for its secure basis to recalibrate his situation. This is separation anxiety. If the toddler's affect gets too strong and dysregulated, her coping mechanisms start to fall apart, and the child has to go back to an earlier place psychologically, a place where she is always safe even if curiosity has to take a back seat for a while. At that moment of "refueling" or "rapprochement" (Mahler, Pine, & Bergman, 1975), the caretaker's reassuring presence optimally allows the child to regain his stride, to place the ratio of curiosity to fear back in favor of exploration, and the child can then move back out into the world.

Think once again about what an advance this is from the previous level of stranger-based anxiety. The child has become not only able to tolerate the world when being held by her comforter (stranger anxiety), she has become able to create some internal representation of this holding person that can be carried around with her as she explores the world. The child's capacity for self-soothing becomes portable: she has progressed from a desktop to a laptop in terms of the mobility of her inner attachments to others. In adult parlance, the person would have the capacity for prolonged periods of work without literally needing the comforts of home or could remain in the company of strangers for reasonable periods of time without profound feelings of alienation or despair. This experience of anxiety-free competence begins tentatively, of course, and is never completely resolved over our lifetime. The toddler grows increasingly able to rely on its robust internal representations of others as comforters and hence can spend more time by itself and/or in the presence of strangers (preschool teachers for example). The world can increasingly become a laboratory for advancing cognitive growth and physical mastery and less and less a sphere where comfort, familiarity and repetition are the

16 Conceptual Links

prime currency of the realm. From another viewpoint, we can say that the toddler, with minimal separation anxiety at any given moment, can take their comforting people for granted, and with this assumption of protection and availability comes an enormous advancement in the capacity for cognitive growth, especially in symbolization and language development. Put in yet another framework, if the baby cannot take her caretaker for granted, if her attachment is insecure, then this cognitive surge is limited in scope and depth (especially in avoidant attachment, which inhibits growth, or in disorganized attachment, which prompts chaotic growth) or linked with what we would call in adults a "manic" lunge toward novelty (as in dismissive attachment). In these precarious states of mind, the toddler is simply too immersed in "protecting the fort" of his inner feeling of calm to take on his world with optimal vitality and spontaneity.

Despite its potentially crippling affects, the existence of separation anxiety compels us to think about how much development has occurred to allow the toddler to be at this relatively narrowed level of anxiety. In order to have separation anxiety you have to first feel comfortable enough to try to separate, and that's a major widening of the world that previously only existed safely when on mom's hip and being held. Separation anxiety implies that the toddler's world is potentially gratifying enough for her to be willing to leave mom and explore. While there's a to and fro between the quest for novelty and the apprehension of finding something too novel to bear, that's still very different from the much more limited experiences willing to be felt if annihilation anxiety or stranger anxiety is the predominant affect.

This paradigm of narrowing (but still deeply and intensely felt) anxieties continues as the child moves into the preschool (ages 2½ to 5) period. Here the principal anxiety is incumbent not upon a simple reaction to the world, but rather intrinsic to moments of taking the initiative in shaping it. Preschoolers are not just interested in going along with the flow but rather with the "Why?" behind a command or suggestion. They seek, moreover, to go beyond face value and to shape the world as they see fit. It's the remarkable egocentricity of the three-year-old that says: "the world should really be the way I want it, and if it's not that way, there's something wrong with the world."

The danger, of course, in wanting the world to be on your terms, of questioning everything, of not taking it at face value, is that power differentials become paramount. What will it feel like if someone bigger/stronger/more intimidating does not succumb to your attempts at setting the frame of interaction? For our purposes, I am calling the affect that comes to the fore when the attempts at power do not hold up, castration anxiety. While Freud's original phallocentric conceptualizations turned this level of anxiety into something specific to a penis and hence turned it into what it meant to be male, the term can be usefully applied more broadly than that. In fact, every person faces issues of what does it mean to take the initiative? What does it mean to have a sense of power? What does it mean to have a sense of being belittled? When I say castration anxiety,

A Conceptual Framework for Assessment **17**

it's perhaps unavoidable that it be linked to the remnants of an only somewhat viable "classical" way of thinking about it in terms of literal castration. I retain the term because the affect phenomenologically experienced by the preschooler during moments of stifled initiative is to feel belittled. Those moments of "defeat" can and do get expressed as a tremendous feeling of suddenly being powerless, victimized, or made impotent. Those affects ring true regardless of what kind of genitalia you possess.

Looked at from a different perspective, this time period is also a critical age in which the conflicts between the reality principle and the pleasure principle are both dramatically felt and most blatantly articulated. While causality can still be magical, especially in moments of emotional intensity, the preschooler has enough of a sense of the rules involved in social discourse to be prone to feelings of guilt should they transgress certain key familial or societal norms. The brilliance of Erikson's (1950) depiction of the key dynamic in the preschool years as initiative versus guilt thus rings as true today as ever. It should be evident here that while fear of being viewed as "bad" is a narrower field of anxiety than those previously described, its depth of visceral intensity can be enormous.

Part of my reason for depicting the hierarchy of anxieties within this domain in such detail is that we most often cannot tease out what level of anxiety is primary to a patient simply by how much distress they feel. Any of these anxieties can be felt as overpowering. It is not simply how bad the patient feels but the degree to which we can place the patient's felt emotions in a situational and interpersonal context that makes a differentiation of the nature of their anxiety more possible. This will hopefully become more self-evident as we more fully articulate the remaining domains and their hierarchies.

The next two rungs in this domain's hierarchy of negative outcomes in response to developmental challenges are still more subtle, yet no less devastating in affect; the fear of losing the love of an essential other and the fear of a loss of meaning. Here we no longer primarily fear the loss of personhood, or an intrusive stranger, or that if I'm away from "home" I can't function, or even the fear that if I take the initiative I'm going to be punished. Critically, fearing the loss of the love of a trea- sured person is not to lose them as a person but to feel that you're not as intrinsi- cally lovable. It speaks to the question of to what extent we disappoint others. We know they still care about us. We know that they're still there for us in certain ways or would be there in an emergency, but do they really love us for who we are in our fullness, and can we really love someone else despite the ways in which they disappoint us? These questions point to how far our now latency-aged child or adolescent has developed. When one is still struggling with castration-level anxieties, the world is a very all-or-none world. Think of the four-year-old who wants to go outside in the snow in his bare feet, and the mother says: "No, Johnny, you can't go unless you put your boots on." If the struggle continues, typically the four-year-old will cry out: "I hate you, Mommy." It's not "I hate that you're mak- ing me wear these boots when I would love to go outside barefoot and feel the

18 Conceptual Links

sensuous experience on the bottom of my feet as they turn blue." No, it's, "I hate you, I obliterate you. You are awful." Moments later, after the child is on to other issues, you may often hear: "I love you, Mommy." It's as if they never hated at all.

Within these two final steps in our hierarchy, however, the child's capacity to hold onto affects and even to allow affects to "speak to one another" permits a very different level of response. Strong affects no longer just disappear. They sit alongside one another and even blend into one another in various shades and colorings. Thus, as we go through adolescence and into adulthood, our task becomes increasingly one of how do we hold onto positive feelings toward people when they disappoint us or we disappoint them? Here we are talking about the capacity for true ambivalence, a critical developmental milestone that suggests that feelings persist over time.

A last, perhaps most developmentally sophisticated level within this domain, is the fear of a loss of meaning. Struggles with the question of purpose and value of life imply a relatively more sophisticated level of cognition, symbolization and perspective than any of the other levels we've discussed. The person must have enough freedom from immediate fears of bodily harm or loss of self/other or initiative to wonder about why they exist and what gives them a sense of purpose, both to themselves and to others. These "existential" anxieties can plague us from adolescence onwards, but appear most acute as the aging process smacks into certain societal milestones (birthdays at each of the ends of decades, for example) or as we suffer the actual losses of loved ones. Once again, these anxieties can be viscerally as painful or immobilizing as any of the others in terms of felt experience. The differences again refer to the content of the worries and the sturdiness of the platforms built by the patient in their handling of early anxiety-inducing dilemmas of living. The greater the sturdiness of the prior platforms, the more capable the patient is in their attempts to get mastery of, or at least a perspective on, the dilemmas with which they struggle.

A Domain and Hierarchy of Positive Object Relations

For the domains I am describing to have any semblance of heuristic value in creating a scaffold for understanding personality, it must again be stressed that each of the domains is in constant touch with every other. This is especially true regarding my depiction of a strand of "negative" and "positive" object relational paradigms. Indeed, it is better to think of each of the previously described anxiety paradigms as having its positive counterpart, with both engaged in an ongoing dialectical relationship. The nature of this dynamic interplay is such that at any moment in time, a given anxiety paradigm and its opposite are in a particular ratio to one another.

Thus, the counterpart to a state of annihilation anxiety is a deep experience of trust. To go back to Winnicott's temporal model, if as a baby you don't go very often into X plus Y time, but if you do go there, you never get to X plus Y plus Z

A Conceptual Framework for Assessment **19**

time, you and your caretaker become predictable or even monotonous. This predictability becomes reliability over time. Beginning perhaps with feeding or holding, an emerging predictability creates an implicit trust between caretaker and baby. This trust builds across multiple modalities, feeding on itself, as it were, so that experiences of caretaker as feeder, as warmth giver, as gaze responder, etc., each become suffused with the reliability that serves as a platform for cognitive growth and an appreciation of, rather than a terror at, novelty. The more varied in type and intensity of the affective conditions you have as a baby that a person can come along and soothe and ameliorate or enliven, the greater an overall sense of trust is created under those widening conditions. Crucially, with each experience of coming to count on a predictable caretaker, the baby also experiences herself as predictable and trustworthy. Things begin to make sense to the baby precisely because her parenting is attuned to what and how she receives and processes stimuli. Importantly, and this is especially crucial in the very first weeks of life, the caretaker's ability to tamp down stimuli, to serve as a stimulus barrier to an impinging world, is every bit as crucial to the child's avoidance of annihilation as what the caretaker actively provides in the way of stimulation. There is nothing quite like watching a confident baby, even as young as three to six months, sitting happily with a sense of anticipation, a sense of, to quote the title of an old Herman's Hermits tune from the 1960s: "Something Tells Me I'm Into Something Good."

This sense of trust is a fundamental antidote to a feeling that the world at any moment could crash and burn. Indeed, trust carries the baby through the first several anxieties. It certainly carries the baby through annihilation anxiety. It carries her through stranger anxiety as well, for the dread that can be evoked by the intrusive "Uncle Sid" can be powerfully mitigated by the warm comforting of the nearby caretaker, whose reliable holding permits the child to slowly sneak a peek back at the intruder and might eventually even lead to a comfort with being held by him. It even carries the baby a long way through separation anxiety, because if the toddler trusts that Mom's going to be there, even when she's not in sight, then, at least for a short period of time, the child may avert panic until the caretaker comes back into view.

There's a story that my old professor, Marty Mayman, one of the true giants in this field, used to tell about a friend of his who had a baby. As I remember the story, Marty was asked by this friend to watch over her baby who was fast asleep in her crib while she went out briefly to the store. Of course what happens within moments of her departure is that the baby starts to fuss and cry. Having little experience with babies, Marty is flummoxed with the child's fussing and grows increasingly panicked as the baby gets similarly panicked with this man she doesn't recognize. Holding and giving toys to distract the child only produces more upset. But he begins to notice that every time he mentions the word "mommy," the child seems to soften her cries just a fraction. It dawns on him that perhaps saying "mommy" briefly engenders in the child the

20 Conceptual Links

memory, the internalization of mommy. So he starts using the word mommy with nearly every other phrase he creates. After a couple of minutes of him doing this, she appeared to recharge her ability to link herself to memories of her mommy and used that to soothe herself. To bring this anecdote back to our discussion of trust, we can easily speculate that the baby's heretofore trusting relationship with her mom allowed her to re-find her mommy in her mind through language, even though her mommy wasn't physically present. So trust allows even separation anxiety to be mitigated, because if a child has had a good solid year of trust, it has access, with an occasional priming through the use of symbolization, to an internalization of mom that can fight off, for a time, an experience of separation.

Further positive counterparts are needed to fully counter the anxieties we've described. Separation anxiety, although mitigated by trust, is more profoundly coped with when this trust is aided by a widening sense of autonomy. It is not a sufficient impetus, in my mind, to posit that the remarkable cognitive and emotional growth of the infant rests solely on a trust he develops with the world. While this would provide the means for a more passive acceptance of any given situation, it would fail to account for the child's great delight in novelty and change. I vividly remember my older son during this time period. After being asked rhetorically many times if he would like to do X by himself, he began to assert before he started almost any activity: "self!" as a way of letting us know he wanted, as a given, to take on this task autonomously.

There is still a further developmental achievement during this period that serves as perhaps the strongest bulwark to an "outbreak" of separation anxiety. This achievement is what Winnicott (1958) termed "the capacity to be alone." As with much of his theoretical conceptualizations regarding the developmental process, the capacity to be alone develops from the consistently and reliably available, "good enough" mother, whose attunement gives the child the emotional and physical space to take her for granted. At first for short periods of time, the child tentatively explores the world around him, increasingly being absorbed by the properties of what he explores. The caretaker hovers nearby, providing a stimulus barrier should his exploration become overwhelming or else simply providing a source of comfort should he momentarily lose track of her. For Winnicott, the paradox to "defeating" separation anxiety lies in the fact that the baby first experiences aloneness while in the mother's presence, well before he has developed the consistent memory traces of her that can withstand her true absence (i.e. when she has become internalized in the form of a stable, easily retrievable mental representation). The smoother this transition to internalization occurs, the less prone the child is to separation anxiety. Obviously no one makes this transition so perfectly that they are immune to anxious feelings regarding separation and loss. Indeed, one could make a convincing argument that the inability to have any experience of such anxiety would suggest a dearth of attachment capacity and hence a profoundly limited hollow shell of existing.

A Conceptual Framework for Assessment **21**

In much the same way that the capacity to be alone and its resulting autonomy are the counterpoints to separation woes, curiosity builds upon autonomy and serves as an apt counterpoint to castration concerns. Curiosity is an incredibly important human characteristic and developmental achievement that certainly has origins in the first weeks of life. But it is in the throes of worries about initiative and anxieties about being belittled for incompetence that curiosity may serve its most crucial developmental function. If you are curious about how things work, then you feel enough of a sense of trust and autonomy to not merely be content with what you are supposed to do but to play with "whatever comes to mind" (I use this phrase purposely, as the freedom to free associate cannot be safely employed in psychotherapy without this requisite curiosity and its accompanying modicum of autonomy and trust). When you watch curious three- or four-year-olds play with a new toy, they're not just content to play with a toy as it is supposed to be played with, but instead they want to see how it works, including taking it apart to see what it's made of. That level of curiosity is a vital antidote to fearing castration, because castration is most commonly operationalized in the form of avoidance and retreat from novelty. The child plagued by castration fears inhibits his actions to avoid belittlement or feeling diminished. Thus a child wrestles between his wish to avoid his limits and his curiosity about potential mastery of the new and unexplored.

In this regard I personally note that the psychologist who had the greatest effect on my early training was a man named Robert W. White. White worked at Harvard for many years, and he wrote a monograph in 1959 called, "Motivation Reconsidered: the Concept of Competence." White argued that the feeling of being effective, what he called effectance motivation, is inherently rewarding, and is an intrinsic drive toward making sense out of the world. I found that to be eye-opening in the helpful way it explains how rapidly babies develop; that it's not just the unfolding of their brain development, but it's also the self-rewarding nature of doing something interesting that makes the baby repeat the activity until it is mastered to their satisfaction. Think of a baby lying in a crib looking at a mobile. If the baby by accident moves her arm, and the mobile shakes, it is markedly likely the baby will repeat the movement to see if she can "cause" the mobile to move. The toddler dropping his spoon to see it crash to the floor, the child hitting a ball off a tee again and again, these repetitive acts suggest a quest for competence and the intrinsic pleasure such competence provides. Competence is thus available from the beginning but perhaps reaches its greatest significance as a bulwark against castration fears. The competent child at any given moment is not inhibited by fears of belittlement, indeed is willing to take on the world full bore to expand her sense of mastery. This sense of competence builds ideally on her foundations of trust, autonomy and curiosity so that by the time the child is five or six years old she is ready for the ultimate crucible of competence testing vs. castration fears – the world of formal schooling. So many of the problems we see in children of this age are an artifact of their inability to sustain competence

22 Conceptual Links

in the face of this crucible, and a good portion of referrals for testing of children center on their difficulties in sustaining competence. In this sense, competence can also be viewed as the summation of the positive hierarchy of relatedness we've talked about: when the baby feels trust in the world, she begins to have a sense of personhood; when she develops this degree of autonomy, she feels curious about the world, and when she feels competent in her exploratory forays, she creates a milieu in which mastery can be obtained through repetition.

There remains to be detailed the two positive counterparts to the fear of the loss of love and a fear of a lack of meaning. For both of these anxieties I would argue that the capacity for empathy, or its more cognitive cousin reflective functioning, is a viable other side of the coin. Although it, too, starts in the first year of life, the capacity to first intuit and later to articulate the affective states and cognitive intentions of others is a crucial tool to viable functioning. Before language, it can be manifest in the baby's "reading" of the mother's mood with its positive sequelae of aiding in mother–baby attunement and its negative connotations if such "reading" leads to an overly compliant false self. With the requisite parental reliability, the child can trust in his experience of others as predictable emotionally and actively. He can then learn over time to read his own states of being and project those states into others. Over time, he can then safely test whether these projections are accurate and trust enough in prior positive dyadic experiences to overcome errors in assessing the feeling states and behaviors of others.

This empathic capacity leads to two profound developments that mitigate the fear of the loss of the love of significant others in two ways. One, an accurate reading of the "other" allows for a minimal number of emotional "blunders" that could lead to a threatened loss of love. Two, if such errors do occur, an accurate capacity to read others' emotions allows for timely reparations to be made if that other is hurt by our actions. Many chronic parent–child dysfunctions have at their root an inability of one or both parties to "read" the others' feelings and intentions, resulting in behaviors that may have the best of intentions but hopelessly miss the mark in terms of creating the rapport that both parties may seek.

I would also argue that this refined capacity for empathy and reflective functioning, capable of beginning to reach its highest forms with the advent of formal operational thinking in early adolescence, is also the counterpart to a lack of meaning or purpose. While I will leave to poets, philosophers and religious figures whether the fear of death can ever be fully assuaged, we do derive our fullest sense of meaning and purpose through our attachments to others. Thus the greater the degree to which we feel emotionally "held" by others; the greater ease with which we can internalize and conjure up these experiences of being "held"; and the greater facility with which we can do the same for others, all serve as ballast in the existential quest for meaning and purpose.

There is a final subset of the capacity for empathy and reflective functioning that may be usefully seen as the amalgam of the two capacities. That is the propensity for altruism. Altruism combines the cognitive capacity to understand the thinking processes of another (reflective functioning) with the more intuitive ability to understand the feelings of another (empathy) into a mode of action that benefits the other. It is the ultimate level of human social functioning, the best we as a species have to offer one another.

These two dialectical domains of object relations provide the conceptual underpinning for the empirical studies to be described below. What is necessary now is to describe the methodologies employed to operationalize these concepts. Chief among these methodologies for me has been the use of the Mutuality of Autonomy (MOA) scale with the RIM (and, in the last chapter, with the TAT as well). I turn now to an early paper that describes the use of this measure.

SECTION TWO

The Projective Tasks Used in This Book

2

MEASURES EMPLOYED TO ASSESS OBJECT REPRESENTATIONS

The MOA Scale

Paper used: Tuber, S. (1992). Empirical and clinical assessments of children's object relations and object representations. *Journal of Personality Assessment*, 58, 179–197.[1]

Mayman (1967) helped make explicit the shift from an emphasis on drive theory as the primary model in projective test research to the study of object representations with projective tests. Mayman spoke of the "reparative process" that occurs when a subject is asked to make sense of the formlessness inherent in a Rorschach inkblot (RIM), for example. This reparative process is manifested through the specific, personal associations reflective of one's inner repertoire of "people, animals and things which fit most naturally into the ingrained expectancies around which [one] has learned to structure his phenomenal world" (p. 17). This hypothesized projection of one's inner repertoire of past, animated interactions onto the RIM suggested the development of a variety of measures to quantify the nature of these interactions between self and others. Object representation scales have been developed with adult, adolescent, and child clinical populations. One of the most widely used measures has been the Mutuality of Autonomy (MOA) scale, a measure that in two recent meta-analyses (Graceffo, Mihura, & Meyer, 2014; Bombel, Mihura, & Meyer, 2009) has been found to have been used in over 900 published papers with strong and consistent reliability and validity. I was the second person to use this measure and the first to apply it to children's RIM protocols. I will now use my 1992 paper to describe the scale.

The MOA Scale

An object representation scale developed by Urist (1977) – the Mutuality of Autonomy (MOA) Scale – was devised to measure the construct validity of the premise that the manner in which individuals represent and construe self–other relationships is consistent and enduring. It is a 7-point scale, with the most adaptive

28 Projective Tasks Used in This Book

scale point being reserved for Rorschach responses that portray simultaneous awareness of self and other in mutual interaction, and the lowest scale point depicting overwhelming, toxic control, and destruction of a calamitous nature imposed on a helpless victim. Inter-rater reliability for the MOA scale has been consistently excellent, falling within the 70%–90% agreement range (Tuber, 1989b, p. 146). The two most adaptive scale points depict interactions in which the autonomy of the self is fully maintained, whether in mutual interaction (scale point 1) or parallel activity (scale point 2). Scale points 3 and 4 reflect impairments in autonomy most closely conceptually linked with Kohut's (1977) work. To be scored on either point 3 or point 4, a response must either involve two figures lacking balance, leaning on one another, or needing external support (a score of 3) or having one figure merely be the reflection or imprint of another (scale point 4). Points 5, 6, and 7 reflect increasing dominance and destruction of one figure over another, closely linked conceptually to the descriptions that Kernberg (1977) used to depict severely disturbed individuals with borderline or psychotic inner experiences. Scale point 5 depicts relationships characterized by control or dominance of one figure over another, without the "victim's" body integrity being severely damaged. A scale score of 6 is reserved for those relationships in which physical destruction of one figure by another in decidedly imbalanced terms is presented. As just described, a scale point 7 response is reserved for those pathological responses in which a figure is dominated by catastrophically malevolent, engulfing forces. The MOA scale assesses the thematic content of interactions on the Rorschach by rating all human, animal, and inanimate relationships (stated or implied) in a protocol along a continuum ranging from mutual, empathic relatedness (1) to themes of malevolent engulfment and destruction (7). As an example, a score of 1 is given to a response to Card II of "two people having a heated political argument." An example of a score of 2 is "two animals climbing a mountain" on Card VIII. Scale Points 3 and 4 indicate an emerging loss of autonomy in interaction in which the "other" exists solely either to be leaned upon (a score of 3) or to mirror oneself (a score of 4). An example of a score of 3 is a response to Card I of "two men leaning on a manikin." A score of 4 is given to the response "a tiger looking at its reflection in the water" to Card VIII. Points 5, 6, and 7 reflect an increasing malevolence and loss of control over one's separateness. A score of 5 is given to responses characterized by themes of coercion, hurtful influence, or threat. An example is "a witch casting a spell on someone" to the top large detail of Card IX. A score of 6 indicates violent assault and destruction of one figure by another – for example, "a bat impaled by a tree" to Card I. Finally, a score of 7 represents a larger than life destructiveness imposed usually by inanimate, calamitous forces as depicted, for example, in the response to Card X, "a tornado hurtling its debris everywhere."

The average MOA score is assumed to express the individual's usual quality of interpersonal relatedness. To reflect a subject's range or repertoire of interactions, we also used each subject's single highest (most pathological) and single lowest (most adaptive) MOA scores in our data analyses.

The MOA Scale **29**

It has been suggested that the MOA scale confuses aggression with autonomy in that the three most pathological scale points do indeed depict highly aggressive interactions. It should therefore be stressed that it is not aggression per se but the imbalance of the "battle" between the figures that is weighed most heavily in scoring a particular Rorschach response on the MOA scale. Thus, a person who describes a highly charged verbal battle among equals could have that response scored as 1, even though the degree of disagreement, competition, or confrontation was significant. It is only when the confrontation involves an imbalanced attack on one figure by another that a more pathological score of 6 or 7 is given.

In marked contrast to most other object representational measures, the MOA scale is applied to any relationship, stated or implied, between animal and inanimate objects in addition to human Rorschach percepts. It is this quality that has made the scale much more relevant to children's protocols, given that children produce very few human movement responses.

In reviewing MOA scale performance across both normal and psychiatric child populations, the scale has demonstrated adequate inter-rater reliability and criterion and construct validity. It appears reasonable now to reassess the scale by reviewing the distribution or scale scores across a number of studies. These distributions provide evidence that allows reexamination of the scale in light of developmental/psychodynamic theory. Three key questions arise that can be addressed by this type of consideration:

1. Is the MOA scale a developmental scale? (If so, MOA scores should, for example, be affected by the chronological age of the child.)
2. Is it a scale of psychopathology? (If so, it should be related to other Rorschach indices of psychopathology, i.e., thought disorder and poor form level.
3. What is the nature of the distribution of MOA scores? (Is the MOA scale an ordinal scale with sequential levels of adjustment, a nominal scale simply measuring modes of adjustment, or an interval scale, akin to an IQ scale?)

Table 2.1 provides the distributions of MOA scale scores for children from a number of the studies just described. A number of implications can be derived from a review of these distributions of MOA scale scores. Clearly the MOA scale is not an interval scale. Every sample had a bimodal distribution in which scale points 2 and 5 were the most commonly scored responses. Scale point 4, responses indicative of reflection, were very rare, accounting for no more than 8% of any of the responses in any of the distributions. Scale point 7 scores were even more rare and were almost exclusively a pathognomonic indicator. Scale point scores of 6 in great quantity also appear to be indicative of psychopathology, but not in small numbers; they were found to at least a small degree in two of the normative distributions. Scale point 3 appears to be a distinct indicator of separation difficulties, as evidenced by its plentiful distribution within the Separation Anxiety Disorder (SAD) group, and appears to be reasonably

TABLE 2.1 MOA Scale Distributions Across a Number of Different Studies

Normative Study

MOA Scale Points	Total Sample[a]		Boys Only[b]		Girls Only[c]	
	#	%	#	%	#	%
1	22	11	6	6	16	17
2	74	38	28	29	46	48
3	31	16	19	19	12	13
4	4	2	4	4	0	0
5	48	25	30	32	18	19
6	14	7	11	11	3	3
7	0	0	0	0	0	0

Separation Anxiety Disorder (SAD)

MOA Scale Points	SAD Only[f]		SAD/GID[g]	
	#	%	#	%
1	0	0	1	1
2	25	34	15	21
3	21	28	10	14
4	3	4	6	8
5	17	23	28	38
6	6	8	9	13
7	2	3	2	3

Children With Imaginary Companions

MOA Scale Points	#	%
1	6	7
2	25	29
3	2	2
4	0	0
5	42	48
6	11	13
7	1	1

Notes: [a]n = 40, [b]n = 19, [c]n = 21, [d]n = 26, [e]n = 18, [f]n = 9, [g]n = 10.
Source: These data are based in part on findings reported in Tuber (1989b), Goddard and Tuber (1989), and Meyer and Tuber (1989), respectively.

The MOA Scale **31**

plentiful among the normative subjects as well. A scale point score of 1 is relatively rare in male samples, whether normal or psychiatric, but appears to be more common in girls.

The MOA scale with children thus appears to be an ordinal scale depicting differing modes of object experience of varying severity. Three distinct modes of object representational scores do exist in studies using male populations: (a) interactions among percepts that are either nonintrusive (a scale point score of 2) or potentially intrusive (a scale point score of 5), (b) dependent interactions (a scale point score of 3), and (c) toxic interactions (a scale point score of 6 or 7). For female populations, a fourth mode of object representation, involving benign, reciprocal interaction (a scale point score of 1) is also common. A review of these distributions of MOA scale responses also provides further data suggesting that the MOA scale does not place object representations on a developmental continuum as Urist (1977) originally suggested. The MOA scale has not been found to correlate with chronological age and the distribution of the MOA scores for the 4- to 5-year-old children with imaginary companions, for example, is not significantly different from that of the latency age samples. This gives further credence to the premise that the MOA scale measures varying levels of adaptive and pathological object representations, but is not linked to a developmental timetable. Conceptually, the depiction of the MOA scale as a developmental continuum implies that the more primitive scale points reflect interactions that took place earlier in life than the more adaptive, "mature" scale points. Although this line of reasoning is in keeping with the psychoanalytic theories of Klein (1937), Mahler, Pine, and Bergman (1975), and Jacobson (1964), it is strikingly incongruent with more recent infant and mother–infant interaction research in which the baby's adaptive and autonomous capacities of self-coherence have been increasingly clearly demonstrated (Beebe & Lachmann, 1988; Emde, 1983; Sander, 1983; Stern, 1985; Zelnick & Buchholz, 1990).

It does appear more correct to describe the MOA scale as a continuum of pathological to adaptive depictions of internalized object representations without the link to a temporally derived distribution of progressive object representational experiences. The MOA scale should therefore be more precisely viewed as an ordinal index of varying degrees of adaptive and maladaptive object representations and should not be viewed as a scale that places these object representations necessarily within a developmental timetable.

Note

1 Copyright 1992, Lawrence/Erlbaum Associates, Inc. Reproduced with permission.

3
USING THE MOA SCALE WITH A NONCLINICAL POPULATION

Paper used: Tuber, S. (1989). Children's Rorschach object representations: Findings for a nonclinical sample. *Psychological Assessment: Journal of Consulting and Clinical Psychology*, 1, 146–149.[1]

Alluded to briefly in Chapter 2, it seemed wise to find a "normative" sample of boys and girls and create a baseline for what their MOA scores would be like. The following paper provided these beginning normative data.

In the absence of data derived from nonclinical subjects, the research applicability of the MOA scale remains limited. In this study, therefore, in a beginning attempt to place the scale on firmer empirical ground, I present demographic and correlational data describing the nature of MOA responses in a sample of nonclinical, preadolescent children. I also present findings that suggest gender-based differences in the quality of object representations in a nonclinical sample.

Method

Subjects were derived from an earlier, larger study by Santostefano, Rieder, and Berk (1984). Their control sample of 40 (21 girls and 19 boys) comprised the subject pool for the present study. Their mean age was 10.5 years ($SD = 1.5$) with an age range of 6 to 13. Full-Scale IQ, as measured by the Wechsler Intelligence Scale for Children – Revised (WISC-R), was 110.88 ($SD = 9.36$). The families of these children had a median income of $25,000. Roughly two thirds of the working parents held managerial-technical jobs or professional positions, 25% were skilled laborers, 10% were semi-skilled, and 5% were unskilled (Santostefano et al., 1984, p. 6). Eighty-five percent of the families were intact. About half the group were

MOA Scale With a Nonclinical Population **33**

Catholic, and the remainder reported Protestant, Jewish, or no religious affiliation. The children's public school records were extensively reviewed, and current teachers were interviewed to rule out the presence of any psychiatric history or academic/behavioral school disturbance.

The children were taken to a specially designated room in their school building where they were administered first the WISC-R and then the Rorschach Inkblot Test. Rorschach inquiry was performed at the end of the standard 10-card presentation as described by Klopfer, Ainsworth, Klopfer, and Holt (1954). For the present study, the Rorschach protocols were disguised as to name, age, and gender and were given to two raters, one a recent PhD in clinical psychology and the other a clinical psychology graduate student. Raters were also blind to the purpose of the study. Rater reliability for the MOA Scale was .93: 85% of all ratings were exact matches, and disagreements in the remaining 15% involved only one scale point. I reconciled these minor discrepancies without knowledge of the identity or gender of the child. (The reader is referred to Tuber, 1988, for a detailed description of the MOA Scale as well as the criteria used for its scoring.)

The total number of MOA Scale scores, the mean MOA score (MOA-M), the single best score (HORS), and the single worst score (LORS) were calculated for each subject. Because the MOA Scale is an ordinal scale (see Tuber, 1983), I used nonparametric statistical procedures to evaluate the MOA-M, HORS, and LORS data by gender, age, and IQ. T tests were used when comparing the subjects' IQ, age, and gender with the total number of Rorschach and MOA Scale responses.

Results

Subjects gave a mean of 20.18 Rorschach responses ($SD = 9.46$); the individual response rate ranged from 11 to 38. The total number of Rorschach responses was not significantly correlated with any of the MOA measures (Spearman correlation coefficients ranged from .13 to .17, $N = 40$). Rorschach productivity was also not significantly correlated with either the age ($rs = .01$) or Full-Scale IQ ($rs = .03$) of the child.

Of the total number of 807 Rorschach responses, 193, or 24%, were scoreable using the MOA Scale. The subjects' total MOA responses ranged from 1 to 15, with a mean of 4.65 responses per child ($SD = 3.3$) and a median of 4. Seven (2 girls, 5 boys) subjects gave only one MOA response; 12 (8 girls, 4 boys) gave two to three MOA responses; 9 (7 girls, 2 boys) gave four to five responses; 8 (3 girls, 5 boys) gave six to eight responses, and 4 (1 girl, 3 boys) had nine or more MOA responses. The mean MOA score for those subjects with fewer than four scoreable MOA responses was 3.17 ($SD = 1.63$); for subjects with four or more scoreable responses, it was also 3.17 ($SD = 1.56$). Gender differences, when compared at each of the number of MOA response categories, were consistent with the overall gender differences, to be described below.

34 Projective Tasks Used in This Book

Half of the total number of MOA responses reflected either of the two most adaptive scale points. One third of the total responses were at the malevolent ("five," "six," and "seven") end of the scale. Notably, however, the vast majority of malevolent scores (48 of 62, or 77%) were of the relatively more benign "five" category, and none of the 40 subjects gave the most maladaptive "seven" score. Scores indicative of dependent, leaning interactions ("three") were relatively plentiful, with nearly half of the subjects giving at least one such response. I checked to see whether the mean age of the 18 subjects whose scores indicated dependency interactions would be significantly younger than that of the children who did not show such dependent-type scores. The mean age of the 18 children who gave "three" responses was 10.3 years, however – nearly identical to the mean age of the rest of the sample of 10.6 years.

Most subjects' responses reflected an extensive repertoire of object representational experiences: Three quarters of the children received a best score of "one" or "two," and 60% received a "five" or "six" for their worst response. Comparison of the HORS and the LORS for each subject revealed a strong tendency among subjects to balance more malevolent scores with highly adaptive scores. Of the 11 subjects whose LORS was a "six," for example, 4 had an HORS of "one" and 5 had an HORS of "two." Only 10% of the sample failed to follow this trend. Of this group of 4, 2 subjects produced a single ratable response of "five," 1 produced two "five" responses, and the other subject two "six" responses. Of the remaining 10 subjects who had a LORS of "five," 9 had a best score of "one" or "two" and the other had a best score of "three."

I then compared the four major MOA variables with age and IQ. The age of the child was not significantly correlated with any of the four MOA variables (Spearman correlation coefficients ranged from .02 to .21). Full-Scale IQ scores were also not significantly correlated with any of the four MOA variables (Spearman correlation coefficients ranged from .03 to .15).

Table 3.1 presents a series of Rorschach and demographic data comparisons by gender. There was a suggestive finding that girls had significantly more benign HORS scores (using the Mann-Whitney U Test, $z = 2.95, p = .0032$, two-tailed), less malevolent LORS scores ($z = 2.43, p = .0152$, two-tailed), and more adaptive mean MOA scores ($z = 3.19, p = .0014$, two-tailed).

Girls' more adaptive overall mean, HORS, and LORS scores are consistently supported by a more adaptive performance than the boys' at each of the individual scale points. Differences at the endpoints of the scale are dramatic, with girls accounting for 70% of the most adaptive "one" responses, and only 21% of the destructive "six" responses. Boys gave an average of 1.79 benevolent ("one" and "two") responses ($SD = 2.50$), whereas girls gave an average of 2.95 benevolent responses ($SD = 1.75$). This was a statistically significant difference (using Mann-Whitney, $z = 2.41, p = .0161$). Boys gave an average of 2.16 malevolent responses ($SD = 2.12$), whereas girls gave an average of one malevolent response ($SD = 1.38$). This difference was also statistically significant ($z = 1.97, p = .0484$). I then

MOA Scale With a Nonclinical Population **35**

TABLE 3.1 Rorschach and Demographic Data Comparisons by Gender

Variable	M	SD
Full Scale IQ[a]		
Boys (N=19)	111.2[b]	8.54[c]
Girls (N=21)	110.6	10.30
Age[a] (in years)		
Boys	10.5	2.3
Girls	10.5	2.3
No. of responses[a]		
Boys	22.7	11.4
Girls	17.9	6.9
No. of MOA responses[a]		
Boys	5.15	4.08
Girls	4.54	3.63
HORS[d]		
Boys	2.74	1.59
Girls	1.43	1.51
LORS[d]		
Boys	5.00	1.20
Girls	3.86	1.59
MOA-M[d]		
Boys	3.83	1.07
Girls	2.67	0.86

Notes: MOA = Mutuality of Autonomy Scale; HORS = single highest object relations score; LORS = single lowest object relations score.
[a]Parametric statistics (t and F tests) used given interval or ratio data. [b]All tests were nonsignificant (two-tailed p). [c]All F tests were nonsignificant. [d]Nonparametric statistics (Mann-Whitney U Test) used given ordinal data. Z scores were corrected for tied ranks and expressed in the text as a normal deviate.

compared the percentage of benevolent responses by gender as a proportion of the total number of benevolent and malevolent responses. Strikingly, the mean percentage of benevolent responses for boys was 27.13 (SD = 33.9), as contrasted with a 78.1% figure for girls (SD = 25.4). This was a highly significant difference (z = 4.04, $p <$. 0001).

Discussion

The MOA Scale has again been found to be a reliably scored measure of object representation for preadolescent children. Data from the present nonclinical sample confirmed previous findings that the quality and range of Rorschach object representations as measured by the MOA Scale are not significantly related to either chronological age (Goldberg, 1989; Goddard & Tuber, 1989) or IQ (Ryan,

36 Projective Tasks Used in This Book

Avery, & Grolnick, 1985). The findings that nonclinical subjects could (a) counterbalance malevolent scores with more benign responses, (b) avoid truly toxic or empty interactive representations, and (c) have a modal response indicative of benign parallel interaction may signify the presence of an inner representational analogue to their nonclinical interpersonal and academic functioning. Also of interest was the relatively large number of responses characterized by dependent, leaning interactions (scale point "three"). Given the age range of the sample, it appears that such object representations, in small quantities, characterize a normative aspect of childhood representations. In this light, I note that the mean of .79 "three" responses per child for this sample is considerably less than the 1.72 "three" responses reported for a comparably aged sample of boys diagnosed as separation anxious (Goddard & Tuber, 1989).

An analysis of mean MOA, HORS, and LORS scores by gender indicated that the girls gave consistently more adaptive MOA scores. A recent article on the implications for developmental theory of gender differences in neonates may begin to provide an explanation for this unexpected finding. Silverman (1987) reviewed the considerable amount of developmental research suggesting that female neonates are "easier to calm, possess greater stability (and) manifest less restlessness" (p. 316) than boys. These differences, Silverman argued, promote a more immediate and sustained bond between mother and daughter than between mother and son. She suggested that this difference in bonding readiness may permit female infants "to experience an earlier awareness of others as significant in their lives (and to) experience the beginnings of the socialization process earlier" (p. 316).

Urist's (1977) mutuality of autonomy construct has been defined as the degree to which the subject can conceive of people in relationships as possessing a self while at the same time recognizing the existence and interdependence of others. Findings from the present study may therefore be a reflection of the sustained "head start" girls have compared to boys in being aware of others in interaction. This gender-difference finding is also consistent with the repeated finding of sex differences in level and quality of aggressive behavior. In a large number of studies of preadolescent and latency-age children, boys have been found to be more physically aggressive than their female peers (Huesmann, Eron, Lefkowitz, & Walder, 1984; Maccoby & Jacklin, 1980). The present findings provide tentative evidence suggesting that boys' more aggressive behavior may correlate with intrapsychic themes of relatively greater malevolence and control.

The present findings are preliminary. Lack of matched clinical comparison groups, relatively small sample size, and the need to consider other potentially confounding variables (e.g., socioeconomic status) render these findings tentative. It now seems advisable, however, to compare gender differences along a number of object representational dimensions, in addition to mutuality of autonomy. Such comparisons might further elucidate the manner in which interpersonal interactions become internalized and, more specifically, might help determine whether gender differences persist across a wide range of interpersonal and object representational domains.

Note

1 Copyright © 1989, American Psychological Association. Reproduced with permission. The official citation that should be used in referencing this material is Tuber, S. B. (1989). Children's Rorschach object representations: Findings for a nonclinical sample. *Psychological Assessment: A Journal of Consulting and Clinical Psychology*, 1(2), 146–149. http://dx.doi.org/10.1037/1040-3590.1.2.146. No further reproduction or distribution is permitted without written permission from the American Psychological Association.

4

USING THE MOA SCALE WITH A SLIGHTLY OLDER POPULATION

Paper used: Blatt, S., Tuber, S., & Auerbach, J. (1990). Representation of interpersonal interactions on the Rorschach and level of psychopathology. *Journal of Personality Assessment*, 54, 711–728.[1]

Having extended the use of the MOA scale to both normative and child psychiatric populations, an opportunity was afforded to me to use the measure with an adolescent/young adult psychiatric population. This study, with Sid Blatt and John Auerbach, not only extended the use of the scale to a different aged population, but it further refined the degree to which we could understand what the measure correlated and didn't correlate with, including measures of symptomatology as well as actual interpersonal behavior. Findings revealed that the MOA scale was strongly related to the Concept of the Object scale, was positively associated with other RIM measures of reality testing and with neurotic and psychotic symptoms but not related to IQ, all of which further substantiated its use as a distinct and construct validated measure of object relations.

Psychoanalysis has increasingly focused on object-relations theories of personality (Kernberg, 1976; Mahler, Pine, & Bergman, 1975; Winnicott, 1958). This perspective, developed in parallel with research on social cognition and person perception in social psychology, places the representation of interactions between self and others at the center of normal and abnormal psychological development. Clinical research based on object-relations theory has made frequent use of projective techniques to assess both the cognitive structure and thematic content of interpersonal interactions (Blatt & Lerner, 1983; Hatcher & Krohn, 1980; Krohn & Mayman, 1974; Mayman, 1967; Spear, 1980; Tuber, 1983; Urist, 1977). A basic assumption of these research efforts is that dimensions of self and object representations on projective techniques provide methods for evaluating interpersonal or psychosocial

MOA Scale With a Slightly Older Population **39**

functioning. One important method of assessing representations of interpersonal interactions, Urist's (1977; Urist & Shill, 1982) Mutuality of Autonomy (MOA) Scale, is the object of this investigation.

Urist (1977) reported significant positive correlations of the MOA scale with independent ratings by ward staff of interpersonal relationships and with aspects of autobiographical descriptions of interpersonal experiences of adult inpatients. He stressed that individuals have a range of object representations that define the limits of their capacity for interpersonal relations. Calculating a mean MOA score, as well as the single most disrupted score and the single most adaptive score, Urist also found that individuals' capacities to give at least one response at the more integrated end of the MOA scale correlated significantly with ratings of constructive interpersonal behavior on the ward, whereas the tendency to give at least one response at the more disrupted end of the scale correlated significantly with ratings of disrupted relationships in autobiographical narratives. In a second study, Urist and Shill (1982) used comprehensive case records to assess the quality of interpersonal relationships of 60 adolescent patients. Developmental and family history reports, as well as clinical progress and nursing staff notes, were assessed with a version of the MOA scale adapted for rating clinical records. Ratings of the clinical case records correlated significantly with the mean and the single most disrupted MOA score on the Rorschach. More disrupted MOA scores on the Rorschach were consistently associated with reports of poorer interpersonal functioning on the clinical units and in past history. The single most adaptive MOA score on the Rorschach did not correlate with any ratings derived from clinical case records.

Harder, Greenwald, Wechsler, and Ritzler (1984) found that the MOA scale correlated significantly with ratings of severity of psychopathology derived from both complex symptom dimension checklists and independent diagnostic assessments according to the *Diagnostic and Statistical Manual of Mental Disorders* (3rd ed. [DSM-III]; American Psychiatric Association, 1980). The mean MOA score derived from only four Rorschach cards (Cards I, II, VI, and VIII) differentiated among schizophrenic, affective, and nonpsychotic conditions. More severe psychiatric disorders were associated with a more disrupted mean MOA score. Spear and Sugarman (1984) used a modified version of the MOA scale that identified differences among infantile borderline patients, obsessive paranoid borderline patients, and schizophrenics. Kavanagh (1985), in an analysis of the test protocols from the Menninger Psychotherapy Project, compared pre- and posttreatment Rorschach protocols of 33 patients receiving either psychoanalysis or psychotherapy. Kavanagh found no difference between admission and termination Rorschach protocols either for the mean MOA score or for the single most disrupted or most adaptive MOA score. Using an independent clinical judgment of subjects' MOA level, however, Kavanagh reported significant improvement at the end of treatment for patients treated both in psychoanalysis and in psychotherapy. Because the MOA scale rates the nature of interactions on the Rorschach

40 Projective Tasks Used in This Book

between animal and inanimate percepts, as well as between human figures, it has also been useful in the study of object representations in young children (Ryan, Avery, & Grolnick, 1985; Tuber, 1983, 1988). Thus, the Urist MOA scale seems to be a reliable and useful measure with adults, adolescents, and children in both clinical and nonclinical samples. MOA ratings correlate significantly with independent assessments of interpersonal behavior from clinical case records (Spear & Sugarman, 1984; Urist & Shill, 1982), ward staff ratings of social interactions (Urist, 1977), psychiatric symptomatology in adults and in children (Harder et al., 1984; Tuber & Goddard, 1989), and ratings of interpersonal behavior in a nonclinical context (Ryan et al., 1985).

The purpose of our study is to investigate further the MOA scale as a method of assessing the quality of interactions represented on the Rorschach by evaluating its relationship to independent clinical assessments of interpersonal behavior and clinical symptoms in a sample of acutely disturbed adolescent and young adult patients admitted to a long-term, intensive, but open residential treatment facility.

Method

Subjects

The sample consisted of 90 inpatients (45 women and 45 men) admitted to a small psychoanalytically oriented private hospital. The patients ranged in age from 18 to 29, with an average age at admission of 21 years. These patients were part of a larger study of psychotherapy change[2] and were selected for the study if they had been in treatment for at least 1 year and had been administered a repeated set of psychological tests, both early and late in the treatment process, that were recorded legibly enough to be used in research. No patient had an IQ of less than 80 or any indication of central nervous system impairment as assessed in a psychiatric evaluation and/or in psychological testing. In traditional diagnostic nomenclature, approximately 30% of the sample were regarded as psychotic, 60% as severe character or borderline personality disorders, and 10% as severely neurotic or depressed. Most of the patients were from at least middle socioeconomic status, were well educated, were of at least average intelligence, and had sufficient family resources or insurance coverage to afford long-term treatment in a private psychiatric facility.

Mutuality of Autonomy Scale

The average MOA score is assumed to express the individual's usual quality of interpersonal relatedness. To reflect a subject's range or repertoire of interactions, we also used each subject's single highest (most pathological) and single lowest (most adaptive) MOA scores in our data analyses. The MOA scale was scored by an expert judge who had established an acceptable level of interrater reliability

MOA Scale With a Slightly Older Population **41**

with this scale on other samples. In this study, the judge scored the MOA scale on the Rorschach without knowledge of the ratings made on the clinical case record. The three MOA scores (mean, highest, and lowest) were correlated with the independent clinical assessments of interpersonal behavior and clinical symptoms made from the clinical case records, as well as with several relevant Rorschach variables.

Independent Clinical Assessment

An extensive admission evaluation was conducted on each patient as part of the clinical process during the first 6 weeks of hospitalization. Data from multiple perspectives were gathered and integrated in a detailed case report. This report included family history (e.g., the history of the parents, siblings, spouse, and children, if any), the developmental history of the patient, a description of the present illness and its onset, the course of any previous therapy, current and past medical evaluations, a description by nurses and activities staff of the patient's initial behavior in the hospital, and a detailed account of the first 6 weeks of the psychotherapeutic interaction.

Clinical symptoms. The narrative case records were assessed for the presence of manifest symptoms with procedures developed by Strauss and Harder (1981) to rate reliably a wide range of disturbances included in the typical case history report. Strauss and Harder (1981) chose items to provide data on 32 symptoms originally derived from factor analyses, modified by clinical judgment, and subsequently validated in several clinical studies. In this procedure, a clinician reviews a case record and rates each symptom as absent or present and, if present, as mild or severe. Two judges in this study (an advanced graduate student in clinical psychology and an experienced master's level social worker) were able to achieve an acceptable level of inter-scorer reliability (item alpha > .65) for rating the total number of clinical symptoms in a case record. Each judge independently rated one half of the case records.

From a replicated factor analysis of clinical characteristics in a representative sample of first psychiatric admissions, Strauss, Kokes, Ritzler, Harder, and Van Ord (1978) identified several highly stable clusters of symptoms that do not correspond to usual diagnostic typologies. Using an orthogonal solution with varimax rotation, Strauss et al. found the following four factors: A Psychosis factor that accounted for 20.5% of the variance, a Neurosis factor accounting for 11% of the variance, and a Bizarre-Retarded factor and a Bizarre-Disorganized factor accounting for 8% and 6.5% of the variance, respectively. Strauss et al. reported that these four factors significantly differentiated among several diagnostic groups (schizophrenics, affective psychotics, and neurotics).

The symptoms on the Psychosis factor included delusions of control, reference, grandeur, religion, and sex; visual, auditory, tactile, and olfactory hallucinations; and suspiciousness, derealization, and depersonalization. Symptoms on the Neurosis

42 Projective Tasks Used in This Book

factor included depression, restlessness, somatic complaints, anxiety, obsession, withdrawal, and some insight into one's problems. The Bizarre-Retarded factor comprised symptoms of retarded movement and speech, flat affect, and bizarre behavior, whereas the Bizarre-Disorganized factor included symptoms of incomprehensibility, unkempt appearance, bizarre behavior, nonsocial speech, and incongruent and labile affect. Because very few of our patients had "bizarre behavior," the names of these last two factors were changed to Flattened Affect and Labile Affect to indicate that the difference between these last two factors in our sample was primarily one of affective tone. Strauss et al. (1978) commented that the first two factors (Psychosis and Neurosis) were particularly robust and stable. In our study, ratings of the patients on the four Strauss-Harder (S1-I) factor scales – Psychosis, Neurosis, Labile Affect, and Flattened Affect – were the measures of clinical symptomatology.

Evaluation of interpersonal behavior. Using primarily descriptions of the patients' daily interactions with other patients and staff, as reported by nursing and activities staff and other members of the clinical team, two judges evaluated the case records for dimensions of social behavior and interpersonal relations. Several previously established procedures were used to rate interpersonal communication and patterns of social behavior and involvement. The first was a measure originally developed by Fairweather et al. (1960) to rate ward behavior in an inpatient therapeutic setting. Items were dichotomous forced-choice assessments of a specific adaptive behavior and its maladaptive counterpart (e.g., "The patient participates in the activities around him" and "The patient ignores the activities around him"). We used a subset of this scale consisting of 32 items related to interpersonal communication, and two judges were able to achieve an acceptable level of reliability (item alpha > .65) in rating this scale. A high score is indicative of poor interpersonal involvement.

Interpersonal behavior was also rated on several scales developed at the Menninger Foundation (Harty et al., 1981) as part of their psychotherapy research project. These scales included an assessment of the patient's motivation for treatment, the capacity for sublimatory activity, the quality of object relations, the degree of superego and the ability to contain impulsivity. Each of these five variables was rated on a 100-point scale comprising several well-specified and clearly defined anchor points for each measure. Two judges were able curate these live at acceptable levels of reliability (item alpha > .65, except for Impulsivity, with an item alpha > .62). Factor analysis of the ratings of these five Menninger scales on our 90 subjects identified two primary orthogonal factors. The first factor accounted for 46.95% of the total variance, and four of the five scales had significant loadings on this factor: Motivation for Treatment, Sublimatory Effectiveness, Superego Integration, and Object Relations. The factor loadings of these four scales on the first factor were .83, .59, .73, and .88, respectively. Scores on the four significant loading Menninger scales were transformed to standard scores and then combined for each subject to get a score for this factor. This factor was labeled

Capacity for Interpersonal Relatedness. Impulsivity had only a minimal loading (-.003) on this first factor. The second factor, comprising the Impulsivity scale with a loading of .95, accounted for 24.49% of the total variance. The other four scales had loadings less than .50 on this second factor.

Other Psychological Test Variables

In addition to the MOA Scale, which assesses the thematic content of interactions portrayed on the Rorschach, the Rorschach protocols were scored for several traditional dimensions, as well as for two recently developed conceptual schemes designed to measure more structural aspects of psychological test protocols. Each of these variables had emerged from a factor analysis of Rorschach scores (Blatt & Berman, 1984) as defining a crucial psychological dimension. These variables included the degree of adherence to reality (F+) (Korchin & Larson, 1977), the extent of thought disorder involving disturbances in boundary articulation (Blatt & Berman, 1984; Blatt & Ritzler, 1974), the degree of affective lability (the weighted sum of color responses) (Blatt & Feirstein, 1977; Shapiro, 1977), and the amount (weighted sum) and mean developmental level of well differentiated, articulated, and integrated human forms that are accurately (OR+) or inaccurately perceived (OR-) (Blatt, Brenneis, Schimek, & Glick, 1976a, 1976b).

The weighted sum and the mean developmental level of the differentiation, articulation, and integration of accurately perceived human forms (OR+) assessed the capacity for investing in appropriate and satisfying interpersonal relationships; the weighted sum and the mean developmental level of differentiation, articulation, and integration of inaccurately perceived human forms (OR-) assessed the degree of investment in inappropriate, unrealistic, possibly autistic fantasies, rather than realistic relationships (Blatt, Schimek, & Brenneis, 1980; Ritzler, Wyatt, Harder, & Kaskey, 1980).

An overall estimate of thought disorder was developed for the Rorschach by differentially weighting several types of thought disorders in terms of severity of boundary disturbance (Blatt & Ritzler, 1974). The most severe boundary distribution was reflected by the contamination response, in which independent concepts or images lost their identity and definition. The next major thought disorder on the boundary disturbance continuum was the confabulation response. In this type of response, an initially accurate perception became lost in extensive, unrealistic, and grandiose personal elaborations and associations. In confabulatory thinking, ideas and images did not merge and fuse as in a contamination; rather, the extensive, unrealistic elaboration indicated a loss of the distinction between the external perception and one's personal associations and reactions to it. The third major, but less severe, level of boundary disturbance was indicated by the fabulized combination response. In these responses, the separate definition of independent objects or concepts was maintained, as was the distinction between the perception and personal reactions to it. But unrealistic thinking was expressed by establishing

44 Projective Tasks Used in This Book

illogical, arbitrary relationships between independent and separate percepts or concepts. Two separate percepts were interrelated simply because they were spatially or temporally contiguous.

Differential weighting of these three types of thought disordered responses allowed construction of a composite measure of the extent and severity of thought disorder on the Rorschach (Blatt & Berman, 1984; Blatt, Ford, Berman, Cook, & Meyer, 1988). This index included the three types of thought disorders and milder manifestations of each type of thought disorder – the thought disorder tendencies. In addition, a distinction was made between two different types of fabulized combination responses, one in which there was an arbitrary relationship between the two independent objects (e.g., a bear standing on a butterfly) and one in which the arbitrary relationship occurred within the definition of a single object (e.g., a bear with a rabbit's head). This latter type of fabulized combination was more like a contamination because it involved a tendency for the two disparate pans to blend into a single figure. It was thus considered to be more serious and more like a contamination tendency (Blatt & Berman, 1984).

All Rorschach variables were scored with acceptable levels of reliability (Item alpha > .65) and have demonstrated validity in prior research. Several Rorschach variables (e.g., thought disorder) were summation scores that reflected the frequency with which a particular type of response occurred in a Rorschach protocol. All summation scores were corrected by covariance to control statistically for total response productivity.

Results

None of the three MOA scores (the mean score, the single most disrupted, and the single most adaptive score) correlated significantly with Verbal, Performance, or Full Scale IQ.

The correlation between the MOA scores and the Concept of the Object scale (Blatt et al., 1976b) presented in Table 4.1 indicated a fair degree of convergent validity between the MOA ratings of the content of interaction responses and the more structurally determined Concept of the Object. The mean MOA score (a reverse scale) correlated significantly with the investment in inaccurately perceived human forms (OR-). The more malevolent the average thematic content attributed to interactions portrayed on the Rorschach, the greater the degree of elaboration of inaccurately perceived human responses (OR-), as measured by both weighted sum and mean developmental level. The mean MOA score, however, did not correlate significantly with the weighted sum or the mean developmental level of accurately perceived human forms (OR+). The single most disrupted MOA score correlated significantly ($p < .01$) with the investment in both accurately and inaccurately perceived human responses, whereas the single most adaptive MOA scale did not correlate significantly with either of the Concept of the Object scales.

MOA Scale With a Slightly Older Population **45**

TABLE 4.1 Correlation of MOA With Concept of the Object Scores

Concept of Object Scores	MOA^a		
	Mean Score	Single Most Disrupted Score	Single Most Adaptive Score
Developmental level (Weight sum)[b]			
OR+	.13	.31**	−.14
OR-	.26**	.21*	−.07
Developmental mean			
OR+	.11	.28**	−.08
OR-	.33***	.34**	−.01

Notes: N = 90.
[a]The Urist is a 7-point reverse scale ranging from most adaptive (1) to most pathological (7).
[b]The weighted sum is corrected by covariance for total response productivity in the Rorschach.
*$p < .01$. **$p < .001$. ***$p < .0001$.

To address issues of multicollinearity and to determine which of the four measures of investment in human responses were the most powerful predictors of MOA scores, we performed stepwise multiple regressions with a Bonferroni adjustment for multiple F tests. Alpha levels were set at .0125. The mean developmental level for inaccurately perceived human responses (OR-) significantly predicted the mean MOA score, $F(1, 88) = 10.95$, $p = .0014$, and the single most disrupted MOA score, $F(1, 88) = 12.05$, $p = .0008$. The mean developmental level for accurately perceived human responses (OR+) also contributed significantly to the prediction of the single most disrupted MOA score, $F(1, 88) = 7.74$, $p = .0066$. None of the measures of investment in human responses, however, predicted the single most adaptive MOA score. Thus, of the three Urist scores (mean and the most and least disrupted scores), the mean score was a more differentiated measure because it correlated significantly with OR-, but not with OR+. The single most disrupted MOA score, in contrast, correlated significantly and positively with both OR- and OR+, whereas the single least disruptive score did not correlate significantly with either OR measure.

MOA Ratings and Independent Assessment of Clinical Symptoms

As indicated in Table 4.2, the mean MOA score correlated significantly ($p < .05$) with the ratings of neurotic and psychotic symptoms as independently assessed from the clinical case record reports. The more the Rorschach responses portrayed malevolent and disrupted interactions, the greater the presence of neurotic and psychotic symptoms.

46 Projective Tasks Used in This Book

TABLE 4.2 Correlation of MOA Scores With Case Record Ratings

Case Record Ratings	MOA		
	Mean Score	Single Most Disrupted Score	Single Most Adaptive Score
Social relations:			
Menninger scales			
Motivation for treatment	.08	.03	.00
Sublimatory Capacity	−.04	.08	−.02
Impulsivity	.01	−.08	−.13
Superego Integration	−.27★★	−.21★	−.02
Object relations	−.03	−.002	−.08
Fairweather scale			
Interpersonal Communication	.10	.05	.20★
Clinical symptoms:			
Strauss-Harder			
Neurosis	.21★	.06	.23★
Psychosis	.35★★	.29★★	.32★★
Labile Affect	.14	.03	.27★★
Flattened Affect	.07	−.06	.14

Notes: All scales, except four of the five Menninger Scales (Motivation for Treatment, Sublimatory Capacity, Superego Integration, and Object Relations), are negative scales. Higher scores indicate poorer functioning. The Urist scale is also a reverse scale; higher scores indicate responses that portray more malevolent interactions. N = 90.
★$p < .01$. ★★$p < .001$. ★★★$p < .0001$.

The analysis of the correlations obtained with the single most disrupted and the single least disrupted MOA score provided further understanding of these relationships. The data presented in Table 4.2 indicate that the level of the single most disrupted MOA response (the level of each individual's most malevolently represented interaction) essentially replicated the findings obtained with the mean MOA score. In contrast, however, the most adaptive score (the level of each individual's least malevolent score) correlated significantly ($p < .05$) with several symptom scales. The more a patient was able to portray at least one interaction as constructive (nonmalevolent), the lower the number of neurotic and psychotic symptoms and the lower the affective lability indicated in clinical case records.

All six possible correlations among the four clinical symptoms measures were significant, Pearson rs(88) range from .25 to .42, ps < .02. To address issues of multicollinearity and to determine which of these four measures were the most powerful predictors of MOA scores, we performed stepwise multiple regressions with Bonferroni adjustment for multiple F tests. Alpha levels were set at .0125.

The Strauss-Harder Psychosis scale predicted the single most disrupted MOA score, $F(1, 88) = 7.92$, $p = .006$, the single most adaptive MOA score, $F(1, 88) = 10.07$, $p = .0021$, and the mean MOA score, $F(1, 88) = 12.43$, $p \leq .0007$.

MOA Ratings and Independent Assessment of Interpersonal Behavior

As indicated in Table 4.2, the three MOA scores did not seem to relate significantly in any consistent manner to estimates of interpersonal, social behavior as assessed from descriptions of the patients' behaviors in the clinical case records. Only superego integration correlated significantly with mean and single most disrupted scores. More malevolent interactions on the Rorschach were correlated with ratings of impaired superego integration. The Fairweather scale of interpersonal communication correlated significantly only with the single most adaptive MOA score. The more patients were able to portray at least on adaptive interaction on the Rorschach, the better their interpersonal communication with clinical staff and with other patients, as assessed by the Fairweather scale. Correcting for rnulticollinearity by using stepwise multiple regressions with Bonferroni adjustment for multiple F tests did not result in significant predictions of social adjustment.

MOA Ratings and Other Psychological Test Variables

As regards other test variables derived from the Rorschach, there was a highly significant correlation between the mean MOA score and measures of reality testing (F+%), thought disorder, and affective lability (Sum Color) on the Rorschach. As indicated in Table 4.3, the more malevolent the average MOA interaction response was on the Rorschach, the more impaired the reality testing ($r(88) = -.41$, $p < .001$), the greater the presence of thought disorder ($r(88) = .49$, $p < .0001$), and the greater the indication of affective lability ($r(88) = .44$, $p < .0001$). These significant

TABLE 4.3 Correlation of MOA Scores and Other Rorschach Variables

Variables	MOA		
	Mean Score	Single Most Disrupted Score	Single Most Adaptive Score
Reality Testing (F+%)	−.41★★★	−.27★★	−.16
Sum Thought Disorder[a]	.49★★★	.50★★★	−.11
Sum Weighted Color[a]	.44★★★	.37★★★	.29★★

Notes: Sum Thought Disorder, Sum Weighted Color, and the Urist MOA are reverse scales; higher scores indicate greater pathology. N = 90.
[a]Rorschach variables that are summation scores are corrected by covariance for total number of responses.
★$p < .01$. ★★$p < .001$. ★★★$p < .0001$.

48 Projective Tasks Used in This Book

relationships between the mean MOA score and these other Rorschach variables seemed to be determined primarily by the patient's tendency to give at least one disrupted and malevolent response, rather than by a failure to give at least one constructive response. The higher the single worst (most malevolent) score, the more disrupted the patient's degree of reality testing, and the greater the presence of thought disorder and indications of affective lability. In contrast, the tendency to give at least one constructive interaction response correlated significantly with only the measure of affective lability (Sum Color). The more a patient was able to give at least one response indicating more constructive interactions, the greater the indication derived from the Rorschach of a modulation of affective lability.

One correlation among these other three Rorschach variables was significant. Reality testing (F+%) correlated with thought disorder (r(88) = -.47, $p \leq$ .0001). The greater the thought disorder, the poorer the reality testing. Stepwise multiple regressions, with Bonferroni adjustments for multiple F tests, were performed to determine which of these three variables were the most powerful predictors of MOA scores. Alpha levels were set at .0167. Thought disorder significantly predicted the mean MOA score, F(1, 88) = 32.20, $p \leq$ .0001, and affective lability contributed significantly to this prediction, F(1, 88) = 25.49, $p \leq$ .0001. Thought disorder also best predicted the single most disrupted MOA score, F(1, 88) = 31.33, $p \leq$ 0001, with affective lability adding to the prediction, F(1, 88) = 21.20, $p \leq$ .0001. Affective lability also predicted the single most adaptive MOA score, F(1, 88) = 7.88, p = .0061.

Table 4.4 presents a more detailed analysis of the relationship between the three MOA scores and thought disorder on the Rorschach. The mean MOA score and the level of the single most disrupted MOA score correlated significantly (p < .05)

TABLE 4.4 Correlation of MOA Scores With Different Types of Thought Disorder on the Rorschach

	MOA		
	Mean Score	*Single Most Disrupted Score*	*Single Most Adaptive Score*
Contamination	.28**	.20*	.30**
Contamination Tendencies	.22*	.28**	.15
Confabulation	.47***	.41***	.16
Confabulation Tendencies	.32**	.27**	.23*
Fabulized to Confabulated	.56***	.54***	.06
Fabulized Combination Regular	.16	.22*	−.03
Fabulized Combination Serious	.27**	.32**	.11

Notes: Each of the different types of thought disorder are summation scores and, therefore, are corrected by covariance for total response productivity on the Rorschach. N = 90.
*p < .01. **p < .001. ***p < .0001.

MOA Scale With a Slightly Older Population **49**

with a wide range of thought disorder scores, thus indicating an impressive range of relationships between MOA performance and the different degrees of boundary disturbance that comprise the composite thought disorder score. It was clear that the mean MOA score and the tendency to give a single response expressing a highly disruptive interaction related significantly to indications of pathological thinking on the Rorschach. The single most adaptive MOA score, however, was relatively independent of the various forms of pathological thought.

To address issues of multicollinearity and to determine which types of thought disorder were the most powerful predictors of MOA scores, we again performed stepwise multiple regressions with Bonferroni adjustments for multiple F tests. Alpha levels were set at .0071. The number of fabulized to confabulated responses predicted the mean MOA score, $F(1, 88) = 40.03$, $p \leq .0001$. The number of fabulized to confabulated responses also significantly predicted the single most disrupted MOA score, $F(1, 68) = 36.50$, $p \leq .0001$. The number of contamination responses significantly predicted the single most adaptive MOA score, $F(1, 88) = 8.84$, $p = .0038$.

Discussion

The purpose of this study was to assess the degree to which patients' representations of interactions on the Rorschach were associated with independent judgments of the quality of interpersonal relationships and psychiatric symptomatology, as well as with estimates of functioning derived from other Rorschach variables. Prior research using the Urist MOA scale suggested that there was a significant relationship between the degree to which interactions on the Rorschach were portrayed as malevolent and disrupted and the degree of interpersonal behavior disturbance observed on the clinical unit (Harder et al., 1984), the need for later psychiatric re-hospitalization of children when they reach adulthood (Tuber, 1983), and the severity of psychiatric symptomatology (Spear & Sugarman, 1984). The results of our study are consistent with these prior findings and indicate that the portrayal of more disrupted interactions on the Rorschach is associated with both greater clinical symptomatology and with psychological test indicators of severe psychopathology. Malevolent content portrayed in interactions on the Rorschach is clearly related to measures of thought disorder, particularly thought disorder that indicates disrupted boundaries among independent ideas, affects, and images. Though the MOA and the thought disorder scores are both derived from the Rorschach, it is important to note that the MOA scores are based on thematic content and the thought disorder scores are determined by structural or formal properties of the responses.

It is also noteworthy that MOA scores are significantly correlated with independent assessments of clinical symptoms, especially with neurotic and psychotic symptoms, but not with independent assessment of interpersonal behavior. Though the MOA scale evaluates the thematic content of interactions between

50 Projective Tasks Used in This Book

people, animals, and things portrayed on the Rorschach, the data of this study suggest that the MOA scale seems to measure more a tendency toward pathological functioning than the nature of interpersonal relationships.

We also examined whether the results obtained with the mean MOA score were a function more of the tendency to give at least one response indicating a very disrupted interaction or of a failure to give at least one response expressing a more benign, benevolent interaction. A comparison of the findings using the single most disrupted and the single most adaptive response reveals that both these scores are less differentiated than the mean MOA score. Unlike these other two scores, the mean MOA score, when correlated with the Concept of the Object scale, relates specifically to measures of an investment in inappropriate interpersonal relationships and not to measures of an investment in constructive, adaptive interpersonal relationships. In addition, the results with the mean MOA score, rather than with the single most disrupted or most adaptive score, capture most of the major findings of our study.

The single most disrupted score appears to reflect a subject's general responsiveness to the Rorschach. It correlates significantly with an investment in both accurately and inaccurately perceived human forms, as measured by the Concept of the Object scale, as well as with the number of accurately perceived human movement responses. The single most disrupted response also correlates significantly with several clinical indications of severe pathology, including psychotic symptoms, impaired superego functioning, and signs on psychological tests of disrupted reality testing, thought disorder, and excessive affective lability. The single most adaptive response, in contrast, correlated significantly with lower scores on several Strauss-Harder symptom scales (Neurosis and Psychosis) and with indications of less affective lability, as assessed from both the narrative clinical case records and Rorschach Sum Color. The single most adaptive interaction responses on the Rorschach also correlated with better interpersonal behavior in the hospital, as measured by the Fairweather scale. These findings suggest that the capacity to represent at least one benign interaction on the Rorschach reflects the capacity for more conventional and adaptive behavior in social situations.

It is noteworthy that the tendency to give one adaptive interaction response on the Rorschach was related primarily to behavioral ratings derived from clinical case records and not to psychological test variables, whereas the tendency to give at least one severely disrupted interaction response correlated more with psychological test estimates of psychopathology. It seems that the single most adaptive MOA response reflects the patients' general ability to respond appropriately in social contexts. In contrast, the single most disrupted response seems to indicate the depth and severity of an individual's psychopathology, as expressed both in clinical symptoms and on an assessment procedure like the Rorschach. In social contexts, individuals seem to express their potential for adaptation, whereas on psychological tests, particularly the Rorschach, individuals seem to present their more pathological potential. The traditional Rorschach variables, at least those explored in this study (F+%, thought disorder, Sum Color), seem to give a view of the individual's more disturbed functioning or pathological potential.

In summary, the assessment of the thematic content of interaction responses on the Rorschach appears to be a valuable differential diagnostic measure. It enhances clinical research by including in the research methodology a reliable measure of how individuals represent the nature of interactions and thereby enables us to assess both the capacity to adapt in social contexts and the potential for more pathological and regressive functioning. The data suggest, however, that the MOA scale, at least with the young adult and adolescent patients in our sample, measures primarily a tendency toward pathological functioning and only secondarily assesses the capacity for interpersonal relatedness.

Notes

1 Copyright 1990, Lawrence/Erlbaum Associates, Inc. Reproduced with permission.
2 These data have been the focus of a large-scale collaborative study of the nature of psychological change during long-term intensive treatments (Blatt, Ford, Berman, Cook, & Meyer, 1988).

5

THE OBJECT REPRESENTATION
SCALE FOR DREAMS (KROHN)

Paper used: Gluckman, E., & Tuber, S. (1996). Object representations, interpersonal behavior and their relation to the dream reports of latency-aged girls. *Bulletin of the Menninger Clinic*, 60, 102–118.[1]

A contemporary of Jeffrey Urist, the creator of the MOA Scale at the University of Michigan, Alan Krohn looked to operationalize object relations utilizing dream reports in addition to RIM protocols as his source of data. Modeling his work on Mayman and Ryan's (1972) use of thematic content and reliance on the clinical judgment of raters, he developed the Object Representation Scale for Dreams (ORSD). It is of curious interest to me to note how rarely the ORSD has been used in empirical work compared to the MOA measure. I myself was reluctant to use it as it appeared to be more suited for work with adults, and most of my research was with children. It provides two very important distinctions from the MOA scale that suggest that its lack of usage is something to address in the field. First, it provides a far more differentiated measure of healthy object representations, as it has three scale points (points 6, 7, and 8 to be described below) that together offer a nuanced depiction of healthy relatedness in contrast with the MOA measure, which provides but one such scale point. More conceptually, it also provides a different picture of what lies at the depth of pathology. For the MOA measure, extreme pathology is measured by malevolence, as a scale point 7 score is described as a percept conveying all-encompassing destruction and annihilation. In that sense, it operationalizes the annihilation anxiety posited in Chapter 1 as the most primitive mode of human interaction. For Krohn, however, the most pathological scale point 1 is described as the presentation of the void, of a nothingness deemed more pathological than the malevolence Krohn provides in his scale point 2 score, which is far more like Urist's scale point 7 score. Krohn's scale point 1 is suggestive of the barrenness of the schizoid state. It would be most worthy of study with severely disturbed adult populations to test whether a sense of void vs. a sense of annihilation was

Object Representation Scale for Dreams **53**

indeed more present in certain cases and to determine whether those cases could be independently measured as more or less pathological.

Throughout human history as well as throughout the history of psychology, the dream, Freud's "royal road to the unconscious," has been viewed as a potential treasure trove of information about the human psyche. Clinicians often look to dream material when in doubt about a diagnosis, when unsure about the meaning of some transference manifestation, or when confused about the course a treatment may be taking. Many clinicians have reported the value of using dreams to assess such variables as, for example, degree of impulsivity (Saul, 1972), chronicity of symptomatology and adaptability of ego functioning (Warner, 1987), diagnosis and prognosis (Sperling, 1971), or intensity of unconscious conflicts (Sarnoff, 1976). However, the metaphorical "transformational grammar" (Chomsky, 1968) through which the clinician's intuitive grasp of the meaning of children's dream material translates into diagnostic knowledge appears to be largely undocumented.

One lens through which to view children's dream material is an object representational framework. Diagnostic knowledge of child development and psychopathology has been substantially augmented by the burgeoning interest in the study of children's representations of self and other both as a potential template of interpersonal relationships and as the thematic content of their fantasy life (Greenberg & Mitchell, 1983; Winnicott, 1971). Largely through the use of projective testing, object representational assessment of children has been notably successful in linking particular modes of representation to diagnostic and prognostic issues in child psychopathology (Stricker & Healey, 1990; Tuber, 1992). The application of object representation scales to children's dream material would seem to offer another means of looking at the relationship between object representations, this time as expressed in dreams, and psychological, interpersonal, and psychopathological variables of the individual dreamer.

One such scale has been used in such research with adults. Krohn (1972), working in conjunction with Mayman, developed an Object Representation Scale for Dreams (ORSD), which he validated using the dreams of adults (Hatcher & Krohn, 1980; Krohn, 1972; Krohn & Mayman, 1974). The scale has reliably differentiated various diagnostic categories of adults from one another (Sands, 1986; Skolnick, 1984), but has not been validated for use with children's dreams.

The ORSD is an 8-point ordinal scale. Krohn conceived various levels of deficit in object representation as failures of the internalization process over the course of the psychological history of the person: "On the least differentiated end [scale point 1] ... manifest dream ... data should reflect a virtual absence of internalizations, a vacant, fluid object world, resulting from a fundamental failure of introjection" (Krohn, 1972, p. 62).

At a slightly higher level (scale point 2), Krohn hypothesized that an inner [relational] world dominated by "'nonmetabolized' introjects would appear ... introjects which retain the undifferentiated, primitive affects experienced during

54 Projective Tasks Used in This Book

the process of these early introjections. Introjected during a period of life characterized by minimal affect regulation and cognitive differentiation, these inner objects often have an overwhelming, malevolent, brutal, all-powerful, or morbid quality" (p. 62).

At scale point 3, the next level of object representation, the "inner world ... [would be] characterized by an absence, fluidity, or insubstantiality of boundaries between self and object representations and among object representations, resulting from an incomplete separation in the introjective phase of development between self and object images" (p. 63). In addition, the object representations at this level are fragmentary, inconsistent, and unstable, because they were internalized before the achievement of the identification process that fuses momentary images into cohesive object representations.

Krohn conceived the next level of internalized objects, at scale point 4, to be "stable and consistent but 'real' and alive only around the gratification of need" (p. 63). Krohn noted that, theoretically, this level of object representation would closely correspond to Kohut's (1971) formulation of a narcissistically cathected object or self object which is "experienced only as it mirrors wished for or rejected qualities of the self. The object representations at this level consist, then, of others only as they gratify needs, worship the self, or extend the self" (Krohn, 1972, pp. 63–64).

"At the next stage [scale point 5], internal objects bear the stamp of early identifications" (p. 64). Ego splitting no longer predominates, and people are seen as cohesive, integrating both positive and negative aspects. At this level, affect tone is modulated, and the self and object representations are seen as having roles within themselves and in complementary relationship to each other.

At scale points 6, 7, and 8, the most advanced levels, object representations "would correspond to Kernberg's stages of consolidation of ego identity, the elaboration, organization, and deepening of object representations. With the stabilizing and maturing of ego structures, object representations take on a greater consistency, complexity, and definition" (p. 64). Therefore, Krohn continued, "The object representations at this stage are sufficiently differentiated to permit a growing recognition and understanding of the motives and feelings of others" (p. 65).

In his study of children's dreams, Foulkes (1982) noted that dreaming is an "index of mental operations and organizations" (p. 8). He added that because children do not know their role in making dreams, they are often not self-conscious about telling them; thus, dreams are "objectified mental acts" that "may be our best window on the inner mental life of children, who otherwise are neither interested in, nor competent at, introspection" (p. 8). In a sense, dreams are the purest form of projective material available, so it is therefore quite surprising that so little has been written on the use of children's dreams as projective material. Further, even less has been written on girls' dreams than on boys' dreams.

In light of this situation, the primary research goal of this study was to ascertain whether measures of object representation level can differentiate between psychologically healthy and psychologically disturbed children when they are applied to their dream reports. Concurrently, this study attempted to validate the use of the ORSD with children's dream material. The first step in this validation process was to determine whether the ORSD can reliably differentiate a group of healthy children from a group of disturbed children. A common mode of discriminating a clinical sample from a "normal" sample would be to use their active utilization of psychiatric services as the independent variable. This mode of discrimination, however, is problematic in that although referral to an emotionally handicapped special education class or to a therapy clinic often indicates emotional disturbance, it is certainly not proof of it. Rather, it might be a sign that a child or family is reacting to a conflictual or crisis situation. The acting-out behavior or symptomatology that brings a child to the attention of school authorities or mental health personnel may, in fact, represent a psychologically adaptive attempt to ameliorate a stressful or traumatic situation. Conversely, the lack of referral for mental health services does not necessarily rule out emotional disturbance. Therefore, the Achenbach Child Behavior Checklist (CBCL) was been included in the study to serve as the criterion for differentiating participants into nonclinical and clinical groups.

A second purpose of this study was to explore the link between the ORSD and behavioral indicators of social competence and abnormality, as measured by the CBCL, with the aim of further clarifying what an object representation scale measures in children and how the scale is related to overt behavior. A fundamental assumption of this study was that no dream report is an absolutely accurate, unbiased, unelaborated, "true" dream, because dreams are apperceived as visual images but retold in words. A translation process is necessarily involved in every dream sample. For the purposes of this study, a recalled dream was considered to comprise some undetermined mixture of sleep mentation, conscious fantasy elaboration, and unconscious but waking mentation, and to stand as a creative mental production that offers, in a fashion similar to other projective data, potentially valuable information about the nature and functioning of psychological processes.

We specifically hypothesized that the ORSD would reliably differentiate a clinical population of girls from a nonclinical population when applied to their recalled-dream reports. The nonclinical group was expected to obtain higher object representation level scores, meaning that the images of people or other figures in their dreams were more humanlike, more benevolent, richer in detail, more expressive of feelings and thoughts, and more empathic of each other than such images in the dreams of the clinical group.

Participants

The nonclinical group was initially composed of 25 students from the New York City public school system who were not being seen in any sort of therapy or counseling and who were screened by their respective teachers as meeting several

56 Projective Tasks Used in This Book

basic criteria of normality. The "clinical" child group was first composed of 26 children who were referred to a community mental health outpatient child psychiatry clinic for psychotherapy because of emotional difficulties. DSM-III-R Axis I diagnoses were obtained for every clinical participant from clinic case records. Using this treatment versus non-treatment dichotomy as an initial distinction, we then evaluated the entire sample with the CBCL. Results from the CBCL were considered a more robust measure of psychopathology than was simply being in psychiatric treatment, and thus they were used as the criterion measure, resulting in a nonclinical group of 24 and a clinical group of 27 participants. All schools and clinics involved in this study were located in stressful, high-crime, inner-city neighborhoods.

The participants ranged in age from 9 years 0 months to 11 years 11 months, with a mean age of 10 years 4 months. They ranged from 2nd grade to 7th grade, with a mean school grade of 4.37. All participants were female. Generally, pathology translates more directly into overt, observable behavior in males than in females. Therefore, the study was limited to females on the assumption that any behavioral indicators of psychological difficulty discovered would be all the more meaningful. In terms of prior research, there is clearly a need for exploratory study of the developmental progression of psychosocial stages and object relations as well as the manifestations of emotional disturbance in the dreams of girls, because most such studies to date have looked at boys (Elkan, 1969; Hickman, 1975; Mack, 1975).

Participants were interviewed with their guardians, who provided demographic information. Forty-three percent of the girls came from intact, two-parent households; 31% of the girls were cared for by single mothers; the remainder lived in foster situations, mostly with relatives. Sixty percent of the participants considered themselves to be African American, 29% Hispanic, and the remainder, Caucasian or mixed. Guardians ranged from 8–58 on the 66-point Hollingshead Socio-Economic Status Index, with a mean index of 26. An attempt was made to match participants in the clinical and nonclinical groups for cognitive, ethnic, racial, and socioeconomic variables. Statistical comparisons of the two groups across these measures revealed no differences between the groups, with the exception of the Laurendeau-Pinard Concept of Dream Questionnaire variable, which will be discussed.

Measures

Object Representation Scale for Dreams (see description above)

Measures of intelligence. A rough estimation of cognitive functioning (prorated Full Scale IQ) was obtained by administration of a shortened form of the Wechsler Intelligence Scale for Children – Revised (WISC-R) to the clinical sample. The shortened WISC-R was composed of the Vocabulary, Similarities, and Block

Object Representation Scale for Dreams **57**

Design subtests. A minimum prorated IQ of 75 was established for inclusion in the clinical participant pool in order to minimize the possibility that cognitive limitations would confound dream-telling ability and/or performance. Participants recruited through the public school system (the nonclinical group) were not permitted by school policy to take the prorated WISC-R. Citywide reading and arithmetic scores were therefore used with this portion of the sample to guard against the potentially confounding variables of cognitive under achievement and/or learning dysfunction. No participants below grade level in reading or arithmetic were selected.

Laurendeau-Pinard Concept of Dream Questionnaire. The Laurendeau-Pinard Concept of Dream Questionnaire (Laurendeau & Pinard, 1962) was used to measure how well participants understand what a dream is. This test was used by Foulkes (1982) for a similar purpose. The Concept of Dream Questionnaire is an interview-format scale comprising a systematic series of questions about the origin, location, cause, and reality of dreams. Scores range from 0–3. Incomprehension or refusal of the questions earns a rating of Stage 0. Stage 1 is that of Integral Realism, in which the child believes that the dream's origin is external to the dreamer and that the dream takes place in reality. Stage 2 is that of Mitigated Realism, a transitional stage wherein the dreamer oscillates between an internal and external localization of the dream. Stage 3, Integral Subjectivism, indicates an "operational" understanding of the idea of the dream (Foulkes, 1982, p. 43) as a subjective phenomenon located in the mind.

Procedure

If a child and her parent agreed to participate, an appointment was scheduled for administration of the experimental protocol to them. Interviewing of the clinical participants took place in the clinics from which the participants were recruited. Interviewing of nonclinical participants took place in either the participant's school or home. During the initial phone contact, the experimenter offered the child a verbal prompt to remember several dreams. Both parent and child were informed that they might discontinue their participation in the study at any time.

After the parent (mother) and child both signed the informed consent, the parent was given a Parent Questionnaire form and CBCL to fill out alone in a separate room.

During that time, the experimenter interviewed the child. The interview format began with filling out the Girl's Questionnaire, a simple form designed to put the participant at ease. Subsequently, the experimenter administered the modified WISC-R. The three WISC-R subtests were administered in randomly rotating order. Afterward, the child was asked to recall several dreams and to speak them into an audiotape recorder. During the collection of dreams, the first author followed a structured dream-inquiry format that she had compiled on the basis of pilot study experiences and other sources (Foulkes, 1982; Krohn, 1972; Spear,

58 Projective Tasks Used in This Book

1978). This format offered some structured flexibility to allow for participants' varying degrees of willingness to be questioned. Finally, the Laurendeau-Pinard Concept of Dream Questionnaire was administered. The sequence of test administration was designed to maximize efforts to put the child at ease early on in the interview, while minimizing any possible contamination of the dream material by intrusions of associations from previous tests.

After completion of the data collection protocol, a debriefing interview was held with the child to address any concerns and answer any questions. With the exception of the WISC-R administration, the procedure was identical for the nonclinical participants. The entire data collection interview with a child generally took about 75–90 minutes.

The experimenter then returned to the parent and reviewed both forms, question by question, to assure that the parent understood each question and answered each one as accurately as possible. Finally, a debriefing interview was held with the parent, similar to the one held with the child. This final interview with the parent generally took about 30–45 minutes.

Although the literature indicates that it is best to take a sampling of several dreams from each child on a number of occasions (Elkan, 1969; Mack, 1975), this study, limited by certain practical considerations, involved the collection of dream samples from each participant on just one occasion.

Coding and interrater reliability

Typed transcriptions of dreams were scored with the ORSD by two judges blind to other information about participants, working independently, after suitable interrater reliability was established. A training format was developed involving children's dreams, which were collected in a pilot study. Several training sessions were held on use of the scales. Pilot study dreams were then scored separately by the raters, in small batches. After each batch, raters met to review their scoring and resolve differences by conference. When raters were unable to resolve their differences, the experimenter, in consultation with several researchers familiar with the use of the scales, resolved the differences.

In scoring the ORSD, raters initially scored the dream material elicited from participants by the experimenter's request to tell a dream ("dream"). Subsequently, the raters scored the dream plus whatever additional material was elicited by the experimenter's structured inquiry ("dream plus inquiry"). The use of inquiry material changed the score in only 14 of 131 cases. Most often, the consideration of inquiry material raised the ORSD score by one or two scale points.

For the ORSD applied to dreams, raters achieved 65% exact agreement, and 85% agreement within one scale point. When raters scored dream plus inquiry, they achieved 64% exact agreement and 86% agreement within one scale point. This level of reliability is consistent with other studies using the ORSD or similar object representation measures (Stricker & Healey, 1990; Tuber, 1992).

Results

Because the samples were originally selected on a treatment versus nontreatment basis, we compared this dichotomy with the CBCL distribution to assess the degree of overlap between being in treatment and psychopathology score. The groups, as expected, were significantly different, not only in their CBCL Health–Pathology ratings (Mclinical = 68.3, SD = 8.9; Mnonclinical = 57.3, SD = 9.7; F[1,50] = 18.37, p < .0001), but also in their CBCL Competence ratings (Mclinical = 39.3, SD = 6.7; Mnonclinical = 47.3, SD = 6.8; F[1,50] = 18.34, p <.0001) as well. There was substantial overlap, however, with eight (31%) of the nonclinical girls falling into the clinical range and seven (27%) of the clinical girls falling into the normal or borderline ranges on their CBCL Total Problem scores. Therefore, the CBCL Total Problem score was used as a more accurate way of dividing the total sample into a clinical and a nonclinical group so as to ensure that those groups would be as different as possible from each other in the variable of behavioral symptomatology. This decision resulted in a clinical group of 27 and a nonclinical group of 24 participants.

The clinical and nonclinical groups differed significantly on the Laurendeau-Pinard Concept of Dream Questionnaire. This discrepancy in Concept of Dream scores between groups was primarily due to the failure of more of the clinical than nonclinical girls to achieve the highest subdivision (Substage 3B; see Table 5.1) of the highest dream concept state. However, a collapsed chi-square test (see Table 5.1), using Fisher's Exact Test, revealed that there was no significant difference between the groups in terms of reaching the final stage, Integral Subjectivism (Stage 3), in

TABLE 5.1 Cross-Tabulation of Laurendeau-Pinard Concept of Dream Scale Score by Substage and by Stage

Concept of Dream Substage	Clinical		Nonclinical			
	n	%	n	%	x^2	$p\star$
Stage						
1 (Integral Realism)	0	0	0	0	–	–
2 (Mitigated Realism)	6	22.2	4	16.7	0.274	.6026
3 (Integral Subjectivism)	21	77.8	20	83.3	–	–
Substage						
Stage 1 (no substages)	0	0	0	0	–	–
Stage 2A	0	0	0	0	–	–
Stage 2B	4	14.8	1	4.2	–	–
Stage 2C	2	7.4	3	12.5	–	–
Stage 3A	10	37.0	2	8.3	8.79	.0331
Stage 3B	11	40.7	18	75.0	–	–

Note: ★Probability values are two-tailed, using Fisher's Exact Test, given cell frequency < 5.

60 Projective Tasks Used in This Book

their conceptual level of understanding of the dream phenomenon. That is, most girls in both the clinical and nonclinical groups were able to understand the dream experience as being a personal, interior, invisible, immaterial phenomenon occurring during sleep, and therefore were not likely, by virtue of cognitive limitations, to confuse the dream with either waking fantasy or waking reality.

Object Representation Scale for Dreams

We hypothesized that the ORSD would differentiate the clinical and nonclinical groups in that the nonclinical participants would obtain higher level object representation scores than their clinical counterparts. This hypothesis was tested by means of a one-way multivariate analysis of variance performed on the ORSD scores representing the single lowest (LOR), single highest (HOR), and mean (MOR) levels of object representation obtained across the sample of from one to five dreams collected from each child.

Clinical participants ranged in LOR scores from 2 to 6, with a mean LOR of 2.7, while nonclinical participants ranged in LOR scores from 2 to 6, with a mean LOR of 3.9. Clinical participants ranged in HOR scores from 2 to 7, with a mean HOR of 6.0, while nonclinical participants ranged in HOR scores from 4 to 7, with a mean HOR of 6.0. Clinical participants ranged in MOR scores from 2 to 6, with a mean MOR of 3.8, while nonclinical participants ranged in MOR scores from 3 to 6.5, with a mean MOR of 4.9. As shown in Table 5.2, the nonclinical participants averaged significantly more adaptive ORSD scores than their clinical

TABLE 5.2 Multivariate Analysis of Variance of Krohn Object Representation Scale for Dreams (ORSD), by Group

A	B	C	D	E	F	G	H	I
ORSD LOR	2.7	1.3	3.9	1.4	9.42	.004	.38	.14
ORSD LOR[a]	2.7	1.3	3.9	1.4	9.20	.004	.38	.14
ORSD HOR	5.1	1.4	6.0	0.7	7.63	.008	.34	.12
ORSD HOR[a]	5.2	1.5	6.1	0.6	6.70	.013	.32	.10
ORSD MOR	3.8	1.1	4.9	0.9	14.25	.001	.49	.24

Legend for Chart:
A – Variable
B – Group, Clinical: (n = 27), M
C – Group, Clinical: (n = 27), SD
D – Group, Nonclinical (n = 24), M
E – Group, Nonclinical (n = 24), SD
F – $F_{(1, 48)}$
G – p
H – omega[b]
I – omega^2
Notes: [a]Based on dreams with inquiry. [b]Approximate correlation estimate.

Object Representation Scale for Dreams **61**

counterparts (Pillais Statistic = 0.24, F = 2.76 (5, 44), p = .03). Therefore, the hypothesis was confirmed, in that the five scores generated from the ORSD did significantly differentiate the clinical from the nonclinical groups.

Correlations Between ORSD Scores and CBCL Subscales

In an effort to explore in more detail the way in which the ORSD corresponded to actual behavioral symptoms in children, a correlational analysis was performed with several ORSD scores and the various CBCL subscales. Referring to the correlation matrix shown in Table 5.3, we see that the ORSD LOR is the most robust of the three ORSD scores examined, in its ability to differentiate a clinically pathological group of children from a nonpathological group. This is consistent with a number of other studies that have used the ORSD and similar scales to discriminate pathological groups from one another (Stricker & Healey, 1990; Tuber, 1992).

In particular, ORSD LOR scores tended to correlate with the presence of social problems, thought problems, attentional problems, delinquent behavior, and aggressive behavior. On the other hand, no ORSD score was correlated with the presence of withdrawn behavior, somatic complaints, anxiety/depression symptoms, or sexual problems. The ORSD then, in general, tended to indicate the presence of externalizing behavior or acting-out behavior, while not necessarily picking up the presence of internalizing behavior or inward-directed symptoms such as psychosomatic problems, depression, or withdrawal.

Notably, the strength of the correlation between the most highly correlated single ORSD measurement (i.e., the lowest of scores obtained over the one to five dreams collected from each participant, or ORSD LOR) and the measure of psychological health–sickness used in this study (i.e., the CBCL) was approximately .37. This correlation is similar to that of .33 originally obtained by Krohn when he correlated the ORSD with a measure of actual behavioral symptoms. The relationship seems to be similar for both children and adults.

Discussion

This study sought to extend the assessment of children's object representations from projective tests to dream depictions. A first step in this process was to ascertain whether the ORSD could discriminate between a clinical and a nonclinical group of children. Our study provides some beginning empirical support for the usefulness of this object representational approach to children's dreams. Overall, nonclinical participants produced, as expected, dream reports whose thematic content was more benign, cohesive, and modulated than that of the clinical participants.

A close look at the correlations between the ORSD and the individual CBCL subscales raises the question of why the ORSD correlates with certain

62 Projective Tasks Used in This Book

TABLE 5.3 Correlations Between Selected ORSD Scores and CBCL Subscales

A	B	C	D
I. Withdrawn	-.13	-.01	-.07
	(.175)	(.461)	(.304)
II. Somatic Complaints	-.13	.00	-.07
	(.178)	(.491)	(.306)
III. Anxious/Depressed	-.25	-.17	-.23
	(.037)	(.115)	(.101)
IV. Social Problems	-.33★	-.22	-.30
	(.01)	(.059)	(.017)
V. Thought Problems	-.37★	-.17	-.34★
	(.005)	(.123)	(.008)★
VI. Attention Problems	-.36★	-.13	-.26
	(.005)	(.194)	(.035)
VII. Delinquent Behavior	-.34★	-.18	-.30
	(.009)	(.101)	(.018)
VIII. Aggressive Behavior	-.35★	-.30	-.38★
	(.007)	(.019)	(.003)★
IX. Sex Problems	-.28	-.06	-.24
	(.023)	(.329)	(.044)
Problem—Internalizing	-.22	-.07	-.15
	(.066)	(.304)	(.142)
Problem—Externalizing	-.37★	-.31	-.40★
	(.004)	(.014)	(.002)
Total Problems	-.35★	-.25	-.34
	(.007)	(.038)	(.008)
Competence—Activities	-.00	.10	.07
	(.491)	(.248)	(.321)
Competence—Social	.16	.10	.15
	(.128)	(.252)	(.153)
Competence—School	.02	.33★	.17
	(.443)	(0.01)	(.114)
Total Competence	.09	.24	.18
	(.259)	(.048)	(.104)

Legend for Chart:
A – Achenbach CBCL Problem scales
B – ORSD LOR[a]
C – ORSD HOR[a]
D – ORSD MOR[a]
Notes: One-tailed probability levels are reported in parentheses. [a]n = 51.
★$p < .01$.

manifestations of pathology and not others. In general, the CBCL subscales
that correlated most strongly with the ORSD – that is, Aggressive Behavior,
Delinquent Behavior, Attentional Problems, and Social Problems (primarily
immature behaviors such as clinging) – encompass behaviors that tend to elicit

Object Representation Scale for Dreams **63**

rejecting or hostile responses from others. One might speculate that low scores on the ORSD correlate with these acting-out sorts of behaviors not only because they indicate the presence of poor internal objects, but also because they may set up negative feedback loops that would seem to perpetuate both poor relationships and poor object representations. That is, the expectation of a malevolent response to a behavior might lead to a defensive action that in fact does antagonize the other, leading to further confirmation that the "object world" is indeed toxic, with this process repeating itself ad infinitum. In light of this speculation, it is interesting that the ORSD also picks up thought problems, because this is more an internally than an externally manifested behavior. In any case, the speculation of a negative object representation feedback loop offers the clinical implication that for children of the preadolescent age range, behavioral intervention at the level of reversing such negative feedback loops would be important.

The lack of correlation between the ORSD and the three CBCL "internalizing" subscales – Withdrawn, Somatic Complaints, and Anxiety/Depression – represents both a disappointment and a puzzle. Troubled girls often go unnoticed and untreated because their symptoms are frequently inwardly directed and so do not attract attention and eventual help. We hoped that this scale would provide a way of identifying these sorts of problems for that very reason, but unfortunately this was not the case. This result raises interesting questions. For example, can one hypothesize the existence of an internalizing behavioral cluster that exists entirely independent of object representational status?

An interesting and unexpected difference between the clinical and nonclinical groups turned out to be cognitive maturity. The clinical girls achieved significantly lower scores than the nonclinical girls on the Laurendeau-Pinard Concept of Dream Questionnaire. Although most girls in both groups achieved the final stage, Integral Subjectivism, in their conceptual level of understanding of the dream phenomenon (i.e., that the dream is personal, interior, invisible, and immaterial), almost one half of the clinical girls still attributed the source of the dreams to external forces such as God (a last vestige of precausal thinking), while most of the nonclinical girls displayed no precausal thinking in their understanding of the dream as an entirely objective phenomenon. In light of these cognitive differences between the clinical and nonclinical groups, one might speculate that some relationship links cognitive maturity, externalizing behavioral symptoms, and lower levels of object representation. Certainly aggressive behavior, delinquent behavior, and attentional deficits are often correlated with learning delays and immature cognitive development in areas such as judgment, insight, and the ability to foresee consequences. In such a model, one would hypothesize that for the developmentally delayed child, cognitive and emotional immaturities conspire just as powerfully as significant external figures to engender and perpetuate the negative object representations seen at the lower end of the ORSD. The implication of such a model for treatment, then, would be to focus as much on compensating for cognitive deficits and on shoring up ego weaknesses as on treating the emotional turmoil, when attempting to treat the behaviorally acting-out or hyperactive child.

Limitations of the Study

The method of dream collection is an important factor in any study about dream content. Foulkes (1982, p. 19) wrote that the collecting of dreams from REM, NREM, or sleep onset nocturnal sleep awakenings (in a sleep laboratory) is the only way to collect accurate, representative dream samples. He held that dreams remembered days or weeks later would represent a biased sampling of dreams, remembered, perhaps, because the participant awoke during or shortly after a dream due to some disturbing factor in the content of the dream or in sleep patterns or because of some other bodily function. In addition, one might assume that dreams recalled after some time would more likely be elaborated by conscious fantasy and distorted by imperfect memory or defensive ego functioning than would sleep-awakening dreams. Foulkes (1982) in fact did observe his dream samples to be less bizarre and disturbing than dream samples generally described in the clinical dream research literature. The impossibility of collecting dreams from nocturnal sleep awakening clearly constitutes a limitation of this study. However, given that the study seeks to provide some way of rating dream material that is accessible to clinicians upon diagnostic examination, the use of "less accurate," "more biased," later remembered dreams can be justified.

Cross-Sectional Versus Longitudinal Study

Foulkes (1982) argued the advisability of the longitudinal research design for any study in the area of dreams. He stated that "age and state related fluctuations in baseline measures of any dream characteristic will obscure cross-sectional results" (p. 191).

The cross-sectional design of this study is a disadvantage, particularly in regard to the matter of state fluctuation. One must assume that a child's dream material is highly reactive to the day's events and mood shifts. Therefore, a series of dream collection interviews spaced out over a significant period of time most likely would have produced a sampling of dream data more characteristic of the underlying personality organization of each participant.

The Confounding Variable of Treatment

To locate a sizable sample of girls known to have exhibited psychopathological symptomatology, clinical participants were recruited from mental health clinics. Therefore, although some of the clinical participants (as judged by the CBCL) were recruited from the public schools and had never been in therapy, most of the clinical sample had undergone a period of psychotherapy. This circumstance constitutes a methodological limitation of the study because it is possible that any finding of a difference between the clinical and nonclinical groups may be attributed to participation in therapy rather than to the greater degree of pathology in the clinical participants. The major area in which this limitation affected interpretation of results involved certain object representation scores wherein the clinical participants achieved higher levels than the nonclinical participants. In these cases, it was impossible to determine whether their higher levels of object representation were related to pathology or to time spent in therapy.

Note

1 Copyright 1996, Guilford Press. Reproduced with permission.

6

THE ANIMAL PREFERENCE TEST

Paper used: Rojas, E., & Tuber, S. (1991). The Animal Preference Test and its relationship to behavioral problems in young children. *Journal of Personality Assessment*, 57, 141–148.[1]

It has always been central to my thinking that it was not the instrument chosen to study that was of primary interest, but rather the assessment of the underlying utility of the domain of object representations that was central. This was embodied in a paper that my colleague Evelyn Baez Rojas and I wrote utilizing the Animal Preference Test.

The Animal Preference Test (APT) was first used with children by Van Krevelen (1955). Each child was asked to name both the animal they would like to be (positive choice) and the animal they would not like to be (negative choice) "if you had to return to this world and you could not be a person." In each case, the question was followed by an inquiry into why the child did or did not want to be that particular animal. Van Krevelen then provided clinical vignettes to illustrate how children project different psychological conflicts onto an animal symbol based on both their emotional needs and their specific notions about that animal's characteristics.

Numerous authors have described the ease with which young children use animals as sources for projection, identification, and/or displacement of their salient emotional needs and wishes. Particularly, Bellak (1986) posited that, for preadolescent children, animals offer a number of advantages vis-à-vis humans that suggest their usefulness in projective rests: They offer some "manifest disguise" (p. 237) for the child's unacceptable wishes and drives; animals are usually smaller than human adults and are thus "underdogs" like children; these emotional relationships to animals are easier for children to handle. Despite the advantages, however, very

The Animal Preference Test **67**

few studies have attempted to provide additional data regarding the clinical utility of the APT, particularly with children. Early studies revealed that positive APT choices reflect a more rational, intellectualized process, whereas the negative APT response appeared less rational and more idiosyncratic in content (David & Leach, 1957); the vast majority of responses for both boys and girls were contained in a relatively small number of everyday animals (Freed, 1965).

After a brief conversation to establish rapport, each child was asked: "If you could no longer be a person, what animal would you most like to be?" Their second and third choices were also requested. The child was then asked "If you had to be an animal, what animal would you never like to be?" A second and third choice was also requested for this question. After giving their responses, the child was then asked why he chose each of the six animals. The test took between 5 and 10 minutes to administer and was responded to favorably by all the children. A brief play period was conducted after administration of the APT while the child's mother was given the CBCL in another room (or if the child was tested at his clinic, his mother was interviewed at another time in her home).

Reasons for selecting a given animal were assigned to one of the four categories derived from the two pilot studies. No other content categories were needed. A response is considered aggressive when an animal is chosen because it attacks, bites, scratches, fights, or is fierce, combative, hostile, and unfriendly. A response is categorized as autonomous when the animal was chosen because of its freedom, independence, large size, muscular vigor, physical efficacy, self-reliance, and/or decisiveness. A response is considered to tap nurturance themes when the animal is chosen because it provides or craves for shelter, protection, love, wellbeing, food and/or support. Last, a response is scored as fitting in the pleasure-beauty category when the animal is chosen because it is beautiful, delicate, graceful, aesthetically pleasing, or leads a good life.

The marked ease with which this "test" can be given and the value animals have as identificatory figures for young children certainly suggest that future empirical work could be useful. Instead, I have used the method in my clinical work with children but never again in empirical work, although in the final chapter to this volume, I will discuss some future studies that will contain this procedure for assessing object relations and use it in comparison with RIM and Thematic Apperception Test (TAT) data.

The paucity of research with this easily administered yet apparently forgotten set of projective questions prompted two pilot studies by the first author of this article (Rojas, 1981 [unpublished manuscript]; Rojas & Mintzer, 1978). These studies determined that the reasons children gave for their positive animal preferences could be categorized reliably as depicting aggression, autonomy, nurturance, and pleasure-beauty themes. Girls were more prone to select animals for their nurturing qualities whereas boys tended to give more aggressive reasons; younger children were more likely to give nurturing responses than aggressive ones; and middle-class children gave more autonomous reasons for their animal preferences

68 Projective Tasks Used in This Book

than lower-class children (Rojas & Mintzer, 1978). Rojas (1981) found that these sex differences were replicated with Black children of low socioeconomic status (SES). However, findings with low SES Dominican children failed to show any significant difference with regard to either age or sex.

The results of these previous studies indicate that the reasons given for animal preference, at least in the non-Dominican samples, may be linked with gender, SES, and chronological age in a meaningful way. These preliminary data, therefore, suggested that the APT may be capable of highlighting salient personality variables in young children. As a first test of this possibility, we decided to correlate positive and negative animal preference with an independent measure of clinical behavior, the Achenbach Child Behavior Checklist (CBCL). We hypothesized that the thematic categories used in describing the reasons for positive animal preference, tapping more conscious, rational motives and identifications, would not differentiate actual child behavior within a clinical child sample. The reasons for negative animal choices, on the other hand, would reveal less well-defended tears, impulses, and wishes. We used three choices in both positive and negative categories and hypothesized that the consistency of theme in the negative choice situation would correlate significantly with the problematic behaviors manifested in these children, as measured by the CBCL. We sought to explore whether this correlation would persist in a clinical population despite the non-significant age and gender correlations reported for the nonclinical Dominican samples.

Method

Subjects

Black (n = 9) and bilingual Dominican (n = 31) 6- to 13-year-old boys were interviewed in this study. The children were recruited from the Morrisania Family Health Care Center, Unitas, and the South Bronx Mental Health Council – all public mental health clinics in lower SES neighborhoods in the South Bronx. The subjects were randomly selected from the active clinic files with age and gender being the sole discriminating factors in selection. Only a very small number of the parents of the children initially selected refused to participate; therefore additional children were randomly selected.

Procedure

The children and their mothers were interviewed either at the outpatient clinic they attended or at their homes. The children were given the APT by the first author, while a trained bilingual interviewer, unaware of the child's APT scores, administered the CBCL to the mothers. Informed consent was obtained from all parents prior to the administration of the APT and CBCL.

The APT

Reliability

Reasons for stating animal preference (positive and negative) were grouped into one of the four categories by two independent raters (one PhD candidate in clinical psychology, another PhD candidate in social work). The raters were unaware of the CBCL scores and the demographic characteristics of the subjects in the study. Interrater agreement for both the positive and negative choices was 91%. Disparate ratings were resolved by the first author by independently scoring the discrepant 22 of 240 responses and using this score as the final one. The first author was blind to the identity of the children giving these responses.

Results

We asked each child for a set of three positive and three negative animal choices, because we were especially interested in the internal consistency or theme dominance within each choice category. Theme dominance was defined as the degree of homogeneity or similarity in the categorization of why animals were chosen for either the three positive or the three negative choices. When all three responses in a given set were assigned the same thematic category, the set manifested full dominance. Partial dominance indicated that two of the three responses had been similarly categorized. No dominance identified those sets of responses where no two responses were placed in the same theme category. We felt that the use of more than one animal choice and the concept of theme dominance would provide a firmer base for understanding animal preference, as opposed to relying on a single positive and negative choice. Table 6.1 provides the groupings for both positive and negative animal choice across each theme category for the subjects. As Table 6.1 indicates, 7 of the 40 subjects chose three different reasons for positive animal preference, whereas 3 of the 40 subjects gave three different themes for their negative animal preferences. Thus, the vast majority of children (82% in the positive choice situation and 93% in the negative choice situation) were quite consistent in the reasons they gave for choosing different animals within the positive and negative choice situation. For 39 of the 40 children, however, the reasons given for positive versus negative animal choices were not identical, suggesting that the positive and negative questions tap different aspects of psychological experience.

CBCL Scores and APT Theme Dominance

Subjects' theme dominance was then compared with CBCL performance. Because of the small sample size, we combined the aggression and autonomy categories and the nurturance and pleasure-beauty categories and compared these two new groups on their CBCL scores. The two newly formed groups – aggression/

70 Projective Tasks Used in This Book

TABLE 6.1 Distribution of Dominant Scores for Each APT Theme Category

Dominance	Aggression	Autonomy	Nurturance	Pleasure-Beauty	Total
Positive choices					
Full	3	8	2	1	14
(3 of 3)					
Partial	2	6	5	3	19
(2 of 3)					
No dominance					
Negative choices					
Full	12	0	2	1	15
Partial	10	1	5	6	22
No dominance					3

TABLE 6.2 Comparisons Between Groups 1 and 2 on Negative Choices

CBCL Scales	Group 1[a] Aggressive/Autonomy		Group 2[b] Nurturance/ Pleasure-Beauty	
	M	SD	M	SD
Anxious	3.52	3.04	4.53	3.04
Depressed	7.72	5.74	14.02	6.81★
Uncommunicative	4.72	3.41	7.13	2.61
Obsessive/Compulsive	8.00	5.80	10.93	5.42
Somatic Complaints	2.64	2.27	3.80	2.62
Social Withdrawal	3.24	2.37	5.87	3.27
Hyperactive	8.52	4.02	11.60	4.07
Aggressive	17.60	8.57	27.53	9.94★★
Delinquent	5.60	4.20	7.93	4.17

Notes: [a]$n = 23$, [b]$n = 14$.
★$p < .05$. ★★$p < .001$, from post-hoc tests.

autonomy (Group 1) and nurturance/beauty (Group 2) – distinguished children whose reasons for positively or negatively wishing to be an animal were determined by aspects of moving away from others versus moving towards others or a preoccupation with the self.

No significant group differences were found on any of the CBCL subscales when examining the reasons for positive animal choices, as was hypothesized.

Table 6.2 compares the two groups' negative APT choices and the nine clinical subscales of the CBCL. An examination of Table 6.2 reveals that all the means for Group 2 on the nine CBCL subscales are greater than the means in Group 1. A repeated measures analysis of variance (ANOVA) revealed a significant main

The Animal Preference Test **71**

effect for group, $F(1, 38) = 9.8, p < .001$. In addition, there was a significant Group X Scale interaction, $F(8, 304) = 5.5, p < .001$, as a consequence of some of the scales distinguishing the groups and others not. Explicitly, from post-hoc tests, Group 2's mean score on the Depression subscale was significantly greater than Group 1's mean score at the $p < .05$ level, based on a Tukey test, whereas Group 2's mean score on the Aggression subscale was also greater than Group 1's at the $p < .001$ level, also using the Tukey test. Thus, the second hypothesis was partially supported with respect to depression and aggression.

Discussion

As hypothesized, themes consistently expressed within the negative animal preference category were linked to actual problematic behavior for a clinical sample, whereas theme expressions within the positive animal preference category were not.

Our findings indicate that negative animal preference appears to be a better indicator of children's behavioral difficulties as assessed by their parents than by responses to the positive APT. This finding supports David and Leach's (1957) work, in that negative APT choices seem to tap more individualized aspects of inner experience, and positive APT choices reflect more conventional, stereotypical, and less variable personality dimensions.

The findings also provided evidence that the children who consistently rejected an animal on the basis of its nurturing, pleasurable, or aesthetic qualities exhibited both more aggressive and depressed behaviors, as measured by their parents, than those children whose rejection of an animal was based on its aggressive, autonomous traits. For the Group 2 children, the disowning of animals for their nurturant or aesthetic qualities was meaningfully related to depressed behavior. We parsimoniously interpret this link as a repudiation of a need for nurturance in the service of maintaining emotional equilibrium. The finding that this repudiation is also strongly linked to more aggressive behavior further suggests that this defensive maneuver is maladaptive. It does not serve as a mechanism that helps buffer these children from exhibiting overtly aggressive behavior.

It is noteworthy that the negative APT could meaningfully subdivide a sample of children who are all psychiatric outpatients and are referred predominantly for their problematic conduct. Even within this clinical population, the rejection of nurturing or physically gratifying aspects of animals appears to tap particularly maladaptive aspects of personality. Further research comparing negative APT theme dominance with other independent measures of ego functioning seems appropriate in this regard.

Given the relatively homogeneous demographic profiles of this sample, the negative APT's ability to discern meaningful behavioral differences is noteworthy. The ease of administration and relatively high interrater reliability further suggests its expanded use in the ongoing attempt to assess and treat troubled children. Care

72 Projective Tasks Used in This Book

should be taken not to generalize our findings to populations other than Black and Dominican 6- to 12-year-old boys. An extension of this research paradigm to other samples of differing sex, age, SES, and cultural background is indicated.

Our study failed to control for the reasons for referral as well as for a more specific depiction of the children's psychiatric diagnoses. This information would have provided another basis for comparing these children in relation to their performance on both the APT and CBCL. Further research linking psychiatric diagnoses, APT performance, and actual behavior is also indicated.

Note

1 Copyright 1991, Lawrence/Erlbaum Associates, Inc. Reproduced with permission.

SECTION THREE
Assessing the Object Relations of Varying Child Populations

Notwithstanding the two forays into using other measures (the Krohn scale in the study with Gluckman) or measures other than the RIM (the APT in the study with Rojas), the use of the RIM remained my primary focus. Having meaningfully used the RIM to assess the object relations of both a normative and a clinical child sample, we sought to expand its utility by studying children with one of a number of specific clinical syndromes. A particular focus was children with Attention Deficit Hyperactivity Disorder (ADHD). In the following paper within this group, Meehan et al. use Human Movement (M) scores on the RIM as a prime measure of the ADHD group's deficits in self-regulation.

7

THE OBJECT RELATIONS OF CHILDREN WITH ADHD

Paper used: Meehan, K., Reynoso, J., Ueng-McHale, J., Harris, B., Wolfson, V., Gomes, H., & Tuber, S. (2009). Self-regulation and internal resources in school-aged children with ADHD. *Bulletin of the Menninger Clinic, 72*(4), 237–261.[1]

The diagnosis of attention deficit hyperactivity disorder (ADHD) has received such widespread interest from both the scientific community and mainstream media sources that it is easy for the average person to conjure a stereotypical image of an easily distracted, fidgety, impulsive, driven-by-a-motor child who can single-handedly disrupt even the most well-managed classroom. Despite its extensive use and application in clinical child populations, the ADHD diagnosis continues to be accompanied by dilemmas regarding its conceptualization, assessment, and treatment (Anastopoulos & Shelton, 2001; Faraone, 2005; Stubbe, 2000; Nichols & Waschbusch, 2004).

Conservatively, ADHD has been estimated to be prevalent in 3%–7% of the child population (American Psychiatric Association, 2000), although rates ranging from 7%–21% have also been reported among community samples (Bauermeister et al., 2007; Baumgaertel, Wolraich, & Dietrich, 1995; DuPaul, Power, & Anastopoulos, 1997; Wolraich, Hannah, & Pinnock, 1996). ADHD-related difficulties have proven to be so seriously pervasive that Barkley (2005) estimated that between 30% and 40% of referrals to child mental health practitioners could be conceptualized as ADHD-related cases.

Complicating matters, there is a high rate of comorbidity between ADHD and other externalizing disorders of childhood. It has been estimated that about half of children diagnosed with ADHD also meet criteria for conduct disorder (CD) and oppositional defiant disorder (ODD) (Biederman, Newcorn, & Sprich, 1991). Children with ADHD also evidence a high rate of comorbidity with internalizing

76 Object Relations of Child Populations

disorders of childhood, with estimates that about one third of these children meet criteria for depressive or anxiety disorders (Jensen, Shervette, Xenakis, & Richters, 1993; Tannock, 2000).

The problems associated with ADHD, which begin in childhood and often continue through adulthood, not only affect academic and professional achievement, but also impact family and peer relationships (Barkley, 2005; Hinshaw et al., 1997a). Indeed, a number of researchers have demonstrated the profound social consequences of ADHD in children's lives, including a greater tendency to be rejected by peers, to misperceive their own social abilities in interactions, and to exhibit patterns of intrusiveness and disruptiveness (e.g., Diener & Milich, 1997; Flicek, 1992; Hinshaw, Zupan, & Simmel, 1997b; Hodgens, Cole, & Boldizar, 2000; Landau & Moore, 1991; Nixon, 2001; Pfiffner, Calzada, & McBurnett, 2000; Waschbusch, Pelham, & Jennings, 2002; Zalecki & Hinshaw, 2004).

Authors have described conceptual models closely tied to the empirical literature that explain social dysfluency in ADHD in terms of underlying problems in affect regulation, management of behavioral intensity, and social reciprocity and communication (Saunders & Chambers, 1996; Pfiffner et al., 2000). In addition, the past decade has seen the ascension of neuropsychological theories explaining ADHD-related difficulties as resulting from impairments in neurologically based behavioral inhibition mechanisms (Quay, 1997). In particular, many theoreticians have come to view ADHD as stemming from a deficit in the arena of executive function (e.g., Barkley, 1997; Shallice & Plaut, 1992). Barkley (1997) offers one of the most comprehensive views of deficits in executive functions associated with ADHD. He argues that ADHD is misconceived as a disorder of general attention and should be conceived of as a disorder of internally regulated, sustained attention, which for some children may be secondary to deficits in behavioral inhibition.

Similarly, Gilmore (2000, 2002) links the organization and integration of ego capacities to problems in ADHD. Drawing from an ego-psychological perspective, she proposes a model that views ADHD and its treatment in the context of the interplay among intrapsychic, developmental, constitutional, and environmental/familial factors. She notes that the capacity to attend is dependent upon the organization and integration of ego capacities, which is not a given but a developmental accomplishment, and that impairment in ego functioning is reciprocally intertwined with attentional impairment, disturbances in object representations, and affect regulation from very early on in life. With low tolerance for intense affect and anxiety, children with ADHD can become easily dysregulated by unexpected changes in their environment and by the dynamic quality inherent in social exchanges. They then may appear either hyperexcitable and anxious, or in contrast, oddly constricted and lacking in anxiety.

The Rorschach Inkblot Method (RIM; Exner, 1993; Klopfer & Kelley, 1942; Rapaport, Gill, & Schafer, 1968) has been used to assess personality domains that are central to the study of this complex disorder. Indeed, a child's cognitive/

perceptual style, stress tolerance and coping resources, quality of defenses, object relational capacities and themes, impulsivity, capacity for delay, and affect regulation have all been repeatedly assessed via the RIM (Bornstein, 2001; Exner &Weiner, 1982; Lerner, 1990; Mayman, 1967; Tuber, 1989a), making it uniquely fit to assess the internal resources necessary to regulate affect and sustain attention.

The small literature of research on assessments of children with ADHD using the RIM (Bartell & Solanto, 1995; Exner & Weiner, 1982) takes its lead from Exner and Weiner (1982), who cited unpublished studies to suggest that impulsivity (defined as lack of control) may be related to several Rorschach variables from Exner's Comprehensive System. These include the D and Adjusted D scores as indicators of stress tolerance and control; the Experience Actual (EA) score as an indicator of available resources to initiate behavior; the affective ratio as an indicator of affective responsiveness and emotional control, and the FC:CF + C ratio as an indicator of modulation of emotional discharge or displays; human movement (M) as an indicator of a capacity for delay and interest in social exchange; and X+% as an indicator of conventional reality testing and perceptual accuracy.

Four previous studies of children with ADHD using the RIM were identified in peer-reviewed journals, three conducted with primarily Caucasian samples from predominantly upper-middle class communities, and one conducted with children in India. Gordon and Oshman (1981) evaluated 40 boys (ages 6 to 11) and found that boys designated as hyperactive produced fewer human movement (M) and human content (H) responses and more animal content (A) responses compared with the nonhyperactive group. Similarly, in a sample of 24 children (ages 5 to 11) diagnosed with ADHD, Bartell and Solanto (1995) found that these children produced fewer human movement (M) responses, poorer form quality (X+%), and a lower Experience Actual score (EA) in comparison to Exner's (1993) norms for children of the same age. Cotugno (1995) compared the protocols of 120 children (ages 5 to 6) that comprised an ADHD group, a non-ADHD clinical control group, and normal control group. He found that compared with the normal control group, children in both the ADHD and clinical groups produced a higher frequency of pure form responses (Lambda), fewer color responses (FC+CF+C), more shading responses, fewer popular responses, fewer depictions of whole humans (H), and overall less accurate responses (X+%). Jain, Singh, Mohanty, and Kumar (2005), in a sample of 224 school children (ages 6 to 11) in India, found that compared with a control group, children with ADHD produced fewer human movement (M) responses, more color responses (FC+CF+C), fewer common details (D), poorer form quality (F+%), less animal content (A), and fewer popular responses (P).

The present study is relatively rare in that the sample comprises children from minority ethnic groups living in a lower- to middle-income American urban community, an underrepresented population in the research literature. Findings from performance-based assessment research using the RIM will be used to examine the cognitive-affective disruptions that are emblematic of this diagnosis, including

78 Object Relations of Child Populations

difficulties accessing internal resources, impairments in children's capacities for control and delay, and problems with the formation of ideational representations of self and others. We will extend the current literature on ADHD and the RIM in a sample of ethnically diverse children from urban communities; we predict that the impairments found in children with ADHD symptomatology (e.g., difficulty with sustained attention, regulation of affect and arousal level, and behavioral inhibition) will be reflected in Rorschach variables sensitive to such vulnerabilities, namely, form quality and movement, as well as ratios that capture children's access to internal resources or ego strengths.

Related to a number of core impairments in ADHD, an examination of children's movement responses and human representations may be particularly useful. Exner (1993), Klopfer and colleagues (1954), and Schachtel (1966/2001) all note that the capacity to represent human movement (M) on the Rorschach is an indicator of a capacity for delay, social interest, and an ability to access and make effective use of fantasy life. In research on child populations, My colleagues and I (Goddard & Tuber, 1989; Tuber, 1983, 1989a, 1992; Tuber, Frank, & Santostefano, 1989) have found that the quality of human movement (M) responses on the Rorschach relate in significant ways to the developmental level and affective quality of children's internal representations of self and others – representations of interactions that may influence their social functioning. Because children with ADHD evidence impairments in their capacity for delay and self-regulation, which impinge on their social fluency, it is expected that these children would respond with fewer representations of social interactions through the use of human movement (M), as well as with fewer depictions of human (or human-like) figures in general [H, Hd, (H), (Hd)].

An assessment of the use of color on the Rorschach is expected to relate to impairments in affect regulation seen in children with ADHD. Schachtel (1966/2001) argued four decades ago that an individual's responsiveness to the stimulation of the bold colors in the Rorschach is indicative of one's responsiveness to internal affectivity. He hypothesized that a lack of responsiveness to color may reflect an aversion to strong passionate affects. Because children with ADHD can become easily dysregulated by affective stimulation, it is expected that these children would constrict their responses and avoid using color to form their percepts, simplifying the stimulus demands of the blot and focusing excessively on form (F) in order to organize their percepts. This would then result in a high percentage of pure form responses (e.g., high Lambda).

Additionally, a number of ratios that sum movement and color responses may be relevant to assessing children's access to the internal resources central in ADHD impairments. Exner (1993) argues that the ability to represent human movement and color indicates an overall capacity to access internal resources (including ways in which feelings are used as well as cognitive capabilities), represented by a variable termed the Experience Actual (EA) score.[2] He also evaluates the capacity to access internal resources in relation to the individual's current stimulus demands, as represented by nonhuman movement determinants, shading, and achromatic determinants (D score).[3] As defined by Exner, stimulus demands draw on the emotional or mental activity of the person and originate from either internal or external sources. Thus, as a measure of the difference between one's available resources and one's experienced demands, a person's D score can be thought of as indicative of capacities of control and stress tolerance. Because children with ADHD have an impaired ability to draw on inner resources to delay gratification, inhibit behavior, and regulate emotional responses (Barkley, 1997, 2005), it is expected that these children would be found to have less adaptive scores on variables signifying resources and capacities of control and stress tolerance (i.e., lower EA and lower D scores).

Finally, in accordance with prior research (Bartell & Solanto, 1995), we predicted that children with ADHD would have less accurate responses in comparison with children without significant ADHD symptomatology, as reflected in lower overall form quality (i.e., lower X+%). Children with ADHD may have particular difficulty forming accurate percepts because it requires the ability to attend to different aspects of the blot simultaneously, while delaying responses beyond initially salient details.

Methods

Participants

The participants for this study were 42 children (15 females and 27 males) between the ages of 7.0 and 10.0 years ($M = 99.40$ months; $SD = 10.46$ months). All children were culled from a National Institute on Deafness and Other Communication Disorders (NIDCD)–funded project at the City College of New York examining attention and language in community children. Most children referred to the study were enrolled in city public schools and were experiencing either behavioral or reading problems in school; children were typically referred by a parent or teacher. All of the children were fluent English speakers enrolled in English-only classrooms, but 14 of the children came from bilingual households. Self-reported ethnicity/race and gender are reported in Table 7.1.

TABLE 7.1 ADHD and Comparison Groups by Gender and Ethnicity

	All Children (N = 42)		Boys (N = 27)		Girls (N = 15)	
	ADHD	Comparison	ADHD	Comparison	ADHD	Comparison
Total	28	14	21	6	7	8
African American	13	7	10	2	3	5
Latino/Latina	11	5	7	3	4	2
Caucasian	3	2	3	1	0	1
No Information	1	0	1	0	0	0

80 Object Relations of Child Populations

Children were excluded from the larger NIDCD project and thus the present study if they had a chronic medical or neurological illness, a history of neurological problems, if they were taking systemic medication, if they received a diagnosis of schizophrenia, major affective disorder, autism, pervasive developmental disorder, or a chronic tic disorder, or if they were not attending school. Children included in the study reported normal hearing and normal or corrected to normal vision, and they passed a hearing screen. Furthermore, the children were excluded from this study if they failed to achieve a score of 80 or better on either the Test of Nonverbal Intelligence – Third Edition (TONI; Brown, Sherbenou, & Johnsen, 1990) or the performance composite scale of the Wechsler Abbreviated Scale of Intelligence (WASI; Psychological Corporation, 1999). Eleven additional children were removed from the data set for the present study because they were found to have an expressive language score below 80 on the Clinical Evaluation of Language Fundamentals – Third Edition or Fourth Edition (CELF-3; Semel, Wiig, & Secord, 1995; CELF-4; Semel, Wiig, & Secord, 2004), because it was unclear how the Rorschach responses of children with expressive language disorders should be interpreted.

Children were categorized as having significant ADHD symptomatology using the 'or' algorithm used by Nigg and colleagues (Huang-Pollock, Nigg, & Carr, 2005; Huang-Pollock, Nigg, & Halperin, 2006; Nigg, Blaskey, & Stawicki, 2004), which integrates information from multiple sources following the *DSM-IV* field trials validity data (Lahey et al., 1994). Parents, teachers, and examiners completed the *DSM-IV* ADHD rating scale (DuPaul et al., 1997). In this study, a symptom was considered present if any of the three informants (i.e., parent, teacher, and examiner) endorsed that particular symptom. This was then aggregated into a total score for the inattentive and hyperactive categories, respectively, reflecting the total number of unique symptoms endorsed by at least one of the informants for each category. Children were then categorized in the ADHD group if they met at least six of the nine criteria specified on the *DSM-IV* checklist in either the inattentive and/or hyperactive categories, and these behaviors were present before the age of 7. Children were categorized in the comparison group if they met fewer than six of the nine criteria specified on the *DSM-IV* checklist in both the inattentive and hyperactive categories. The children in the ADHD group are better conceptualized as "at risk" for ADHD, or showing clinically significant signs of ADHD, rather than carrying the diagnosis proper.

Using this algorithm, we determined that 28 children met criteria for significant ADHD symptomatology, and 14 children met criteria for the comparison group. It is important to stress that dividing the sample in this manner results in groups with a small magnitude of differences, giving any potential Rorschach discrepancies a greater heuristic power and value. In terms of gender, 21 boys and 7 girls met criteria for ADHD, and 6 boys and 8 girls met criteria for the comparison group.

Measures

DSM-IV Attention Deficit Hyperactivity Disorder (ADHD) Rating Scale (DuPaul et al., 1997). The ADHD Rating Scale, used to assess symptoms of ADHD, was completed by each child's parent, teacher, and examiner. The self-report scale includes the 18 *DSM-IV* ADHD symptoms, which were assessed on a 4-point scale. Such scales have been used by numerous investigators (Conners, 1999; DuPaul et al., 1998a, 1998b; Hinshaw et al., 1997b; Wolraich, Hannah, Baumgaertel, & Feurer, 1998), and have been found to be highly reliable and to have excellent validity.

Schedule for Affective Disorders and Schizophrenia for School Aged Children (KSADS; Kaufman et al., 1997). Parents of subjects were given the KSADS, a clinician-administered structured diagnostic interview, which was used to assess comorbid diagnoses in the sample. With the interview children were assessed on the following diagnoses: anxiety disorder, depressive disorder, oppositional defiant disorder, and conduct disorder.

Rorschach Inkblot Method (RIM; Exner, 1993; Klopfer & Kelley, 1942; Rapaport et al., 1968): The RIM is a standard performance-based measure used to assess many aspects of an individual's internal experience. It was administered to the participants in the standardized manner as outlined by Exner (1993) with the exception that an inquiry was conducted following administration of each card as recommended by Ames and colleagues (1974) for young children. The RIM has demonstrated strong test–retest reliability (Gronnerod, 2003, 2006), interrater reliability (Meyer et al., 2002; Meyer, Mihura, & Bruce, 2005), and clinical utility (Viglione & Hilsenroth, 2001).

To minimize the potential for chance findings arising from multiple comparisons (Weiner, 1995), the Rorschach variables used in this study were restricted to number of responses (R), human movement (M), human content scores [H+(H)+(Hd)+Hd], accuracy (X+%), percentage of pure form responses (Lambda), EA score, and D score.

Two expert raters, who were blind to the clinical status and social functioning of the children, coded the protocols. One rater coded 24 of the protocols; the other rater coded 28 protocols, 10 of which had been coded by the first rater. Interrater reliability was estimated for 10 of the 42 protocols (146 percepts) by comparing the ratings of the two coders and calculating kappa coefficients (Cohen, 1988). The κ coefficients were 0.90 for Location, 0.89 for Determinants, 0.70 for Form Quality, 0.87 for Contents, and 0.94 for Popular, indicating strong interrater agreement. These results were consistent with interrater reliability results reported by Meyer and colleagues (2002). Scores of the more experienced rater were used in the data analysis when discrepancies between the raters occurred.

Procedure

Testing was performed in a small, quiet testing room. Each child was administered the RIM as part of a battery of language, attention, and intelligence testing, which

82 Object Relations of Child Populations

was completed over two morning sessions. The RIM was usually administered toward the end of testing on the second day. Responses were transcribed and tape-recorded for confirmation of written transcription.

Data Analysis

Outlier analysis indicated one subject outside of the 95% confidence interval around the mean on a number of variables. To ensure that this outlier was not unduly influencing the findings, variables were reanalyzed without this outlier with negligible changes in findings.[4] Therefore this outlier was retained in the analyses.

Descriptive statistics indicated a non-normal distribution of the majority of the variables. Therefore Mann-Whitney tests for independent samples variables were conducted to compare the ADHD and comparison groups on Rorschach variables and ratios associated with problems with inattention and hyperactivity.

Due to the non-normal distribution of the majority of the variables, a log transformation procedure (log [Xi +1]) was used on all variables with the exception of the D score because it is represented as a z-score. The log-transformed variables were reanalyzed with no changes in findings (Mann-Whitney U equal for all transformed and non-transformed variables); therefore the non-transformed variables were retained in the analyses.

To test the effect of two potential confounding variables, gender and comorbid ODD diagnosis, Factorial Analysis of Variance was utilized, with gender and ODD diagnosis entered as fixed factors, respectively, into the analysis of the ADHD and comparison groups on Rorschach variables and ratios.

Results

Table 7.2 displays the comorbidity of diagnoses in the ADHD and comparison groups; KSADS data were not available for one child. Overall the ADHD group was not found to have more comorbid diagnoses than the comparison group. There was a trend toward the ADHD group having significantly more children diagnosed with ODD than the comparison group, but the groups were not found to differ in terms of conduct disorder, anxiety disorder, or depressive disorder.

Table 7.3 displays the means, standard deviations, and group differences on the RIM variables. It is important to note that the two groups did not differ in terms of the number of responses (R) given, and therefore group differences cannot be simply attributed to overall productivity.

As predicted, the ADHD group was found to have significantly fewer human movement (M) scores than the comparison group. However, no significant differences between the groups were found on the human content scores [H+(H)+(Hd)+Hd].

Object Relations of Children With ADHD **83**

TABLE 7.2 KSADS and ADHD Diagnoses Crosstabulation ADHD Dx

KSADS		Normal	ADHD	Total	χ^{2a}	p
ODD	No	13	21	34	5.87	.053+
		31.0%	50.0%	81.0%		
	Yes	0	7	7		
		0%	16.7%	16.7%		
	NA	1	0	1		
		2.4%	0%	2.4%		
	Total	14	28	42		
		33.3%	66.7%	100.0%		
Conduct disorder	No	13	26	39	3.00	.223
		31.0%	61.9%	92.9%		
	Yes	0	2	2		
		0%	4.8%	4.8%		
	NA	1	0	1		
		2.4%	0%	2.4%		
	Total	14	28	42		
		33.3%	66.7%	100.0%		
Anxiety disorder	No	12	24	36	2.40	.301
		28.6%	57.1%	85.7%		
	Yes	1	4	5		
		2.4%	9.5%	11.9%		
	NA	1	0	1		
		2.4%	0%	2.4%		
	Total	14	28	42		
		33.3%	66.7%	100.0%		
Depressive disorder	No	13	26	39	3.00	.223
		31.0%	61.9%	92.9%		
	Yes	0	2	2		
		0%	4.8%	4.8%		
	NA	1	0	1		
		2.4%	0%	2.4%		
	Total	14	28	42		
		33.3%	66.7%	100.0%		

Notes: Cell entries are n's and column percentages, NA for no KSADS data available.
ODD = Oppositional defiant disorder. +trend at $p < .10$. [a]Pearson's Chi-Square.

In terms of percentages and ratios, there were no significant differences between the groups in terms of accuracy (X+%) or percentage of pure form responses (Lambda). With regard to ratios reflecting children's access to internal resources, the ADHD group was found to have significantly lower EA scores than the comparison group, suggesting that the ADHD group displayed poorer access to internal resources. There was a trend toward a significant difference between

84 Object Relations of Child Populations

TABLE 7.3 Differences Between ADHD and Comparison Groups on Rorschach Variables

	ADHD (n = 28)		Comparison (n = 14)		df	Analyses		
	M	SD	M	SD		U^a	p	r^b
# Responses	19.79	6.13	20.79	5.86	40	176.50	.60	−.08
M	1.54	2.10	3.50	3.46	40	117.00	.03★	−.34
H+(H)+Hd+(Hd)	2.14	1.94	3.57	2.95	40	142.00	.14	−.23
X+%	52.36	22.07	56.64	19.28	40	171.00	.50	−.10
Lambda	1.20	1.10	.88	.80	40	163.00	.38	−.14
EA score	2.91	2.59	5.32	3.98	40	110.50	.02★	−.35
D score	−1.14	1.18	−.36	1.45	40	134.00	.08+	−.27

Notes: ★significant at $p < .05$. +trend at $p < .10$ [a]Mann-Whitney test for independent samples. [b]Cohen's d is the between group effect size.

groups on the D score, with lower scores in the ADHD group relative to the comparison group. Although this finding was non-significant and therefore should be viewed cautiously, it may suggest lower stress tolerance and less control in the ADHD group relative to the comparison group.

Table 7.4 displays the Factorial ANOVA of ADHD and gender on Rorschach variables and ratios, testing for the potential confounding effect of gender on findings. As can be seen, the main effect of differences between the ADHD and comparison groups on the variables of human movement (M) and EA score remained when the factor of gender was added as a covariate, albeit not at the trend level, which indicates that between-group differences cannot be better explained by general sex differences in responses on the Rorschach than by ADHD symptoms. There was a trend toward gender differences on the human content score [H+(H)+(Hd)+Hd], with boys producing fewer scores ($M = 2.04$, $SD = 2.16$) than girls ($M = 3.67$, $SD = 2.50$), but otherwise no main effects for gender on Rorschach variables were observed. Furthermore, no interaction between the factors of ADHD and gender was observed.

Table 7.4 also displays the Factorial ANOVA of ADHD and ODD on Rorschach variables and ratios, testing for the potential confounding effect of a comorbid diagnosis of ODD on findings. As can be seen, the main effect of differences between the ADHD and comparison groups on the variables of human movement (M) and EA score remained when the factor of ODD was added as a covariate, and the trend toward significance on the D score remained, which indicates that between-group differences cannot be better explained by the presence of an ODD diagnosis in responses on the Rorschach than by ADHD symptoms. Furthermore, no main effects for ODD on Rorschach variables were observed. The interaction between the factors of ADHD and ODD could not be evaluated because there were no comparison subjects who received a diagnosis of ODD.

Object Relations of Children With ADHD **85**

TABLE 7.4 Factorial ANOVA of ADHD and Gender, as well as ADHD and ODD on Rorschach Variables

	Gender		ADHD		Gender* ADHD		ODD		ADHD	
	F	p	F	p	F	p	F	p	F	p
# Responses	1.41	.24	.01	.91	.02	.88	.93	.34	.00	.96
M	2.36	.13	3.54	.07+	1.12	.30	2.25	.14	4.08	.05*
H+(H)+Hd+(Hd)	3.76	.06+	2.02	.16	1.46	.24	2.45	.13	2.82	.10+
X+%	.13	.72	.22	.64	.01	.92	1.41	.24	.16	.69
Lambda	.23	.64	1.40	.25	.59	.45	.00	.99	.80	.38
EA score	2.35	.13	3.47	.07+	.39	.54	.58	.45	5.23	.03*
D score	.49	.49	2.24	.14	.02	.89	1.18	.29	3.94	.06+

Notes: *significant at $p < .05$. +trend at $p < .10$.

Discussion

This study extends the current literature on ADHD and the RIM in a sample of children who are predominantly from minority ethnic groups living in lower- to middle-income urban communities. As such, it is one of only a few studies of this type using an ethnically diverse sample of urban, community children, a population that is poorly represented in the research literature, and thus the fact that our findings are consistent with other studies of white, predominantly Caucasian, middle- and upper-class school-age children (e.g., Bartell & Solanto, 1995; Cotugno, 1995; Gordon & Oshman, 1981) is notable.

As predicted, the RIM responses indicate that children with greater ADHD symptomatology evidenced less access to internal resources (EA) than the comparison group. These findings are consistent with the notion that children with ADHD symptomatology have difficulty accessing internal resources in the face of high stimulus demand in order to organize, process, and represent their experience. Also as predicted, children in the ADHD group generated fewer human movement responses (M), reflecting impairments in their capacity for delay and ideational resources, as Exner (1993) would suggest. It also may be the case that because they are easily dysregulated by mutual social exchange, children with ADHD symptomatology may tend to shy away from percepts of an interpersonal nature. The finding of relatively fewer human movement responses may also reflect impairments in the internal representations of self and others in children with ADHD symptomatology (Tuber, 1983, 1989a, 1992).

These findings likely have significant implications for our understanding of the development of internal resources and of self-regulation in the context of the parent–child and teacher–child relationships. Are these children having greater difficulty representing interactions between self and other and, if so, are they then

86 Object Relations of Child Populations

less able to make use of internal relational models to regulate themselves? It may be, for example, that problems in the self-regulation of arousal and affect, as well as deficits in executive functions such as sustained attention, may disrupt the normal developmental progress that shifts sources of self-control from the external world of the child to the internal world (cf. Ruff & Rothbart, 1996). As a result, such deficits may complicate the internalization of experiences of coregulation with caregivers and teachers. This may leave children with a diminished capacity to evaluate their own actions and may further undermine their ability to draw on inner resources to delay gratification, inhibit behavior, and regulate emotional responses – abilities that are crucial to engaging in mutual social interactions. These impairments in ego resources may result in a reciprocal cycle in which the child's dysregulation of arousal, attention, and affect disrupts coregulatory experiences with adults and the internalization of those experiences, and impairments in socially developed internal resources inhibit a child's capacity to understand and represent object relations –further hampering healthy emotional development. It is highly likely, then, that their classroom experience will suffer as they will not be able to bring their full arsenal of resources to bear upon their educational experiences in a consistent, coherent manner.

Contrary to predictions, the ADHD group did not differ from the comparison group in terms of their accuracy of percepts (X+%) or percentage of pure form responses (Lambda). It is important to note that the comparison group in this study comprised mostly children who were self-selected by parents for evaluations because of learning or behavioral difficulties at school, rather than a group comprising a random cross-section of the community population or a strictly symptom-free child population. This may partially account for the non-significant differences between groups on variables that were linked to ADHD in other studies that compared ADHD children to a normal control group (e.g., Cotugno, 1995). In terms of the non-significant comparison between groups on the percentage of pure form responses (Lambda), it is also possible that the dynamic interplay between children's deficits in executive function and affect regulation was not captured by this variable. We had predicted that children in the ADHD group would avoid the use of color by constricting their perception of the cards to predominantly pure form responses. However, it may be, for example, that children with problems with attention and impulsivity have a more complicated relationship to color stimuli that is not reflected in whether the child simply represents color or not over the entire protocol. For children who are highly reactive to intense stimuli, their performance may be context dependent, and as such, it may be important to focus on the child's performance on chromatic cards relative to achromatic cards. It may be the case that the degree to which the child relies on a strategy of simplifying the stimulus by focusing excessively on form is dependent upon the complexity and intensity of stimuli; in this conceptualization, an individual child may have a bimodal way of coping with the world: one strategy of simplification and constriction, and a second strategy of acknowledgment of

Object Relations of Children With ADHD **87**

some vitality and affect, which then overwhelms the child. In this scenario, the quality of the child's responses would be heavily influenced by the stimuli in the environment, as likely occurs for the child in different contexts. This is consistent with the ADHD child's actual performance in the classroom, which is often highly variable, inconsistent, and unpredictable.

Finally, the non-significant comparison between groups on variables such as accuracy of percepts (X+%) and percentage of pure form responses (Lambda) may be a result of the most significant limitation of this study – the sample size. As a result of the small sample size, the study may be underpowered, increasing the possibility of our failing to detect differences in this sample that may in fact exist in the population. Future research should replicate these findings in a larger sample to ensure adequate power to detect between-group differences. Future sampling should seek randomly selected children from the community, as the participating families in this study were self-selecting. This sampling method might also yield both normal and clinical comparison groups of children to contrast responses on the RIM with those of children with ADHD symptomatology.

Another potential limitation of this study stems from the non-significant differences in comorbidity of the diagnoses between groups. There was a trend toward the ADHD group having significantly more children diagnosed with ODD than the comparison group, which is not surprising given estimates that about half of children diagnosed with ADHD also meet criteria for ODD (Biederman et al., 1991). In fact, given the rates of comorbidity in the population, it is surprising that the rates of comorbidity were not higher in this sample. However, the trend toward comorbidity between ADHD and ODD in this sample may limit the degree to which we can attribute group differences to attentional deficits alone. Although it was found that group differences were not better explained by ODD than by ADHD symptoms, future research should attempt to disentangle the relationship between attentional and oppositional symptoms and their relative contribution to the social and emotional functioning of children with ADHD.

These questions warrant further investigation in future research, and we believe that moving toward a more dynamic and complex approach to empirical studies of the RIM with children with ADHD will be a fruitful avenue toward capturing the kind of variability in functioning and self-regulation we see in these children, variability that is partially dependent on the nature of the child's environmental context. In this way, analyzing data based on different types of stimuli (e.g., chromatic vs. achromatic cards) or identifying several common patterns of coping with stimuli (e.g., bimodal approach of constriction vs. flooding, mainly constriction, or mainly flooding) may provide us with a more nuanced understanding of how these children struggle with their particular deficits in the classroom.

Another direction for future research might include a longitudinal design that would look at the development of these children over time, as the current study only provides a snapshot of children's functioning in latency. These children may look very different in adolescence, especially because some symptoms of ADHD

88 Object Relations of Child Populations

abate with time while others do not (DuPaul et al., 1998b). Future empirical research using the RIM would also benefit from an examination of the different patterns of self-regulation seen in these children's responses to the different types of stimuli presented in the RIM. It may be that careful analysis would reveal several strategies or patterns in the ways in which children struggling with ADHD symptomatology attempt to manage the world around them. This would not only help to capture the variability we see in children's functioning at school, home, and the consulting room, as sensitive as these children are to their environmental contexts, but this approach to research would also help to integrate the pockets of strengths and access to internal resources that these children do possess and to identify the conditions that allow these strengths to emerge so beautifully. We might then move beyond our own limitations in empirical, bimodal functioning in which children are seen as either ADHD or normal, with or without associated deficits in total. To this end, the integration of empirical research and case material from performance-based measures like the Rorschach and treatment (see Harris, Reynoso, Meehan, Ueng-McHale, & Tuber, 2006, for example) may provide valuable data on the dynamics underlying ADHD children's self-regulatory difficulties and the ways in which these impairments affect their capacity to access and make use of their fantasies, to experience and contain affect, and to relate well to their peers, teachers, and family members.

Notes

1 Copyright 2009, Guilford Press. Reproduced with permission.
2 The EA score represents the total number of human movement responses and a weighted sum of the chromatic color responses.
3 The D-score represents the EA score minus the sum of all nonhuman movement determinants, the shading and achromatic determinants.
4 Responses: U = 176.5 with outlier, U = 175.5 without outlier; M: U = 117.0 with and without outlier; H+(H)+Hd+(Hd): U = 142.0 with and without outlier; X+%: U = 171.0 with outlier, U = 162.0 without outlier; Lambda: U = 163.0 with outlier, U = 160.0 without outlier; EA score: U = 110.5 with and without outlier; D score: U = 134.0 with and without outlier.

8

ASSESSING NARCISSISTIC PATHOLOGY IN CHILDREN USING THE RIM

Paper used: Weise, K., & Tuber, S. (2004). The self and object representations of narcissistically disturbed children: An empirical investigation. *Psychoanalytic Psychology*, 21, 244–258.[1]

In a paper with Karen Weise, a more cognitively focused assessment of object relations was used to examine another specific syndrome in childhood that has been linked conceptually to deficits in object relations. Here Drew Westen's Social Cognition and Object Relations Scale (SCORS; Westen, 1995) measure was used. Because there has been relatively little published on the nature of narcissistic pathology in children, especially as it can be assessed via projective methods, I include the literature review from this paper in full detail. It is also crucial to note that the assessment instrument used in this study was the Thematic Apperception Test (TAT), not the Rorschach Inkblot Method (RIM). Much as we discussed in describing the use of the APT, it is not the projective method per se that is of prime importance in these works, but rather the psychodynamically informed underlying concepts that stress the heuristic value of the assessment of object relations in an enhanced understanding of personality development.

Although the vicissitudes of narcissism continue to be a major focus of the psychiatric literature, particularly among psychoanalytic clinicians (Kernberg, 1975; Kohut, 1968; Modell, 1975), the literature addresses narcissistic pathology in children to a much smaller degree. The absence of such a focus could be attributable to several factors, including a scarcity of developmental and clinical descriptions to facilitate conceptualizations and a hesitation to diagnose characterological disorders in children (Egan & Kernberg, 1984). In addition, a great number of these children are treated only for their overlying Axis I disorders (with medication, short-term treatment, etc.), and therefore any underlying personality factors are left unaddressed (Rinsley, 1980). Although a few authors have examined

90 Object Relations of Child Populations

narcissistic traits and disturbances as they emerge in children (Bene, 1979; Beren, 1998; Bleiberg, 1984, 1988; Egan & Kernberg, 1984; Rinsley, 1980; Wilson, 1988), and their clinical descriptions can be remarkably consistent, there is not yet an agreed-on definition of a narcissistic disorder in childhood.

Narcissistically disturbed children have been found to vary greatly in their interpersonal adjustment and observable behavior and often present to the clinician with diagnosable Axis I disorders reflecting their problems in the management of anxiety, moods, or conduct. As is true for adults, a disorder of narcissism as a primary clinical diagnosis is relatively unusual in both inpatient and outpatient settings (Gunderson, Ronningstam, & Smith, 1991). However, in the midst of this diagnostic diversity, common and specific features are apparent. For example, clinical descriptions converge in their emphasis on narcissistically disturbed children's lack of empathy for others, over or undervaluation of themselves, and precocious or uneven areas of ego development (Bene, 1979; Beren, 1998; Bleiberg, 1984, 1988; Egan & Kernberg, 1984; Rinsley, 1980). Parents and teachers refer narcissistic children to treatment for a variety of symptoms, including

> disturbances in interpersonal relationships; coldness, exploitativeness, and excessive efforts to control and manipulate; impulsivity and poor tolerance for frustration; school problems (usually underachieving); mood swings, irritability and lability in self-esteem; persistent lying, stealing and chronic violation of rules; exhibitionism, haughtiness, arrogance and a constant need for attention and admiration; self-doubts and intense envy.
>
> *(Bleiberg, 1984, p. 504)*

Many of these children meet some or all of the criteria for narcissistic personality disorder in adults as defined in the fourth edition of the *Diagnostic and Statistical Manual of Mental Disorders* (*DSM-IV;* American Psychiatric Association [APA], 1994), which includes the following: grandiosity, preoccupation with fantasies of success, a sense of entitlement, shame/rage reactions to criticism, and a tendency to be interpersonally exploitative (APA, 1994).

Narcissistic Disorders in Children

Although narcissistic injuries are an inescapable part of both normal and pathological development, for some children, narcissistic difficulties are the central feature of their psychopathology. At this point a brief case illustration might be useful.

Kevin, aged nine, was referred for assessment of multiple long-standing difficulties in the context of two parents with character difficulties of their own and a severely disturbed marriage. Kevin was described by his mother as a distractible child, who easily became tearful and angry if something went

> wrong. Unlike in his younger years, he did poorly in school and constantly complained of boredom; he had tantrums and would "make a scene" in front of anyone; was totally self-absorbed and would eat nonstop. He was clingy and demanding and would not let his mother out of his sight, expressed fears of the dark and of spiders, and had long-standing sleep difficulties. He had no friends and was easily upset by other children. Kevin seemed particularly eager for adult attention and was universally unable to tolerate frustration or failure. In initial diagnostic interviews his enormous insecurities were apparent, and the assessing clinician was struck by the quality of his communications and the relationship he made, attempting to identify himself with the adult or with their perceived expectation of him. He tried very much to maintain an adult style of interaction throughout his assessment and to appear a seasoned expert at clinics, tests, therapy, and whatever else might present itself. Kevin's treatment was characterized by his ineffective grandiose defenses and omnipotent, controlling fantasy play that excluded his therapist. Work with the parents, though largely unsuccessful, was aimed at understanding that their relationship with him was based largely on his fulfilling their own needs and identifications with him (e.g., as a misunderstood child prodigy).
>
> *(K. Weise, 1992, unpublished case material)*

In narcissistic children such as Kevin, grandiose fantasies and self-absorption serve to maintain a pathological equilibrium that interferes with differentiation and integration (Egan & Kernberg, 1984). These children are seriously compromised in accomplishing the developmental task of acquiring a relatively stable self-esteem (Bleiberg, 1984) and, though they may appear haughty and self-assured, are prone to feeling like worthless failures. Children who experience such narcissistic dysregulation often exhibit extremely rigid coping mechanisms that involve reliance on an omnipotent sense of self, refusal to acknowledge personal failures, projection of disowned self-experiences onto others, and demands for affirmation of their power (Bleiberg, 1994, p. 38).

As described previously, the diagnosis of a narcissistic personality, or character, in childhood is problematic. An important question is whether we can really consider children, still in the throes of developmental forces, as having a fixed set of personality characteristics, as is implied by the diagnosis of a personality disorder. The *DSM-IV*, although having no category of personality disorders for children, does state the following:

> Personality Disorder categories may be applied to children or adolescents in those relatively unusual instances in which the individual's particular maladaptive personality traits appear to be pervasive, persistent and unlikely to be limited to a particular developmental stage or an episode of an Axis

92 Object Relations of Child Populations

I disorder. It should be recognized that the traits of a Personality Disorder that appear in childhood would often not persist unchanged into adult life. To diagnose a Personality Disorder in a person under 18, the features must have been present for at least one year.

(APA, 1994, p. 631)

It is unclear whether personality disorders in childhood are identical to the adult disorders of the same name. For example, narcissistic children do not necessarily have a child-sized version of the better-known adult classification of narcissistic personality disorder, and they will not definitively go on to become adults with a diagnosable narcissistic disorder. Because the origin of these disturbances is early childhood, it seems intuitively sound to suppose that we are, in fact, seeing a future adult disorder in its infancy. However, it is important to keep in mind that this is not clear and that the adult and child with narcissistic, borderline, or antisocial psychopathology may look different. One explanation for changes in overt symptomatology is that although one's clinical presentation may change (owing to intervening events and normal developmental forces), the underlying psychic "organization" may remain unchanged.

Characteristic Object Relationships

In the clinical case literature, the narcissistic child's sense of self and identity is characterized by a lack of authenticity (Bleiberg, 1994). Children's experience of who they are is not based on an integrated sense of themselves but instead on an idea of what others expect, or what will gain them admiration and special advantages. Narcissistic children often have particular qualities that make them more likely to be selected for a special role in their families. These qualities increase their odds of being invested with their parents' narcissistic aspirations and make it more likely that they will be called on to play a unique role in maintaining their parents' self-esteem (Beren, 1998). They may be treated as a source of pride and gratification, which fosters their omnipotence and sense of uniqueness. They are often treated as "as if" children (Deutsch, 1942) by their parents and "may begin to experience those aspects of the self that elicit the parents' delighted response, but cannot integrate the range of more troubled feelings, needs and self-images into the core sense of self" (Bleiberg, 1988, p. 10).

All feelings of sadness and vulnerability are kept at bay, and grandiosity emerges in their illusion of not needing anyone and of controlling every aspect of themselves and their environment. We turn, for example, to material from an early session with Kevin:

Narcissistic Pathology in Children **93**

> When we first walked into the treatment room Kevin looked at the play materials on the table but chose to go and sit behind my desk. He made a show of stretching and making himself comfortable, and talked about getting some pictures to brighten the room up a bit. I said something about maybe it feeling good to come and sit and be the big boss behind the desk. He agreed and excitedly talked and acted out being the boss in an office filled with files and computers, giving orders to his employees in a world-weary voice. He described how all he would have to do is look at them (and demonstrated this) and they would do whatever he wanted. His excitement grew and he spoke of grapes being put into his mouth, and leaned back in his chair opening his mouth as if to receive them. Next he began to look at the computer and using the full name and serial number, commented that his computer at home was much larger than this, maybe the largest in the country. He hesitated briefly after saying this and said, "well, maybe the largest in the city." He started to draw it for me and became flustered when he was not able to produce something that he was satisfied with. He scribbled and erased, looked somewhat anxious and ripped up the paper. When I commented on his perhaps feeling dissatisfied with what he had done (in what I tried hard to be a gentle and light manner) he threw himself on the couch and told me to shut up.
>
> *(K. Weise, 1992, unpublished case material)*

These children defensively sever any emotional connection that might lead them to experience themselves as helpless or dependent and are rarely conscious of what lies beneath this "false self" (Winnicott, 1965c). In this way their sense of self is less developed and more vulnerable and dependent on outside approval than normal children's (Beren, 1998). The simultaneous over- and undervaluation of their needs results in alternating feelings of grandiosity and worthlessness. Because of earlier expressions of vulnerability or sadness being ignored or rejected in favor of the fostering of a sense of uniqueness, the narcissistic child achieves an inner coherence only at the expense of a balanced, integrated personality (Edwards, Ruskin, & Turrini, 1991).

By virtue of their beauty, talent, or precocity, some narcissistic children are able to secure vitally needed admiration, but this may never be enough. They find themselves in an impossible dilemma – they require external approval to feel good yet are threatened by such dependency because their grandiosity and fear of vulnerability requires an illusion of independence (Egan & Kernberg, 1984). These children have enormous difficulty expressing and experiencing love, gratitude, and an interest in others. Their grandiosity may be related to a need to devalue others, in order to keep from seeing themselves as defenseless and to keep vulnerability at bay. Reality testing is compromised in the service of maintaining a grandiose self-image; rules and regulations are discarded and others are manipulated and

94 Object Relations of Child Populations

devalued with no constraints or guilt. The attention to rules that typically characterizes latency children, for example, is conspicuously absent. This grandiosity becomes a nucleus around which to establish a sense of self, and the world becomes a stage that reinforces this (Bleiberg, 1988).

In normal development, young children show genuine attachments and interest in others and have the capacity to trust significant figures. In disturbances of narcissistic regulation, concerns about being ignored, often coupled with doubts about being able to evoke responses from others, result in others being seen as a means to an end – as tools in the fight to stave off inadequacy and helplessness. This intense self-absorption and need to be the center of attention has an enormous impact on relationships with others, who may find narcissistic children provocative and controlling. Others are not regarded for their attributes but are needed in order to replace "the functions of the mental apparatus which had not been established in childhood" (Kohut, 1968, p. 89). Attempts to recreate an early relationship with a parent who inflated the child's omnipotence and rewarded exhibitionistic displays of competence are largely unsuccessful, and this longing for a self-object typically causes these children a great deal of difficulty. Therapeutic relationships with these children, for example, are frequently characterized by strong countertransference reactions of boredom and exploitation. It has been suggested that such feelings are the hallmarks of treatment of those with underlying narcissistic disorders, no matter what their original clinical presentation (Beren, 1998).

The Assessment of Narcissism and Narcissistic Modes of Relating

Several authors have called for research concerning the differential diagnosis and treatment of individuals suffering from character pathology (Blatt & Lerner, 1983; Kernberg, 1975; Westen, 1991). All have stressed the importance of careful diagnostic assessment of these individuals, especially using psychological testing, for treatment planning and the management of issues related to transference and countertransference, as noted above (Hilsenroth, Hibbard, Nash, & Handler, 1993). Though narcissistic personality disorder was first included as a diagnostic category in the third edition of the *DSM* (APA, 1980), empirical research on narcissism has lagged behind theoretical interest, and the literature on narcissistic disorders is composed for the most part of case material. In the absence of research, the value of the category has rested solely on the attributions of clinical utility from psychodynamically informed clinical literature. However, recent efforts have begun to systematize and describe the characteristic features of narcissistic personality disorder and aid in differentiating it from related personality disorders (e.g., borderline, histrionic, and antisocial; Gunderson et al., 1991).

The majority of assessment tools used to measure narcissistic symptomatology are checklists and self-report questionnaires. Projective testing has been used only infrequently, but several studies are worth mentioning. In 1958, Grayden

(1958) used the Blacky Picture Test to assess narcissism and several other variables. This measure consists of a series of drawings that are thought to correspond to Freudian psychosexual stages. Exner (1969), in an attempt to classify narcissism, gave a sentence completion test to a group of subjects to determine whether they were egocentric and then studied their Rorschach responses. He found that there were significant differences between responses of different groups on the dimension of reflection (i.e., the frequency of seeing mirror responses in the stimuli). A few recent studies have used the Rorschach in differential diagnostic research for narcissistic personality disorder (Hilsenroth et al., 1993). In general, it seems that the Rorschach may be helpful in comparing narcissistic personality disorder patients to various other clinical groups. For example, in relation to patients with borderline personality disorder, narcissistic patients display higher levels of object representations, use less primitive and severe defenses, and project less aggressive imagery (Hilsenroth et al., 1993). Berg (1990) found a narcissistic group less grandiose in their Rorschach responses, and Gacono, Meloy, and Berg (1992) noted that a narcissistic personality disorder group produced a larger number of idealization responses than a group of borderline personality disorder cohorts. Farris (1988) found that compared with borderline personality disorder patients, narcissistic personality disorder patients showed significantly higher cognitive–perceptual functioning, body narcissism, and phallic–oedipal issues.

A few studies have used the Thematic Apperception Test (TAT; Murray, 1943) to more closely examine character pathology. The first study to evaluate the usefulness of the TAT in the assessment of a narcissistic character style was the work of Leary (1957), who used TAT stories to determine an "interpersonal style." Though this work predated current diagnostic classification systems, Leary characterized certain stories as "narcissistic" or "exploitive." Harder (1979) used early memories, the TAT, and the Rorschach in the assessment of an "ambitious narcissistic character style." He scored these in conformity with theories of narcissistic character (Reich, 1933). The Narcissism-Projective (NP), developed by Shulman, McCarthy, and Ferguson (1988), is a measure with four parts in which subjects are asked to write descriptions of two TAT cards and share two early memories. They are then interviewed and identified as either high or low narcissists.

Each of the protocols and interviews is next scored according to criteria adapted from the *DSM-III* definition of narcissistic personality disorder. Clinical validity of the NP was indicated by 85% agreement for NP and interview ratings of narcissism.

Narcissistic modes of relating – as opposed to narcissistic characteristics – have been assessed via measures developed to look at object representations. The unconscious representations of object relations can be inferred from projective sources that elicit information on relationships. A variety of psychological tests and scoring systems have been developed with this in mind, including those using the Rorschach, the TAT and the Early Memories Test (Mayman, 1968). For a more detailed review of the literature on the projective assessment of object relations, see Stricker and Healey (1990).

96 Object Relations of Child Populations

On the basis of an extensive review of the literature and a convergence of clinical descriptions, an assumption was made that there is a correlation between clinical assessment of narcissistic personality disorder and underlying object relationships, and an attempt was made to provide empirical support for this clinical presumption by a measure developed to explore self and object representations, a distinctive area of difficulty for these children. The most recent version of Drew Westen's Social Cognition and Object Relations Scale (SCORS; Westen, 1995) was used to compare the TAT responses of a group of narcissistic children with a clinical comparison group. It was predicted that narcissistic children would (a) depict fewer relationships, of poorer quality; (b) exhibit a lower investment in values and moral standards; (c) demonstrate difficulty with the experience and management of aggressive impulses; (d) manifest unstable self-esteem; and (e) exhibit problems with the development of a stable identity when compared with the nonnarcissistic clinical group.

Method

Subjects

The sample consists of 32 subjects drawn from a population of elementary school-aged boys and girls of low to middle socioeconomic status. All had been referred for psychological assessment at one of two outpatient psychological centers. These children were referred for a variety of symptoms and were assigned diagnoses such as attention-deficit disorder, obsessive–compulsive disorder, and oppositional defiant disorder. Of these 32 children, 16 were found to meet behavioral criteria for narcissistic personality disorder as outlined in the *DSM-IV*, including problems in self-esteem regulation, a lack of empathy, and an omnipotent denial of vulnerability, by the clinicians involved in their assessment or treatment (all a minimum of master's level child therapists trained in assessment and treatment of this age group). These children's symptoms were stable and long-standing (duration of at least 1 year), as outlined in the *DSM*.

To test the reliability of the identification of eligible subjects, two independent clinicians were asked to blindly assess 18 cases potentially able to be included in the sample. After reviewing diagnostic interviews of potential subjects to determine whether they met the criteria for a narcissistic diagnosis as defined for this study, the independent raters confirmed that 16 were eligible for inclusion. The 16 members of the control group had been referred for treatment of similar *DSM-IV* Axis I diagnoses, including those characterized by depression, behavioral acting out, learning difficulties, and hyperactivity, but they did not meet the criteria outlined here for a disturbance in narcissism. Of the 16 subjects in each group, 8 were male and 8 were female. The mean age for the data group was 10.9 years (*SD* = 2.15); the mean age for the control group was 12.1 years (*SD* =2.01). Exclusionary criteria included evidence of psychosis or an IQ below 70. Material used in the assessment process included diagnostic interviews, school reports, and psychological testing.

Materials

Data used in this study were archival and included behavioral summaries, social histories, and IQ tests (mostly WISC-Rs, with some Stanford-Binets). These 32 records are complemented by TAT protocols that were administered by several examiners with formal coursework in psychological assessment, affiliated with one of two psychological centers – a hospital outpatient department and a child guidance center. TAT administration was consistent with the procedure recommended by Bellak (1986), with probes generally limited to characters' thoughts and feelings and story antecedents and outcomes (Ornduff & Kelsey, 1996). Prompting was minimized. All legal guardians of subjects gave informed consent to each institution at the time of the assessment, and participant' identities were kept strictly confidential. Permission to use material was granted by each agency. Examiners were unaware of each child's ultimate diagnosis at the time of the administration.

The TATs of the 32 subjects were assessed using the SCORS, developed by Drew Westen et al. (1985). This scale focuses on dimensions of object relations and social cognition as measured from TAT responses. The SCORS has been revised several times since its inception in 1985. The present study used the latest version, which is made up of eight variables (or subscales). These are as follows: Complexity of Representation of People, Affective Quality of Representations, Emotional Investment in Relationships, Emotional Investment in Values and Moral Standards, Understanding of Social Causality, Experience and Management of Aggressive Impulses, Self-Esteem, and Identity and Coherence of Self. The theoretical underpinnings of this scale are rooted in object-relations theory. The concept of object relations in psychoanalysis refers, most broadly, to interpersonal behavior and the cognitive and affective processes mediating the capacity for relatedness to others (Westen et al., 1991, p. 400). Object relations theorists propose that many individual differences in this area reflect developmental differences, and they attribute severe interpersonal disturbances to early developmental failures. Patients with severe personality disorders, for example, would evidence lower levels of development in their object relations. As explained in prior sections, it is hypothesized that narcissistic children would have just such gross disturbances in their self and object representations and that this is due to early problems in the parent–child relationship. The SCORS thus shares our developmental perspective and aims to measure the level of distortion caused by such early failures.

Five of the eight dimensions seem especially important to a study of narcissism in children and were used here. Two dimensions seem particularly relevant: Emotional Investment in Relationships and Emotional Investment in Values and Moral Standards. (Note that in the original scale, these two dimensions were combined.) The first assesses the extent to which the person transcends a need-gratifying orientation toward relationships and is capable of forming mutual bonds with others in which there is a real involvement and investment in others (Westen, 1991, p. 62). The latter dimension measures how much an investment in behaving

98 Object Relations of Child Populations

in a thoughtful, compassionate way toward others is evident in the story told. In addition, we used the subscale Experience and Management of Aggressive Impulses, which assesses how much anger is depicted and how this is dealt with by the characters in the story. The final two dimensions we included measure the Self-Esteem (from negative to positive) and the Identity and Coherence of Self (from unstable to stable) attributed to characters. The three SCORS dimensions for which data were not analyzed, Complexity of Representations of People, Understanding of Social Causality, and Affective Quality of Representations, were excluded from this particular study because upon examination they did not seem likely, a priori, to be as useful in elucidating characteristics of narcissistic individuals or relationships. This conclusion was reached after an extensive review of the literature and careful consideration of the thinking behind the variables in question.

The reliability and validity of the SCORS to rate TAT stories has been demonstrated in a number of previous studies investigating the object relations of a wide range of psychological conditions (in Ackerman, Clemence, Weatherill, & Hilsenroth, 1999). These studies have validated the original measures with both normal and clinical populations and both adult and adolescent samples (Ackerman et al., 1999; Ackerman, Hilsenroth, Clemence, Weatherill, & Fowler, 2000; Barends, Westen, Byers, Leigh, & Silbert, 1990; Cogan & Porcerelli, 1996; Hibbard, Hilsenroth, Hibbard, & Nash, 1995; Westen, Lohr, Silk, Gold, & Kerber, 1990; Westen, Ludolph, Block, Wixom, & Wiss, 1990; Westen, Ludolph, Lerner, Ruffins, & Wiss, 1990; Westen, Ludolph, Misle, Ruffins, & Block, 1990; Westen et al., 1991). Other studies have found developmental changes between 2nd and 5th graders and between 9th and 12th graders on all dimensions except for affect–tone (as predicted; Westen et al., 1991). Another found a systematic relationship between object relations assessed in adolescence and several developmental history variables, such as disrupted attachments in childhood (Westen, Ludolph, Block, et al., 1990). More recently, studies using this measure have undertaken to point out important differences in the object representations of both sexually and physically abused children/adolescents and subjects with both borderline personality disorder and major depression (Hibbard et al., 1995; Ornduff, Freedenfeld, Kelsey, & Critelli, 1994; Ornduff & Kelsey, 1996).

Procedure

Two raters blind to the age, gender, and diagnostic category of the participants coded all of the TAT responses. Personal information on each subject was kept on a master code sheet, which was kept separate until the analysis of coded data began. Coders were given typed stories organized in a random order, and four TAT cards were coded on five dimensions: Experience and Management of Aggressive Impulses (AGG), Self-Esteem (S-E), Emotional Investment in Values and Moral Standards (EIV), Identity and Coherence of Self (ICS), and Emotional Investment in Relationships (EIR). Four cards (1, 2, 3BM, and 4) were chosen on the basis

Narcissistic Pathology in Children **99**

of their representation in each of the protocols to be evaluated and their appearance in several previous well validated SCORS studies. Each scale has seven levels, with Level 1 representing the most primitive response and Level 7 the highest level response. Scoring requires extensive training using a comprehensive manual (Westen et al., 1985) that includes standards for establishing scorer reliability (Westen, 1991).

Reliability

Reliability was established via intraclass correlation coefficients (Shrout & Fleiss, 1979), as outlined in the SCORS manual (Westen et al., 1985). The two coders employed for the present study had extensive prior experience in the development of the modified SCORS, and interrater reliabilities for their ratings ranged from .81 to .96, demonstrating that scores for each of the variables used in this analysis were highly reliable (EIR = .96; EIV = .84; AGG = .81; S-E = .95; ICS = .89). When necessary, differences were discussed and reconciled by agreement.

Results

Pearson correlation coefficients (r) were used to check the intercorrelation of the independent variables (see Table 8.1).

Correlations among scales revealed moderate degrees of interrelationship, as expected. Five correlations emerged, with the key finding being that the EIV variable was significantly correlated with three of the other variables. The most significant relationship (.62 at $p < .01$) was between the AGG and EIV variables. This indicates that there is a strong potential of overlap between scale dimensions measuring the management of aggressive impulses and how likely one is to behave selfishly or without remorse (i.e., to be poorly invested in values and moral standards). This significant correlation does not discount any findings but rather suggests that results obtained may be less powerful. The ICS variable was also shown to be correlated

TABLE 8.1 Intercorrelations of Thematic Apperception Test Scores

Dimension	1	2	3	4	5
1. EIR	—				
2. EIV	.02	—			
3. AGG	.15	.62★★	—		
4. S-E	.12	.56★★	.31	—	
5. ICS	.34	.51★★	.57★★	.42★	—

Notes: $n = 32$. EIR = Emotional Investment in Relationships; EIV = Emotional Investment in Values and Moral Standards; AGG = Experience and Management of Aggressive Impulses; S-E = Self-Esteem; ICS = Identity and Coherence of Self.
★$p < .05$, two-tailed.
★★$p < .01$, two-tailed.

100 Object Relations of Child Populations

with three of the other variables (EIV, AGG, and S-E), and two of these relationships reached significance ($p < .01$). Significant differences between groups being studied were also investigated. No significant differences were found between gender of subjects, coders, or gender of subjects by coder on a series of chi-square tests.

Three of the five hypotheses were borne out in the expected direction. The hypothesis that narcissistic children exhibit a low investment in values and moral standards was investigated via the SCORS variable EIV. A lower score on this dimension may indicate that a subject behaves in a selfish manner with little evidence of remorse or guilt – the higher the score, the more likely is the subject to think abstractly about moral questions or be compassionate toward others. The narcissistic group had a significantly ($p < .01$) lower mean score on this variable ($M = 13.00$, $SD = 2.10$), as predicted, than the clinical control group ($M = 15.81$, $SD = 1.72$). Also significant ($p < .01$) were findings for the AGG variable, which demonstrated that narcissistic children have more difficulty with the management of aggressive impulses ($M = 13.75$, $SD = 2.02$) than peers with a similar symptomatic presentation ($M = 15.81$, $SD = 1.38$). The final hypothesis to achieve significance in the predicted direction ($p < .01$) was that the narcissistic group ($M = 14.69$, $SD = 2.27$) would show less stable self-esteem (the S-E variable). Higher scores are seen in subjects who tend to have a more realistic range of positive and negative feelings about themselves, as was evident in the control group ($M = 16.69$, $SD = 1.58$).

One finding, though significant ($p < .028$), was in the direction opposite to that predicted. The hypothesis that narcissistic children would depict fewer relationships, of poorer quality, than their non-narcissistic peers was investigated via the SCORS variable EIR, in which a lower mean score indicates that a subject is more focused on his or her own needs or has "shallower" relationships. The narcissistic group showed a significantly *higher* investment in relationships ($M = 12.75$, $SD = 1.73$) than the control group ($M = 10.81$, $SD = 2.83$). Though this finding was contrary to predictions, mean scores for both groups were substantially lower than for other scale variables.

The final hypothesis, that narcissistic children show less self-cohesion and have problems with identity, was tested by examining ratings on the SCORS variable ICS. A low score on this item indicates that a subject may have a fragmented or fluctuating sense of self. There was a trend toward significance ($p < .09$) on this item, with the narcissistic group ($M = 16.44$, $SD = 1.90$) showing more of a tendency toward identity instability than the control group ($M = 17.63$, $SD = 1.89$).

Discussion

The primary purpose of this study was to investigate whether there is a correlation between the clinical assessment of narcissistic personality disorder in children and related underlying object relations as represented on the TAT. Using a clinical sample, children who met some of the behavioral criteria for an adult narcissistic personality disorder (i.e., problems in self-esteem regulation, a lack of empathy, omnipotent denial of vulnerability) were compared with a second group of

Narcissistic Pathology in Children **101**

referred children for whom narcissistic issues were not determined to be primary. Given that disorders of narcissism are thought to develop in the context of early relationships, the assumption was that observed narcissistic characteristics are manifestations of underlying self and object representations laid down and consolidated during early life, and that these representations could be investigated via the TAT.

The SCORS was used to look at representative TAT stories of both groups of children. Five related scale dimensions were used to measure levels of self and object representations.

The prediction was that, no matter the overt diagnostic presentation, children who met the study criteria to be described as narcissistic would score lower than the clinical control group on each SCORS dimension. Three of the hypotheses were statistically significant in the expected direction, indicating that the narcissistic children in this sample did indeed appear to have more trouble maintaining empathy for others (EIV variable), managing their aggressive impulses (AGG), and regulating self-esteem (S-E). These findings provide empirical support for the clinical literature, which has described these children as exhibiting a profound self-preoccupation and lack of concern for the feelings of others. An unevenness of self-feelings, which vary from omnipotent to helpless, is also evident in the relationships of narcissistic children, as is a difficulty in the management of aggressive impulses (e.g., narcissistic rage). These children, even before school-age years, replace developmentally appropriate efforts to regulate self-esteem with a defensive fantasy. They develop their sense of self around an illusion of perfection and invulnerability, and they rigidly persist in disowning any experience in which the self fails to measure up to the ideal. Experiences of helplessness, envy, or pain are completely denied when feasible. When this is not possible, they may fly into rages or strike out at others in a desperate attempt at self-protection.

One hypothesis, that narcissistic children would represent fewer relationships, and of poorer quality, than their non-narcissistic peers, was not substantiated. In fact, the data group showed a significantly higher investment in relationships than the control group. The significant finding that the narcissistic group showed a higher EIR, which was contrary to the hypothesis, may be related to some ambiguity in how this variable is interpreted. According to information compiled in a review of the relevant literature, it seemed reasonable to predict that the *quality* of relationships depicted by the data group would be poor (e.g., focused primarily on their own needs). On closer examination, however, the EIR scale variable is also concurrently measuring the *quantity* of relationships depicted in the stories. For example, the more relationships are mentioned, or the more a character seems to be striving to form relationships (of any sort), the higher the score will be. Although it is true that narcissistic disturbances typically include strong defenses against significant object relationships (e.g., omnipotent denial of need), narcissistic individuals are also known to exhibit a kind of "object hunger" (Modell, 1975). So, though the narcissistic children in this study may be prone to problematic, precarious relationships – characterized by little capacity for give and take – they are also thirsty for objects whose confirming and admiring responses will nourish them. This object

102 Object Relations of Child Populations

hunger may be especially relevant for a child sample, for it is more developmentally relevant and natural for any child to seek out parent surrogates and the like.

Finally, there was a trend toward significance for the hypothesis measuring stability of self-concept in the data group, signifying that the narcissistic children in this study showed more of a tendency toward identity instability than the control group. The hypothesis that a predominance of narcissistic concerns would interfere with the establishment of a secure sense of self was not fully borne out. It is possible that this finding did not achieve significance because, whereas narcissistically disturbed individuals may fluctuate greatly in the quality of their self-feelings, their self-concept may be more firmly established around a perhaps well defined, yet rather grandiose, presentation.

Conclusion

Recent research has found psychoanalytically informed assessment to be an accurate predictor of ultimate diagnostic understanding and treatment outcome (Sugarman & Kanner, 2000). One of the most valuable contributions is in the measurement and description of internal representations of self and other (Blatt, Tuber, & Auerbach, 1990). Variables measured by a psychoanalytic approach to testing can then be applied to the treatment setting. For example, the therapeutic process that a particular patient will create in psychotherapy may be determined by the same personality variables as those measured by such tests as the SCORS (e.g., the EIR variable). Although there has been some disagreement about the use of projective testing to "estimate personality characteristics" (particularly in children), this seems to be more a warning against using such material as the exclusive tool in the assessment of psychological disorders (Klein, 1986).

There were a number of limitations in the design and execution of this study, which are important to touch on here. First, generalizability of results obtained may be limited by the relatively small sample size. Additionally, data collected and analyzed were from three archival samples, and several examiners, in more than one assessment location, administered tests. This may have influenced the quantity and quality of material produced. For example, although all testing administrations were documented as "standard" (i.e., queries were limited to asking about characters' thoughts and feelings and about story antecedents and outcomes), there was no way to account for differences in styles of examiners, or for requirements of clinical settings. It is possible that more systematic probing may have allowed for closer evaluation of the range of subjects' functioning at both ends of the object relations continuum. Similarly, the inclusion of more TAT cards may have provided a better sampling of the representational world of subjects.

A related issue concerns the use of the SCORS with young children, a population that the scale has not been extensively validated for (Freedenfeld, Ornduff, & Kelsey, 1995; Ornduff & Kelsey, 1996). The stories children produce to projective stimuli are often shorter, and less detailed (especially affectively), than those given by adults. On the SCORS, default codes are assigned when a subject does not give

Narcissistic Pathology in Children **103**

enough information to score a particular dimension, and these scores could have had an impact on the results (Westen et al., 1985). For example, on the EIR dimension, if no relationships are depicted, a score of 2 is coded (on a scale from 1 through 7). This relatively low score would be seen as indicating a poor investment in relationships. On the AGG variable, if no angry feelings are mentioned, a score of 4 is coded, suggesting that the subject manages his or her aggressive impulses in neither a noticeably positive nor negative manner. Although this method of scoring seems intuitively correct, the likelihood that the SCORS is giving an accurate portrayal of children's object relations could be called into question if there were a preponderance of defaults. This did not seem to be the case in the present study, where default ratings were assigned for approximately 35 responses, or 3% of all responses given. And, as the current study compared two similarly aged groups, results obtained informing us about their relationship to each other should not be greatly impacted. In addition to age, IQ has been shown to affect the length and level of detail in projective responses (Klein, 1986). This potential problem was addressed in part by excluding subjects with IQs below 70. In fact, IQ data were available for many of the subjects, and these scores tended to be in the average to high average range. As data were collected from outpatient mental health facilities where children were primarily referred for psychological evaluation and screening for psychotherapy, it is likely that most IQs would have been in this range.

The implications and limitations of this work suggest many potential areas for future research. To provide an even fuller picture of narcissistic children at the referral and assessment stage, data from other projective measures (e.g., the Rorschach) and object relations scales could be combined to obtain more information on these children's functioning.

Data from outcome studies of work with narcissistic children would also be of value and might validate or expand on findings in this study. The literature on the treatment of these children is predominantly anecdotal and available only on a case by case basis. Psychological assessment of children with underlying narcissistic vulnerabilities and modes of relating through projective testing during the assessment process would aid clinicians in devising a treatment plan suited to their particular needs and limitations. Even given the limitations of this study, the SCORS has been shown to be a useful tool in highlighting the self and object representations of such children, and it may contribute to the quality of diagnostic and therapeutic work with this challenging group.

Note

1 Copyright © 2004, American Psychological Association. Reproduced with permission. The official citation that should be used in referencing this material is Weise, K. L., & Tuber, S. (2004). The Self and Object Representations of Narcissistically Disturbed Children: An Empirical Investigation. *Psychoanalytic Psychology*, 21(2), 244–258. http://dx.doi.org/10.1037/0736-9735.21.2.244. No further reproduction or distribution is permitted without written permission from the American Psychological Association.

9

ASSESSING THE OBJECT RELATIONAL WORLD OF PRESCHOOLERS WITH IMAGINARY COMPANIONS

Paper used: Meyer, J., & Tuber, S. (1989). Intrapsychic and behavioral correlates to the phenomenon of imaginary companions in young children. *Psychoanalytic Psychology*, 6, 151–168.[1]

A most fortuitous set of circumstances permitted us to use the Rorschach Inkblot Method (RIM) with a very special child population in terms of their evincing a set of behaviors with direct links to the domain of object relations. Typically, preschool children's Rorschach protocols are as mercurial and labile as the egocentric, preoperational cognition of such youngsters would suggest, making a RIM assessment of their object relations problematic. However, preschool children with explicit imaginary companions could potentially be a fascinating group to study in that their "symptom" (their companion) is an inherently object relational phenomenon. Jodie Meyer and I thus wondered whether children with such precociously explicit inner worlds would produce a RIM protocol that would be far more immersed in object representational productions than their same-aged peers. The following study proved enlightening in that regard.

Since the late 1800s, educators, psychologists, and sociologists have made reference to a particularly intriguing form of childhood fantasy known as imaginary companions. These imaginary companions provide compelling data regarding the boundary between reality and fantasy and hence the development of both reality testing and pretend play. Researchers have taken two disparate approaches to this phenomenon. One approach provided demographic data regarding imaginary companions themselves, the children who create them, and the children's familial background. The second approach focused on case reports and/or vignettes describing imaginary companions. Both approaches have also attempted to determine the functions of the imaginary companion and hence the degree of

Preschoolers With Imaginary Companions **105**

adaptation or psychopathology associated with its use (Manosevitz, Prentice, & Wilson, 1973; Munroe, 1894; Nagera, 1969; Sperling, 1954; Svendsen, 1934).

Shortcomings of the demographic approach include its failure to depict both the phenomenology of the experience and the specific function it serves for a given child. The idiographic approach, while providing rich material regarding the function the imaginary companion serves in a given child, is limited by its lack of generalizability and its focus on children with differing degrees of preexisting or concomitant psychopathology.

This article, through the use of both behavioral and projective test data, has a threefold purpose: (a) to study a group of young children whose demographic background resembled that of earlier studies; (b) to obtain a quantitative measure of the degree of behavioral disturbance, if any, in a sample of children with imaginary companions; and (c) to use the Rorschach Test to assess the degree to which these children's inner experience, of which the imaginary companion plays such a rich and important part, may differ from that of their peers without imaginary companions.

Definition and Characteristics of the Phenomenon

Svendsen (1934) defined the *imaginary companion* as "an invisible character, named and referred to in conversation with other persons or played with directly for a period of time, at least several months, having an air of reality for the child but no apparent objective basis." Svendsen went on to note that "the imaginary playmate is a visual or auditory idea that becomes as real and vivid as a visual or auditory percept, but that the child nevertheless always recognizes its unreality" (p. 986).

There has been significant disagreement as to whether the presence of an imaginary companion is a pathognomonic indicator. Bettelheim (see Pines, 1978) believed that the imaginary companion is symptomatic of underlying disturbance. Svendsen (1934), Ames and Learned (1946), and Manosevitz et al. (1973) all presented data in support of their finding that imaginary companions are used by children who are especially lonely. Nagera (1969) noted that an intense fantasy life frequently implies a withdrawal from the real world into a more satisfactory inner world. He distinguished the use of imaginary companions from this more maladaptive use of fantasy by reporting that "having found a new solution, the child brings his imaginary companion back into his real life and tries to have it integrated with and accepted by his object world" (p. 195).

To date, only two studies attempted to address the issue of the relative functioning of children with imaginary companions. Manosevitz et al. (1973) reported no significant group differences in either the mean number or type of behavioral problems reported between children with and without imaginary companions. This finding is limited, however, by the author's informal method of collecting data on behavior problems, using a list of 22 symptoms that each parent reported as present or absent. In another study, Singer (1973) noted that

106 Object Relations of Child Populations

children with imaginary companions differed in several ways from those who did not have them. The former group was less aggressive and more cooperative, smiled more, showed a greater ability to concentrate, was seldom bored, and used richer, more advanced language. Singer's study, however, focused more broadly on imaginative play in somewhat older (ages 6 to 9) children, in which having a make-believe friend was only a small portion of the data used to compare "high fantasy" children with "low fantasy" children. The relative level of functioning of preschool-aged children with imaginary companions is therefore still largely unknown.

Although disagreement still exists as to the underlying degree of adaptation in children who have an imaginary companion, near unanimity exists regarding the use of the imaginary companion as a defensive phenomenon with many possible functions. Sperling (1954) described the function of imaginary companions as a means of communication whereby children can express their wishes and fears without taking responsibility for them. Fraiberg (1959) believed that an imaginary companion permits the ego to operate freely, without being restricted by avoidance and phobic symptoms. Nagera (1969) compared the imaginary companion to other forms of fantasy and stated that "both are used in the attempt to solve conflicts and restore, at least transitionally, [an] inner equilibrium before excessive stress forces a path into symptom formation, regression or other disturbances" (p. 192). Nagera went on to note a wide number of functions that an imaginary companion can serve: (a) as a superego auxiliary; (b) as a "vehicle for the discharge of impulses that are no longer acceptable to the child" (p. 177); (c) as a scapegoat, becoming the recipient of the child's "badness" and negative impulses; (d) as a means of allowing the child to prolong his or her sense of control and omnipotence; (e) as a representation of the child's primitive ego ideal (i.e., it can be imbued with characteristics in which the child feels lacking, e.g., goodness, strength, or intelligence); and (f) as a way to counter feelings of loneliness and neglect, including coming to the aid of the child in the process of separating from his or her primary caretaker.

The Imaginary Companion as an Aspect of Symbolic Play

The phenomenon of imaginary companions is also intertwined with the developing capacity for symbolic or make-believe play. Piaget's (1945) initial depiction of the cognitive mechanisms underlying symbolic play was consonant with his model of early cognitive development. After the development of object permanence, the child developed a capacity to "try on" others' roles or activities as a by-product of "expanding knowledge of feelings, object properties and social rules, setting the stage for increasingly organized and integrated play" (Slade, 1986, p. 542). This view led to the assessment of the level of the child's play as an index of its emerging representational capacity (Bretherton, 1984). Developmental researchers (e.g., Fein, 1975; McCune-Nicolich, 1981; Nicolich, 1977; Wolf & Gardner, 1979) thus

Preschoolers With Imaginary Companions **107**

studied both normative emergence and timing of role play and individual variations in symbolic play capabilities (Lowe, 1975; Slade, 1987).

Recent research on symbolic play has also attempted to place its development in a more social, mother–child interactional context. Werner and Kaplan's (1963) description of the differentiation process of self from other as inherently linked with symbol formation was of major heuristic value in this area. Their depiction of the mother–child relationship as the "primordial sharing situation" provided symbol development with two intrinsically social meanings: (a) only as differentiation from her proceeded could the child employ symbols as internal replacements for mother and (b) the use of symbols (through play and language) allowed the child to more adeptly share his or her inner experience with his or her mother. Similarly, Winnicott's (1971) depiction of the "potential space" between mother and child as the origin of the symbol (p. 96) affirmed the inherently object related context of developing symbolic representation. More recent psychoanalytic researchers, from the framework of separation-individuation theory, suggested that the process of symbol formation is motivated by the symbol's usefulness as a means of simultaneously maintaining an emotional tie to mother while promoting the first, tentative physical separateness (Drucker, 1975, 1979). In this context, the development of an imaginary companion is a striking use of symbolic representational capacities to create a "being" with whom the child can try out important aspects of the self–other relationship. Developmental and psychoanalytic research on symbolic play places the earlier finding that imaginary companions appear during the third year of life in a cognitive, motivational, and social context.

Hypotheses

It seems clear that "the imaginary companion serves a variety of functions depending on the special needs of the child who creates it" (Nagera, 1969, p. 175). This article seeks to maintain the clinical flavor and richness of the idiographic approach, while deriving more objective data through the use of behavioral and projective test material. We hypothesize that our sample would be able to avoid overt behavioral disturbance through the use of their imaginary companions, but would have a pattern of Rorschach test responses indicative of both the underlying concerns they struggle with and the particular psychological strengths they use to cope with them. More specifically, we hypothesize that the children would all fall within the normal range across a wide variety of behaviors, as measured by the CBCL (Achenbach & Edelbrock, 1983). We further hypothesize that there would be a significantly greater number of human movement responses in these children, the presence of which would indicate their relatively greater inner resourcefulness and creativity compared to peers without imaginary companions. We hypothesize that their Rorschach protocols would show signs of regressive and conflict-laden responses as measured by a Rorschach object representation scale (Urist, 1977)

108 Object Relations of Child Populations

that assesses the quality of interaction between human, animal, or inanimate figures in a Rorschach percept. Finally, we hypothesize that less adaptive Rorschach performance would also be indicated by the presence of large numbers of animal and inanimate movement scores and by a poorer capacity to accurately represent a given percept (form level). Due to a lack of funding, our sample of children is compared, when possible, not to a matched control sample, but to the normative data of comparably aged children provided by Ames et al. (1974).

Method

Sample

The study employed a sample of 18 children (12 girls and 6 boys), who ranged in age from 3 years, 10 months to 5 years, 2 months. At the time of the study, all of these children had at least one imaginary companion that met Svendsen's definition. Their families were all in the top three (of nine) social class divisions as determined by the Hollingshead (1957) Scale.

This sample shared a large number of demographic characteristics with those reported in previous research in this area. Two thirds of the subjects were girls, following reports by Svendsen (1934), Ames and Learned (1946), and Manosevitz et al. (1973) indicating that between 50% and 75% of all children with imaginary companions were girls. Several authors (Ames & Learned, 1946; Jersild, Markey, & Jersild, 1933; Manosevitz et al., 1973; Vostrovsky, 1895) reported that although imaginary companions can be human, animal, or personified objects, most children tend to have human imaginary companions. In this sample, 83% of the children had imaginary companions that were human, whereas 11% had both animal and human imaginary companions. One child had an imaginary companion that was first an animal and then changed into a human.

Frequently, authors have described the sense of reality and vividness that the imaginary companions have to their creators. According to the informants in this study, all the companions were real, but they (the children) knew them to be imaginary. Previous researchers also reported this imaginary realness.

Our sample's age of creation of the imaginary companion was also similar to previous reports. All of the children in our sample had their companions by the age of 4, with the youngest age of first appearance at 2 years. Thirteen of the 18 children created their imaginary companion between the ages of 2 and 3; most authors have reported a similar distribution.

It has also been reported that imaginary companions are more prevalent among first-borns and only children. In our sample, 38% were only children and 78% were only and/or first-born. Previous investigators found that imaginary companions tend to be either the same age or older than their creators, or have an indefinite age. In this sample, only one child had a companion who was younger. Finally, the attitude of parents toward their child's imaginary companion was similar to

Preschoolers With Imaginary Companions **109**

other reports in the literature. Twelve of the 18 parents were either pleased by or actively encouraging of the phenomenon.

Subject Recruitment

Subjects were recruited via directors of several New York City preschool programs. These directors sent home a note to the parents describing the study. We unfortunately had no way of knowing how many parents of children with imaginary companions did not wish to participate and hence did not respond. Every parent who did respond, however, completed the study. The only criteria for inclusion in the study were that the child have an imaginary companion and that she or he be between the ages of 4 and 5. None of the children had ever been in psychiatric treatment.

Procedure

In the initial contact with parents, we presented a brief description, including both the purpose of the study and an explanation of what their participation would entail. After they gave written consent, a meeting was scheduled for both parent and child interviews. On three occasions a parent interview was conducted over the phone, and the children were seen at a later date. The 30- to 45-min parent interview focused on a questionnaire assessing the ways the child used his or her imaginary companion and what the parent's attitude was toward the phenomenon. We also obtained a detailed vignette describing the way in which the child typically described and interacted with the companion. We also gathered relevant demographic data regarding the child and the family. During the interview with the child, the parent was asked to complete the CBCL (Achenbach & Edelbrock, 1983) described next.

We interviewed the child in his or her room, at a time of day when the child was alert and cooperative. We began with a free play period to establish rapport. We then administered the Rorschach and the Peabody Picture Vocabulary Test (PPVT). We followed the tests with a brief play period as a means of ending the interview pleasantly.

CBCL

The CBCL is a questionnaire designed to obtain parents' description of their children's behavior in a standardized format. Achenbach and Edelbrock (1983) described their development and standardization of the CBCL in detail. It is composed of 112 items that describe various behaviors. The parent is asked to circle whether the given behavior is *not true* (0), *somewhat or sometimes true* (1), or *very true or often true* (2) of their child. The items then collapse into eight subscales that have been standardized and named for the behavioral syndrome that each measures.

110 Object Relations of Child Populations

In addition, a total sum score is computed. The subscale scores and the total sum score for each subject are then compared against the established norms to decide whether a given child's performance is in the normal or clinical range.

Rorschach Test

The Rorschach Test was administered according to the manner described by Ames et al. (1974). Given the age of the children, inquiry was done after each card. The Rorschach was scored using the method described by Klopfer et al. (1954). Each Rorschach was scored by two independent raters who did not know the identity of the subjects nor the purpose of this study. After the percent agreement between the two raters was calculated for both the Klopfer and Mutuality of Autonomy (MOA) scores, differences in scoring were reconciled by discussion between the raters and the second author of this article.

Peabody Picture Vocabulary Test – Revised (PPVT–R)

Substantially below-normal intelligence can play a confounding role in both the quality and quantity of Rorschach responses (Allison & Blatt, 1964; Friedman, 1953). Vocabulary scores are an effective general predictor of children's over-all intelligence (Kaufman, 1979; Wechsler, 1974). Therefore, the PPVT–R was administered as a brief but concise way to screen for below-normal intelligence.

The PPVT–R consists of 5 training items followed by 175 items arranged in order of increasing difficulty. The child is shown a page of four simple black and white illustrations arranged in multiple choice format. The child's task is to select the picture considered to best illustrate the meaning of a stimulus word presented orally by the tester.

Normative Data Comparison

We compared the Klopfer system responses of children with imaginary com-panions to the normative data provided by Ames et al. (1974). Ames et al.'s study consisted of the testing of 650 children; they tested 25 boys and 25 girls at half-year intervals from ages 2 to 6 and annually thereafter through 10 years of age. We used the children Ames et al. tested at ages 4, 4½, and 5 (a total of 150 children, 75 boys and 75 girls) as a source of comparison with the imaginary companion sample. These 150 children had a median IQ in the Superior range (116 to 125). As measured by the Minnesota Scale of Paternal Occupation, the median socio-economic status was in the professional or "higher" status category. Given the identical number of subjects at each of the three age ranges, their mean Rorschach scores for each of the Klopfer determinants were added together and divided by three to come up with the overall mean score that was then compared with our imaginary companion sample.

We also wished to compare the distributions of the major Klopfer determinants across groups. Ames et al. (1974) did not, however, provide standard deviations for any of their Rorschach determinants. They did provide the range, median, and quartile scores at each age. These descriptive statistics, without individual subject data, preclude statistical significance comparisons between the Ames et al. data and our sample. We will, however, compare the quartile data from the two samples.

Results

CBCL

CBCL scores are reported both as an overall normality score, and as a series of eight subset scores. All of the children fell within the normal behavior range on the total sum score. Seventeen of the 18 children also scored within the normal range on each of the eight subscale categories. One subject scored in the pathological range on the sex problems subscale, but within the normal range on the other seven subscale categories. Given the checklist's comprehensive nature, the normative nature of the children's behaviors is noteworthy.

PPVT–R

The PPVT–R IQ scores ranged from 99 to 134, with a mean of 118 and a standard deviation of 10.83. These scores are strikingly similar to the IQ data reported by Ames et al. (1974). Levitt and Truumaa (1972) reported a significant correlation between IQ and the human movement Rorschach score. The correlation between the PPVT–R IQ scores and the human movement response for our sample, however, was not statistically significant, $r(16) = .158, t = .648, ns$.

The Rorschach Test

The percentage of interrater agreement on the Klopfer et al. (1954) scoring system was 87%. The corrected for chance agreement was $N = 18, - k = 0.79, SE = 0.13$. Percent agreement on the MOA Scale was 89%, with a corrected for chance agreement of .80. These results suggest a solid degree of interrater reliability.

Table 9.1 provides a summary of each subject's performance for each of the Rorschach determinants we studied.

Table 9.2 summarizes the imaginary companion group's performance on several Rorschach determinants considered important in the assessment of both inner resourcefulness and anxiety. The table compares this group's performance with the data provided by Ames et al. (1974).

The comparisons between the imaginary companion sample and the Ames et al. data are obviously crude, given that data by individual subject were not available for the Ames et al. sample. Nevertheless, certain dramatic differences

TABLE 9.1 Rorschach Determinants by Subject

Subjects Rorschach Determinants

R	F%	F+%	M	FM	m	FM+m	FC	CF	C	Sum C	M: Sum C	H%	A%	P%
1	18	56	70	1	3	1	1:4	0	2	0	2	1:2	6	17	17
2	20	60	25	2	6	0	2:6	0	0	0	0	2:0	10	60	20
3	27	30	63	4	4	1	4:5	0	1	7	8	4:8	4	15	19
4	15	13	100	0	8	3	0:11	0	1	1	2	0:2	0	53	27
5	12	75	44	1	2	0	1:2	0	0	0	0	1:0	25	33	33
6	17	59	40	4	3	0	4:3	0	0	0	0	4:0	12	18	18
7	25	40	40	5	4	2	5:6	0	1	1	2	5:2	12	16	8
8	20	25	80	0	9	2	0:11	2	1	0	3	0:3	0	65	30
9	19	53	50	1	8	0	1:8	0	0	0	0	1:0	5	53	16
10	06	50	100	0	0	2	0:2	0	0	1	1	0:1	0	50	17
11	17	41	43	3	3	0	3:3	0	0	4	4	3:4	12	41	18
12	27	41	64	5	6	1	5:7	1	2	1	4	5:4	7	37	30
13	15	53	38	1	3	3	1:6	0	0	0	0	1:0	7	20	7
14	14	36	60	3	4	1	3:5	0	1	0	1	3:1	8	36	29
15	19	32	57	2	6	2	2:8	0	1	0	1	2:1	5	32	32
16	17	24	0	1	4	6	1:10	1	4	0	5	1:5	6	24	29
17	18	28	40	6	5	2	6:7	0	0	0	0	6:0	6	17	17
18	10	70	43	1	2	0	1:2	0	0	0	0	1:0	10	30	30

TABLE 9.2 Intergroup Comparisons on Rorschach Determinants

Rorschach Determinant	Imaginary Companion Group[a]					Ames et al. (1974) Group[b]			
	M	SD	25%	50%	75%	M	25%[c]	50%	75%
R	17.56	5.26	14.5	17	20	14.3	11	13	17
F+%	52	24	40	44	63.5	73	63	76	85
M	2.22	1.84	1	3	4	.47	0	0	1
FM	4.44	2.29	3	4	6	1.00	0	1	2
m	1.44	1.50	0	1	2	.17	0	0	0
FC	.22	.53	0	0	0	.23	0	0	0
CF	.78	1.03	0	0	1	1.03	0	1	2
C	.83	1.77	0	0	1	.23	0	0	0
Weighted Sum C	2.13		0	2	6.5	1.90	0	1	1

Notes: [a]N = 18. [b]N = 150. [c]No standard deviations reported by Ames et al. (1974), quartile ranks are given.

Preschoolers With Imaginary Companions **113**

between the imaginary companion group and the demographically comparable data provided by Ames et al. are noteworthy. The data regarding Rorschach productivity (R) reveal that the imaginary companion sample was more productive. This difference in Rorschach productivity, however, was subsumed by the striking difference between the two groups in the average number of human, animal, and inanimate movement responses. Human movement responses were nearly 5 times greater on the average than those reported by Ames et al. Similarly, animal movement responses were almost 4½ times greater for the imaginary companion sample than for the Ames et al. sample. Last, the average number of inanimate movement responses was over 8 times greater than that reported by Ames et al.

These group differences in mean values are mitigated by the relatively large standard deviations of the imaginary companion sample, making it possible that none of the differences in the mean scores would attain statistical significance. A comparison of the distribution of R, M, FM, and m scores did, however, suggest relatively little overlap between groups. In the Ames et al. sample, 25% of the 4- to 5-year-olds had 17 or more responses, while 50% had at least 13 responses (1974, p. 37). For our sample, 12 of the 18 subjects (67%) had 17 or more responses, while 84% had at least 14 responses. The two groups had less overlap in the distributions of their movement responses. Only 27% of Ames et al.'s sample had at least one M response (p. 38), compared with 83% of our sample. In our imaginary companion sample, only one subject (6%) had no FM responses; 17 of 18 (94%) had at least 2 FM responses. Less than 25% of Ames et al.'s sample had 2 or more FM responses and a full 54% had no FM responses (p. 40). The distributions of inanimate movement (m) responses also were quite dissimilar. Less than 13% of Ames et al.'s sample had at least 1 m response (p. 40), while two thirds of our sample did. The criteria for scoring FM and m responses were identical across groups. However, Ames et al. include "people existing" but not in movement (p. 58) as an M response, thereby inflating the number of M responses for their sample relative to the imaginary companion sample. Eleven of the 65 M responses reported by Ames et al. for this age group would not be scored as M using the Klopfer scoring system. This suggests even less overlap between groups in the distribution of human movement scores.

The strikingly plentiful human, animal, and inanimate movement responses of the imaginary companion sample may be highlighted in another way. Levitt and Truumaa (1972) reported a strong linear relationship between movement responses and age. In this light, it is notable that the number of movement responses given by the 4- to 5-year-old imaginary companion subjects are greater than the mean values for 10-year-olds as reported by Ames et al. ($1.7M$, $1.7FM$, and $.4M$). Only 70% of Ames et al.'s 10-year-olds, moreover, had at least one M response and 25% had three or more M responses. Eleven of our 18 subjects (61%) had three or more M responses while, as stated above, 83% had at least one M response. Indeed, the mean number of human movement responses for the imaginary companion

114 Object Relations of Child Populations

sample is roughly comparable to the normal expectations of an adult Rorschach protocol (2 to 3M; Ames et al., 1974, p. 265).

The comparison between the two groups on the percentage of form only responses rated as accurately perceived (F+%) is also notable. In Ames et al.'s sample, 25% of the 4- to 6-year-olds had F+%s greater than 85%, while 75% of their subjects had an F+% of greater than 60% (Ames et al., 1974, p. 40). In contrast, only 2 of our 18 subjects (11%) had an F+% above 85% and only one third of the subjects had an F+% greater than 60%. The mean F+% of 52% for our sample is nearly identical to that reported by Ames et al. for their sample of 2-year-olds (54%), an age at which Rorschach responses have been described as perseverative and magical in their arbitrary and capricious character (Fox, 1956, p. 89). It is important to note that the raters were advised of Ames et al.'s distinct criteria for scoring form level quality in children aged 4 to 6 (Ames et al., 1974, pp. 20–26). Thus, the scoring of the F+% variable used here is specifically geared to the preschool-aged child and not a simple application of older children's or adult norms. The relatively poorer performance of the children with imaginary companions is thus viewed as indicative of relatively greater disruption in their capacity to perceive accurate form.

Table 9.3 describes the performance of our sample on the MOA Scale. The table first gives the number of responses at each of the 7 scale points. It then provides the distribution of human, animal, and inanimate movement responses within each scale point.

The difference in the quality of interactions when the subjects give human movement, as opposed to animal or inanimate movement responses, is striking. To quantify this M versus $FM + m$ content distinction, we compared the dichotomous categories of benign (scale points 1 and 2) versus malevolent (scale points 5, 6, and 7) MOA responses with the human versus animal/inanimate movement response dichotomy. Human movement responses were significantly more likely to be benign and autonomous than the animal/inanimate movement responses, χ^2 (1, N = 85) = 9.79, p < .005.

TABLE 9.3 Number and Distribution of Mutuality of Autonomy (MOA) Scale Scores

MOA Scale Point & Theme	Total No. of MOA Responses	MOA Scores With M	MOA Scores With FM	MOA Scores With m
1 (reciprocal interaction)	6	6	0	0
2 (benign but parallel)	25	12	13	0
3 (dependent, leaning)	2	1	1	0
4 (reflection)	0	0	0	0
5 (controlling, menacing)	42	13	26	3
6 (attacking, damaging)	11	0	4	7
7 (catastrophic violence)	1	0	0	1
Totals	87	32	44	11

Discussion

This study sought to obtain a sample of young children with imaginary companions that were similar enough to prior studies to permit some generalization of the data we derived from the CBCL and Rorschach test. The demographic data of our sample were notably consistent with data reported in earlier studies on the imaginary companion (Ames & Learned, 1946; Griffiths, 1935; Hurlock & Burstein, 1932; Jersild et al., 1933; Manosevitz et al., 1973; Schaeffer, 1969; Svendsen, 1934). The similarity of our data to prior research serves to enhance the generalizability of this work to those previous research efforts. It also suggests a rather striking uniformity of demographic characteristics of these children across a wide variety of samples.

All of the subjects, except for one subject on one subscale, scored well within the normal range on the CBCL. Even the subject with one discrepant score was within the normal range on the other seven subscales as well as on the total sum score. These findings strongly suggest that the existence of an imaginary companion is not to be equated with pathological behavioral symptomatology. The CBCL generates a comprehensive depiction of behaviors and has standardized normative values. These results therefore provide compelling data indicating that having an imaginary companion in children of this age is not pathognomonic. This fact encouraged us to compare the Rorschach results of this sample with that of the extensive normative data gathered by Ames et al. (1974).

We hypothesized that these children's Rorschach records would show evidence of both significant ego strength and internal conflict. These results were confirmed by the crude comparison of our sample with the available normative data. The comparison was particularly noteworthy regarding the far greater number of movement responses given by our sample, although we were unable to assess this difference for statistical significance. Although some semantic and clinical differences in the interpretation of the human movement (M) response do exist, "the consensus of experts holds that M reflects emotional adjustment with most of its conventional connotations and specifically, capacity for empathy, self awareness and the ability to use fantasy as a defense mechanism" (Levitt & Truumaa, 1972, p. 49). Ames et al. (1974) argued that an individual with a rich supply of M responses "feels a personal role in forming his own fantasies [and has] some development of a concept of a self" (p. 57). The capacity to produce M responses has been positively correlated with age (Levitt & Truumaa, 1972) to the extent that few if any M responses would be expected in the preschool years. The weak correlation between their number of M responses and their PPVT–R IQ scores suggests that the high intelligence of our sample was not a dominant factor in their capacity to produce these creative responses.

The presence of many M responses in our sample provides a perceptual correlate to the mechanism whereby the imaginary companion itself may be produced. The findings regarding the quantity and content of the FM and m responses,

116 Object Relations of Child Populations

moreover, suggest a way to understand the motivation behind the creation of the imaginary companion, at least for this sample. Whereas the number of *FM* responses commonly exceeds the number of *M* responses in early childhood, Rorschach theorists interpret animal movement responses as more impulsive, less deliberate, and less safely identified with than *M* responses (Ames et al., p. 59). Ames et al. described inanimate movement (*m*) responses as reflecting an even greater disowning and projecting outward of unacceptable fantasies (Ames et al., p. 60). It is thus typical to find in normal children that *FM* and *m* percepts are more active and sometimes more violent than *M* responses. Nevertheless, the markedly greater malevolence of the *FM* and *m* responses and their relative lack of differentiated and autonomous interaction suggest a more pronounced disowning of more powerfully conflictual feelings in our sample. The finding that these youngsters also have considerably lower *F+%s* – an indicator of less accurately perceiving reality (Levitt & Truumaa, 1972) – lends additional support to the notion that these children experience greater than normal internal tension and conflict.

Normative data on the MOA Scale with preschool-aged children is presently not available and this certainly highlights the tentativeness of the present findings. It is striking, however, that the MOA distribution of *FM* and *m* responses is similar to that of clinical samples of children aged 6 to 12 (Goddard & Tuber, 1989), whereas the MOA distribution within the *M* response category is quite compatible with normative MOA data on latency aged children (Tuber, 1989). This dichotomy of benign *M* versus malevolent *FM* and *m* responses is consistent with the clinical findings of Nagera, Sperling, Fraiberg, and others that the imaginary companion serves simultaneously as a means of disowning "bad" self-representations while sustaining "good" ones. This "good self" may then more easily create and sustain a safe and hence ego-enhancing tie to significant parenting figures as it adapts to the developmental demands of early childhood. The finding that these children's behavioral performance, as measured by the CBCL, is consistently non-pathological suggests that the creation of imaginary companions, at least for our sample of children, is a highly adaptive, symptom-free means of negotiating intensely felt inner struggles.

Note

1 Copyright © 1989, American Psychological Association. Reproduced with permission. The official citation that should be used in referencing this material is Meyer, J. R., & Tuber, S. (1989). Intrapsychic and behavioral correlates of the phenomenon of imaginary companions in young children. Psychoanalytic Psychology, 6(2), 151–168. http://dx.doi. org/10.1037/0736-9735.6.2.151. No further reproduction or distribution is permitted without written permission from the American Psychological Association.

10

ASSESSING THE OBJECT RELATIONS OF BOYS WITH SEPARATION ANXIETY DISORDER

Paper used: Goddard, R., & Tuber, S. (1989). Boyhood separation anxiety disorder: Thought disorder and object relations psychopathology as manifested in Rorschach imagery. *Journal of Personality Assessment, 53,* 239–252.[1]

A paper written with my colleague Rodger Goddard has been repeatedly cited in a number of the works already presented. It was one of the very first articles written that linked a specific syndrome in childhood to Rorschach Inkblot Method (RIM) findings using the Mutuality of Autonomy (MOA) scale.

Although Separation Anxiety Disorder (SAD) was formally introduced as a diagnostic category in the DSM-III, controversy still exists over the meaning, degree of pathology, and contributing factors involved in the etiology of this symptom complex. Prior to 1980, research findings in this area were confounded by the tendency of investigators to group school phobics with SAD children in their studies. The DSM-III defines separation anxiety disorder via nine possible areas of subjective distress the child may experience when physically separated from an attachment figure, with a minimum of three areas needed to make the diagnosis. School phobia is listed as one of these nine areas. School phobia is therefore neither a necessary nor sufficient condition for SAD. Early investigations in this area are thus plagued by the possible inclusion of disparate psychiatric disturbances within a given sample of children. Regardless of the exact nature of their subjects, however, both theorists and researchers have endorsed widely diverse viewpoints regarding this syndrome.

Gittleman-Klein and Klein (1973) viewed pathological separation anxiety as being biologically and neurochemically determined. They based their viewpoint on empirical data in which 35 6- to 14-year-old school phobic and separation

118 Object Relations of Child Populations

anxious children, treated with medication and family counseling, had lower relapse rates than children treated with placebo and family counseling.

Other authors have asserted that pathological separation anxiety does not develop from the child's individual psychological or neurochemical makeup but, rather, arises from an acting out of a disturbed family interactional pattern or older family members' psychopathology (Baideme, Kern, & Taffel-Cohen, 1979; Davidson, 1960). Empirical studies have supported the contention that these children come from families with at least moderate family member psychopathology and disturbed interactional patterns (Pritchard & Ward, 1974). Waldron, Shrier, Stone, and Tobin (1975), for example, found the school phobic children they studied to be of greater importance to their mothers than their husbands were, in comparison to the mothers of their control group.

Others have asserted that the family's reinforcement of separation anxious behaviors leads to the conditioning of these behaviors (e.g., Fowler, 1978; Lazarus, Davidson, & Polefka, 1965; Miller, 1972; Vaal, 1973). These authors pointed to their successful counterconditioning techniques with school phobic and separation anxious children to support their viewpoint.

Psychoanalytic and psychodynamic authors have presented case studies in support of their views that excessive gratification, early oral fixations, and oedipal conflicts contribute significantly to the child's displacement of anxieties onto school and situations of separation from their parents (e.g., Klein, 1945; Skynner, 1974; Sperling, 1967). Empirical studies have found that these children and their mothers do possess heightened dependency needs; that these mothers tend to inappropriately gratify their sons, often while neglecting their husbands; and that these mothers tend to be separation anxious themselves and overprotective with their children (Berg, McGuire, & Whelan, 1973; Berg, Nichols, & Pritchard, 1969; Pritchard & Ward, 1974).

Several authors have viewed aggression and hostility in the child as having great importance in the etiology of pathological separation anxiety (Coolidge, Tessman, Waldfogel, & Willer, 1962; Estes, Haylett, & Johnson, 1956; Goldberg, 1977; Miller, 1961). These authors generally viewed the child as not overindulged or overgratified, but as frustrated and angry. These authors viewed the child's clinging and dependent behavior as an attempt to psychologically protect his mother and himself from his rage. Research in this area has been limited yet suggestive that the child does possess heightened aggressive feelings or conflicts over aggression (Waldron et al., 1975).

Other writers have suggested that inadequate psychological and cognitive development in these children are the responsible and supporting elements of this symptomatology. These authors have viewed the responsible agents as inadequate ego development and functioning (Coolidge et al., 1962; Radin, 1974; Szyrynski, 1976), pathological internal object relations (Angel, 1972; Waldron et al., 1975; Weiland, 1966), and poor self-concept development (Leventhal & Sills, 1964; Miller, 1961; Radin, 1968, 1972; Weinberger, Leventhal, & Beckman, 1973).

Boys With Separation Anxiety Disorder **119**

Empirical observations and studies support the notion that these children do have faulty character development. In particular, studies noted that these children have an archaic, grandiose, and omnipotent sense of self, poor self-esteem, identity diffusion, high self-expectations, inhibition of fantasy expression, manipulative and controlling behavior, and intense depression (Eisenberg, 1958; Levenson, 1961; Leventhal & Sills, 1964; Waldron et al., 1975). Coolidge et al. (1962) concluded that, in general, these mothers indulged their children's feelings of omnipotence, leading to cycles of resentment, anger, explosiveness, guilt, repression of their hostility, and eventually, more compensating overindulgence of the child's sense of grandiosity. Conclusions concerning these studies, however, are limited by a lack of more objective evidence of characterological disturbance in the child and are based almost exclusively on subjective clinician's judgments of individual cases without controlled comparisons.

Thus, studies investigating SAD have been found to hold widely disparate etiological conceptualizations. Whether or not the just-mentioned studies stressed external or intrapsychic factors, however, it is clear that the causal agents are complexly multi-determined, and for a particular child they are likely to consist of multiple factors with specific degrees of salience. We take the position that regardless of its various etiological agents, the further clarification of the intrapsychic correlates of SAD is of heuristic value in fully understanding this syndrome.

The degree of subjective distress these children experience when physically separate from an attachment figure is understood in the context of their inability to successfully sustain or evoke an internal representation of a soothing "other" during the period of separation. This failure in evocative or sustaining representation has been linked theoretically with failures in the development of a coherent and/or fully differentiated sense of self and other (Kohut, 1977; Mahler, Pine, & Bergman, 1975). Subjective feelings of abandonment are likely to prevail when the child's sense of inner coherence is based primarily on the actual physical presence of an important "other" and that "other" is not physically available. A lack of inner self-cohesion and differentiation has been viewed theoretically as potentially deleterious to children's autonomous ego functions (Kernberg, 1977). Disruptions in self-cohesion are likely to also be disruptive of their cognitive/perceptual accuracy, differentiation, and clarity as reflected in Rorschach verbalizations and imagery. The nature of the SAD children's Rorschach representations was therefore hypothesized as capable of revealing their dependency needs, their lack of self-cohesion and differentiation, their perception of interpersonal interactions as potentially dangerous when a familiar "other" is not available, and their disorganized inner experience and thinking in general. Our study was undertaken to assess these hypotheses. More specifically, it was hypothesized that separation anxious boys, as compared to normal controls, would show greater psychopathology as measured by: (a) the poorer quality and greater number of thought disordered verbalizations, and (b) a greater degree of more disturbed representations of self

120 Object Relations of Child Populations

and other in interaction. The Rorschach test is used to measure these aspects of personality functioning.

Method

Subjects

Nineteen urban, middle and low SES boys, between the ages of 5 and 13, who were being treated at an outpatient child psychiatry department, were included in this study. The children were all assessed as part of the routine diagnostic process at the clinic; the psychiatric staff was unaware that a research effort regarding these children would be undertaken. These boys were selected both by use of psychiatric case summaries and, when possible, by a survey of their present clinic therapists. Psychiatric diagnosis was verified by comparing chart notes and therapists' surveys with the behavioral criteria as listed in the DSM-III. The DSM-III diagnoses of the subjects were decided on independently from psychological test data, including the Rorschach. Ten of these subjects had an additional secondary DSM-III diagnosis or gender identity disorder of childhood. This percentage was in accord with previously found percentages of gender identity confusion in samples of separation anxious and school phobic boys (Levenson, 1961; Waldron et al., 1975). The children, tested within 2 years of each other, had been given a battery of psychological tests as part of their initial evaluation. The test batteries included the Wechsler Intelligence Scale for Children – Revised (WISC-R), Figure Drawings, Bender-Gestalt Test, and the Thematic Apperception Test (TAT), in addition to the Rorschach. The verbatim protocols were transcribed manually. Fourteen control subjects were also administered psychological testing for research purposes at the clinic. These subjects were gathered from local schools. Their parents were paid for their child's participation in the study. These subjects and their parents were interviewed to rule out the presence or history of overt psychiatric symptomatology in either their own or their family's background. Major academic or social difficulties were also ruled out.

Psychological Testing

All psychological testing was performed by doctoral level psychology externs and interns who were blind to the nature of this study. Rorschach were administered according to the method described by Klopfer et al. (1954), with a modification of the inquiry procedure as described by Tuber (1988). The separation anxious and control groups were compared on a number of demographic variables. No significant differences were found to differentiate the two groups on any of the variables we tested: age, overall I.Q., verbal I.Q., performance I.Q., SES (Hollingshead measure), grade in school, number of siblings, sibling rank, religion, ethnic group, intactness of family, and private versus public school attendance. Comparing the two groups on chronological age was particularly important given Ames, Metraux, Rodell, and Walker's (1974) findings that "odd combination" responses (i.e., thought disorder responses) do occur in normal populations with children between the ages of 4 and 5½, although they "virtually disappear" by the age of 6. A post hoc review of our two samples revealed four subjects in each group between the ages of 5 and 6, suggesting that age-range differences between the groups would not affect possible group differences on the thought disorder measure. A preliminary review of normative findings regarding chronological age differences on the Mutuality of Autonomy Scale (MOA; Tuber, 1992) has also found no differences in the number and quality of MOA scale scores within this age range.

Rorschach Scoring Procedure

The Rorschachs of these children were evaluated by rating scales that assessed thought disorder and object relations. All scoring was done by a doctoral candidate in clinical psychology (who was paid for her work by a research grant from the clinic; and Rodger Goddard (the senior author). The outside rater was blind to the hypotheses of the study and to which group the various Rorschach protocols belonged. Reliability between the two scorers on both the MOA and the Rorschach thought disorder scale was found to be good, ranging between 80% and 86% agreement. Differences in scoring between both raters were reconciled by Steve Tuber (the second author), who was blind to the identity of the subjects in question. The scores were then statistically analyzed by nonparametric procedures to evaluate differences between the groups. The Mann Whitney U Test was utilized to perform the comparisons. The Kalter and Marsden (1970) method to determine if controlling for Rorschach productivity is necessary was employed in this study. In accordance with the Kalter and Marsden procedure, evaluation of inter- and intragroup correlations determined that there was no need to control for Rorschach productivity on the scales used in this study.

Thought Disorder Rating Scale

Blatt and Ritzler (1974) developed an "overall estimate of thought disorder … by differentially weighting different types of thought disorder based on the severity of boundary disturbance" (Blatt & Berman, 1984, p. 231). The scale was designed to measure various levels of cognitive boundary disturbance which they believed "relate to disruptions in reality testing, impairments in cognitive processes, and the capacity to become involved in interpersonal relationships" (Blatt & Ritzler, 1974, p. 373). The hierarchical scale points of Blatt's thinking disturbance scale, from most pathological to mild distortion responses, are: contamination, contamination tendency, fabulized combination serious, confabulation, confabulation tendency, fabulized to confabulation, fabulized combination benign, and fabulized combination tendency (see Blatt & Ritzler, 1974, for examples of each of the scale points).

122 Object Relations of Child Populations

Blatt and Ritzler (1974), Blatt and Berman (1984), and Harder, Greenwald, Wechsler, and Ritzler (1984) successfully used this hierarchy as an aid in subtle diagnostic discriminations. Blatt and Ritzler (1974), Wilson (1985), and Lerner, Sugarman, and Barbour (1985) conceptualized the contamination and fabulized combination serious responses as indicative of self–other boundary confusion. Confabulation responses are seen as connoting confusion in the boundary between reality and fantasy, whereas fabulized combination benign responses depict a more general laxness of boundaries This tripartite distinction has received empirical support from the work of Wilson (1985) and Lerner et al. (1985) in that schizophrenic subjects demonstrated the more pathological self–other confusions, whereas borderline subjects had greater reality–fantasy confusions of the confabulation type.

Results

Table 10.1 summarizes the results of the intergroup comparison of the subjects using Blatt's hierarchy of thought disturbances. As hypothesized, the separation anxious boys produced a significantly greater total number of thought disorder responses than the control subjects. This significant intergroup difference was also found on the fabulized combination serious, confabulation, and fabulized combination regular responses. Table 10.2 gives some examples of the separation anxious boys' thought disordered responses to illustrate the nature of their verbalizations.

Table 10.3 summarizes the intergroup differences on the MOA. The separation anxious boys produced significantly more pathological object relations scores than the normal controls as measured by this scale. As hypothesized, separation anxious boys had a significantly poorer mean MOA score. The single lowest (most adaptive) MOA score was also poorer for the separation anxious boys. Concerning individual scale points, the separation anxious subjects produced significantly fewer of the most adaptive object relations scale point (a score of 1) than the

TABLE 10.1 Comparison of Thought Disorder Scores Between Groups

Variable	z^a Values	SAD M	SD	Controls M	SD
Total number thought disorder responses	2.43★★	6.84	6.21	2.00	2.72
Contaminations	ns	.37	.60	.14	.36
Fabulized combinations-Serious	1.19★	1.68	2.03	.57	1.02
Confabulations	2.03★	2.37	2.75	.57	1.09
Fabulized combinations-regular	2.13★	1.63	2.31	.89	.47
Fabulized to confabulation	ns	.58	1.17	.29	.61
Confabulation tendency	ns	.21	.54	.14	.05

Notes: [a]Value using Mann Whitney U Test given large sample size. Mann Whitney U Test corrected for tied ranks and expressed abnormal deviant.
★$p < .05$. ★★$p < .01$.

Boys With Separation Anxiety Disorder **123**

TABLE 10.2 Examples of SAD Boys' Thought Disordered Responses

Contamination	"a grizzly dog," "a rainbow man."
Fabulized combinations – serious	"a spider with human hand," "a skeleton with a hippopotamus mouth," "blood coming out of a cloud."
Confabulation	"a bat…in the haunted house, a skeleton…I am the witch. I'm cooking the skeleton." "An ordinary bird…it jumped out and is eating a dog. Reminds me of it…I saw it in Alaska, a bird attacks a dog and flies away with it."
Fabulation to confabulation	"That looks like a building. A very nice building. That's where I live. I live in California and this is California, New York City."
Fabulized combinations – regular	"Two cockroaches pushing a rocket ship up," "A monster (with) x-ray vision…it shoots bullets…it eats people, a man taking off his shirt inside him, maybe people live inside him."

TABLE 10.3 MOA Scale Scores Across Groups

Variable	z^a Values	SAD M	SD	Controls M	SD
Mean object relations scores	1.92★	3.82	.80	3.16	.95
Number 1 scores	2.16★	.06	.24	.50	.86
Number 2 scores	ns	2.06	2.16	1.93	1.39
Number 3 scores	3.12★	1.72	1.18	.43	.65
Number 4 scores	ns	.50	.86	.50	1.09
Number 5 scores	ns	2.44	2.50	1.50	1.79
Number 6 scores	ns	.89	1.37	.79	.99
Number 7 scores	ns	.22	.55	.07	.27

Notes: [a] Value using Mann Whitney U Test given large sample size. Mann Whitney U Test corrected for tied ranks and expressed abnormal deviant.
★$p < .05$.

controls. Strikingly, the separation anxious boys also produced a far greater number of object relations scores in which dependent clinging of one figure upon another was preeminent (a MOA point 3 score). There were no other significant differences between the groups on any of the other MOA points. Table 10.4 gives some examples of the separation anxious boys' object relations responses, illustrating the clinical nature of these verbalizations.

Discussion

The objectives of this study were to determine whether Rorschach assessments of cognitive distortions and low-level object relations in the projective test data of urban, middle and low SES boys could distinguish SAD boys from a normative

124 Object Relations of Child Populations

TABLE 10.4 Examples of SAD Boys' Urist Object Relations Responses

Urist 7	"A tremendous explosion, here, that the people are running…and these are the hands and heads of the people…they're under attack."
Urist 6	"Two scientists…had to shoot a bear…they have its heads…as a trophy."
Urist 5	"Spiders holding Japanese beetles (who are) just right, plump. That's the way… Everything has to die. The spiders are holding them to eat." "Butterflies are chained to the pink rocks…chained by the unidentified monsters."
Urist 4	"A man and a woman falling in love…wearing the same hat, they're twins, made twins, they know they were twins and they got married."
Urist 3	"These two clouds are not separate. They're both attached because they use a magic formula to attach them." "Those things to hang coats on, that's the stick, those are the coats." "Three people holding onto each other." "A bat hanging." "A mask that you hang up."
Urist 2	"Two people singing."
Urist 1	"Two bunnies looking at each other going their own ways (given by a non-SAD subject)."

sample. Results strongly supported the contention that these boys have a greater incidence than normal boys of disordered thinking and a generally poorer quality of object relations projective imagery. The finding that separation anxious boys gave significantly more pathological thinking disordered responses than normal boys is especially noteworthy. Athey, Fleischer, and Coyne (1980) noted an important distinction between "thought organization as the formal organizing principle for structuring the representation and expression of psychological experience and object relations as the thematic relational content that is thereby organized" (p. 277). Our findings suggest that children with SAD manifest disturbances in both of these intertwining personality constructs. These findings suggest potential impairment in cognitive and perceptual thought processes. These boys' thought disordered responses on the Rorschach demonstrate a potential for these children to possess thinking and imagery that is boundary compromised, idiosyncratic, bizarre, arbitrary, psychotic-like, and blurred. Ideas and images that should merit their own stability and independence, in order to be contrasted with other ideas and images, may lack discrete boundaries for these children. The finding that SAD children had greater numbers of all three types of thought disorder (Wilson, 1985) suggests impairments in the boundaries between self and other (their greater number of fabulized combination serious responses), between reality and fantasy (confabulation responses), and in a more general laxness of boundaries (fabulized combination benign responses). These results imply that these children may have difficulty with both effectively distorted and cognitively confused thought processes. The possession of thoughts and ideas that are boundary compromised by these children is directly analogous to their clinging and overly dependent behavior. We speculate that their clinging behavior may serve as a manifestation of their attempt to use others as an auxiliary ego to fill in the gaps of their confused and/or distorted cognitive functioning and as an attempt to have a physically present "other" solidify a sense of self in the face of such a chaotic and unstable internal world.

The results of this study also indicate that the object representations of these boys were, on the whole, more pathological than the controls. These boys were also more likely to have far fewer instances of benign and empathic interactive representations. This study suggests that the projective, interpersonal, interactional imagery of these children tends to be dependently or symbiotically merged and, on the whole, more pathological in comparison to normal boys.

The far greater number of dependent or clinging object representation scores in the protocols of the separation anxious boys are likewise viewed as a striking intrapsychic correlate to their behavioral need to rely on familiar others to reduce their anxiety. We speculate that these children have not fully developed an intrapsychic sense of themselves as stable and differentiated. Rather, the intense presence of dependent and symbiotically merged projective object imagery in these children's Rorschachs suggests the possibility that their sense of self and self-images are enmeshed and intertwined with their objects. These children may therefore be deficient in the internal psychological structures and imagery that would enable them to function independently. These children may be lacking the interpersonal interactions and environmental experiences (e.g., feedback, personal verification, enhancement of self-esteem, and granting of responsibility) that brings about greater internal self–other differentiation. The relatively larger number of dependent and clinging MOA responses in the Rorschach protocols of these children (i.e., scores of 3) suggests the possibility that the presence of such responses may be used as a diagnostic/pathognomonic indicator of SAD in middle-childhood and preadolescent boys. Thus the prevalence of scale point 3 responses may prove useful in discriminating separation anxious children with gender confusion from separation anxious children without gender identity problems.

In summary, the results of this study strongly suggest that pathological object relations and cognitive thought disturbances may play a significant role in SAD in boys. Whatever environmental or biochemical factors may act as formative or sustaining of SAD, they do not appear to act in isolation or account for the etiology of the entire syndrome. These children are likely to be deeply psychologically troubled. It is strongly suggested that further research and psychological intervention in this area address itself to the affective and cognitive functioning of these children.

Note

1 Copyright 1989, Lawrence/Erlbaum Associates, Inc. Reproduced with permission.

SECTION FOUR

Assessing Object Relations With Child Populations Under Extreme Duress

The following five studies share an interesting characteristic: each one assesses a population under significant duress. In the first paper, this duress was chronic in that latency-aged children disturbed enough to be in a long-term inpatient setting were assessed upon admission using the RIM and then their RIM performance was compared to their functioning at follow-up as adults. Two papers with Paul Donahue then follow which assess the object representations of homeless children, another chronic source of extreme duress. We then switched to a study of children under more short-term or immediate duress as this sample of children were about to undergo surgery, in a paper written with Sebastiano Santostefano and Mary Ann Frank. The fifth paper, with Debra Munczek, assessed the RIM tasks of children in Honduras whose fathers were assassinated or "disappeared" during political unrest.

11

USING THE MOA SCALE WITH A CHILD INPATIENT POPULATION

Primary paper: Tuber, S. (1983). Children's Rorschach scores as predictors of later adjustment. *Journal of Consulting and Clinical Psychology*, 51, 379–385.[1]

The following paper was my first attempt at translating the potential value of assessing object relations into an empirical investigation. It was also the first time the Mutuality of Autonomy (MOA) scale was used with children, an approach that has now become a standard part of assessing children with the Rorschach Inkblot Method (RIM), even so far as to be included, in a modified form, within the new Rorschach Performance Assessment system (Meyer & Eblin, 2012).

The Rorschach Inkblot Test has been generally recognized as the most commonly used projective technique in the psychodynamic/developmental assessment of children. Nomothetic empirical research with the Rorschach in follow-up studies of child clinical populations has, however, been quite rare. Cass and Thomas (1979) attempted to gauge the usefulness of psychological test data in predicting the later adjustment of 200 adults who were originally seen on an outpatient basis as children. Ratings from test battery material, which included the Rorschach test, were found to be of only minor value in assessing adult adjustment.

The present study also applies the Rorschach test as a post hoc predictor of later adjustment in a child clinical population. It specifically employs the Rorschach as an index of thought organization and object relations. Object representations and thought organization have been considered key aspects of underlying personality organization (Kernberg, 1977). Their capacity to be assessed with the Rorschach test suggests their potential usefulness in follow-up research.

130 Child Populations Under Extreme Duress

A number of Rorschach scales have been employed to assess aspects of these two broad personality indexes. Mayman's (1962) manual differentiating Rorschach form level and his later (1967) measure of object relations both apply complex psychoanalytic principles to certain Rorschach configurations. Blatt and Ritzler (1974), Harder and Ritzler (1979), and Goldfried et al. (1971), among others, have described a hierarchy of disturbances in thought organization on the Rorschach that has successfully differentiated among subtly different diagnostic groups. Friedman (1953) developed a thought organization measure based on Werner's (1948) developmental theories. This measure was found capable of distinguishing variations in thought organization among schizophrenic and normal adults and normal, preadolescent children. I used it, therefore, in the present investigation.

The thematic object relations scales employed in many studies have relied almost exclusively on the quality of Rorschach human movement responses as indicators of object experience. This would limit the effectiveness of such a scale in work with preadolescent children, who typically produce few such responses (Levitt & Truumaa, 1972). Urist (1977) has developed, however, an object relations scoring system that uses both animal and human movement responses. Because this scoring system appears particularly promising in the nomothetic assessment of children's object relations, I used it in the present study.

Psychiatric re-hospitalization was chosen as the criterion to measure later adjustment. The degree of emotional dysfunction that would necessitate re-hospitalization (given a population matched on demographic, family background and treatment variables) is thought to be associated with an extreme state of distorted organizational activity and relatively primitive object relatedness. The thought organization and object relations measures chosen for the present study are expected to be useful in differentiating subjects along these dimensions of personality structure. The either-or quality of the re-hospitalization criterion, moreover, appears consonant with the limitations of our ability to make longstanding predictions on the developmental process. Predictive research (e.g., Mellsop, 1972) and Rorschach research (e.g., Frieswyk & Colson, 1980) both provide empirical precedents for the use of re-hospitalization as an outcome criterion.

It is specifically hypothesized that higher Rorschach object relation and thought organization scores will be associated with the avoidance of later re-hospitalization. Lower scores on these scales would be linked with re-hospitalization. The combined use of these scales, by providing a more complete overview of personality organization, is expected to enhance the capacity to predict behavior as compared to the separate use of the scales. Simple quantitative sums or proportions of the Rorschach determinants, based largely on the number and not the quality, content, or sequence of Rorschach responses provide only a small portion of the information to be derived from a Rorschach analysis. It is therefore hypothesized that these data would not discriminate the sample groups on the adjustment criterion.

Method

The present study uses a subsample of the residential treatment center population studied by Mordock (1978). Forty-one of the 400 children in residence some time during the period of 1953–1973 were documented (by actual contact with the subject or relative) to have spent a considerable amount of time (at least 6 months) in a psychiatric residential facility (not including group or foster homes) at some point between discharge and 5- to 20-year follow-up. The age of these children at the time of initial assessment (psychological testing was routinely performed on all the children within the first month of admission) ranged from 6 to 11 ($M = 9.83$). The age at follow-up ranged from 17 to 30 ($M = 23.86$). A 6-month minimum for both Astor Home placement ($M = 2.41$ years) and later re-hospitalization was arbitrarily established in an effort to prevent brief and/or inappropriate placements from confusing the data. A minimum of five years post-discharge from the Astor Home ($M = 11.62$) was also established so that a relatively long-term assessment of the subject's post-Astor history could be engendered.

The child's initial Rorschach test was used to prevent the confounding effects of retesting. Of the 41 subjects originally selected, four records could not be used as their Rorschach tests were illegible. A minimum full scale IQ of 75 (based on the Wechsler Intelligence Scale for Children) had been pre-established so that cognitive limitations would not confound either Rorschach performance or later adjustment. This ruled out two additional "re-hospitalized" records. The final results consisted of 35 re-hospitalized subjects who formed the "experimental group" (Mednick & McNeil, 1968) in this study.

I obtained a control group in the following manner. Each child admitted to Astor had been given a code number from 1 to 400 on the basis of their admission date. For every child found to fit the criteria of the hospitalized group, the next code number was reviewed. If that child had a legible Rorschach test, an IQ above 75, had been discharged from Astor for at least 5 years, and had documentation that directly noted no further psychiatric services, then the child was included in the control group. This procedure was continued until 35 non-hospitalized children's records were obtained.

The 70 children were given the following admitting diagnosis by the Astor Home staff: "passive-aggressive personality" (8 re-hospitalized, 8 not); "schizoid" (7 and 6); "child schizophrenia" (5 and 12); "adjustment reaction" (11 and 7); "hyperactive" (2 and 1); and "over-anxious reaction" (1 and 1). One male re-hospitalized subject's diagnosis was not available.

The re-hospitalized group was also found to have the following racial and sex characteristics: 29 boys, of whom 23 were white, 3 Puerto Rican, and 3 black, and 6 girls, of whom 4 were white, 1 Puerto Rican and 1 black. The children of the "control" group were selected so that these same racial and sex characteristics would be extant. Notably, however, no more than five code numbers above or below a given re-hospitalized child's code number were needed to obtain this half

132 Child Populations Under Extreme Duress

of the sample. The sexual and racial matching of the two sample groups did not appear, therefore, to distort the relatively unbiased process by which the control group was obtained.

Following their selection, I compared the two groups on a wide variety of demographic, family background, and treatment variables. These variables did not significantly discriminate between these sample groups (Tuber, 1981).

Procedure for Scoring the Rorschach Protocols

The identities and group classification of all 70 children were disguised before their Rorschach performance was evaluated. The Rorschach tests of the entire sample were first scored using the Klopfer et al. (1954) scoring system. They were then rescored using the object relations scale of Urist (1977) and the thought organization scale of Friedman (1953). Becker's (1956) modification of Friedman's scale was also employed, as it had been found to be particularly useful in nomothetic research applications (Goldfried et al., 1971). A randomly selected subsample of 20 records were then sent to another rater, a PhD psychologist, to assess the interrater reliability of the scoring systems employed in the present work. After the percentage of agreement between raters was calculated, differences in scoring on those 20 records were reconciled by discussion between the raters. On completion of this procedure, the Rorschach test results were then compared across groups for the entire sample, for boys only and for girls only. The Mann-Whitney and Fisher exact probability tests were employed in these comparisons (Siegel, 1956).

The relative strength of these Rorschach measures to predict later adjustment was assessed by employing the index of predictive association measure (Goodman & Kruskal, 1954). The combined effectiveness of any two or three or all three scales in predicting re-hospitalization was also assessed. As a final check of the predictive utility of these Rorschach measures, a comparison of their predictive efficiency with that of the Astor Home's diagnosis for each child was also engendered.

The Rorschach Scales

The Klopfer method for scoring the Rorschach test has been described in detail elsewhere (Klopfer et al., 1954) and will not be described here. Friedman's scoring system uses Rorschach location and determinants as its departure point. These scores are then classified according to the "percept's level of diffuseness, articulation [and] integration" (Goldfried et al., 1971, p. 21). Eight classifications of each of the two major locations scores ("W" and "D") are possible in Friedman's system, three considered developmentally "high" or "mature" and five deemed "low" or "immature" developmentally.

This study also summarizes Friedman's scoring categories using Becker's (1956) weighted scoring system. Wilensky (1959) has slightly modified Becker's system by computing an average developmental level score for each of the Rorschach

A Child Inpatient Population **133**

cards. These cards are then totaled and an average score for the entire record is obtained. This modification results in a highly reliable but more variable distribution of scores (Goldfried et al., 1971).

I also used the object relations scale developed by Urist (1977) in the present investigation. Although Urist used parametric statistical procedures with his scale, the state of knowledge of the range and vicissitudes of object experience is considered too tentative to assume equal intervals along a relationship continuum. The Mann-Whitney test was therefore used to assess the relationship between this scale and the adjustment criterion. Three object relations scores were obtained for each child: a median score, the single highest score (HOR) and the single lowest score (LOR).

Results

I assessed interrater reliability by comparing the ratings of the author and a PhD-level psychologist on a randomly drawn and completely disguised subsample of 20 Rorschach protocols. Percentage of agreement levels were obtained for the Klopfer (92%), Friedman (87%), and Urist (73% "exact hits," 90% agreement within 1 scale point) scale scores. These results suggest a solid degree of interrater reliability for all three measures.

I then initially compared the sample groups on the total number of Rorschach responses and the number of object relations responses. The groups did not differ significantly in the mean number of total responses (hospitalized mean = 17.6; non-hospitalized mean = 19.3; $t = 1.22$, ns).

No differences between sample groups were also reported on the number of object relations scores, $t(68) = -.97$, ns. I then compared the number of Rorschach responses given by each child across the entire sample with the number of object relations responses these children gave. These scores were also not significantly associated with one another, $r(68) = .12$, ns. Last, following a method of controlling for Rorschach productivity devised by Kalter and Marsden (1970), I subtracted the number of object relations responses for each child from his or her total number of responses. I then compared the resulting distribution of total number of responses minus object relations responses with the outcome groups. This association was also not significant (using Mann-Whitney test, $z = .09$, ns). These findings suggest that Rorschach productivity did not significantly influence the patterning of object relations scores. No correction for Rorschach productivity was therefore necessary.

Table 11.1 summarizes the results of the intergroup comparisons between the three object relations scores and the outcome criterion. As hypothesized, the single highest and lowest Rorschach object relations scores were significantly related to later re-hospitalization at follow-up.

Thought organization, as measured by Wilensky's adjusted scoring system, was significantly associated with follow-up adjustment for the total sample ($z = -1.72$,

134 Child Populations Under Extreme Duress

TABLE 11.1 Object Relations Scores (O-R) and Outcome Criterion

Variable	Total sample (N = 70)		Boys only (N = 58)		Girls only (N = 12)	
	z^a	p	z	p	U^b	p
MOR	−1.43	ns	−1.42	ns	7	.047
LOR	−2.48	.0066	−2.71	.0034	14	ns
HOR	−2.20	0.139	−2.40	.0082	11	ns

Notes: MOR = median O-R score; LOR = lowest O-R score; HOR = highest O-R score.
[a] z value using Mann-Whitney U test given large sample size.
[b] U value of Mann-Whitney test given small sample size (cf. Siegel, 1956).

$p < .05$) and boys-only subgroup comparison ($z = -1.89, p < .05$), but not for the girls-only comparison ($U = 17$, ns).

I also performed intergroup comparisons using Friedman's measure of Rorschach thought organization scores. Of the 16 Friedman variables for the total sample, 13 were in the hypothesized direction. Only 1 of these 16 associations, however, attained significance at $p < .05$, a figure expected by chance alone. A hypothesized, none of the Rorschach determinants (human movement, color, shading, or proportions therefrom) significantly discriminated between the two groups.

The relative strength of association between those Rorschach scores that were significantly linked with re-hospitalization was then measured using Goodman and Kruskal's (1954) index of predictive association (or "lambda"). The values of all three Rorschach scores were, therefore, separately ranked for all 70 subjects. A median value for each of the scores was thereby obtained. To permit uniformity of reporting, a "high" value will be regarded as that half of the median "split" that is considered indicative of adaptive functioning. A "high" LOR score is, therefore, applied to those subjects whose lowest single object relations score is still relatively adaptive. The small sample size of the girls-only subgroup does not make it appropriate to use this measure. The predictive comparisons are applied, therefore, only to the total sample and boys-only subgroups. Table 11.2 summarizes the results of both individual and joint Rorschach comparisons with the adjustment criterion.

The use of the Rorschach object relations scales individually did, as hypothesized, meaningfully predict later re-hospitalization or its avoidance. The conjoint use of the measures, again as hypothesized, substantially improved the capacity to predict re-hospitalization as compared to separate use of the scales. This improvement was most evidenced when the two object relations indexes were combined. The developmental level measure alone did not predict re-hospitalization. It actually decreased predictive utility when combined with both object relations indexes.

A Child Inpatient Population **135**

TABLE 11.2 Intergroup Comparisons: Predictive Association Measures

Variable	Total Sample					Boys Only				
	Overall		"Best"			Overall		"Best"		
	x^{2a}	λ	x^2	N	λ	x^{2b}	λ	x^2	N	λ
HOR	2.80*	.23	–	–	–	3.40	.28	–	–	–
LOR	5.74**	.31	–	–	–	5.60**	.34	–	–	–
DL	2.06	.20	–	–	–	2.50	.24	–	–	–
HOR/LOR	11.42**	.34	10.76**	38	.47	12.46**	.38	11.76***	31	.57
DL/LOR	10.04*	.31	9.80**	37	.50	9.74**	.31	7.84**	30	.42
DL/HOR	6.28	.26	6.16*	47	.35	7.78*	.31	7.64**	39	.42
DL/HOR/LOR	14.22*	.40	12.67**	38	.56	16.07*	.45	15.19**	32	.69

Notes: Overall comparison gives chi-square value for overall contingency table; "best" comparison gives chi-square value for most predictive partition of the overall contingency table, following the Bresnahan-Shapiro equation (1966).
HOR = highest single objects relations score; LOR = lowest single object relations score; DL = developmental level score.
[a]n = 70 for each overall comparison.
[b]n = 58 for each overall comparison.
*p < .05. **p < .01. ***p < .001.

One of the primary emphases of this research has been to assess whether the use of these Rorschach scales would meaningfully improve our diagnostic acumen. A comparison, albeit crude, of the predictive utility of the Rorschach scales vis-à-vis admission diagnosis was, therefore, undertaken. In keeping with prior predictive research on child pathology, all children diagnosed by the Astor Home staff as "child schizophrenic," "schizoid personality," or "inadequate personality" were placed in a "poor prognosis" category. Similarly, all children diagnosed as "neurotic," "passive-aggressive," "hyperactive," or "adjustment reaction" were placed in a "good prognosis" category. These categorizations were then compared with the outcome criterion. In 20 of the 38 subjects (53%), the Astor diagnosis was correct in matching a child with its outcome group. The combined use of the Rorschach scales, in contrast, correctly predicted outcome for 30 of the 38 subjects (79%). This is a statistically significant difference, $x^2(1) = 8.74, p < .01$.

Discussion

The underlying premise of this study is that the assessment of object relations and thought organization would help elucidate the inner template of a child's actual experience at a given time. Knowledge of this experience would then improve our understanding of the child's personality organization, thereby improving our capacity to predict his or her later adjustment. This basic hypothesis was largely confirmed for the boys in the present study.

136 Child Populations Under Extreme Duress

A significant positive association was reported between the highest single object relations score and the avoidance of later re-hospitalization. In certain respects, re-hospitalization may be considered a failure in an individual's interpersonal support system to provide an intra-system haven for acceptable functioning. A higher object relations score, then, may suggest that these individual's early internalized representations of others were benign enough to enhance the likelihood of generating equally benign relationships later in life. A higher such score would therefore be a relatively strong counter-indicator of later re-hospitalization.

A strong positive association was also reported between the existence of relatively "low" object relations scores and later re-hospitalization. These low scores reflect an experience of object relations where the autonomy of the self is under siege. Representations of self and others are therefore depicted as experiences of malevolence, depletion, or disintegration. One could speculate that the avoidance of malevolent object representations would provide an inner sanctum in times of stress. The existence of such a low score may, conversely, be conceived of as "predisposing" the child to expect later experience to be as malevolent as his or her present inner representations of reality. It would likely take exceptionally fortuitous later circumstances to avoid a "poor" outcome.

A positive association between Becker's developmental level summary measure and later adjustment was also described. Cognitive organizing capabilities, which the developmental level measure has been shown to reflect, have been conceptualized as the medium through which object relations and other aspects of the ego functioning are composed. The availability of more integrated and accurate perceptions of reality in childhood may be related to the later ability to avoid the intrusion of primary process thinking and the "blurring" of intrapsychic boundaries (Blatt & Ritzler, 1974). This blurring would make an individual more prone to distortions of ostensibly equal environmental circumstances. Relatively less mature scores were thus expected to be associated with a later inflexibility in cognitive functioning significant enough to help foster re-hospitalization.

The conjoint predictive utility of the developmental level measure was, however, relatively limited compared to that of the two object relations indexes. This result suggests that Rorschach measures of cognitive structure may not be compatible with Rorschach content measures. The marginal predictive utility of the developmental measure itself contrasts with its effectiveness in research with adult populations (e.g., Levine & Cohen, 1962). Further research is indicated to assess whether these discrepant findings are a function of demographic/psychological issues and/or simply error variance.

There are a number of limitations to this study that restrict the generalizability of its findings. The outcome criterion, re-hospitalization, is a discrete behavioral manifestation that is very likely a summarization of a complex interaction among intrapsychic, familial, and environmental factors. The manifold influences on re-hospitalization may not depend solely or even largely on the intrapsychic resources or deficits of the individual. Thus, it is to be reasonably expected that

Rorschach indications of personality structure would account for only a part of the variance that can accurately predict this complex outcome. In the present study, information on environmental circumstances and personality resources prior to re-hospitalization was not available. To the extent that these unavailable sources of data directly affected re-hospitalization, the findings of the present study must be viewed cautiously.

The results of the present investigation clearly depict a strong sex difference in the effectiveness of the Rorschach to predict outcome. By and large, the Rorschach scales were not significantly effective in predicting outcome for the girls in the sample. No sex differences in predictive utility were hypothesized for this sample. These findings therefore mitigate the empirical support this study lends to the construct validity of the Rorschach. The relative homogeneity of the two girls-only subgroups may also, however, be a function of its small sample size. Further research with a larger sample of girls is warranted to assess the viability of these Rorschach scales in work with female populations.

At present, the findings of this study suggest that the object relations and thought organization constructs, as represented on the Rorschach test, have predictive utility for boys only, and for the prediction of later re-hospitalization only. Further generalizations are not indicated. The use of nonparametric statistics and the exclusively linear association of independent with dependent variables further implies that additional research linking early object representations and thought processes with later adjustment is indicated. The positive findings of the present study suggest that such research may provide fruitful data to aid in the understanding of the developmental process.

Note

1 Copyright © 1983, American Psychological Association. Reproduced with permission. The official citation that should be used in referencing this material is Tuber, S. B. (1983). Children's Rorschach scores as predictors of later adjustment. *Journal of Consulting and Clinical Psychology*, 51(3), 379–385. http://dx.doi.org/10.1037/0022-006X.51.3.379. No further reproduction or distribution is permitted without written permission from the American Psychological Association.

12
RORSCHACH ASSESSMENTS OF HOMELESS CHILDREN

Primary paper: Donahue, P., & Tuber, S. (1993). Rorschach adaptive fantasy images and coping in children under severe environmental stress. *Journal of Personality Assessment*, 60, 421–434.[1]

Paul Donahue and I produced the following two papers that looked at the internal world of inner-city, homeless children. This population is often profoundly neglected in research protocols, especially protocols that seek to assess their underlying personality dimensions. It is as if the dire circumstances they wrestle with on a sociological level make it easy to avoid studying their experience at the level of unconscious processes. Yet another insult thus laid upon people from disadvantaged backgrounds is that psychological research commonly treats their internal experience as not worthy of the same depth of approach as is done for more privileged populations. Methodologically speaking, it is also useful to note that the first paper utilized both the human movement score and the MOA scale as its measure of inner life, in this case, access to fantasy. We sought to understand resilience in the face of dire hardship as a function of the inner relational dynamics within the child, speculating that the ability to retain benevolent imagoes of others can become a sanctuary in the face of adversity and a beacon to look for further support to deal with crises.

Beginning with the pioneering work of Anthony (1974), clinicians and researchers have come to recognize that some children remain resilient in the face of intense situational crises, and that a subgroup of invulnerable children appear to be resistant to even the most severe traumas. Most researchers attribute their successes to three overlapping variables: temperament (Murphy & Moriarty, 1976; Rutter, 1983), the strength of the mother–child relationship (Anthony, 1987a; Cicchetti & Aber, 1986; Garmezy, 1983), and the quality of social supports (Anthony, 1974, 1987b; Rutter, 1983; Wallerstein, 1983).

By most accounts, resilient children are endowed with a number of attributes that allow them to cope with stressful circumstances. They are emotionally secure and have positive self-images (Garmezy, 1983). Though often in the midst of chaos, they feel in control of their lives and rely on their own self-comforting mechanisms (Anthony, 1987b; Cohler, 1987). They are not necessarily more intelligent, but they are more alert and have greater perceptual abilities than do their peers (Murphy & Moriarty, 1976). Resilient children are less impulsive than their counterparts (Kagan, 1966), and they are capable of planning ahead and utilizing mental trial and error (Cohler, 1987).

Largely overlooked in the various descriptions of resilient children is their adaptive use of fantasy to withstand and overcome the painful circumstances in which they dwell. Among those who have studied patterns of invulnerability in childhood, only Anthony (1987a, 1987b) placed emphasis on children's use of fantasy to internally transform and repair their fractured environment. He attempted to fit the notion of *creative competence* into Piaget's framework of intellectual development. Anthony commended the use of fantasy as an effective means of making sense of traumatic events and long-term stressors (such as parental schizophrenia) and integrating them into existing schemata. He cited as examples the triumphs of major literary figures, including Hans Christian Andersen, who entered a fantasy mode so that his "unpalatable reality could be altered and assimilated into the inner representational system," and whose use of "symbolic dramatizations allowed him to select bits of experience over which he had ultimate control" (Anthony, 1987b, p. 37).

Ultimately, however, Anthony relegated the use of fantasy to a form of *pseudoresilience* in which there is an "illusion of powerfulness, of immunity from stresses, and of well-being" (Anthony, 1987b, p. 26). Although he suggested that a child's creative reservoir can operate as an autonomous ego function, Anthony regarded fantasy activities as regressive endeavors that eventually must be replaced by more goal-oriented actions. His conception, in fact, is less an integration than an either/or proposition, in which a child must choose to either accommodate to the world or escape into fantasy.

Other developmental theorists painted a broader picture of the adaptive role of fantasy in helping children cope with traumatic experiences. Singer (1973) argued that not only do fantasy play games allow children to gain a sense of mastery over the traumas they have experienced, but these fantasy activities also give them an opportunity to test new roles and attitudes that may help them overcome future stressors. Santostefano (1988b) contended that play and fantasy activities form the cornerstone of a more developed system of mental representation through which children (and adults) interpret interpersonal events and evaluate their attempts to negotiate the environment in which they live.

Though few studies have specifically examined the ways in which the adaptive use of fantasy enables children to cope with stressful events, considerable data suggest that this could be a fruitful area of inquiry. Researchers have consistently found that children who actively engage in fantasy and dramatic play have more

140 Child Populations Under Extreme Duress

developed means of organizing and interpreting new information (Dansky, 1979; Ghiaci & Richardson, 1980), greater impulse control and longer attention spans (Freyberg, 1973; Saltz, Dixon, & Johnson, 1977), higher thresholds for aggressive behavior (Biblow, 1973; Townsend, 1968), and more adaptive interpersonal skills (Connolly & Doyle, 1984; Saltz et al., 1977).

To test the hypothesis that children's use of adaptive fantasies is associated with an enhanced ability to withstand the effects of chronic environmental stress, a sample of homeless children from New York City was selected for study. In recent years, homeless children in New York have been subjected to some of the most devastating living conditions imaginable. In her comprehensive report on the lives of the city's homeless children, Molnar (1988) reported that many of the children were undernourished, and few were properly immunized. Diseases such as lead poisoning, diarrhea, asthma, and pneumonia were fairly common in the welfare hotels and shelters that she surveyed.

Molnar (1988) also found that many homeless women suffer from depression, and she observed that the mothers living in the hotels and shelters often did not have the emotional resources to care for their children. The tasks of parenting are made all the more difficult by the dangers inherent in most of the hotels and by the overcrowded living conditions, which leave little room for a mother and child to have private moments together. As a result, attachment patterns between homeless mothers and their young children are often disrupted or more permanently impaired (Molnar, Rath, & Klein, 1990).

A number of researchers have recently documented the impact of homelessness on children. Studies have indicated that homeless preschoolers have short attention spans, poor impulse control, and speech delays (Molnar, 1988) and have more cognitive delays and behavior disturbances than do other impoverished children (Rescorla, Parker, & Stolley, 1991). A study of children living in shelters in Massachusetts found that more than half were in need of psychiatric care, based on their responses to scales of depression and anxiety (Bassuk & Rubin, 1987). A similar number suffered from learning disabilities. Researchers in St. Louis found that 45% of the children they tested were at, or below, the borderline range of intelligence (Molnar, Rath, & Klein, 1990).

Measuring Fantasy – the Rorschach Human Movement Score

Attempts to measure fantasy activity directly have produced equivocal results. Among the methods used in research have been dream recall, daydreaming, creative story-telling techniques, and tests of associative fluency and divergent thinking. Though each of these measures has its merits, they all suffer from difficulty in distinguishing the capacity for fantasy from environmental restraints and personality variables, including intelligence, verbal fluency, motivation, and insightfulness. These methods also tend to assess the ability to produce a product; they do not evaluate the creative process involved, nor do they identify variables that underlie the production of fantasy images (Taylor, 1988).

This research has also been hindered by the lack of a precise and widely accepted definition of fantasy. Unconscious mentation, conscious creative thinking, regressive play, free association and goal-directed imagery have all been used as conceptual or operational definitions of fantasy. In this article, fantasy is defined in relatively broad terms as a cognitive process that includes both conscious and unconscious thoughts, images, and ideas that assist in reworking areas of conflict, choosing among current behaviors, and planning future activities.

In our study, the Rorschach human movement score (M) was used as a measure of adaptive fantasy. Though it is subject to some of the same criticisms as the methods previously described, there is relatively strong evidence that the M score is indicative of creative potential and imaginativeness, as Rorschach (1942) postulated in his most detailed discussion of the test. The M score can be parsimoniously interpreted in this manner, not as a measure of the full extent of creative resources or capacity for fantasy, but as an index of underlying potential to formulate complex, animate mental images.

Although there is evidence that the M score reflects developmental differences (Ames et al., 1974; Levitt & Truumaa, 1972) and intellectual capacity (Exner, 1986; Levitt & Truumaa, 1972), it has been more highly correlated with fantasy measures in a wide variety of clinical and empirical studies (Cocking, Dana, & Dana, 1969; Dana, 1968; Levitt & Truumaa, 1972). Researchers reported strong correlations between the number of M responses and creative story telling on the Thematic Apperception Test (King, 1958; Singer & Herman, 1954). Studies showed that the M score also correlates highly with measures of creativity (Weissberg & Springer, 1961), and that it predicts children's level of imaginative play in the short term (Moran, Sawyers, Fu, & Milgram, 1984) and over time (Shmukler, 1983). Children who have an imaginary companion are more likely to produce M responses than are their peers (Meyer & Tuber, 1989). The M score has also been used to identify people who are more likely to daydream (Page, 1957) and to recall their dreams (Schonbar, 1965).

In this study, the $M+$ score was chosen in preference to the overall M score to ensure that the responses were well formed and well articulated and could more readily be viewed as adaptive representations. Use of the M score generally assumes a high degree of organization in these responses, but studies with adult clinical populations suggest that M responses with good form are clinically distinct from those with poor form (Blatt & Berman, 1984). Discrepancies in the form level of children's M responses have not been investigated thoroughly, but the $M+$ score was chosen as a more conservative indicator of their capacity for adaptive fantasy.

Hypotheses

The primary purpose of this study was to determine whether the subjects' $M+$ scores could predict their levels of functioning in four separate domains that are key indicators of children's ability to survive and prosper under stressful circumstances. These include their ability to respond to reality demands in unstructured situations, their capacity for attention/concentration, their ability to maintain well-integrated

142 Child Populations Under Extreme Duress

object representations, and their facility in social situations. Homeless children in particular must be competent in each of these areas if they are to successfully navigate through their chaotic and often frustrating environment and not be overwhelmed by the violence and dangers that surround them.

Method

Subjects

Subjects were drawn from an after-school program at one of the large welfare hotels in midtown Manhattan. A total of 46 children were tested, ranging in age from 5 years 8 months to 13 years, with a mean of 9 years 5 months. Of this group, 24 were Black (10 boys and 14 girls), and 22 were Hispanic (14 boys and 8 girls). The mean length of homelessness was 10 months, with a range from 1 to 26 months. The mean length of stay in the hotel was 7 months, with a range from 1 to 22 months.

Little information about the subjects' parents was available; however, the hotel records did indicate that nearly all of the children lived with their mothers. The mean age of these mothers when they gave birth was 20 years 9 months. Of the 43 children for whom records were available, only 2 had fathers who were currently living with the family. Five children had another male present in the household.

Participation in the testing was voluntary, and all the children in the after-school program were eligible as long as they had signed permission from one of their parents. The children generally enjoyed the testing, and most of them were eager to participate. Two of the children left the hotel before they completed the testing.

Procedure

The children were tested by four advanced doctoral students in clinical psychology. All of the testing sessions were held in an office down the hallway from the main classroom on the second floor of the hotel. The office was partitioned with a large screen so that two testings could proceed simultaneously. The majority of the sessions were conducted without incident, but on occasion, there were disturbances in the hall that disrupted the testing, and in a few instances, the sessions had to be postponed temporarily. Relative to the chaotic and tense atmosphere in much of the building, however, the classroom and the testing area were remarkably calm during most of the testing period.

Independent Variables

This study was designed to evaluate the relative contribution of the children's capacity to form well-articulated fantasy images in predicting outcome on the indices of adaptive functioning. The subject's age was also included as an independent variable in the analyses to determine the impact of developmental differences on the children's performance. Sex was included to measure the potential impact of gender differences. A brief measure of nonverbal intelligence, the Raven's test (Raven, 1977), was used to control for the possibility that the $M+$ score was primarily a function of the children's level of cognitive development.

Rorschach human movement score. As discussed, the Rorschach $M+$ score was used as a measure of adaptive fantasy. The Rorschach test was administered according to the guidelines provided by Ames and associates (1974). Movement responses were scored according to the method outlined by Klopfer and Davidson (1962).

Raven's Colored Progressive Matrices. The Raven's Colored Progressive Matrices (Raven, 1977) has been widely used as a brief nonverbal measure of intellectual ability. Researchers have found that it correlates highly with the Wechsler verbal (Martin & Wiechers, 1954) and performance IQs (James, 1984; Martin & Wiechers, 1954) and the California Achievement Test (Powers & Barkan, 1986). The Raven's is less culturally biased than most cognitive instruments and does not appear to discriminate markedly between minority and nonminority groups (Powers & Barkan, 1986).

Dependent Variables

Fruit Distraction Test. The Fruit Distraction Test (Santostefano, 1988a) is designed to measure field articulation, the ability to selectively attend to a particular stimulus while ignoring irrelevant information. The test requires that the child quickly name color patterns on a series of cards while ignoring peripheral stimuli. The first card serves as an introduction to the task. Card 2 serves as a baseline measure, and the time and error (misnaming) differentials between this card and the two experimental cards provide the key scoring indices. Card 3 is designed to measure a child's ability to handle external distractors, and Card 4 is intended to be an index of a child's capacity to manage internal stimuli.

In his summary of the research on the Fruit Distraction Test, Santostefano (1988a) reported that young children tend to be distracted by irrelevant data, whereas older children are better able to maintain their focus on the task. He also found that this test successfully distinguished between normal and learning-disabled children. In factor analytic studies, the Fruit Distraction Test has loaded with other tests of selective attention. Children's scores on the test have also correlated significantly with performance on the Marble Board Test (Strauss & Lehtinen, 1947) and the Benton Visual Memory Test (Benton, 1955), both of which require children to attend to select information for extended periods.

Rorschach form quality. High form quality *(F+)* responses are indicative of an individual's ability to concentrate on the inkblots, to attend to memory images, and to select from them a response that is fitted to the stimulus. A substantial body of clinical evidence (Rickers-Ovsiankina, 1977) and factor analytic studies (Blatt & Berman, 1984) support the notion that the percentage of *F+* responses

144 Child Populations Under Extreme Duress

is a measure of the subject's ability to evaluate critically and respond to the reality demands of the task. Form quality can be reported for both pure form responses ($F+$ percentage) and all responses with definite form, including movement, color, and texture responses (extended $F+$ percentage). Research has suggested that the extended $F+$ percentage is a more valid index in records where there are few pure form responses (Exner, 1986). In this study, the form quality of the responses was rated according to the system devised by Mayman (1962).

Object relations – the Mutuality of Autonomy Scale. The Mutuality of Autonomy (MOA) Scale was developed by Urist (1977) to assess the extent to which a person's internal representations of relationships reflect interactions in which the participants maintain their separateness and their individuality.

Teacher's Rating Scale: Self-Perception Profile. The Teacher's Rating Scale (Harter, 1985) provides measures of children's scholastic competence, social acceptance, athletic competence, and behavior. Each item on the questionnaire is rated on a 4-point scale. In two studies using an earlier version of the scale, Harter (1982) found that the teachers' ratings showed high internal consistency in each domain, and consistently produced four distinct factor loadings. The children were rated by two staff members of the after-school program in which they all participated.

Reliability

The Rorschach protocols were scored by two advanced doctoral students who participated in training sessions with Paul J. Donahue (the first author). The agreement percentage for the number of responses across all subjects was .92 and for $F+$ responses, .87. For identifying responses that qualified as human movement, their level of agreement was .80. For the MOA scores, their reliability score was .62 for exact agreement and .88 for agreement within 1 scale point.

Results

A series of multiple regression analyses was conducted using the $M+$ score, the Raven's score, and the subjects' age and sex as independent variables. All of the regression equations utilized the stepwise procedure, which calls for the entry and removal of variables from the regression model according to designated criteria. Because our study was designed as a preliminary investigation, these were set at fairly liberal levels ($p < .15$ to enter, $p > .165$ to remove). The correlation matrix of all variables entered into the regression equations is displayed in Table 12.1.

Fruit Distraction Test

The Rorschach $M+$ score was the only variable that predicted the outcome on the external distractor score (time on Cards 3-2) of the Fruit Distraction Test, and it accounted for a significant portion of the variance on this measure: $R2 = .091$, $F(1, 42) = 4.21, p < .05$. The results of this analysis are summarized in Table 12.2.

Rorschach Assessments of Homeless Children **145**

TABLE 12.1 Correlations Between Variables in the Regression Analyses

	M+	Age	Sex	RAV	FDE	FDI	F+	XF+	MOA
M+		.26	−.13	.38	−.32	−.04	.22	.46	−.40
Age	.26		−.27	.63	−.29	−.26	.31	.46	−.05
Sex	−.13	−.27		−.20	.15	.07	−.18	−.10	−.00
RAV	.38	.63	−.20		−.23	−.07	.31	.43	−.20
FDE	−.32	−.29	.15	−.23		.49	−.41	−.49	.23
FDI	−.04	−.26	.07	−.0?	.49		−.08	−.15	.18
F+	.22	.31	−.18	.31	−.41	−.08		.72	−.25
XF+	.46	.46	−.10	.43	−.49	−.15	.72		−.42
MOA	−.40	−.05	−.00	−.20	.23	.18	−.25	−.42	

Notes: FDE: Fruit Distraction External Distractibility score. FDI: Fruit Distraction Internal Distractibility score. XF+: Extended F+ percentage. MOA: Mutuality of Autonomy score.

TABLE 12.2 Predictors of Fruit Distraction External Distractibility Score: Final Regression Statistics

Variable	Beta	B	t
Rorschach M+	−.30	−3.21	−2.31★

Notes: A lower differential score on the Fruit Distraction Test indicates greater attentiveness.
★$p \leq .05$, two-tailed.

None of independent variables was significantly correlated with the internal distractibility score (Cards 4-2) or with the misnaming error scores on the Fruit Distraction Test.

Rorschach F+ Percentage

The percentage of both the pure form ($F+$) and extended form responses were used as dependent variables. Age proved to be the only independent variable that predicted outcome on the former. Though not so powerful a predictor as the subjects' age, the $M+$ score was significantly correlated with the extended $F+$ percentage, and after it was entered on the second step, $R2$ increased from .21 to .33 (See Table 12.3). Again the subject's sex and Raven's score did not reach the criterion levels for inclusion in the final regression equation.

Object Relations – The MOA Scale

The Rorschach $M+$ score was the only variable in the regression equation significantly to predict outcome on the MOA scale. By itself it accounted for a significant portion of the variance on this measure: $Ji2 = .16$, $F(1, 39) = 7.56$, $p < .01$.

146 Child Populations Under Extreme Duress

TABLE 12.3 Predictors of Rorschach Extended $F+$ Percentage: Final Regression Statistics

Variable	Beta	B	t
Age	.36	0.02	2.75*
Rorschach $M+$	.36	0.03	2.72*

Note: *$p \leq .01$, two-tailed.

Teacher's Rating Scale: Self-Perception Profile

The biases of the raters and their limited knowledge of many of the children precluded the use of this measure in the analyses. The two raters both tended to be exceedingly lenient in the scores they gave the children, viewing the vast majority of them in uniformly positive terms. The few children who were rated in a negative direction were given low scores in all categories. In addition, each of the raters was familiar with only about half of the children in the sample, and the interrater reliability for the subjects whom they both observed was at unacceptably low levels.

Discussion

The index of adaptive fantasy, the Rorschach $M+$ score, played a significant role in predicting the outcome on the three dependent measures. Of the four independent variables, it was the only one that was significantly negatively correlated with the measure of external distractibility, derived from the Fruit Distraction Test. This score reflects an individual's ability to screen out irrelevant information in the immediate environment, a critical task for homeless children who live in large congregate shelters and are barraged by competing stimuli.

The correlation between the $M+$ score and the internal distractibility score, a measure of the extent to which an individual's private thoughts and fantasies interfere with the ability to attend, was extremely weak ($r = -.04$). This lack of relationship suggests that the children with more developed fantasies were not more susceptible to these types of intrusions, as may have been expected.

The $M+$ score accounted for a significant portion of the variance on an index of reality testing, the Rorschach extended $F+$ percentage. This relationship is confounded somewhat by the fact that both scores are derived from the Rorschach and by the fact that they overlap. Although the $M+$ score is included in the extended $F+$ score, it accounted for only a small portion of the $F+$ total. The mean of $M+$ for the entire sample was 2.2, whereas the mean of $F+$ for the sample was 14.6. In addition, research with adults has indicated that the $F+$ and $M+$ scores load on different factors and do not share much common variance (Blatt & Berman, 1984). The $M+$ score was also the only independent variable to predict outcome on a

Rorschach Assessments of Homeless Children **147**

measure of object relations, the MOA scale. The MOA score is an index of the level of mutual relatedness in an individual's mental representations. Again there is some overlap between this measure and the M score, but an MOA score can be given to any Rorschach response and is theoretically an independent measure of the quality and not the quantity of mental representations. Logic dictates, however, that to receive an MOA score, a child must have the ability to create, structure, and retain an image. The production of the M response can be viewed as the necessary cognitive precursor to the MOA score, regardless of its affective content.

The MOA scale may also tap into two other areas of strength of children who can create adaptive fantasy images. First, it requires a good degree of sensitivity to appreciate and to respect another's boundaries and separateness. As the research of Saltz and his colleagues (1977) demonstrated, imaginative children tend to be more empathic and more attuned to the cues of other children. In addition, they have the cognitive skills necessary to mentally assume another's perspective and to step into a role that they have occupied previously (Tower, 1983). With these advantages, children with well-developed fantasies should find it easier to maintain images of people who share a mutual respect for one another.

The $M+$ score proved to be a significant factor in each of these regression analyses, and it was not subsumed under the other independent variables. Although both the Fruit Distraction Test and the extended $F+\%$ are to a large extent developmental indices, the $M+$ score made an independent contribution in predicting the subjects' performance on both of them that went beyond or added to the variance accounted for by their age. It is important to note that the independent measure of intelligence, the Raven's test, was not significantly correlated with any of the dependent measures in the regression analyses. The strength of the correlations between the dependent variables and the $M+$ score in this study cannot therefore be primarily attributed to the latter's role in assessing general intelligence or global developmental functioning.

The results of this study are particularly striking in light of the reported incidence of psychopathology among homeless children. Given the extent of the traumas and deprivation that they have endured, one might have hypothesized that the fantasies of the current sample would be either markedly deficient or grossly distorted. Yet their actual level of M production ($M = 2.80$, $SD = 1.96$) exceeded the levels of both a sample of inner-city minority children and a middle-class sample (Ames et al., 1974). Those children who were able to utilize fantasy might have been expected to attempt to withdraw or escape from their environment. The fact that the $M+$ score was positively correlated with attentiveness and well-developed reality testing casts doubts on this argument and suggests instead that the capacity for adaptive fantasy may be a key indicator of children's ability to withstand the stress of homelessness.

Reflecting on the variables that contribute to resiliency, it is worth considering their role in fostering children's capacity for fantasy. Young children who have good relationships with their mothers and other adults in their social

148 Child Populations Under Extreme Duress

system are provided not only with a facilitating environment for cognitive and emotional growth, but also with a context in which they can develop symbolic representations of these relationships (Stern, 1985; Winnicott, 1965b). Developmental theorists contend that these symbols are continually transformed in childhood and later form a more sophisticated representational system through which children interpret their experiences, prescribe behaviors, and check the results of their actions (Bretherton, 1984; Santostefano, 1988b). Although the M score does not capture the full extent of a child's representational capacity, it can be viewed as a fairly concise measure of the success of the child's early symbolic strivings. It is also likely that high M production in latency-age children is a reflection of their continued exposure to and identification with mature and capable adult figures.

The fact that the Teacher's Rating Scale could not be used limited our analyses to the relationship between children's test scores and precludes a discussion of the impact of the children's access to fantasy on their social skills and their behavior. Future studies must be more focused on this issue, so that the relationship between children's representational capacity and their actual coping behaviors can be examined more fully.

Further research also is needed to refine the conceptual and operational definitions of fantasy. Studies should attempt to clarify which aspects of the cognitive-affective process involved in fantasy, including the creation of mental imagery, the relational context, the motivational features, and the goal-directedness of the images, are the key elements to its adaptive function. The measurement of each component must also be more carefully delineated. It is within this framework that the ultimate significance of the M response could be judged more fully.

In summary, the capacity for adaptive fantasy, as measured by the Rorschach $M+$ score, was positively correlated with three measures of adaptive functioning in a sample of homeless children. The $M+$ score made a unique contribution in predicting success on each of the dependent variables in regression analyses that controlled for the effects of age, sex, and intelligence. The results of the study suggest that the capacity for adaptive fantasy can be viewed as an important factor in resiliency in children. These findings also offer a potential means of evaluating clinical interventions with homeless and other disadvantaged children.

Note

1 Copyright 1993, Lawrence/Erlbaum Associates, Inc. Reproduced with permission.

13

ANOTHER STUDY OF HOMELESS CHILDREN

Paper used: Donahue, P., & Tuber, S. (1995). The impact of homelessness on children's levels of aspiration. *Bulletin of the Menninger Clinic, 59*, 249–255.[1]

In this second study with Paul Donahue, we looked at the relationship between how long a child was forced to stay in a homeless shelter and their level of aspiration, in this case a willingness to take on harder tasks. We then added in TAT responses from four of the youngsters, two homeless for a considerable period of time and two with relatively shorter stays, and showed how prolonged stays impacted their object relational experience.

Over the past few years, the developmental delays, educational deficits, and behavioral and emotional disturbances of homeless children have been well documented (Bassuk & Rubin, 1987; Molnar, 1988; Rafferty & Shinn, 1991). Homeless children also face a severely limited future; research has demonstrated that children who do not live in a protective environment are not as likely to have achieved the sense of security and self-confidence necessary to develop and pursue challenging goals (Aber & Allen, 1987; Pynoos & Eth, 1986; Terr, 1991). Recent clinical reports suggest that the violence and unpredictability inherent in shelter life have a profound impact on homeless children's feelings of control and self-efficacy, and can lead to states of passivity and learned helplessness.

Given the level of stress that homeless children endure, we hypothesized that increasingly lengthy stays in the shelter system would be negatively correlated with one aspect of children's motivation and self-concept—their level of aspiration. We predicted that children who had extended stays in shelters would prefer to attempt less challenging tasks than children who had been homeless for a shorter period.

Method

Subjects

Subjects were drawn from an after-school program at one of the large "welfare" hotels in New York City. The initial sample included 46 children, ranging in age from 5 years, 8 months to 13 years old (mean: 9 years, 5 months). Of this group, 24 were black (10 boys, 14 girls) and 22 were Hispanic (14 boys, 8 girls). The mean length of homelessness was 10 months (range: 1–26 months).

Level of aspiration

A modified version of the Block Design subtest of the Wechsler Intelligence Scale for Children-III (Wechsler, 1991) was used to assess the children's cognitive functioning as part of a larger research protocol (Donahue & Tuber, 1993). This task entails assembling blocks to match geometric designs. In this study, five patterns of graduated difficulty (Block Design items 1, 2, 4, 7, and 10) were used. After completing the five designs, the children were asked to choose the pattern that they would like to attempt again, and the difficulty level of the design they chose (ranging from 1 to 5) was deemed their level of aspiration score. The Raven's Colored Progressive Matrices (Raven, 1977), a brief, nonverbal measure of intelligence, was used in this study as a control measure of cognitive ability.

Results

Of the original 46 children, only 39 completed both facets of the level of aspiration task. Their level of aspiration scores were distributed fairly evenly across the five scores, with slight elevations at the lowest score (n = 11) and the highest (n = 10). As predicted, the level of aspiration score was significantly negatively correlated with the length of time the children had been homeless ($r = -.41$, $p \leq .05$, two-tailed). The level of aspiration score was also significantly correlated with the children's scores on the modified Block Design test ($r = .43, p \leq .01$, two-tailed) and the Raven's ($r = .48$, $\leq .01$, two-tailed). Subsequent analyses (using partial correlations) that controlled for the effects of these variables revealed that the correlation between level of aspiration and length of homelessness remained significant (Block Design: $r = -.34, p \leq .05$, two-tailed; Raven's: $r = -.35, p \leq .05$, two-tailed).

Discussion and Clinical Implications

The picture that emerges from this research fits with that of other recent clinical portraits of homeless children. Although some children living in shelters can stave off the impact of the traumas they experience by their superior intelligence and resourcefulness, the vast majority are unable to weather the chaos and frequent

Another Study of Homeless Children **151**

environmental insults, particularly as these persist over time. Visions of academic achievement or career aspirations tend to get overshadowed by the harsh realities they face daily, and most homeless children do not set their sights too high.

To illustrate the impact of length of homelessness on these children, we selected two Thematic Apperception Test (TAT) stories (Card 1, a boy staring at a violin; Card 2, a young woman in a farm scene) from each of four subjects, two who had been homeless for just a few months, and two who had been homeless for an extended time. These protocols were not chosen at random, but were selected to capture the typical themes of aspiration of the children in each group. The subjects selected were similar in age, ethnicity, and cognitive ability.

Extended Homelessness

The first subject is a black female, age 8 years and 3 months, who has been homeless for 24 months.

Protocol. Card 1: He's sad, maybe because he can't play the violin. It doesn't work. He wants the violin to work. (led up to?) He must have dropped it. (thinking?) Maybe he should quit or not. (future?) He might not quit.

Card 2: I think there's a lady thinking about something while the man is working on the farm. I think this is a statue right there [woman by tree]. (thinking? feeling?) He's feeling hot, he's thinking what she should do with the farm. (led up?) Some of the animals burned in the fire. (future?) They're going to do something with the farm and have a house to live in.

Commentary. In Card 1, both the subject and the object (the broken violin) are sad and ineffectual. His tool doesn't work because of his own mistake. The dilemma is whether to quit, and there is little notion of accomplishing anything. The subject's response to Card 2 is disjointed, and she idiosyncratically adds a deadly fire. Here there is a wish to do something, but the level of aspiration is mired by the basic wish to have a home, a stark personalizing of the effect of being homeless.

The second subject is a Hispanic male, age 10 years and 2 months, who has been homeless for 15 months.

Protocol. Card 1: He's bored, hungry, tired. He's feeling that he wants to run away. In the past, he thinks he's going to die. (past or future?) Future. (beginning?) He was playing his violin and he got bored with it. After that, he stopped and he was thinking that he was going to run away. (future?) He can have all the money he wants. (from?) Working, unless be steals it. (?) He'll work.

Card 2: She looks like she's a Christian. She [girl] got the Bible in her hand and she [woman] looks like a statue—serious! She does! And she [girl] just came from church. (beginning?) She came out of church. (thoughts? feelings?) Yeah. This man don't like Christians. (why?) Because he's not one. (thinking?) She [girl] is. She's thinking that the man is saying that, but she don't really know. (future?) Her future is that he's going to die.

152 Child Populations Under Extreme Duress

Commentary. The subject's confusion in the first story over past and future suggests a distortion in his ability to aspire. His playing leads to no ambition, only to empty boredom. His wish to flee and steal suggests a desperation at not having his needs met. His story to Card 2 is totally devoid of aspiration and filled with disconnection and the disparity between Christians and non-Christians.

Short-Term Homelessness

The third subject is a black male, age 10 years and 4 months, who has been homeless 4 months.

Protocol. Card 1: The boy is thinking how he's going to play the violin, and the boy, his mother wants him to play the violin so he'll grow up to be a musician. His father's a musician and he wants to follow in his father's footsteps.

Card 2: The girl is looking at the statues and wondering if she's going to look like that, while the farmer's plowing with his horse beside him while he plants corn and wheat. It's going to be a wonderful field of corn and wheat and he's going to sell it to the store man and the store man will give him money to buy food and clothes.

Commentary. This subject's story to Card 1 is strikingly different from those of the previous two subjects. He shows a notable degree of identification with his accomplished father and a ringing endorsement by his mother of his aspirations, coupled with a strong future orientation. On Card 2, the subject also identifies strongly with the man, who is seen as productive. The field is rich and fertile, and although its net result is a somewhat limited, concrete enhancement of self via clothes and food, the story is more future-oriented and hopeful than those of Subjects 1 and 2.

The fourth subject is a Hispanic female, age 10 years and 5 months, who has been homeless for 2 months.

Protocol. Card 1: What is this? (violin) He looks like he wants to play it. (beginning?) A teacher gave him the violin because he told her he could play the violin, but he really couldn't. So he's sitting there trying to think of a way to play the violin. (future?) He's going to try to play it and see if he could play. (end?) He's going to discover that he could play it, but he never knew how to play it. (?) He just wanted to make his teacher happy with him. (impress her?) Yeah. (?) At first he didn't know how to play it. He only had 3 days. And then when he started practicing and practicing, he got it. (thinking? feeling?} He's thinking that he can't do it, but when he really puts his mind to it, he finds out that he could play.

Card 2: She goes to school? (your story) She works as a secretary. She takes notes and writes letters. (story?) About a girl that lives on a farm and works as a secretary. (now?) She's holding books in her hands. (?) She's standing. (thoughts? feelings?) She looks sad. (?) 'Cause she lost her job. (thoughts?) Thinking that she's going to try to get her job back. (future?) Should I let her get her job back? She gets her job back! She starts working good. She's retiring in a couple of weeks. At

Another Study of Homeless Children **153**

her last week, she retires and moves. She moves to a farm. She gets married and she lives happily ever after with her job and husband. (retired?) She did. (?) What I mean is that she retired and they promoted her to a better job. (beginning?) She lived and worked on a farm.

Commentary. The level of aspiration in the first narrative is extremely high, to the point where it seems to protest too much. Mastery of the violin in 3 days is obviously unrealistic, but the focus on practicing hard and "putting his mind to it" suggests an ambition and sense of purpose that seem reality-based, attainable, and full of hope and confidence. This story also includes the notion of making his teacher happy, much like Subject 3. Also, her response to Card 1, unlike the stories of Subjects 1 and 2, suggests the availability of a mother who endorses and even presses for the child's accomplishments.

The subject's story to Card 2 is more fluid and rife with confusion between past and present, suggesting more conflict regarding aspiration than in the previous story or those of Subject 3. There is, however, no hint of despair or malevolence as there was in Subject 2's story. Subject 4 acknowledges her sadness and misfortune and, interestingly, she asks the tester rhetorically how she should end the story, again suggesting a capacity for distancing herself from sadness and taking a positive tack. She resolves the dilemma in a Pollyanna-ish way that is not as convincing as it was for her on Card 1, but it is full of positive aspiration and accomplishment.

In summary, Subjects 1 and 2 have little or no sense of realistic aspiration, purpose, planning, problem solving, or future orientation, and are consumed instead by either despair and inefficacy (especially Subject 1) or malevolence, betrayal, and death (as in Subject 2). Subjects 3 and 4, in contrast, reveal significant ambitions, wishes, and hopes for the future, along with plans to enact these wishes. Both also have mothers in the stories who support and push for these wishes. Although Subject 3 seems sturdier, less conflicted, and more realistic in his strivings than Subject 4, they both are confident and enthusiastic about their future prospects.

Conclusion

It would be far too facile to attribute the differences in these subjects' level of aspiration solely to the length of time they have been homeless. Any conclusive statements would have to be based on more in-depth analyses of their previous achievements, their intellectual capacities, and their family histories. The stories of these subjects might overly dramatize the differences between the two groups, but they exemplify how homelessness exerts its influence over time, limiting children's sense of accomplishment and curtailing their hopes for future success.

The diminished level of aspiration of these homeless children has serious implications for their ability to cope with their present situation and for their approach to future challenges. Clinicians now recognize that to successfully master traumatic events, individuals must have an image of a future with brighter

154 Child Populations Under Extreme Duress

possibilities and they must have a strong desire to achieve their goals. Part of this process involves accepting the discrepancy between one's current self-concept and the self that one would hope to become. If homeless children tend instead to increasingly inhibit their ambitions over time and to remain firmly rooted in their present level of functioning, they are unlikely to be able to transcend their current situation.

Note

1 Copyright 1995, Guilford Press. Reproduced with permission.

14

RORSCHACH ASSESSMENTS OF CHILDREN ABOUT TO UNDERGO SURGERY

Paper used: Tuber, S., Frank, M., & Santostefano, S. (1989). Children's anticipation of impending surgery: Shifts in object-representational paradigms. *Bulletin of the Menninger Clinic*, 53, 501–511.[1]

This paper provides a most interesting contrast to the others included in this volume, in that it uses the RIM as an explicit measure of state and not trait and hypothesizes that the RIM can detect very recent shifts in object relational experience as a function of a short-term trauma, in this case a surgical procedure. The paper is intriguing in that historically, researchers using the RIM have shied away from using it as an indicator of short-term change. This paper lends credence to the possibility that the RIM can measure more recent or even sudden shifts in experience.

The psychological sequelae for children following hospitalization or a surgical procedure have been amply addressed in both the clinical and research literature (Coleman, 1950; Levy, 1945; Poznanski, 1979). The psychological vicissitudes of impending surgery, however, and the adjustments that children make internally in the face of trauma that can be anticipated are far less well known.

A variety of specific complaints, fears, distortions, and fantasies have been reported in children anticipating surgery. Anna Freud (1952) noted that "any surgical interference with the child's body may serve as a focal point for the activation, reactivation, grouping and rationalization of ideas of being attacked, overwhelmed and (or) castrated" (p. 74). In their study of 143 children facing tonsillectomy or adenoidectomy, Jessner, Blom, and Waldfogel (1952) found that the anticipation preceding these operations constituted "an important and stressful experience for each child, activating the great childhood fears – of abandonment, of mutilation, and of death" (p. 166). Solnit (1984) described how children

156 Child Populations Under Extreme Duress

need ongoing assistance to cope successfully during hospitalization, because the children's limited resources "can deal with detrimental events only by obliterating their impact of adapting various defensive devices that do not lead to true mastery" (p. 630).

Several other studies have assessed the degree to which hospitalization itself may be traumatic for young children. Davenport and Werry's (1970) questionnaire sent to mothers indicated that children undergoing a brief stay for tonsillectomy did not show evidence of post-hospitalization upset. They noted, however, that more subtle expressions of anxiety and stress occurred during the hospital stay. Skipper and Leonard (1968) found evidence of heightened stress in hospitalized children as measured by elevated temperature, pulse rate, and blood pressure. They also reported postoperative disturbed sleep patterns and extended recovery time. Bourling and Collipp (1969) focused on developing an anxiety hierarchy for hospitalized children. Children in this study were between 15 months and 10 years of age; changes in their heart rates were used to assess stress. Notably, while procedures with needles were the most stressful, the next most stressful procedure was the admission examination. Children's intense anxiety at admission is also demonstrated in a large number of case study reports of pre-surgery fantasies (Kliman, 1968).

These idiographic and nomothetic reports have provided evidence, either through psychological or clinical/anecdotal methods, of the stress that children experience when they undergo even a minor surgical procedure. In this study, we provide a broader assessment of the overall quality of children's psychological reaction to surgery. In keeping with an emphasis on the essential role that a person's inner repertoire of interpersonal interactions plays in the personality (Blatt & Lerner, 1983), we are specifically interested in assessing children's quality of object-representations in the face of an impending surgical procedure. The relative paucity of research of how children return to pre-surgical patterns of object-representations suggested that this aspect of recovery should also be investigated.

Consistent with the recent theoretical emphasis on an individual's conceptions of self and other (Kernberg, 1977) has been a concomitant emphasis on psychological testing procedures that evaluate aspects of "object relations" (Krohn & Mayman, 1974; Tuber, 1983; Urist, 1977).

We hypothesized that in children about to undergo surgery, the anticipation of imminent bodily injury and assault would result in a short-term but acutely felt anxiety, which would particularly affect the quality of children's inner experiences of self and other. We also hypothesized that the fear of malevolent intrusion described anecdotally by others would influence the interactive content of these subjects' Rorschach responses, resulting in an increase in malevolent, controlling, and toxic representations as measured by the MOA scale. Finally, we hypothesized that in contrast to a control group, a surgical group would not differ significantly on the MOA scale either well before or after the surgical experience, but would show a significantly poorer mean MOA score when tested immediately prior to surgery. In the surgical group, we expected a significant worsening of MOA scale

Children About to Undergo Surgery **157**

scores between our first measure, one week before surgery, and our second one, immediately before, with an improvement in scores on our third measure, three weeks after surgery.

Method

Subjects

Subjects were chosen from an earlier, larger study by Santostefano (1978), who studied 28 male, white children, ages 7 to 11. Our experimental group (surgical group) consisted of 15 boys who were scheduled for hernia surgery. The names of the boys were obtained from several pediatric surgeons in a large metropolitan area who notified the original investigators when a child was scheduled for elective hernia repair. We then sought permissions from the parents for the child's participation in the study. The 15 boys were selected over a period of 6 months and had a mean age of 8.8 years, with a standard deviation of 1.3 years. The control group consisted of children attending a parochial school whose parents gave permission for their participation in this study. The children in the control group were selected to match the ages of the children in the surgical group, with the control group having a mean age of 9.1 years and a standard deviation of 1.4 years.

The control group was also selected to match as closely as possible the intelligence level of the surgical group. Four subtests of the Wechsler Intelligence Scale for Children (WISC) were administered (Similarities, Vocabulary, Picture Completion, and Block Design). The surgical group revealed the following scale score means and standard deviations: Similarities = 12.8, SD = 2.1; Vocabulary = 11.7, SD = 2.6; Picture Completion = 11; SD = 2.3; and Block Design = 10.8, SD = 2.8. The control group's respective scores were: Similarities = 12.1, SD = 2.1; Vocabulary = 11.8, SD = 3.4; Picture Completion = 10.7, SD = 3.2; and Block Design = 10.9, SD = 3.3. Prospective subjects for the control group were eliminated if their WISC scale scores deviated markedly from the average range. Accordingly, the mean intelligence scores of these children closely matched those of the surgical children.

The histories of these subjects, all of whom came from middle-class families, contained no evidence of physical or emotional disability that could affect the study. As noted, the control group of students was enrolled in a parochial school; the children of the surgical group attended public school.

In the original procedure, subjects were administered tests individually at three different times. The surgical children were tested in their homes approximately one week before hospitalization (Time 1). The battery was re-administered in the children's hospital rooms at bedside one day before the scheduled surgery (Time 2). Three weeks after discharge, the procedures were re-administered to the children in their homes (Time 3). Except for the control children being tested in their homes all three times, the protocol was identical to that followed in the assessment

158 Child Populations Under Extreme Duress

of the surgical group. In addition, during Time 1 all 28 children were administered four subtests of the WISC.

Present Procedure

The three protocols of the 28 subjects were disguised both as to their group identity and time sequence. Two doctoral candidates in clinical psychology were then asked to score each protocol, using the Mutuality of Autonomy scale developed by Urist (1977). Both raters were blind to the purpose of this study. Kappa coefficients and percentage-of-agreement figures were computed between the two raters ($N = 28$, $K = .80$, $SE = 0.14$; percentage of agreement $= 90\%$). No differences were found in either the corrected-for-chance-agreement or the percentage-of-agreement figures across the three time intervals. Differences between the raters were reconciled by the first author, who, although aware of the purpose of the study, was unaware of both the group identity and time sequence of any given protocol when he was reconciling the disagreements between the raters.

In keeping with the original nature of the MOA scale (see Tuber, 1983), we used nonparametric statistical procedures to analyze the data. We first performed within-group comparisons on the surgical group to assess the impact of the temporal proximity to surgery on the mean MOA scale scores. The Friedman two-way analysis of variance by ranks (Siegel, 1956) measured the overall effect of time on the subjects. A significant difference across conditions using the Friedman procedure then permitted us to make pairwise comparisons of Time 1 versus Time 2, Time 2 versus Time 3, and Time 1 versus Time 3 using the Wilcoxon matched-pairs signed ranks test (Siegel, 1956). We used an identical procedure to make a within-group comparison over time for the control group. We then performed intergroup comparisons at each of the three testing times, using the Mann-Whitney U test for independent samples.

Results

Repeated measures ANOVAs for Rorschach productivity revealed no significant differences between the two groups at any of the three testings. A similar repeated measures analysis revealed no significant differences between the groups on the number of MOA scores. Following Kalter and Marsden's (1970) method for controlling for Rorschach productivity, we subtracted the number of MOA responses for each child from his total number of responses at each testing. The resulting distribution of total number of responses minus MOA responses was then compared between groups over the three testings. We found no significant differences. These findings suggest that Rorschach productivity did not significantly influence the patterning of the MOA scale scores. Therefore no correction for Rorschach productivity was necessary.

Children About to Undergo Surgery **159**

TABLE 14.1 Intergroup Comparisons on Mean MOA Scale Scores

Group	Mean MOA[a]	MOA SD	z[b]	p[c]
Time 1				
Surgical	2.67	1.43	0.75	.23
Control	2.73	1.05		
Time 2				
Surgical	3.97	1.67	−2.09	.02
Control	2.59	.55		
Time 3				
Surgical	3.45	1.49	0.66	.26
Control	2.96	1.08		

Notes: [a]MOA scales have a range of 1 to 7, the higher the score, the more malevolent the object-representation. [b]Mann-Whitney U test corrected for tied ranks and expressed as normal deviate. [c]One-tailed tests.

The within-group comparison of the surgical group using the Friedman test revealed that MOA scale performance was significantly related to the time of the testing relative to the surgery (the mean rank of the subjects at Time 1 was 1.43; at Time 2, 2.50; and at Time 3, 2.07; (X^2 (2, N = 15) = 8.63, P = .013). We then conducted pair-wise comparisons using the Wilcoxon matched-pairs procedure. Subjects' mean MOA scale scores were significantly more malevolent at Time 2 than at Time 1 (z = -2.98, p = .003, two-tailed). Differences in mean MOA scores between Time 2 and Time 3 were not significant (z = -1.33, p = .091).

Within-group comparisons for the control group revealed no observed overall significant effect on the mean MOA scale score as a function of the time tested (the mean rank for Time 1 was 2.08; for Time 2, 1.73; and for Time 3, 2.19; X^2(2, N = 13) = 1.50, p = .472). This non-significant overall difference precluded the use of the pair-wise comparisons for the control group.

Table 14.1 provides the means and standard deviations for the mean MOA scale scores of our subjects and summarizes the results of the intergroup comparisons using the Mann-Whitney U test at each testing time. As we hypothesized, the groups did not differ in the ranking of their mean MOA scale scores at Time 1 or at Time 3. At Time 2, however, the surgical group had significantly less adaptive and more malevolent mean MOA scale scores.

Discussion

The results of this study support our hypothesis that the anticipation of imminent surgery generates specific disruptive fantasied representations, suggesting a brief shift in a child's inner representational world.

Themes of relatively less autonomy and paradigms of loss of control and expectation of malevolence were significantly more prevalent in the children preparing

160 Child Populations Under Extreme Duress

to undergo surgery than in the control group. These findings provided quantitative support to case studies showing that even brief hospitalization for a minor surgical procedure has a disruptive effect on a child.

The fact that the groups did not differ from one another at Time 1 indicates that they were roughly equivalent to each other psychologically prior to the upcoming surgical procedure. The fact that the groups were not significantly different at Time 3, although the surgical group had a poorer MOA scale score, suggests that the disruptions in the children's object-representational world were short-lived. Again, not knowing how well the children were prepared for the surgery limits our ability to know whether adequate preparations before or discussion just after the surgery minimized the duration of that disruption. We strongly suspect that the surgical group's relatively rapid recovery was because the surgery was elective and the degree of physical pain was minimal. Such recovery is consistent with Davenport and Werry's (1970) finding that hospitalization per se is not traumatic if the physical discomfort is relatively mild.

A caveat to this study is that the surgical group may be an atypical sample. Logic suggests that the concern about the psychological effects of surgery that motivated the parents of these children to electively participate in the study might similarly render them more sensitive to their child's need for adequate preoperative preparation and for continued postoperative emotional support. If that is true, the difference between the two groups at Time 2 is a telling example of the disruption evoked by the hospitalization/surgical procedure.

The object-representational disruptions reported at Time 2 for the surgical group highlight the need for a pre- and postoperative psychological intervention strategy based on the assessment of a child's cognitive coping style that may prove useful in limiting psychological scarring from a hospitalization/surgical procedure. Child patients with a propensity for denial may benefit, despite their preference for avoidance, from exploring both concrete realities and their more idiosyncratic fantasies regarding the procedure. Children who are more likely to bring an increased awareness to the procedures should not be discouraged from this process, because it may enable them to "metabolize" the experience more fully after surgery.

This study also demonstrates the relative sensitivity of the MOA scale to even brief, short-lived disruptions in object-representations, and thus suggests the scale's potential usefulness in studies that compare different techniques for preparing children for surgical procedures. More generally, the study shows that the scale need not be limited, as it historically has been, by its capacity to provide a summary measure of enduring object-representations. By underscoring the relevance of this scale for future studies of short-term fluctuations in object-representations, this study extends the applicability of the MOA scale, and hence of the Rorschach, in clinical research.

Note

1 Copyright 1989, The Guilford Press. Reproduced with permission.

15

CHILDREN'S MOA RESPONSES UNDER EXTREME POLITICAL OPPRESSION

Primary paper: Munczek, D., & Tuber, S. (1998). Political repression and its psychological effects on Honduran children. *Social Science & Medicine,* 47, 1699–1713.[1]

Of any project I've ever been a part of, the paper I co-authored with Debra Munczek was by far the most original and remarkable. Dr. Munczek's indomitable will and character led her to immerse herself in Honduras at a time of great political upheaval and carve out a study that used, among other measures, the MOA scale as an alarming and powerful index for assessing her subjects' traumatized object representations. In this case, the difference between knowing one's father is dead (even if via assassination) vs. the even more dreadful not knowing if he's dead or "disappeared" chillingly revealed itself in the RIM responses these children presented. The article will be abridged somewhat to focus exclusively on the findings using the RIM and scoring it with the MOA scale.

Most Latin American countries, plagued for decades by military regimes or civilian governments beholden to military and economic elites, have begun to reestablish democratic institutions only in the past decade. Repressive regimes exercised violent state power in a number of ways, including physical intimidation, jailing, murder and disappearance. Tens or hundreds of thousands of dissenters and political opponents were assassinated or disappeared, kidnapped, tortured, incarcerated in clandestine jails and murdered, their bodies dumped at sea or hidden in unmarked graves (Amnesty International, 1994). What are the psychological effects of these methods of political repression on the families, specifically the children, of the disappeared and assassinated? This study, conducted in Honduras in collaboration with the Committee of Family Members of the Detained and Disappeared of Honduras (COFADEH), evaluates and compares two groups of

162 Child Populations Under Extreme Duress

Honduran children whose loss of a parent was the result of political violence: children of forcibly disappeared and children of assassinated parents.

Effects of Political Violence on the Survivors

Political repression has an impact on an entire society, but the impact is greatest for those most directly affected. Those who have been tortured or imprisoned or whose family members have suffered from state violence all too often had to confront a double source of anguish. One is the original pain of the experience or of the loss; the other is the social denial of these events and the social segregation and isolation imposed on affected individuals and families (Farina, 1987).

When natural and technological catastrophes occur, societal supports and rituals permit the grieving for the dead. In contrast, the social denial of the political catastrophes of disappearance, torture and execution may lead to keeping the loss private, with accompanying feelings of stigmatization, shame and confusion. These problems are of social origin and the experiences and losses are both personal and social. Yet when people are confronted with a reality that does not recognize the existence of the individual and family trauma and instead faults the victim, the process of grieving and coping with the consequences of the experience are particularly difficult. Grieving becomes a state, not a process (Neuman et al., 1990).

The loss of a loved one often causes intense feelings of pain, confusion and disbelief. But forced disappearances and human-induced deaths are more stressful for family survivors; horror and terror are common responses to these events (Lyons, 1991).

In Latin America and other politically repressive regions of the world, the anguish of mourning a disappeared or assassinated loved one has often been compounded by the family's fear of continued persecution. Instead of receiving recognition and support, families have often been subject to ostracism and isolation by friends and acquaintances. Family members may lose their jobs or have to flee for safety. Because of the danger, the family may not be able to hold a funeral for the deceased; it may even have to keep the disappearance or death a secret. Silence and lies are the usual official responses to the circumstances surrounding the disappearances and deaths. Afterwards, severe economic and social hardships are the norm for these families. These losses occur in the context of, and/or provoke, multiple other losses and stresses (Weinstein et al., 1987; Kordon et al., 1988).

Becker et al. (1987) note that feelings of rage are a normal aspect of the grieving process, but that these feelings tend to decrease with time. They observe that with politically motivated assassinations, rage is one of the most intense emotions experienced by family survivors due to the sense of impotence and injustice brought on by the circumstances of the loss and the government's lack of accountability for its actions. In these cases, hate can become a permanent, self-destructive state. Krystal (1988) speaks of hate addiction, referring to similar feelings in concentration camp survivors.

Spiegel (1988) notes that a common feature of stress response syndromes is a sense of spatial and temporal fragmentation. The forcible disappearance of a loved one usually entails not knowing precisely what has happened and, if the person was jailed, tortured and killed, when, where, how and why it happened. This fragmented sense about the disappeared reinforces family members' sense of fragmentation and inability to move forward emotionally, cognitively and behaviorally. According to Kordon et al. (1988), these families are forced to function in a psychotic-like ambiguity and face an eternal question with no answer. Quirk (1992) and Quirk and Casco (1994) in 1990–1991 interviewed 140 members from 25 families of the disappeared in Honduras, along with two control groups, one consisting of families who had lost a family member due to accident or illness in the last ten years and the other comprising of families who had not suffered such a loss. They questioned families about their levels of stress and their health status. Stress-related symptoms were almost equal in the two control groups, but were twice as high in the families of the disappeared. Significant differences for the last group were found in many areas, particularly in measures of increased arousal, such as nervousness and tremor (30%), chronic headaches (24%) and insomnia (17%). Children of the disappeared were also more affected than the controls, as evidenced by frequent mood swings (21%), a drop in school performance (20%) and prolonged bed-wetting (16%).

Fear, a sense of stigmatization and social isolation were frequent themes for these families. Sixty-four percent reported receiving threats after the disappearance and 61% feared that their neighbors were police or police-informers. While 19 of 20 disappeared families said relations with neighbors did not change or worsened after the disappearance, 19 of 22 families from the control group with a death reported receiving food, loans and other moral and material support from their community.

Trauma in Children

Children are deeply affected by a variety of traumatic experiences, such as natural and human-induced accidents and disasters, victimization, observation of violence, loss of loved ones, deprivations and separation experiences. Children's initial reactions to traumatic events have been far better studied and are better understood than the long-term consequences. It appears that, as with adults, there is often no simple resolution to children's traumatic experiences. The defense mechanisms employed to ward off intense affects associated with psychic trauma can eventually become integrated into children's developing personalities, leading to the formation of defensive structures which impair psychic functioning (Terr, 1990; Pynoos, Steinberg, & Goenjian, 1996). For both children and adults, the development of

164 Child Populations Under Extreme Duress

post-traumatic stress disorder (PTSD) after severe trauma requires no preexisting psychiatric symptomatology (Benedek, 1985).

Forced disappearances, assassinations and other forms of political repression frequently lead to temporary or permanent separation of children from their parents and other close family members. Therefore, it is not surprising that research on children and political repression reveals a high incidence of depressive symptomatology (e.g., Allodi, 1980; Kinzie et al., 1986; Schirmer, 1986; Dawes, 1990; Macksoud, 1992). Headaches, stomach-aches, enuresis, nightmares and other sleep disturbances are some of the common somatic complaints found in these children, as literature on Latin America, Cambodia, South Africa and elsewhere reports. Developmental regression has been noted in younger children following traumatic political events (Allodi, 1980). Increased irritability and/or aggressive behavior have been found in many studies, although it seems to be mediated by gender, developmental level and cultural norms (Allodi, 1980; Kinzie et al., 1986; Schirmer, 1986; Macksoud, 1992). In a study of El Salvador that has suggestive implications for other contexts, Martín-Baró (1994) observed that the socially traumatizing results of institutionalized violence and psychological warfare particularly affect children, since they must construct their identities and develop their lives within the network of these dehumanizing [social] relations.

Research examining the psychological effects of political disappearance and assassination on surviving family members has been largely descriptive; there are very few systematic studies with non-immigrant, non-refugee, non-clinical populations. The present research intended to address some of these weaknesses and help build a body of literature on this subject.

The Human Rights Situation in Honduras

Honduras, located in Central America, is one of the poorest countries of the western hemisphere. Until recently, it had only nominally democratic governments. In the 1980s, Honduras was of great geopolitical importance to the United States because it is surrounded by Guatemala, El Salvador and Nicaragua, where civil wars were raging and where the Reagan administration was attempting to roll back leftist and progressive forces. The country's strategic position in the heart of the region made it the ideal site for an expanded U.S. military presence. In return for massive amounts of U.S. aid, Honduras permitted both U.S. and Nicaraguan *contra* military operations on its territory.

Although Honduras faced similar, or worse, social and economic conditions to its neighbors, it did not experience the same level of broad-based domestic unrest, insurgency and civil war. Nonetheless, the late 1970s and 80s were marked by a very oppressive, highly militarized environment: popular, student, peasant and labor movements were repressed, scores of people disappeared at the hands of the Honduran armed forces and many others were jailed, tortured and killed.

With the infusion of millions of U.S. counterinsurgency dollars in the 1980s, the military further consolidated power, acted with impunity and institutionalized unprecedented levels of corruption. In 1988, Honduras earned the dubious distinction of being the first government condemned by the Inter-American Human Rights Court for politically motivated forced disappearance. The governments of the 1990s have become increasingly democratic and political parties and popular organizations have resurfaced. However, elite power, bureaucratic inefficiency, corruption, military impunity and desperate poverty are still firmly entrenched.

The Present Study

Initially upon deciding to study children of both the disappeared and assassinated, we had planned to include a control group of children who had experienced another kind of parental loss. Our intent had been to isolate the effects of political repression from the experience of parental loss in order to gain a deeper understanding of the phenomenon of state terror. Difficulty of access, as well as economic, time and travel constraints made it impossible to find subjects who met the requirements for a true control group: children who matched the test subjects on most criteria, but whose parental loss was the result of human violence that was not politically motivated. The research was therefore limited to an exploratory and comparative field study of the two psycho-politically affected groups of children.

A Committed Psychology

Psychological work in oppressive societies is unavoidably also human rights work. Mental health professionals in Chile (Weinstein et al., 1987; Becker et al., 1989; Becker, 1995), Argentina (Movimiento Solidario de Salud Mental, 1987; Kordon et al., 1988), Uruguay (Patrón and Etchegoyhen, 1990) and El Salvador (Martín-Baró, 1994), working since the 1970s with survivors of political repression and their families, have developed a socially and ethically committed psychology or psychology of liberation which views survivors' suffering and traumatizations as the result of sociopolitical occurrences that have been transformed into mind-damaging processes. This does not deny the influence of people's own pre-trauma conflicts and personality structures.

These Latin Americans (as well as others, e.g. Portelli, 1991; Lykes, 1994; Bracken et al., 1995; Summerfield, 1995; Weine et al., 1995) question notions of neutral, value-free science and charge that the narrow application of scientific method can amount to reductionist medicalizing, separating health and illness from their social roots. In a study of Guatemalan refugees in Mexico, Miller (1994) argues that, from a pragmatic standpoint, non-neutrality is necessary. For the individuals and communities with which one works, political neutrality

166 Child Populations Under Extreme Duress

does not exist, one is either explicitly on the side of the oppressed or distrusted and denied access. The political position taken by the researcher, including neutral, shapes the attitudes and responses of those interviewed. To work effectively with survivors of human rights abuses, researchers and clinicians must abandon absolute neutrality and acknowledge and condemn the injustice and brutality of their experience. The challenge is to do this without imposing on those we study and treat our expectations about their opinions, emotions, symptoms or experiences.

A socially and ethically committed mental health framework also stresses symmetrical, egalitarian, horizontal relationships with those we study, assess and treat. Throughout this project, we were open to sharing skills and information, to mutual exploration and reciprocal learning and to empowering those we worked with to change their life conditions.

Methods

Subjects

Although there are 197 reported cases of forcibly disappeared persons in Honduras (Commission on Human Rights, United Nations, 1996), only a small percentage of these people had children living in the country during the time of the interviews in 1992–1993. This was due to several factors: most of the disappeared were quite young at the time of their abduction and only a minority of them had children; a high percentage were foreigners from other Central American countries, such as El Salvador, Nicaragua and Guatemala and their families lived in their native countries; many of the families went into exile abroad after their relatives' disappearance; and contact has been lost with some of the families and their addresses were unknown.

The number of victims of political assassination and the whereabouts of their families are hard to ascertain. Human rights organizations have better records for the families of the disappeared. Most of the families with assassinated members isolated themselves in fear of further persecution or fled the country, making it difficult to find them for the purpose of the study.

In the first recruitment contacts and interviews in 1992, the first author was usually accompanied by a COFADEH staff member who had previously met the families, but soon began making telephone, telegram or in-person contacts directly, introducing herself to the mother, another family member or the adolescent child as a mental health professional who worked with COFADEH. Both the child and the mother or guardian were told that we were interested in: (1) discovering if and how children had been affected by the disappearance or assassination of their parent and by the changes in their life brought on by this event and (2) documenting the multi-faceted psychosocial consequences of their experiences. Those interviewed were told that the results of the study would be made

Children Under Political Oppression **167**

public, but that their names would remain confidential. Interestingly, several of the subjects insisted that they did not want anonymity; they wanted their father's situations and their individual and family's trials and tribulations known, recorded and remembered.

When the research interviews took place, the democratization process in Honduras was already under way. However, selective persecution of human rights, labor, peasant and Indian leaders continued. Years of persecution, fear and hardship made many or most family survivors distrustful and cautious about revealing their experiences of political persecution and loss to someone they did not know well. Yet, all but one of the members of either the disappeared or assassinated group consented to be interviewed. This was very likely because of the committed psychology stance we assumed in our work and because the research was conducted under the auspices of the Committee of Family Members of the Detained-Disappeared in Honduras, a major human rights organization with strong, popular support and many members and adherents among the interviewees.

Whenever possible, the children and mother were asked to come to the COFADEH office in Tegucigalpa, the capital of Honduras. Many people did not have telephones and lived away from the capital; in these cases, visits or telegrams were the initial means of contact. In some instances, we did not even have an address, just a town or neighborhood. In these situations, we canvassed the town or neighborhood, asking neighbors the whereabouts of the family. Several families were never located.

The diagnostic interviews with children and mothers/guardians were conducted in Honduras between July 1992 and May 1993. Twenty-seven children were interviewed: 16 children from 9 disappeared group families and 11 children from 9 assassinated group families. Of the 18 mothers or guardians, 16 (parents of 22 of the children) were interviewed. The remaining 2 were unavailable; 1 was living abroad and the other was uncooperative. 15 male and 12 female children were interviewed. The disappeared group had 10 males and 6 females; the assassinated group had 5 males and 6 females. Twenty-six of the 27 subjects had lost their father; only 1 subject, a girl, had lost her mother to assassination. This reflects the fact that very few women were disappeared or assassinated and most were childless. Table 15.1 lists information on children's ages at the time of the loss, length of time since the loss and ages at the time of interview.

The difference in the length of time since the two types of parental loss reflects changes in the Honduran government's repressive methods: in the early 1980s, forced disappearance was widely utilized, and the lack of physical evidence facilitated official denials of responsibility. But families desperately looking for their loved ones paradoxically maintained the disappeared alive through their publicized search and demands for justice. Eventually, assassination became the preferred method of permanently silencing dissenters.

168 Child Populations Under Extreme Duress

TABLE 15.1 Ages of the research samples and time since event/loss

Age in months	Disappeared n = 16	Assassinated n = 11
At time of event		
Minimum	0*	84
Maximum	135	190
Mean	65	137
95% CI	24–106	100–174
At interview		
Minimum	123	127
Maximum	238	249
Mean	175	186
995% CI	143–207	152–220
Time since event/loss		
Minimum	42	10
Maximum	143	129
Mean	112	49
95% CI	90–134	9–89

Note: *Mother was six months pregnant with the child at the time of her husband's disappearance.

Procedure

All but 3 of the children and 2 of the caretakers were interviewed in their own or a relative's home; the rest were interviewed at COFADEH. The request for privacy was always made and usually honored. Child interviews lasted 1½–4 hours, were tape recorded and transcribed. Most interviews were conducted in one session; several took 2 or 3 sessions to complete. Interviews with mothers took ½–1½ hours. The first author conducted all interviews, in Spanish, with children and 12 of the interviews with mothers/caretakers. COFADEH staff members conducted the rest. On several occasions, there was limited time to conduct interviews of one family. In those cases, the child was interviewed as fully as possible and the time with the mother-guardian was limited.

Measures

The child interview consisted of several different instruments, including semi-structured and open-ended questions about the emotional, developmental, social and familial impact of the loss and repression; an adaptation of the post-traumatic stress reaction checklist (PTSRC), child version in Spanish; an adaptation of the child behavior inventory (CBI), child version in Spanish; and Cards I, II, III and VIII of the Rorschach inkblot method (RIM). The parent interview included a structured and semi-structured questionnaire devised for this study and adapted parent versions in Spanish of the PTRSC and CBI. Only the findings for the RIM will be presented.

Children Under Political Oppression 169

TABLE 15.2 Rorschach MOA scale

Score	Description	Example[a]
1	reciprocal acknowledgment	two people who are eating at a very elegant table, and I imagine that they are conversing about something very important (Card III)[b]
2	benign parallel interaction	two polar bears that are climbing over a mountain (Card VIII)
3	leaning or dependent relationship	two little bears glued together… that have the little beak glued so (Card II)
4	mirroring oneself	a feral pig, standing in the water, looking at its reflection (Card II)
5	coercive, hurtful influence or threat	two slaves with their arms bound behind with their head leaning forward, tired from so much suffering (Card III)
6	violent attack or destruction of one party by another	this looks like a bat… and these are the wings, but like it was injured, that they ripped off these two parts [of the wings] (Card I)
7	catastrophic event, often by larger-than-life forces	under the table there is a nuclear explosion (Card III)[b]

Notes: [a]All the examples were taken from protocols obtained in this study. [b]Of note, the verbalizations used as examples for scores of 1 and 7 were one subject's responses to Card III.

Rorschach MOA Scale

The Rorschach test can help reveal unconscious mental processes not easily accessed in questionnaire or interview formats. Rorschach protocols were scored using the MOA scale (Urist, 1977) (see Table 15.2).

In this study, the Rorschachs of the 27 subjects were independently scored using the MOA scale by 2 raters: the first author and a trained Spanish-speaking psychology doctoral student who had been told that the subjects had been evaluated in Honduras, but was otherwise blind to the study. Interrater reliability for exact agreement was 93%. Differences were decided by a third rater.

Results

Although most of the measures in this study used ordinal data, a normal distribution with little skew led us to analyze the data utilizing t-tests for independent samples, rather than non-parametric tests, because t-tests are more robust measures and provide more information than non-parametric tests. Differences in the means were then checked for significance.

MOA Scale Findings

MOA scale results were obtained for all 27 children. The children of the disappeared, on the whole, presented less adaptive, more malevolent images of relationships than the children of the assassinated on the Rorschach, as indicated by significantly higher scores on the MOA scale (Mdiss = 3.46, CI = 2.37–4.55; Massas = 2.73, CI = 1.93–3.53, P = 0.035).

Discussion

This article recounts some of the psychological, familial, socioeconomic and societal-political conditions faced by Honduran children with forcibly disappeared and assassinated parents. Although the disappeared and assassinated groups differed on a key dimension, they shared the powerful experiences of the violent, human-induced loss of their parent, the frightening, isolating, politically repressive environment surrounding and following their loss and related long-term familial, social and economic disruptions. Children of both groups described a profound sense of loss and yearning for their lost parent and for what their life might have been had their families not experienced political violence and persecution. They struggled with a sense of difference, damage and psychic pain and with strong feelings of unhappiness, anger and distrust. These issues are partially revealed in the symptom and behavior scales, but better understood through the Rorschach and child interview data.

In every measure administered, as well as in the answers to open-ended questions, the youths acknowledged multiple fears, pervasive worries and an ever-present concern about having the remaining parent close by. While all traumatized people feel fearful, helpless and concerned with loss, these issues are particularly pronounced in children, who lack the physical, emotional and cognitive resources to care for themselves. The violent loss of their parent, the ensuing disruptions to their families and the continuing threats to their safety increased their sense of defenselessness, danger and dependence on adults.

The two groups of children differed on two important dimensions: the type of parental loss, disappearance or assassination and the length of time since the loss. We had anticipated that the longer period of time since the loss would provide the disappeared group more opportunities to rebuild their lives and that these children would report fewer loss-related disturbances and symptoms than would the children of the assassinated. Indeed, more of the disappeared group mothers had remarried than had the murdered group mothers. The disappeared fathers were currently mentioned less frequently by their children and families than was the case for the assassinated group children and families. Yet, the disappeared group families reported greater family conflict than the other group and the children of the disappeared group produced more malevolent interactions on the RIM.

Children Under Political Oppression **171**

These results run counter to most research on bereavement in children. Although post-traumatic symptoms are known to persist for long periods of time, we had nonetheless expected a decrease in their intensity, since children's developmental maturation provides them with more opportunities for change than adults. The absence of significant differences between the two groups may be due to some or all of the following reasons: consistent with the psychological literature on the effects of disappearance and with our observations, family members become paralyzed in a limbo state and are unable to move forward with their lives; continuing repressive conditions and related hardships impede the return to more normal, age-appropriate concerns; the small number of subjects made it impossible to establish significance-level differences In addition, these measures were originally developed for children living under war conditions and may therefore fail to pick up the subtleties and subtle group differences of less extreme conditions.

The children with assassinated parents appeared to be, consistent with the recent occurrence of their loss, less able to concentrate and make plans. Nonetheless, there was an unexpectedly high degree of similarity found between the children of the disappeared and assassinated, particularly considering the significantly different lengths of time since the loss of their parent and the difference in age at the time of the loss. Past literature on the psychological effects of disappearance on family members stresses the severity and persistence of psychological disturbance. The present study tends to confirm these earlier findings.

Moreover, the children of the disappeared presented greater unconscious disturbance and as more traumatized in some ways: they evidenced less adaptive, more malevolent unconscious images of relationships on the Rorschach MOA scale than did the children of the assassinated group. If politically induced trauma were a monolithic entity, we would not expect this result. This finding reveals the highly emotionally disturbing nature of having a parent forcibly disappeared and the tremendous difficulties that these children and families have moving forward with their lives.

The children of the assassinated have the firm knowledge of their parent's death; they can mourn and hopefully achieve some resolution of their loss. The children of the disappeared are unable to do this; they are forced to function in a zone of psychotic-like ambiguity and face an eternal question with no answer (Kordon et al., 1988). The MOA scale, applied to the Rorschach projective technique, is a subtle measure that appears far better able to tap into underlying psychological experience than the symptom and behavior/attitude scales do. The disappeared group, in particular, reports experiencing fewer trauma-related symptoms than in the past when their loss was more recent. However, both the Rorschach MOA scale results and the child interview reveal quite impaired internal worlds, with high levels of emotional conflict and distress.

Spiegel's (1988) observation that a common feature of stress response syndromes is a sense of spatial and temporal fragmentation is compatible with our subjects' repeated lament that they need to know precisely the when, where, how

172 Child Populations Under Extreme Duress

and why of what has happened to their disappeared father. If he was indeed killed, they want to know his burial site so they can visit his grave. The children's fragmented sense about their disappeared parent reinforces their own sense of fragmentation and their inability to move forward emotionally. Our results are also consistent with the Quirk and Casco (1994) assertion that the increased stress and distress of the families of the disappeared results from the atmosphere of fear and isolation that they face.

Apart from these specific results, our findings are generally congruent with other research on political repression and trauma. The Honduran children and their families have been deeply, irrevocably affected by the loss of their family member, the circumstances surrounding that loss, the hostility, persecution, economic hardship and social isolation they experienced subsequent to the event and the lack of social, political or legal response to and reparations for the injustices they have suffered.

Note

1 Copyright 1999, Pergamon. Reproduced with permission.

SECTION FIVE

Using Projective Methods in N of 1 Case Studies

The next section will focus on a number of case studies that used either intensive studies of entire RIM and/or TAT protocols (the Cases of "Lisa" and "Jim") or summarized/partial records (the six vignettes described in Chapter 19). Such idiographic studies have long been the mainstay of psychodynamically informed uses of projective methods, often to the great chagrin of researchers who focus on nomothetic analyses with larger samples. It is almost a cliché to note that both approaches are not only viable means of empirical study, but that each type of work enhances the other. The often provocative, if idiosyncratic, nature of findings from idiographic research naturally warrant follow-up with larger samples to track down these "leads" to possible refinements to theory and practice. The suggestive correlations among variables in larger studies often warrant closer examination "on the ground" to best capture the actual experience (Escalona, 1968) or phenomenology of the correlations reported.

In the cases of Lisa and Jim reported next, we have an added advantage rarely given to idiographic works. The Children's Apperception Test (CAT) protocol of Lisa and the RIM protocol of Jim, both taken when they were children, were linked to their treatment as adults. Such longitudinal data are a treasured commodity in the field and give the idiographic assessments of their protocols an added vitality.

In Chapter 18, we provide two briefer case studies of children with ADHD.

16

USING THE CHILDREN'S APPERCEPTION TASK AS AN IDIOGRAPHIC INDICATOR OF TREATMENT THEMES OVER TIME

Primary paper. Tuber, S. (2004). Projective testing as a heuristic "snapshot" of themes in child and adult psychoanalysis: The Case of Lisa. *Journal of Infant, Child and Adolescent Psychotherapy*, 3, 486–508.[1]

There is a rich tradition of comparison between projective tests and psychoanalytic case material. Rapaport and his colleagues (Holt, 1968), in their seminal work in the 1930s and 1940s, linked psychological test data with psychodynamic conceptualizations in a way that gave more credibility to applied psychodynamic theory. Looking back, these developments served as important rationale for the use of projective testing by psychologists in psychiatric and Veterans Administration hospitals in the 1950s. At that time, psychodynamically informed projective test analysis became intimately intertwined with the treatment of severe psychopathology in private psychiatric hospitals (e.g., Menninger Clinic, Austen Riggs Center, Chestnut Lodge). Psychological testing of each patient shortly after admission at these institutions was common, if not required. Patients were tested at various times during their inpatient stay and frequently tested as part of their discharge process. Later, as some of these institutions began to embark on follow-up studies of former patients, they often referred back to projective test data as a way to reflect on the original treatment predictions (Blatt and Ford, 1994).

More recently, there has been a growing preponderance of nomothetic assessments of inpatient progress and outcome that utilize projective testing with increasing sophistication. Blatt and Ford (1994), for example, who compared Rorschach and Thematic Apperception Test (TAT) protocols of patients at the Austen Riggs Center at admission and again 15 months after treatment, began with a variety of behavioral and clinical measures of patient progress. These test data were meaningfully linked with changes in the quality of interpersonal relationships and

176 Projective Methods in N of 1 Case Studies

the lessening of clinical symptomatology. Similar nomothetic comparisons were derived from an analysis of the data from the Menninger Psychotherapy Research Project. In that study, the Krohn and Mayman (1974) Object Representation Scale proved effective in predicting follow-up two years after discharge for 40 patients selected from the Menninger study (Frieswyk and Colson, 1980). Menninger testing protocols were also used in a later study that reclassified patients as having anaclitic or introjective personality configurations (Blatt, 1992). In comparing the two types, Blatt reported that introjective patients experienced less symptomatology and more adaptive functioning in a psychoanalytically oriented treatment, whereas anaclitic patients were more successful in supportive psychotherapy.

Heinicke (1990) compared children in three-times-per-week psychoanalytic treatment with those in once-weekly treatment. Rorschach data were collected pretreatment and posttreatment for both groups. Improved Rorschach performance was found more commonly in the intensively treated child group. Tuber (1983) assessed the quality of children's Rorschach Mutuality of Autonomy (MOA) object representation scores and effectively used them as a predictor of their later re-hospitalization as adults. He reported that children whose Rorschach tests showed an absence of benign object representations at admission to a child residential facility were more likely to be re-hospitalized than a group of matched cohorts treated at the same facility (please refer to Chapter 11 for a fuller description of this study).

Idiographic or case study use of projective test data in child and adult psychoanalytically informed treatment has had an equally long, and perhaps more extensive tradition than the nomothetic comparisons. For example, Diamond and colleagues (1990) applied the Object Representation Inventory (ORI), a measure used to operationalize concepts from separation-individuation theory, to the Rorschach at the beginning and end of four one-and-a-half to two-and-a-half-year treatments of borderline adolescents. These authors were able to trace shifts in descriptions of self and other to Rorschach shifts in organization and representation. Tuber (2000) studied the Rorschach protocol of Jim, an eight-year-old seen in both child analysis and later in adult treatment with the same therapist. This post hoc analysis revealed profound impairments in the quality of Jim's object representations that presaged his relatively poor outcome as an adult (see Chapter 17).

It is no coincidence that studies of this kind converged conceptually with the emergence of object relations theory as a core paradigm in understanding personality development from a psychoanalytically informed perspective (Greenberg and Mitchell, 1983). The focus of this theory on the conceptions of self and other in interaction and the affects generated by the internalizations of these interactions have been concomitant with the development of a similar framework in projective testing. The cognitive imagoes of these affect-laden interactions form mental object representations or templates of inner experience. These representations, in turn, become manifest in future interactions within the self as well as with others. In treatment, they form the basis of both "real" and transferential configurations.

In projective testing, these representations imbue the visual stimuli of inkblots and/or ambiguous pictures with personally meaningful content and process. The object representational measures (e.g., ORI, MOA) just described are among the most commonly employed instruments of this paradigm in the field of projective testing (Stricker and Healey, 1990).

The ability of projective test data to take a heuristically helpful "snapshot" of personality organization at a given point in time and to integrate this snapshot into an overall assessment of personality functioning is intrinsic to the projective hypothesis from which projective testing was first developed. Projective test material is viewed here first and foremost as providing another, somewhat standardized realm of data from which to test a given view of personality theory. The studies cited earlier regarding projective testing and psychoanalysis suggest that it is viable to leap from testing as a snapshot to testing as a potential enduring marker of personality over time. If projective test performance can usefully identify themes as well as limitations and problems in treatment, it may provide cross-validation of the utility of certain key psychodynamically informed explanations of personality organization and growth. The study of the following projective test protocol, albeit a post hoc predictor of a treatment experience, offers another view of the dynamic relation between testing and treatment data.

The Case of Lisa

At age eight, Lisa entered a five-session-per-week analytic treatment with a female analyst that lasted two years. After a nine-year break, she resumed analysis with a different analyst, also a woman, from the same clinic (Hampstead). In this sense, the continuity of her treatment had a direct institutional, but not personal, link. Lisa's second treatment as a young adult was more extensive, lasting a total of six years. Before Lisa began her first treatment, she was given the CAT as part of the routine initial consultation process. By reviewing her verbatim responses on a card-by-card basis, the reader is afforded a catalog of some of the conscious and unconscious conflicts at work simultaneously. As I try to demonstrate, certain key themes emerge from her words that would later prove crucial during both analyses. This examination offers us the chance to revisit material that may have been more valuable than might have been guessed at the time. I intersperse Lisa's actual response to each card with an analysis of her response.

Let me add a word about my method of CAT analysis. In most respects, it is comparable to the process of understanding case material from a therapy session. Inasmuch as each CAT card presents its own interpersonal dilemma to be solved, the salient questions asked of each response are to what extent can Lisa acknowledge each dilemma and create a response that "solves" the interpersonal "problem" depicted. The degree to which her "solution" invokes a developmentally appropriate richness and aliveness is the means by which Lisa's potential capacity for adaptive handling of actual interpersonal and intrapsychic dilemmas is assessed.

178 Projective Methods in N of 1 Case Studies

Lisa's CAT Card Responses and Analyses

Card 1: Three Chickens Around Meal Table and Shadowy Figure of Hen or Rooster in Background

> Once upon a time … once upon a time there were three chickens and they had … they had some porridge one morning. One day they went out and when they came back they found that somebody had eaten all their porridge so they went to the store and they bought more and they bought two packets of it and their pot was full and they eat it all up.

Lisa begins with a well-defended version of the "Goldilocks" story. Interestingly, however, when the chickens return to find their oral supplies gone in her version, they competently double their supplies and fill their pots. Lisa then makes a point of saying that they eat it all. Thus, not only do the chickens double their compensation for this oral loss, they also need to eat it all up. The gorging behavior of the chickens has an overly vigilant and urgent quality, as if they couldn't leave some porridge for another time because their supplies might be taken again. Here we can begin to see how the experience of hunger may trigger some immediate, impulsive attempt to ward off these hungry feelings. Importantly, the well-defended "niceness" in the story denies the presence of the often menacing, shadowy chicken in the background. Lisa's defensiveness, though somewhat adaptive, comes at the cost of a heavy set of blinders. To what degree this defensiveness is typically age appropriate or indicative of a more pervasive guardedness remains to be seen.

Card 2: Three Bears in Tug-of-War

> There were … after the porridge they went up the mountain and they heard some bears fighting there … and they said, "Stop it, bears, stop it." And they said, "But this is *my* rope." And they got so mad that the little bear can hear it all the way from the cottage and he ran up to pull on his daddy … on his mummy's side. And then they started pulling and pulling and pulling but grandfather was getting more of the rope. And they said, "I bought this rope at the grocery store … but I bought it at the grocery store," and they all went back home … and they left the rope on the ground.

Here Lisa offers a thoroughly confused story. It appears that the blatantly aggressive and unresolved quality of the scene on this card disrupts her temporal continuity. Pronouns and references are elliptical and obscure to the extent that the characters' identities become fluid and undifferentiated. She begins the story with

The CAT as Indicator of Treatment Themes   **179**

an attempt to stop the bears from fighting. The noise is so great that the little bear hears it from far away and wants to stop the fight. This has a strongly personalized flavor, much like a self-reference. Her ambivalence as to what side of the fight she should take is notable. In the end, the animals try to justify to whom the rope belongs but leave the rope behind and, in doing so, render the fight and the prize meaningless. Here we see a quick and pronounced denial of desire, where the passionate tugging ends in abrupt dismissal. No one becomes satisfied, and arguments appear futile. One may wonder if arguments simply serve as a means to express distance or differentiation, or are more indicative of the difficulty of getting one's needs met. Furthermore, what does it mean to be desired and treasured, and how does it feel to be abandoned? Overall, there is an overwhelmed quality to the affect brought on by these issues, and we are left with a fragmented lack of resolve that seems more concerning than the problem-solving, albeit restrictive, aspects of card 1.

Card 3: Lion on Throne and Small Mouse in Hole at Back

> Then the bears and the three chicks went to the castle where the lion lives and they asked the lion who was the one to get the rope, and the lion thought and thought and thought and he couldn't really figure it out. So he said, "Who bought it?" And then the grandfather said, "I did," and the little boy's father said, "I did," and then the king said, "Well, if you're going to argue about it, I'm going to have to break it in half and give it to both of you." So the king took the bears and chicks and the baby bear where the rope was and he brought a knife with him when he went and he broke it in half and he said, "Here's your half." And then the grandfather said, "This is smaller than his." So he said, "If you start quarreling, I'll chop both of your heads off."

The lack of satisfaction in the previous story becomes something Lisa seems determined to resolve. Here she tells the story of "King Solomon" and gives card 2 some coherence. In this story, both sides want the supplies, but clearly one side is lying; they both couldn't have bought the rope. Only here, when Lion "Solomon" cuts the rope, the grandfather still feels deprived, whereupon the king threatens to kill both the father and the grandfather. Again, as we have seen in card 2, there is the strong sense that disputes cannot be resolved, that there is never enough to go around, and that loss and dissatisfaction are inevitable. Also notable is the quickness with which the arbiter loses patience and becomes vindictive. Again, aggression is undirected, dangerous, and overwhelming. We also can see more overt identification with the rope that is being fought over. In the end, the rope is just not long enough and therefore simply unable to satisfy those that fight over it.

180 Projective Methods in N of 1 Case Studies

Card 4: Mother Kangaroo with Baby in Pouch and Small Kangaroo Following on Bicycle

The chicks' friend, Mrs. Kangaroo, and baby kangaroo and Timmy Kangaroo were paying a visit. They were looking and looking for the chicks in their house, but they couldn't find it so they said … the baby said, "Where is their cottage?" And the mother said, "They don't live in a cottage. They live in a tree," and the baby kangaroo said, "But I've never been in a tree, and a tree isn't a house anyway." And then Timmy Kangaroo said, "Just be quiet. We just want to get there because it's going to start storming in a minute."

A new theme, of separation anxiety and being lost, is begun on this card. Here the baby kangaroo feels that even if they find the house, it won't be satisfactory. The older sibling hushes the baby and adds the dimension of an oncoming storm to the story, which gives a more ominous tone to the consequences of not finding the house soon. The combination of being hushed and dismissed when expressing anxiety about the impending storm is especially troublesome. Not only is there a profound lack of empathy toward the anxious baby, but the gravity of the external world overtaxes the "adults," so that no one is cared for.

Card 5: Two Small Bears on Cot in Foreground, Large Double-Bed in Background, and Ambiguity Whether Anyone Is in Large Double-Bed

Then they finally got to the … they finally got to the tree and they knocked on the door but nobody was in. So they had to walk and walk and walk until they came to the cottage and they went into a little room in the cottage and they found two bears sleeping in a bed and they said, "This is probably a bear's house. We had better get out of here quick." And then the bears woke up and said, "Where are you going? And then they said "Well, well, we … we thought this was the chickies' house." And then the bears said, "We know where the chickies' house is." So they showed them to the chickies' house and they said, "We've already been there, but they're not in." So the two bears knocked on the door in the proper way, and they said, "You must talk … knock in the correct way." And they said, "Oh, thank you." So then they got in the chickies' house.

What is most striking in this story is the degree to which the typically salient theme this card calls for, that of nighttime separation and loss, is denied probably as a reaction to card 4. Interestingly, the bears turn out to be friendly and teach the kangaroos the proper way to reach their destination as opposed to the aggressive bears of card 2. At the same time, there is tension from being unsure who one can trust and who one should fear. In an effort to ensure safety, there emerges a

The CAT as Indicator of Treatment Themes   **181**

Pollyannaish quality, where "acting" with good manners provides access to things that one's real self may not.

Card 6: Small Bear Lying by Himself in Foreground and Shadowy Figures of Two Large Bears in Cave

> The mother bear and the two cub bears ... the mother bear and her kids were waiting in the cave for the baby bear to come back. The baby bear finally came back, and the mother started shouting at him, "Where have you been? Where have you been?" And they said, "Oh, we showed ... we showed Mrs. Kangaroo where the chickies' house was." And then the mother spanked them very hard and said, "What did you do that for? You shouldn't go away from the cave any more." Well, after that they never quarreled any more.

Here she distorts the scene on the card and again denies the themes of loneliness, smallness, and danger implicit in the illustration. The two large bears are made into a mother, and one lone cub is converted into two cubs. In this card, the baby's competent helpfulness on the preceding card is squashed by the anxious mother, whose anxiety over loss gets expressed as rage. Again, punishment is harsh, unexplained, and absolute in the face of panic. There is an imitative quality to the dialogue, as if we are hearing tidbits of what may occur between the parents. One might wonder whether dad doesn't "get in trouble" for abandoning "the cave," and so forth. Also, there are hints at fusion between self and mother, as suggested by the confusion over how many bears are actually punished, when the number of parent bears gets exchanged with the number of baby bears. Again, note the punitive consequences for having strivings toward separation-individuation.

Card 7: Large Fierce Tiger Chasing Monkey

> Once upon a time there was a tiger who was a very very tough tiger. Anybody who saw him used to run away and never come back. One day two monkeys were making fun of ... one monkey was right in front of the cave making fun of him and the lion wasn't very happy and he tried to eat up the monkey but the monkey got up the tree and then after that he went back to his cave and it was the next morning.

Another important thematic shift occurs on this card. The first three cards focus on loss, battle, and failed reparation over oral supplies. The next three cards dwell on separation fears and their dismissal and punishment. Now the underlying rage and aggression regarding unmet needs and the shifting identifications between aggressor and victim become primary. Here she can acknowledge the fierceness

182 Projective Methods in N of 1 Case Studies

and intentions of the tiger, but strikingly has the monkey act provocatively while knowing full well of the tiger's fierceness. The themes of danger, desire, and excitement become merged as part of a seduction. Her identification lands firmly with the monkey, who is able to escape without harm. Importantly, the now transformed "lion" (she's perseverating both with the lion from card 3 and with two monkeys being like the two bears of card 6) makes no attempt to get revenge at this time, a wish that cannot be maintained by the end of the protocol. Again, the confusion over what and who are safe continues to resonate: Will the lion attack? Is the tree really protective? Also, we begin to see a heroic tone, where a fearless provocateur seems fleetingly magical and all powerful. Here bravery masks neediness, and grandiosity serves as attempted compensation for fear and self-doubt.

Card 8: Three Large Monkeys and One Small Monkey at Tea Party

Then the monkey went straight back home and told his mother. Mother said to him, "You should never ever go near that cave or else he will eat you up in two seconds." And while they were talking the grandma and grandpa heard them and they were chattering because they thought that their niece was going to get killed.

The wished-for safety of card 7's resolution is extended to include a concerned, but not punitive, mother and set of grandparents. The overly dramatic quality of the adults has an exciting tone to it, suggestive of a pattern whereby the child's counterphobic behavior may have had important secondary gains by granting the child both attention and the experience of engendering the concern of others. Her tremendous wish to be taken care of despite her provocative behavior is much in evidence.

Card 9: Rabbit Sitting Up in Bed and Looking Through Open Door

Then the tiger went to his friend … then the monkey I mean … went to his friend's house, rabbit, and told rabbit all about it and then he left the room. Rabbit was very scared so rabbit decided to get up. He got up and went to the tiger's cave and there was the tiger sleeping and the tiger had a big jewel in his house and bunny wanted to take it so bunny touched it and the lion woke up and went, "Grrr, grrr." And then the rabbit was really getting … rushed back into his room but he didn't shut the door and he was sitting up in bed watching for the tiger.

This card condenses much, if not all, of what has gone on in the previous two cards: It continues the narrative to make one whole story; it confuses

The CAT as Indicator of Treatment Themes **183**

aggressive and passive animals (the monkey is called a tiger), suggesting her own fleeting identifications with both the sadistic and masochistic aspects of her aggression and it acknowledges the rabbit's fear but demonstrates that the counterphobic impulse is to go directly into the lion's den in any case. This card adds one final theme; the tiger has a big jewel, which has both a sexual and an asexual longed-for specialness attached to it. Her cutting off in mid-sentence about "the rabbit getting…" is especially mysterious and evocative in this regard; is the act scary, exciting, or both? What is she suppressing? She ends the story clearly acknowledging the posture of the rabbit in the scene, watching vigilantly, and perhaps expectantly, for the tiger. This is the first and only time in the record that she acknowledges negative affect, and even here the affect is somewhat mixed with the excitement aroused. There is something haunting in the image of an isolated rabbit that fears the return of a vengeful tiger, the parental imago. This appears to echo the ominous quality in card 4 of the lost kangaroos with a storm rapidly approaching. It is important to recognize that in the face of impending danger, the door is left open. A complex blend of impulsivity, masochism, longing, and manipulation are clearly in evidence.

Card 10: Large Dog Spanking Small Dog, Across His Knee, With Lavatory at One Side and Bath in Background

> And after that the rabbit got the monkey and he said, "Why don't we go and tell the puppy dogs," and then they said, "Okay," and then he rang the doorbell of the puppies' house and then the puppy started scraping the door and went "woof woof" and then mother said to her dog, "Don't worry, somebody's at the door." So the mother went to the door and found the monkey and the rabbit and told them all about it and then they all went there and the baby puppy stayed home and the mother puppy stayed at home and while they were there they touched the diamond … before they could get out of the cave the lion ate them up.

Here she goes into a rather long introductory period of regulating her story as she completely denies the explicitly aggressive (abusive) nature of the card. As in cards 2 and 5, pronoun references are confused, and the spatial sequence is distorted as well; it becomes unclear who told whom about the tiger and who went to the tiger's cave to touch the diamond. Unlike in cards 8 and 9, the lion finally swallows up its provocative prey. Suddenly, aggression becomes consuming as rigid defenses fail. Impulses have broken through, as if the storm that had been brewing, this pressured, impending external malevolence is met by irresistible, uncontrollable internal urges, and the collision proves utterly devastating.

Summary of Lisa's CAT and Implications for Treatment

Lisa's protocol can be summarized by the following seven points:

1. Prominent oral hunger and neediness combine with fantasies of replenishment that seem weak and Pollyannaish.
2. Scenes with aggressive content disrupt spatial, temporal, personal, and linguistic boundaries within her narratives and cause personalization of the content in the stories. A portrait of intense anger, quarreling, and chaos in her home is given, with the child having to choose sides and with the resolution of mutual deprivation resulting only in further unhappiness, hopelessness, and threats of violence.
3. Separation anxiety that no one soothes instead becomes suffused with an ominous quality (card 4) or is denied and turned into a wished-for helpfulness from others that seems forced and even unreal. More salient is the theme of an overanxious, prohibitive mother who becomes enraged and abusive when frightened.
4. Counterbalancing the anxious, frightened, unsoothed child is the counterphobic, provocative, eroticized blending of longing for "father" and fearing his orally engulfing destructiveness. The fine line between fearful and fearless is met with a mixture of risky and self-protective behaviors – clearly a deeply ambivalent pose, in which heroic bravado and a flimsy conviction of uniqueness mask deep feelings of inadequacy and neediness.

In addition, there are three points to be made specifically regarding the process of her narratives, though these processes overlap with the content areas described above:

5. She ignores or denies either the conventional affect tone or the typical theme evoked by many of the cards in favor of her own projections.
6. In a number of her stories, the manner in which conflictual material disrupts her secondary-process thinking leads to an illogical use of time, space, and sequence.
7. There is a definite need for all the cards to be linked as a cohesive story, even if the plot must be stretched. Here one can see her discomfort with gaps; empty spaces must be avoided. These gaps are filled with fanciful, exciting plot twists, where the outside world may be used dramatically to enliven a feared and helpless, perhaps deadened, internal world.

These themes suggest that her treatment will be highly charged. Her oral neediness is intense and will doubtless be expressed throughout the treatment. The expectation of failed soothing, the conflict between the expression of the wish and its expected dismissal will create an intense push pull in the treatment. This tension will create difficulty for Lisa's therapist vis-à-vis the transference. Lisa is afraid of yet drawn to aggression, and this conflict will also suffuse the treatment. The intense yet pointless and unresolved quarreling evident in the CAT suggests that Lisa will need to fill the sessions with battles. The counterphobic content and her often disrupted narratives suggest a degree of impulsivity, a loosening of reality testing, and a loss of distance to the point where these battles will likely threaten the existence of a treatment framework. There is also the danger that the therapist may be too kind and thus must be rejected. The sexualized quality of her last two cards will also enter the treatment. It will likely take the form of sexually provocative play within the sessions or a sadomasochistic stance that gives Lisa some means of staying connected to the therapist while simultaneously avoiding too close an attachment.

On the positive side, the occasional helpfulness of others (the bears) and the clear presentation of an overanxious mother who can show concern, provides some means for the therapist to be empathic that may be acceptable to Lisa. It is also worth noting the enjoyment Lisa seems to get from telling a story and having the tester's sustained attention. Her fairytale-like wording reveals the imaginative entertainer in her, and this precocious rendering provides a glimpse of an active inner world as well as a rather ample vocabulary. This verbal fluency and relative access to inner processes bode well for psychodynamic treatment. Last, although her pronoun confusion and fluidity of characters may be due in part to identity confusion, it may also be indicative of a certain capacity for empathy, in which she can identify with a large number of characters. This ability to step outside of herself could be helpful in developing a relationship with her therapist.

I now turn to a brief review of Lisa's two treatments vis-à-vis the themes evoked by the CAT protocol.

Lisa's Treatment at Time 1

Lisa's symptomatology and early history are noteworthy in light of the themes expressed by her CAT. Her presenting symptoms consist of provocative demandingness, enuresis, fears at bedtime, and aggressive verbal and physical behavior at school. Although both anxiety and aggressive symptoms exist at home, her school behavior suggests a reliance on aggression and a notable absence of overtly depressive symptomatology. Why does she shift from anxiety to aggression, a pattern more in keeping with a same-age boy's reaction, and not become withdrawn or lethargic? In the same vein, her analyst sees her father as threatening, yet soft in manner. The implications of this contrast seem central to understanding Lisa, especially because he is described as "doing it all" for Lisa during her earliest months.

Lisa's mother is initially described as girlish, frightened, and non-maternal. Especially striking is mother's deep anxiety about her early days of mothering. She does not have a sense of having been "good enough." Her anger at her induced delivery and her expectation of a lack of caring by others are all strongly reminiscent of Lisa's stories in which anxiety is met with dismissal or rage. Mother appears

186 Projective Methods in N of 1 Case Studies

to express her postpartum depression via anxiety, which is complementary to Lisa's inability to acknowledge themes of aloneness on the CAT. It appears likely that Lisa provokes those around her to avoid aloneness and emptiness.

Lisa's first year of life is described in contradictory terms. She is described as placid, yet always running; climbing too high, yet always knowing when to stop; in control of herself, yet spoiled; and so forth. Notably, her mother denies a seizure disorder Lisa had in early childhood as a potential worry.

Mother describes herself as "forgetting" what Lisa's toddler period was like. From a diagnostic point of view, one could probably equate periods of mother's forgetfulness of Lisa's behavior as blind spots in her recollection of dysphoric ties between them and, consequently, as "holes" in Lisa's experience of coherency across different affective states. In this context, Winnicott might argue that Lisa's placidness may be the beginnings of a false self-compliance and suggest that her running everywhere as a toddler indicates a lack of capacity to be alone. Importantly, however, Lisa's described ability to "always play by herself" may indicate a diagnostic strength for her or it may point to a tendency to withdraw. Either way, it is significant that, though she can be alone, she cannot necessarily maintain separateness in the presence of another, as in the Winnicottian (1965b) idea of the true capacity to be alone.

Numerous other examples in the history speak to a pattern of unintegrated and incoherent affective experiences and a failure to be sufficiently "held" by her parents while attempting to cope with them. (The reader is asked to read both Tobier, 2000, and Parsons, 2000, as companion pieces to this article for a complete depiction of Lisa's history and treatment.) On one hand, Lisa becomes irritable when mother goes to work. On the other hand, the description of Lisa screaming in the back of their car and being tossed candies for comfort by her father when being driven to and from her child-care arrangement is chilling. Similarly, Lisa's response to losing a peer while in nursery school by taking long naps of up to four hours in length speaks to her depression and her inability to openly express her loss. These naps will later take the form of other, more troubling escapes to mind numbing mental states (e.g., her tendency toward using alcohol and marijuana, as well as "losing herself" in romantic relationships). Furthermore, it is fascinating that she experiences depression at the loss of a peer but turns cranky and irritable at the loss of her parents. One might surmise that at this stage of development, the threat of experiencing this fundamental a loss is simply too overwhelming, and she musters some semblance of control by feeling her anger, rather than her need. This reaction may be exacerbated by the fact that it may have been difficult for her to feel a true loss if her tie to her parents had been unstable and disorganized from birth. It begs the question of whether she could really mourn the loss of something she never had. She appears to have already learned that depression is simply not permissible within her family, especially to her mother, but that provocativeness, especially sadomasochistic provocativeness, keeps attachment alive, even if it is largely unsatisfying and ultimately abusive.

The sadomasochistic quality of Lisa's interactive style deserves special mention. Winnicott (1965a), in describing the role of "climax in ego-relatedness," noted that a "deprived child with antisocial tendency, or any child with marked manic-defense restlessness, is unable to enjoy play because the body must become physically involved. A physical climax is needed, and most parents know the moment when nothing brings an exciting game to an end except a smack – which provides a false climax, but a useful one" (p. 35). The application of this description to Lisa's restlessness and deprivation seems apt, and the "smack" fits with the physical beating father applies to Lisa when she is "unsettled" at bedtime. Her inability to get to sleep also speaks to her difficulties in being alone and in self-soothing. The fact that she is abused by the parent described as most available sheds light on her tendency to resort to eroticized physical play as a means to establish connection with him. Perhaps this explains her sadomasochistic interpersonal style, one that serves as a repetition of parent–child interaction as well as regression to her original method of recreating attachment during moments of fear and aggression in her toddler years.

During Lisa's first analysis, these themes enter the transference in a full blown manner. The very fundamental equation for Lisa of sad = bad speaks directly to her need to turn passive into active. Her analyst initially describes her as full of coy, seductive, disdainful facial expressions and as behaving very physically in the room. Her needy demandingness and her certainty that the therapist can't or won't satisfy these needs is striking. She transforms the treatment into something dangerous and seductive, reifying her experience of her mother as the unreliable supplier, and her father as the eroticized, dangerous love object, as she plays out maternal and paternal aspects of the transference. For example, early in the treatment, Lisa's analyst interprets Lisa's nonchalant veneer when confronted with dysphoric experiences. Lisa responds by asking her to join her in watching for trains out the window, thus establishing a degree of parallel play as a first step in eventual trust. Here we see Lisa's first attempts to negotiate the tricky space between together and separate, as she tests herself and others to withstand her desire and fear of intimacy.

Similarly, an interpretation of her sadomasochistic experience with a treasured doll results in Lisa's reenacting early unempathic feeding experiences with her mother along with sexual desire and aggressive impulses toward her father. This working through of early preoedipal difficulties leads to oedipal wishes to be a sexualized partner to her father. Thus, acknowledging her dissatisfaction and frustration with her mother allows for a desire to replace mother. In fact, Lisa's first treatment seems to be dominated by a series of repeated provocative enactments of early oral neediness and lack of trust, coupled with counterphobic denials of her sense of inadequacy. When these denials are interpreted, we see a shift to oedipal-level depictions of her longed for, yet frightening, father. This strongly parallels themes developed within her CAT narratives, which also begin with issues of orality and separation anxiety and end with eroticized conflicts with a vengeful "lion."

I am also struck by the depiction much later in this first treatment of her uncontrollable sexual impulses, which remind me of the "bunny's" need to touch the lion's "jewel" on cards 9 and 10 of the CAT. The repeated juxtaposition of these sexual feelings with fears of loss also harken to card 9 and the bunny's lonely wait for the lion to reappear after her sexualized touching of his "diamond." Similarly, her physicality with her analyst speaks to the restlessness and need for climax described by Winnicott in children who have survived repeated "holes" in their early interactions with mothering figures. The notion of holes in Lisa's inner coherence is vividly depicted in her recurring dream of an amoeba closing in on her, which seems to recreate a preverbal experience of being engulfed. This dream may also speak to the boundary confusion that will later lead to her confusion over issues of identity. Notably, after describing this dream she comments on not knowing her gender, reinforcing the suggestion of core gaps in her identity.

The degree to which Lisa progresses in her treatment along the dimension of increasing trust and greater tolerance for dysphoric and eroticized affect is shown in several ways: a limited but real capacity to discuss feelings of depression and helplessness, an emerging treatment alliance regarding her fear of a nervous breakdown, and a willingness to experience feelings around termination. Not only can she speak of her sadness over the impending loss of her therapist and her worry about being easily forgotten, she can create an imaginary companion to help work through the loss. Given the modal age of two to three for the typical creation of imaginary companions (Meyer and Tuber, 1989) and their most common usage as a type of transitional phenomenon to cope with feelings of loss and aggression, one can argue that her first treatment helped bring her to a more adequate working through of early oral issues and to the important though fragile plateau of the beginnings of libidinal object constancy. Her wish for a tunnel to connect to her therapist after termination speaks to the still somewhat magical and thus far from fully coalesced sense of self that remains after her first treatment ends. The poignant scene in which she leaves her last session with a wagon full of transitional objects posits her acknowledgment of her own need to stay connected and her acceptance of these objects in their role of helping her to tolerate sadness and loss. The depth of pathology evident in her history and the parallels in the issues expressed in her CAT narratives suggest that the change in this first treatment is a substantial developmental move forward, with still much more work to be done in her subsequent treatment.

Lisa's Treatment at Time 2

At age 19, Lisa returns to five-times-per-week analysis after both a breakdown in college along severe obsessional lines, and the breakup of a destructive, abusive relationship with a boyfriend that appears to recreate the worst aspects of her tie to her father. Her second analyst (M. Parsons) sees the following as central to her pathology: her experience of being invisible, having no true self, swinging from states of emptiness to hollow grandiosity, acting impulsively, and exhibiting sadomasochistic behavior. Notably absent in this initial depiction is the oral hunger so present in her first treatment. Is this a function of developmental growth, the gains derived from her first treatment, or a combination of the two? When Lisa describes, 16 months into this second treatment, how she feels like a shattered windshield and is burdened with the enormous task of putting herself back together, I am struck by the degree to which this self appraisal fits with the lack of cohesion described in her first treatment. I am also struck by her capacity to reflect on this state and especially to acknowledge the great sadness and helplessness involved in the task of reparation. Clearly a shift in the capacity for self-awareness and in her tolerance for negative affect has taken place since the end of her last treatment.

Notably, her second analyst makes no reference to the role of her father as the mothering person at the beginning of her life. It may be worth considering that his availability as an oral supplier contributes significantly to the hopefulness she does have, and mitigates against her mother's unavailability during her infancy. Her father's capacity for nurture strongly contributes to the complexity of her sadomasochistic behavior, which can be seen when he is abusive or arousing (or both at once) toward her during her late toddlerhood. Throughout this treatment, the degree to which men offer the hope of satisfaction and gratification may stem, in part, from this early mothering and the lack of dismissiveness on his part. I am reminded of the sought-after jewel the lion possesses on the CAT as a metaphor for father's "preciousness."

Although her analyst did not focus on it, the early days in Lisa's second treatment reveal the oral neediness of her early history. She brings her own "supplies" to treatment, refuses to believe that anyone else could "feed" her, stretches and yawns almost as a wish to go to sleep in the presence of her "holding" therapist, and gorges on food, drink, and marijuana outside the sessions. In contrast to her first treatment, however, she is able to talk about her wish not to be spoiled and to have her analyst be firm with her. Importantly, her pervasive dread of attachment and dependency fits precisely with the sequelae of being parented by someone with a dismissive attachment style (Slade, 2000). One can imagine that interactions with such an unavailable self-absorbed mother might create in Lisa feelings of being "unreal." We can see her struggling with these feelings as she retreats to her poignant depiction of giving her dolls "special treats." She then laments that her dolls "didn't know she existed," amplifying the meagerness of her attempt to self-soothe. As Parsons cogently notes in the title of her paper, Lisa searches for a "good enough" self, yet paradoxically cannot find it without another's help. The degree to which her analyst can help her feel that she can begin to create this self, as opposed to it being imposed on her, is thus the goal of her treatment.

Before turning to how Parsons goes about helping Lisa create this good enough self, there are two additional comments Lisa makes regarding her parents that deserve mention. The first is her mother's gesture of throwing away her favorite toys at the end of her first analysis. This seems paradigmatic of mother's lack of empathy for Lisa's transitional objects and thus of Lisa's need for continuity. The second is Lisa's observation that fighting with her mother leaves her feeling nothing because she does not care what mother thinks, but that she hates fighting with father because in those moments she believes that they are not friends. This speaks once again to father's positive role with Lisa and to her feelings of concern for him that mitigate against a total feeling of emptiness. Each of these vignettes serves to clue in the analyst to Lisa's internal working models of her parents. Importantly, Parsons responds to these two depictions by acknowledging Lisa's emptiness and linking it to her fear of losing her therapist if she were to become attached to her. This comment is met by Lisa's sharing her memory of riding her tricycle down the stairs, knowing that she will hurt herself, yet needing attention at any cost. Her fantasy here, of breaking into little pieces, speaks again to her lack of body coherence or sense of having an integrated "self."

At this point in the treatment, Parsons makes a clinical decision that makes exceptional sense diagnostically. Lisa laments her profound craziness and her disappointment that "one hundred Sigmund Freuds" couldn't help her. Instead of interpreting this as contempt of the therapist or even obverse grandiosity that her problems are so special in their awfulness, Parsons acknowledges Lisa's deprivation and presents herself not as ideal, but as a "good enough" therapist. The success of this interpretation can be understood when we look at Lisa's CAT material. I spoke earlier of two maladaptive processes that occur in her narratives: her denial of dysphoric affect tone and her primary process disruption of logical sequence in the face of aggressive content. Parsons's interpretation of Lisa's rage or fragile grandiosity at that point in treatment would have, I believe, evoked the disorganization and primitive denial evidenced on her CAT.

Shortly after these interpretations, Lisa begins speaking of her internal struggles with conscience and willfulness. Here, for the first time, she is able to locate the struggle internally, as opposed to constantly externalizing difficulties onto a battleground filled with parents, boyfriends, or food and alcohol. She also begins a litany of somatic complaints. Both these shifts connote an emerging feeling that she does, in fact, have a body, however damaged and pained it may be, and that she no longer experiences herself as an empty shell. Notably, her sense of having a body and thus some solidity occurs concomitantly with her first acknowledgment of her wish to have her therapist see her as special and to have more of her outside the therapy hour. Thus, with a step away into her body, her immense oral hunger and need to be "held" come more to the foreground. I am reminded in this context of Winnicott's (1965b) formulation that when working with a patient whose primary diagnosis is the lack of a true self, a period of "extreme dependence" inevitably emerges. The therapist must be there for the patient in an extraordinary way so that the emergence of the true self can occur safely and without collapse by the patient. I believe Parsons did this beautifully.

The remainder of the treatment involved the working through of these key treatment and diagnostic paradigms. Interpretations of her emptiness and deprivation increasingly revealed how she turns to sexual excitement to feel some modicum of aliveness, even if painful. Although father could tolerate her orality and may have even encouraged this seductive interaction, he could not always tolerate her willful wishes to control and dominate him. Mother, moreover, could not tolerate her hunger and could only distort or dismiss her wishes for autonomy. As Parsons interprets the avenue leading to her reliance on sexuality and masochism, Lisa becomes better able to evoke memories of deprivation and begins to describe her need to spit out everything her mother would give her. Then she can enact in the transference the wish to spit out or flee Parsons as well. With further interpretation of this transferential paradigm, Lisa can begin to see the dire consequences of not being "fed" by her mother. Indeed, she regresses so fully that she wants to die or else escape to a maladaptive tie to a boyfriend when her neediness for Parsons becomes too intense. Similarly, she speaks at this point of throwing away her mother's lunches to deny her own need for even these concrete manifestations of being provided for by her mother.

Later in the treatment, her visualization of herself as a ball of clay provides another literal representation of her emerging sense of solidity. This solidity, in turn, fosters her refinement of the capacity to internalize her struggle between punitive superego structures and her intense neediness. Not having to act out these battles permits her, in turn, to further her development of the capacity for concern, thereby permitting a more complete working through of her father's sexual abuse. At this point, she becomes able to remember her mother trying to stop some of the father's beatings. This "new" memory of her mother can be viewed as Lisa's growing recognition that mother can tolerate some aspects of her need for control and autonomy and can thus be differentiated from her father in this important arena of her life. This, in turn, obviates Lisa's need to destroy whatever her mother actually gave to her, making it more likely that their relationship might become more satisfying in the future. The fact that mother could, at that point in treatment, tell Lisa of the first daughter given up for adoption, strongly supports this growing acceptance, where mother is no longer seen as wholly good or bad. Lisa's need to connect with her mother now became tolerable enough to overpower her need to stay so angry. Interestingly, Parsons notes in her closing review of the treatment that Lisa begins to enjoy reading as a by-product of the analysis. This again speaks to Lisa's development of the capacity to be a "solid" and thus to be alone and to enjoy the solitary work/pleasure inherent in reading. With this emerging self comes the capacity for expressing real kindness, as in the case of her giving Parsons, as her "most important gift," a ribbon that she herself wove. Here she has found enough of a sense of intactness to give willingly a part of herself to her analyst.

Conclusion

The treatment of Lisa by both analysts is a strong, complex, and highly valuable example of the manner in which accurate diagnosis effectively points the way toward treatment goals and processes. Disruptions in Lisa's core experience of coherence and the marked lack of safety it engendered are evident in her history and are clearly depicted on her CAT. The CAT analysis described here focused on the quality of Lisa's object representations and the affects her defenses permitted her to experience in the context of these representations. The degree to which interpersonal interactions outside of treatment are evidenced in the object representational paradigms of her projective test material is substantial. The ways in which these paradigms are repeatedly manifested in her treatments are equally impressive. It is especially confirming of the heuristic value of test data to psychoanalytic treatment, inasmuch as Lisa's greater ability to attach without denial or provocation suggests improvement along the very dimensions seen as most salient and vulnerable in her CAT material. It would have been most welcome, obviously, to have further test material available, either from the end of her first treatment or at some point(s) in her second treatment. This type of follow-up test data would have made the links between treatment process and test performance far more rigorous than the post hoc analysis described here.

As a side note, it is important to consider the cognitive and emotional changes that occurred as a function of the shift from childhood to adulthood between the two treatments. The degree to which verbalization replaced play, as well as the benefit of Lisa's emerging capacity for self-awareness, introspection, and empathy, even during the vulnerable beginning of her second analysis, are critical in this regard. Having further testing would have enabled us to distinguish developmental changes from the shifts in her self-coherence that occurred as a function of her first analysis. This would help keep our understanding of treatment progress distinct from that of the cognitive and emotional maturation that is bound to occur over such a long, crucial time period.

In summary, projective test material for Lisa, viewed principally through an object representational lens, captures salient aspects of her personality organization and sheds light on the dynamics and process of her treatment. Parallels between test content and process and later treatment are consistent with the growing literature linking test data with changes in psychoanalytically informed treatment (e.g., Tuber, 1983, 1992; Heinicke, 1990; Blatt, 1992; Blatt and Ford, 1994). Of course the exercise in this article was a retrospective one, and it is thus frightfully easy to make initial diagnosis and later treatment fit together relatively seamlessly. I would like to acknowledge concretely that I am in no way advocating the unique, magical properties of projective testing as a *predictor* of later treatment paradigms. It is instructive, I hope, however, to note the continuity between themes and processes revealed by the projective testing and the paradigms evoked in her treatments as both child *and* adult. As we move forward in attempts to assess formally the effectiveness of child psychotherapy and analysis, we should strongly broaden the use of projective testing as a most helpful tool in both case study and larger group comparisons.

Note

1 Copyright 2004, Analytic Press, Inc. Reproduced with permission.

17
USING THE RORSCHACH AS A PREDICTOR OF CHANGE

Primary paper: Tuber, S. (2000). Projective testing as a post hoc predictor of change in psychoanalysis: The case of Jim. In *Psychoanalytic Study of Lives Over Time*. Eds. J. Cohen & B. Cohler. New York: Academic Press, 283–308.[1]

In this paper, a RIM protocol is studied intensively. I am grateful to the editors of the volume from which the paper came, Bert Cohler and Jonathan Cohen, for giving me the unique opportunity to publish such an extensively elaborated-upon RIM protocol. The paper also allowed me to conduct an analysis of Jim's RIM protocol both with and without a focus on his MOA scale scores, a process that I always use in my clinical work and supervision with the RIM.

Treatment of patients with significant psychopathology has been of special interest to authors with an interest in linking projective test data with psychodynamic treatment process. Bridging projective test scores and patterns to the process of psychodynamic treatment has been reported by several authors: by Hatcher and Krohn (1980) with neurotic and borderline adult patients, by Spear and Sugarman (1984) with borderline and schizophrenic patients, and by Thomas (1987) with borderline and attention-deficit disordered children. In another interesting study in this area, Smith (1980) linked Rorschach test configurations with the impact on the psychotherapist of the borderline patient. Gorney and Weinstock (1980), moreover, showed how impasses in treatment with borderline patients could be foreshadowed by the Rorschach data of these patients.

It is no coincidence that the surge in studies of this kind converges with the emergence of object-relations theory as a core paradigm in understanding personality development from a psychoanalytically informed perspective (Greenberg & Mitchell, 1983). The focus of this theory on the conceptions of self and other in interaction, and the affects generated by the internalization of these interactions, has been concomitant with the development of a similar framework in projective testing. The object-representational measures discussed above are among the most common operationalizing instruments of this paradigm in the field of projective testing (Stricker & Healey, 1990).

Thus, the conceptual underpinnings and the measures chosen for study in the present chapter have a rich clinical tradition. The ability of projective test data to take a heuristically helpful "snapshot" of personality organization at a given point in time and to integrate this snapshot into an overall assessment of personality functioning is intrinsic to the projective hypothesis from which projective testing was first developed. Linking change in psychodynamic treatment with shifts in test performance or using test performance as a predictor of psychotherapeutic change may thus provide confirmation, from two overlapping arenas of study, of certain key psychodynamically informed explanations of personality organization and growth. The study of Jim's projective test protocol, albeit a post hoc predictor of his treatment experiences, may provide another contribution to the important work in this area.

The Case of Jim

Creating a viable bridge from assessment and diagnosis to treatment has been a long-heralded clinical ideal. The case of Jim provides us with compelling idiographic data to address this issue, as Jim's projective test protocol, given prior to the beginning of his child analysis, has been made available. In this chapter, Jim's Rorschach will be examined in light of how he fared in the "supportive" treatment beginning 13 years after the end of his first treatment. A psychodynamically informed approach to the test material will be used. Although this clearly is an exercise in "20-20 hindsight," it is hoped that the data will speak for themselves in a manner that will be useful to a discussion of the nature of, and impediments to, the concept of change in psychodynamic psychotherapy and psychoanalysis.

Jim's RIM Protocol

Jim's assessment was performed by a psychodynamically oriented clinical psychologist and consisted of a WISC, Rorschach, and TAT. Jim's WISC performance will not be described other than to note that his Verbal IQ was in the bright average to superior range, while his Performance IQ was in average to bright average range.

The quantitative analysis of Jim's record uses a combination of scoring procedures developed by Klopfer (1954) and Mayman (1960) and is thus wedded to a psychodynamic framework. Table 17.1 provides Jim's Rorschach protocol, and Table 17.2 provides the "face-sheet" summary of his Rorschach scores. The salient

TABLE 17.1 Jim's Rorschach Protocol

Protocol	Inquiry
CARD I 60 sec 1. A mask. (Go ahead.) (15 seconds) That's all.	1. Had eyes and everything – and it was all weird – had a weird face. (?) It was black and had four eyes. (Else, weird?) Not really.
2. All right, then l.l. a bird. Can I turn it upside down?	2. There was two birds – because they had beaks out to the side – (see). They didn't have any eyes – had a thick beak – had legs – didn't have wings. (Birds?) The beak and the legs – just l.l. them. His helmet – (?) Well, he was playing skydiver (laughs) and he needed protection – birds really have helmets sometimes (laughs). He might if someone put it on him.
3. v. Then it l.l. a four-eyed monster. (Go ahead.) That's all (45 seconds) – I can't find anything else.	3. v (Q) (Laughs) – a four-eyed monster – Well, it had four eyes. Its face was all yucky and black. (Just face?) I just saw the face. (Yucky?) It was black and it l.l. it was burnt. (?) Because it was black and it l.l. its eyes were burthout because it was white. (Eyes burnt out?) Right.
CARD II 85 sec 1. Ohh – uh – Let's see – uh (22 seconds) It l.l. two monsters playing patticake – with their legs too and it l.l. their heads aren't attached to their bodies.	1. (Monsters?) Because they had red heads and their mouth was really weird. (Weird?) It just looked so ugly – like they didn't have any teeth. (Anything else – monster?) Their bodies are playing patticake – because only monsters play patticake. (?) Because it's a corny game. (Heads not attached?) Because it wasn't, because you didn't see any attachments. (Heads red?) Because a luture was shot by a bow and arrow and all blood fell on their heads. (Laughs) (How do you know that?) I took a guess.
2. And there's a stingray in the middle and they're punching the stingray. (Laughs) (card cover) (more?) That's all I can find.	2. Because it had tail. (Anything else?) It was swirly and it had a head like a stingray. (Swirly?) It wasn't on position. It was in motion. (Motion?) Should show you? (Describe) Describe – well – what made it look like it was in motion – uh – well the tail was moving. It wasn't in a – in one position. (?) Because it was moving.

(continued)

TABLE 17.1 (*Cont.*)

Protocol	Inquiry
CARD III 60 sec. 1. Ooh. (Laughs) See. It l.l. two humans with long noses. Men with duck feet are playing hit with each other with – 2. the rocks. 3. And it was raining blood. That's all I could find.	1. (Men?) Because they l.l. men. (?) They just l.l. it (?) How? They had a head and a body and two legs and arms. That's all. (Why men?) Men are – like to hit each other with rocks. 2. (Rocks?) Should I show you? (Tell me.) Right below their hands (?) Shaped like rocks. 3. It had little plops on the side. (?) They were red. (Raining blood there?) Yeah. (How could it be raining blood?) (Laughs) I don't know. (Raining blood?) Oh— Well – No – I don't know. It's just something – it's not – (laughs) – It's so hard to describe. (?) Well some special kind of birds were flying up in the sky and someone started to throw rocks at them and it started raining blood. (Special birds?) They were cuckoo birds.
CARD IV 85 sec Well, how many more of these do we have? (20 seconds) This l.l. a gargantuan – with holes in his arms – with boots on. That's all. (45 seconds) (Else?) He has a stumpy head. He's all black and he doesn't have any eyes or anything. (Anything else?) Nothing – That's his chair.	(What's a gargantuan?) A monster – a hairy monster. (Look hairy?) The little punctures out of his skin. (Punctures?) The needles coming out from his skin. (Holes in arms?) He bit a hole in his arms one day because he was so hungry.
CARD V 60 sec A bat – with – with mouths coming out of his arms – wings – and he has tentacles and so the tentacles has legs – He has big tentacles – He's black.	(Bat has mouths on his wings?) This is a special kind of a cookoo-ca-ca-keecho bat – (Really such things?) No. (Tentacles?) Big ones on his arms – on wings. And that's how he catches his food – birds fly right into his things – he catches them all and eat them up.
CARD VI 70 sec (Laughs) A cat – with four legs – he has his mouth like this (wide open mouth) and you can see his whiskers – It looks like an animal and it looks like his fur and he's black.	(Animal?) Because it l.l. a cartoon. (?) Because it didn't have straight outlines like pictures do. (Else cartoon?) Because in real life cats can't open their mouths like that. How many more do we have? (Furry?) It had a little pin needles sticking out. (Else, fur?) No. (Nothing in the body itself?) No. (If the outline is smooth, is it still fur?) No.

TABLE 17.1 (*Cont.*)

Protocol	Inquiry

CARD VII

70 sec 1. Poodles bowing to each other with their ears sticking up. (25 seconds) That's all (Else?) v < v.
2. v. Oh, yeah. It l.l. two lady dancers with big hairdos, high – Nothing much else.

1. (Describe) They had their ears sticking up – they were just regular poodles. (?) They had all curlies in their hair. (?) It sort of went like this (outlines rough shape) (Outside?) Outside. (Outside smooth – the curls?) No.

CARD VIII

180 sec 1. Oooh, neat. v. This l.l. – should I show how I see this? This l.l. a bull dog with cheeks hanging down – his arms – and two little legs – no fingers – no four. (More?) (Puts card down and ties his shoe).

2. A Russian house. (More?) Should I tell you why it l.l. a Russian house? (Learning the process?) I can't find anything else.
3. Oh yeah. This doesn't l.l. an animal. This does l.l. a chipmunk. Here's a leg. Here's a leg, etc. Here's his tail. Here's his eye.

1. (Good picture of a bull dog?) Yes. It's animated. (?) Because it was in colors. (?) Well because I'm sure a bulldog is going to have different colored skin – fur maybe – little legs. It looked so funny. (?) Because it was so small for such a big dog. (Then why say they are part?) Because it was a dog from outer space – Are we almost done? Are we halfway through it?

2. Two chipmunks. Two were doing a dance and it was different colors so it was animated. (Russian?) Well, it l.l. a Russian house. IT was pretty interesting. Because I've seen pictures of Russian houses and they l.l. it. (Different colors?) Yeah.

CARD IX

70 sec 1. A cow – a cow with horns – these are just heads of animals.
2. v. A cross-eyed African elephant, oh – with clothes on and everything – He has a trunk too. That's all I can find.

1. (Like a cow?) Well, the head was shaped like a cow. (Head?) Yeah. (Else). No.
2. Ears, eyes, trunks, arms. (Arms?) He's deformed – only has two legs. (Deformed?) He was born on the moon. (Two legs?) He was deformed. (Deformed?) Born at the moon. (Not enough oxygen up there! (Clothes on him?) They were colors and everything. (Looked funny, clothes on arms?) His arms.

(*continued*)

TABLE 17.1 (*Cont.*)

Protocol	Inquiry
CARD X 170 sec 1. Oh! It just l.l. a bunch of germs. That's all. (Tell me in more detail.) They're different-colored germs, I guess – (Point that out.) This, this. (points to each quickly) Are you keeping up with me? (Laughs) Okay, I'm finished. 2. Pieces of bodies cut off. That's all. (more?) 3. These l.l. two bugs arguing over this thing – I don't know what it is. 4. v. (green?) Shrimp – that's all.	1. Well – They weren't anything – so far I just assumed they were germs – Fair with you? (l.l. germs?) Yeah. They were all weird. (Pay attention.) Yes. They really did look like germs – They weren't any type of human being type of things – I just assumed they were germs. (Germs?) Because I have a microscope at home. (?) That l.l. what I see under the microscope at home. (?) Because it was what I saw under my microscope a few days ago. (Tell me as if this were under the microscope.) Things that move around under the microscope – so germs. 4. Looked like shrimp (?) Had bodies like shrimp. 2. Bodies, human bodies?) A leg and hand. That's all that I know. They l.l. it (Human bodies?) They just look like piece of bodies cut off.

points to be derived from this "quantitative" analysis will be presented first, followed by a sequential analysis of Jim's record.

Quantitative Analysis

This is a highly charged record in which Jim's high productivity suggests too great an aliveness and an overlay raw, even over-related, quality that is derived from the following quantitative features of his record. These features are best viewed as part of an interrelated dynamic process and not as separate static components.

1. Too few of his responses (F% = 30) use only the shape of the blot to explain the response. When these form-only responses are used, only half (F+% = 50) are of an acceptably accurate form-level. Taken together, these two factors suggest that there are difficulties holding back (repressing, on a more unconscious level) intensely felt inner experience. This process of suppressing the repressing, when attempted, does not ensure accurate efficient cognitive functioning. Thus, there is a press to interact and to enliven, which seems to indicate more need than predilection.

Using Rorschach as a Predictor of Change 199

TABLE 17.2 Some Selected Rorschach Summary Scores for Jim (Age 9 Years, 8 Months)

$R = 22$
$M = 2$ (1 spoiled, 1 plus)
$FM = 6$ (2 spoiled, 1 weak minus, 2 ordinary and 1 plus)
$Fm = 3$ (1 spoiled, 1 vague plus, 1 minus)
$FC = 4$ (2 ordinary, 2 arbitrary)
$CF = 3$ (2 vague, 1 spoiled)
$Fc = 3$ (2 ordinary, 1 weak minus)
$FC' = 5$ (2 ordinary, 1 plus, 1 weak minus, 1 spoiled)

$F\% = 30$ H: (H) etc. 1:7
$F+\% = 50$
ext. $F\% = 96$
ext. $F+\% = 46$

$H = 1$ $(H) = 1$ $H/In = 1$
$Hd = 1$ $H/A = 2$ $(A) = 3$

Five thought disordered responses:
3 Fab ----- Confab; 1 Fab Comb. Severe and 1 Confab

13 Mutuality of Autonomy Scores:
1 (4 of them)
2 (1 of them)
5 (1)
6 (7)

2. With Jim's F% so low (normative values for boys Jim's age are 67% (Ames et al., 1971), the percentage of responses imbued with movement, color, and/or shading is naturally elevated. Fully half (11 of 22) of his responses involve movement, 9 of the 11 are of the more impulse-dominated, anxiety-suffused, animal, and inanimate movement subtypes. Importantly, the form-level of this type of response is either strikingly exact or dramatically arbitrary and of poor quality. Jim seems to live in two starkly different worlds: one richly interactive, accurate, and enlivened, and one equally animated but distorted and indicative of gaps in his reality testing.

3. This dichotomous pattern continues when he uses color to help define his perceptions. Five of his seven color responses are poor in form-quality and/or suggest arbitrary "stretches" to rigidly use color when it is unrealistic to do so. His other two responses are quite adaptive in their use of color to add richness to his percepts.

4. The all-or-nothing overly charged persona I'm posting is qualified, notably, by the quality of his shading and achromatic color responses. First, these responses are quite plentiful, suggesting a capacity for inner awareness and a strongly felt inner tension. Second, they are better in form-level than the movement

or color responses. Only one of these responses is of poor form; two are rated mediocre or "weak" form. In such a rigidly dichotomous record, his shading and achromatic color responses are a welcome sign of some ability to let down his guard without being swamped by primitive fantasy and feeling.

5. The degree to which Jim can feel overwhelmed is evidenced by his five thought-disordered responses, four of which imply an overelaborated personalized affective response. Here he is at his most vulnerable—these responses indicate a serious disturbance in his capacity to keep his more primitive disruptive inner experience at bay.

6. There is also a noteworthy imbalance between those responses seen as fully human ($H=1$) and those in which human or animal content blur into one another and/or are replete with mythical or fantastic attributes ((H) = 1, (A) = 3, H/A = 2, H/In = 1). This implies a disruption in his capacity to effortlessly identify with what is wholly human, consistent with his overly plentiful animal and inanimate movement responses.

Taken together, these six points frame the following questions:

1. Why can't he repress or inhibit his inner world more effectively or efficiently?
2. What prompts his almost exclusively dichotomous response pattern of terrifically adaptive responses intermingled with disrupted, arbitrary, even dereistic ones?
3. How do we understand the relative impairment in his capacity to generate fully human responses, given how vivid his fantasy life appears to be?
4. Given the self-awareness implicit in his shading/achromatic color responses, is this charged quality an at least partially conscious attempt to escape inner pain, and, if so, what are the implications of this awareness for this treatment?

It now makes sense to take a look at the content of his record to help begin to address these questions and set the stage for his treatment. Content will be examined first by a review of the entire protocol and then by a special focus on the quality of his object-representational paradigms using the MOA Scale. It may be useful to describe my thoughts for each card by a "thinking out loud" method, whereby I create and reject hypotheses as the protocol "presents itself" to me. This clinical processing strongly parallels a therapist's process during treatment and therefore may be of heuristic value in and of itself in our understanding of Jim's treatment experience.

A Content Analysis of Jim's RIM Protocol

Card I. He responds dysphorically to the black and shadowy qualities of the blot, first by distancing (a mask and not face) and then by moving to the sides of the blot to make a beak. (Is he getting away from the "eyes," does he feel looked at by the card? By the examiner?) He sees a bird without wings: a castration theme? But then he gives it a helmet, protecting its head when all else is vulnerable? He laughs when making the bird into a more human skydiver who needs help to be protected, but he then is drawn back to his original dysphoric response and focuses on its black burnt-out eyes, implying a longstanding, painful, melancholic quality.

Card II. He begins with an excellent degree of mutuality and relatedness, but then it crumbles. First, the heads are not attached (again a loss, here a mind/body lack of integration that again feels longstanding), and I am struck by how literal he is and how he lacks sufficient repression. Lack of attachment is then followed by a focus on the percept's ugly repulsiveness and weirdness, as he becomes more estranged. Associations become still more primitive as he resorts to autistic logic to explain the "childish" game of patti-cake. This disavowal of regressive play only leads to further disruption, however, as a bloody vulture sadomasochistically stirs his laughter. (The symbol of death is itself killed. Is this the bird on Card I in his associative process?) He then gives a peculiarly vague rationale for the stingray response, as if the tail had become motion itself. The primitive malevolence stirred up by the vulture response seems to have affected the very quality of his language, while the motion of the stingray seems to be driven by ambiguous pervasive anxiety.

Card III. Almost duplicating Card II, he begins with active humans relating to each other and then deteriorates. Interaction becomes malevolent, and the people become blends of human and animal, creating a thought-disordered response in which the boundaries maintaining fully integrated beings are grossly violated, with the perseverative and malevolent "blood-raining" then depicted. The pattern of mutuality leading to un-integration and sadistic body-damaged malevolence, coupled with anxiety-ridden laughter, connotes far more than castration anxiety—it feels as if his very self is imperiled when mutuality is expressed.

Card IV. A new theme emerges here, with a response to shading that is noteworthy. A "popular" response is first made defective through a self-imposed oral mutilation and hunger. Then its hairiness and potential softness is replaced by its opposite: a puncturing suit of needles, which simultaneously repels others and pierces itself. How could such a monster (self? father? males?) ever be approached? How could it ever be at peace? Does he attack (self and/or others) to forestall/ evoke being attacked? Would this pattern manifest itself in his treatment or within his family, if at all?

Card V. Even on this simplest of cards, he spoils his conventional response by projecting an oral hunger (mouths out of wings), which leads to anal "baby talk." Again, he can't repress or inhibit in the face of the dysphoria-induced blackness, much as he cannot successfully defend against the harsh redness and the affect it generates in Cards II and III.

Card VI. Although the cat's mouth on this card perseverates on his oral hunger theme, there is at last no malevolence, and he is able to reasonably sublimate these concerns into a cartoon. Once again, however, as on Card IV, fur is described as "little pin needles." Such an uncommon way to transform textural softness and to perseverate in this way on the two cards most commonly imbued with texture is striking. It can best be called "textural denial," implying a doing/undoing defensive process regarding an unconscious experience of what it might mean to him to feel or wish for visceral closeness. Does he fear being enveloped if he drops his shield of needles? Does he experience himself as damaging those he seeks closeness with if he comes too close?

Card VII. His response to this card presents him at his most adaptive. There is humor and mutuality in his poodle response, and his mention of "curlies" implies an experience of texture without its needle-like, sadomasochistic quality. He then gives his only fully human response and his only human movement response with good form in the record. This card is commonly viewed as relatively more "feminine" in character, and certainly the color of the card is less starkly black than the other achromatic cards. Is there evidence here to suggest a safe/toxic dichotomy as a function of gender? Or does the lightness of the card allow for far better defensive functioning? What might the implications of this capacity be for his treatment, especially during moments of tenderness or vulnerability?

Card VIII. Each of his responses to this card and the remaining two pastel-colored cards has a quality that distinguishes them from the rest of his Rorschach performance. The last three cards lack the stark reds, black, and textural qualities of the first seven cards. His responses mirror this blander quality. There is no trace of malevolence, but this is replaced, as it were, with vagueness, lack of integration and specificity, and, most importantly, an inability to use intellectualization convincingly, so that almost all his responses feel weak and arbitrary. I am made more hopeful by this lack of clarity, as it implies a lack of "calcification" and hence some potential to flounder in his affective experience that his therapist may use to help him. Yet it also implies a psychological fatigue; he seems to be losing his capacity to be self-critical in a positive sense.

Card IX. The description to the previous card applies well here, but the whimsical elephant cannot stay intact and instead becomes deformed and effectively castrated, with a dose of autistic logic employed to explain this deformity.

Card X. His first response is a strong attempt at intellectualization and personalization in the face of persistent inquiry. The oddness of his logic—"they weren't any type of human being things, I just assumed they were germs"—make sense as a defense against the dismembered body parts he can no longer repress and reveals his reliance on his intellectual interests to avoid pervasive body-integrity concerns. Interestingly, on Cards II and III, he began with a fully interactive percept that quickly became damaged and prone to sadomasochistic concerns; here he acknowledges dismemberment first and from this creates a fully interactive response—the "arguing bugs." This implies a restorative capacity that should be a boon to his treatment. Why it occurs here may be linked with the absence of harsh black and red hues to the card itself, which tap his intense dysphoria and great fear of affective storms respectively.

Summary of Rorschach Sequence and Its Implications for Treatment

What can we make of this sequence of Rorschach responses, and what are its implications for this upcoming treatment experience? A number of summarizing points can be made first:

1. Jim attempts, usually unsuccessfully, to ward off a seemingly longstanding sense of dysphoria and hurt, appearing at times much like a "burnt child," who has repeatedly hoped for greater connections with protecting enhancing others but, by and large, has been hurt in his experience with them. There is a sense of a need to protect himself from closeness and a great dread of malevolence that closeness can bring—a damage to one's very body integrity. Jim appears to use this potentially engulfing force and/or a sadomasochistic rendering of this potential damage as a means of maintaining a sense of aliveness.
2. Castration fears are prominent, but they are usually more easily laughed off and seem more containable than the annihilation-like fears described above.
3. Themes of oral hunger and oral envelopment appear to parallel a denial of texture. There is an undoing of textural softness that turns it into its opposite, a shield of piercing and self-puncturing needles. Talking for Jim may be his best means of obtaining closeness. Yet, there appears an unintegrated mind/body split, whereby his voice and mind can maintain or create connection, but his body is felt as simultaneously hurtful and untouchable yet profoundly vulnerable.

At his worst, these three points suggest the following treatment paradigm. If attachment experiences seem replete with hunger, dysphoria, and malevolence, and if sadomasochistic sensation is an attempt to defend against body-integrity damage and dread, then he must preserve his sense of self at all cost and barricade it from overexposure. This places him at risk, given his relatively high Verbal IQ, his propensity of intellectualization, his longing for and yet fear of closeness and loss, and the readiness with which primary process material can intrude, for a "false self" presentation in treatment, that is, Jim may seek an overly rapid compliance to preserve his vulnerable "core self."

What might be presented by Jim within this notion of a "false self"? Certainly, the facility of his words and his longing for support may lead to a rapid "sizing up" of what is expected of him in psychoanalysis. Should he take this to mean generating "insight" or overly quick acceptance of the analyst's interpretations, a profound part of him will stay hidden in much the same manner as the porcupine quality of a number of his percepts hides the soft underbelly of his chronic sense of loneliness.

More specifically, I wonder whether a willingness to talk about his castration fears paradoxically may hide more primitive aspects of his fear of body damage and lack of cohesion. These types of fears are abundant enough in his protocol to be felt as a profound relief for him to master (and of course they would be). The discussion of these fears would appear noteworthy to any psychoanalytically informed clinician and could therefore likely be reinforced by the analyst. This reinforcement and support would likely prove amenable to symptom relief yet fail to address the more primitive aspect of his fears of body damage. This dichotomizing of castration-level vs. annihilation-level anxiety is of course overly linear, yet it suggests a need to eventually assess the treatment process, at least in part through the lens of the quality of his object-relational capacities. This level of analysis will help determine the levels of relatedness the treatment did or did not touch. Before leaving Jim's Rorschach, I would like to add to this discussion a more specific focus on the nature and quality of Jim's Rorschach object-representational and interactive percepts, as measured by the MOA Scale.

The MOA Scale

The sequence of Jim's MOA scores will be presented via the same "thinking out loud" format that I used previously to analyze the content of his RIM protocol. These scores are presented in Table 17.3.

An Analysis of Jim's MOA responses

Card I. Interaction begins only in the inquiry, as it appears that the original bird he saw as a whole response gets lost in the affective associations he has to the weird monsters. The helmet he puts on the bird implies a dangerous interaction and hence a score of 5. What's most striking is the degree to which an entirely natural phenomenon of a bird in flight becomes a dangerous journey—the sense of failed competence is powerful. The four-eyed monster response shifts the danger of malevolence from an acute impending fall to a chronic, harsh, blinded state. Interaction so far provides only pain.

Card II. On this card and then again on Card III, he responds in a very unusual way vis-à-vis more common MOA performance. He begins with a highly adaptive score of 1, with the game of patti-cake intrinsically involving benign reciprocity. This rapidly shifts to the destroyed vulture, which receives a score of 6, aptly characterizing its butchered state. Most boys who are capable of scoring 6s on their protocols rarely have the capacity to experience the mutuality of a 1 response (Tuber, 1992). Whatever blend of benign and toxic object-relations Jim has apparently internalized, they are striking for their unintegrated nature; indeed, it raises the question of whether or not it is possible for a child (or adult) to integrate this degree of contrasting experience with any cohesiveness.

Card III. Here we have almost a duplication of Card II. High mutuality becomes malevolent and thought disordered with the preservative fantasy attack and blood-raining speaking to his intense acute anxiety. I am also struck by his calling the bird "cuckoo." Is he to be attacked for his "craziness" by the examiner?

TABLE 17.3 Jim's Mutuality of Autonomy Scale Scores

Response	Inquiry	Score
I. It l.l. a bird.	There were 2 birds, they had beaks out to the side, they didn't have any eyes, they had thick beak and didn't have wings and he was wearing a helmet because he was playing skydiver and he needed protection because he was going to fall.	5
I. A 4-eyed monster	It was all yucky and black. (?) It was black and it was burnt—it l.l.its eyes were burnt out because it was white.	6
II. 2 monsters playing patticake and it l.l. their heads aren't attached to their bodies	Because they had red heads and their mouths was really weird – it just looked so ugly like they didn't have any teeth. (heads red?) Because a vulture was shot by a bow and arrow and all the blood fell on their heads.	1,6
II. And there's a stingray and they're punching the stingray.	Because it had a tail. (?) It wasn't in one position, it was in a mount (?) The tail was moving, it was all moving.	5
III. It l.l. 2 humans with long noses, men with duck feet, area playing hit each other with the rocks and it was raining blood.	Some special k.o. birds were flying up in the sky and someone started to throw rocks at them and it started raining blood. They were cuckoo birds.	1,6
IV. L.l. a gargantuan with holes in his arms, with boots on, he has a stumpy head, he's all black and doesn't have any eyes or anything.	A hairy monster (?) the little punctures out from his skin (?) the needles coming out from his skin. (?) he bit a hole in his arms one day because he was so hungry.	6
V. A bat with mouth coming out of his arms, wings and he has tentacles, big tentacles and he's black.	This is spooky bat, a cookoo bat. (Tentacles?) That's how he catches his food. Birds fly right into his things and he catches them all and eats them up.	6
VII. Two poodles bowing to each other.		1
VII. (V) L.l. 2 lady dancers with big hairdos, high.		2
X. Pieces of bodies cut off.	Human bodies (?) a leg (pink) a hand (brown) –just l.l. pieces of bodies cut off.	6
X. These l.l. 2 bugs arguing with each other over this thing, I don't know what it is (top gray).		1

Has he been the subject of attack (real and/or imagined) for thoughts and feelings that are ego-alien to him as well?

Card IV. Here again is a percept in which body-integrity damage rates a score of 6. In this percept, however, the damage is imposed by the self. I wonder if this is an extension of his feeling "cuckoo"? Does his inner torment puncture him, while keeping others at a distance, only to create such a loneliness and hunger that he must bite himself? This biting, which simultaneously feeds and punishes, may also be an attempt to let himself feel something and maintain a sense of aliveness.

Card V. This is the third consecutive malevolent depicted interaction. He has now produced seven instances of interaction, and each one has been or become malevolent. Here again the oral-engulfing nature of the malevolence provides additional evidence of the preoedipal quality of his fears and pain. In this context, Winnicott talks of experience of aliveness and writes that people whose earliest years did not provide a "good enough" holding environment would have lives "characterized by a sense of futility born of compliance" (Phillips, 1988, p. 127). Winnicott goes on to note that feeling real is "more than existing, it is finding way to exist as oneself, to relate to objects as oneself and to have a self into which to retreat for relaxation" (p.127). We will need to look at Jim's treatment within this context to best address our concerns that his MOA scores reveal deficits in his feeling truly alive.

Card VII. Jim is at his best here. The two poodles are a 1, although I wish he felt safe enough to have made them fully human. He then turns to intact fully human percepts (the lady dancers) for the only time in his record, but his MOA score becomes one of parallel interaction. Parallelism allows him a haven, it seems, to be fully human in representation in a way that mutuality does not. Again, will treatment that allows him to remain parallel make him look more intact but not get at that which lies "underneath"? This also raises important questions as to the purpose of psychotherapy, both in general and with children. How complete is it possible to be?

Card X. Yet again we have the dichotomy of a 6 and a 1. Now, however, we see a shift from a part-object dismembered percept to a "recovery" in which bugs are capable of arguing with each other. As in Card VII, the recovery seems to occur when animals are seen rather than people.

A more general point needs to be made, connecting Jim's MOA performance with that of similarly aged children. The preliminary normative data collected on MOA responses in children Jim's age (Tuber, 1992) suggests a bimodal distribution, with children giving scale point 2 responses most commonly and then scale point 5 responses are next in frequency. This makes intuitive and clinical sense given the Rorschach's predilection for exposing the most pathological content relative to other test material and the defended parallel quality of a scale point 2 response. Jim, strikingly however, has only one 2 and one 5 response. He has four 1s and seven 6s, however. This all-or-none pattern is very worrisome to me. Is this a Rorschach analogue or representational splitting into all good or all bad interactions? Is it another indication of his inability to repress or leave beings alone? Scale point 2 responses seem to be a healthy non-charged way of just being, of having a self in the presence of others. Jim instead seems to be either disproportionately aware of others or malevolently predisposed to be hurt or to produce hurt on them.

Summary of Jim's RIM Protocol

Jim suffers from disturbances in effective regulation and expression. Affects are only minimally attributed to internal states of mind and are thus easily made arbitrary. When fragmented and non-cohesive in this way, Jim can easily become suffused with dysphoria and just as easily isolate affects from one another. At his worst, on both records, he can become immersed in primary process content, with apparent lapses in reality-testing and with sadomasochistic features to the malevolence he presents. His very language can become vague and ambiguous and his temporal sense disoriented, speaking to lapses in autonomous ego functioning. His inner effective world appears markedly confused at times, with intense neediness being expressed, often oral in nature.

While at times a number of his Rorschach responses speaks strongly to phallic-castration-superego concerns, his predominant mode of functioning as derived from this test suggests to me a level of object-relations of a strongly preoedipal nature. Struggles with self-cohesion of a very early nature seem at the core of these test data.

Thus, we need to turn to his treatment with two broad questions. (1) Can we see signs of his touching his fears of annihilation, his inner effective confusion, his hunger for others, his fear of piercing attack, his being the piercer to get his needs met, his acknowledging the neediness of his "True Self"? (2) Conversely, will he focus on modes of compliance or on less threatening conflicts that keep his core fears hidden and thus minimize his aloneness and hunger?

Jim During his First Treatment: A Brief Comment

Although I want the focus of this paper to be Jim's second treatment, there is a key moment during his first treatment that I would like to comment on first. We are now about 180 sessions into the treatment. Work on Jim's oedipal longings for his mother and his curiosities about his parents' sex life are the focus of the work. Powerfully, Jim takes a family vacation away from treatment, and the analyst notes how Jim never expresses, either before or after this or any other vacation (Jim had four 3-week vacations each year), any feelings of missing the analyst or the treatment. The analyst does note that this is "partly defensive against preoedipal feelings of dependency and aggression but also the result of a deep sense of security in relationship to primary objects and continued gratifying interaction with them. Development during the preoedipal years," he goes on to say, "was essentially smooth and positive, particularly in regard to the separation-individuation process" (Colarusso, 2000).

This statement speaks to the key disparity between the analyst's emphasis on what is to be worked on with Jim and what I am stressing after a reanalysis of Jim's Rorschach. To his analyst, Jim is diagnostically a preoedipally intact youngster with a well-bounded neurotic conflict. The analyst clearly then conceptualizes the treatment as working through Jim's experience of (a) a hostile oedipal father who wishes to control, castrate, and make him passive, and (b) a seductive mother who wants to "cuddle" and talk of sexual themes with him. All of his affects are therefore quite thoughtfully interpreted as anger, fear, aggression, and libidinal excitement within an oedipal context. At the end of 356 sessions, the patient is described, moreover, as a confident early adolescent who has worked extremely well in dealing with these issues. He has made friends at school, and is mature and thoughtful, successful academically, and well versed in preadolescent sexual issues. The kindness of the therapist towards this child is constantly apparent, moreover, and their termination seems complete and strong. Yet I have described series of object-representational projective test responses that do not fit with an oedipal-level ego structure, but do seem to fit more neatly with those aspects of the treatment that deal with possibilities of aloneness, lack of attunement, the creation of a compliant false self, and other characteristics of preoedipal missteps toward personhood.

Jim's Second Treatment

This leads us to Jim's second treatment, 13 years following the end of his first one, when Jim calls his analyst, asking to see him because he is having difficulty deciding on a choice of career. I assume that by now you can see where this is all heading and why I've called this exercise such an unfair one. Despite the seeming clarity, strength, and fullness of Jim's first treatment, Jim's reporting of how his life has gone post-treatment is striking for its impoverishment and difficulty. We are not told of any external traumas in Jim's subsequent life—there is no death, illness, etc. Yet Jim describes having had only one brief intimate relationship with a woman in the intervening years, being bitter over the possibility of marriage, and having few, if any, male friends of any meaning to him either. He states, moreover, that he has been a heavy user of marijuana and alcohol since high school, as it "makes him happy with the status quo," that his schoolwork was mediocre, and that he was undecided about whether he should be a golf pro or try a career as an elementary school teacher. He is presently unhappy working as a salesclerk and often relies monetarily on his parents. He also reports continued estrangement from his father and describes his mother as "just wanting everyone to be in harmony." Interestingly, he describes his younger brother as going through significant depression and identity crisis similar to his upon leaving home and going off to college.

The nature of Jim's second treatment is also noteworthy. Despite being able to articulately and poignantly note his difficulties, Jim refuses to resume intensive treatment and instead sees the therapist for supportive sessions 2 to 3 times per month from 1989 to 1992 and then once every 2 or 3 months to 2000. The therapist notes Jim's going "cold turkey" from pot and alcohol a month after treatment begins, ascribing this to the power of "positive transference." Treatment focuses on Jim's career plans. After four years of his second treatment, he has recently been able to secure a teaching position he likes and has yet to develop an important intimate relationship with anyone, sexual or nonsexual, but does not appear significantly happier than he was at the beginning of his second treatment.

I am obviously surprised by the lack of intimacy in Jim's life and will get back to it shortly. I'd like to focus first on his avoidance of more intensive treatment. Why would he avoid this, given his very positive tie to his therapist, his alleged capacity for strong attachment, and the presumed positive foundation of his earliest years? I would argue now that his now chronic avoidance of attachment is revealed to us in many ways in this second treatment:

1. Towards his analyst, Jim describes not continuing to "think analytically on his own during adolescence ... or early adulthood," which is attributed to his need to separate from him. But why deny the self-analytic *process* unless this thinking could not be sustained without the analyst's presence, unless, perhaps, a compliant false self was largely at work here, with a resulting lack of full object-constancy. Is this a case of imitation, rather than true internalization and/or identification, indicative of a less than fully developed preoedipal life? I argue that Jim adopted the therapist's self too easily and readily as a way of easing his core loneliness but could not sustain this "imitation" after he had been away from the therapist for a time.
2. In the second treatment, Jim's mother is conspicuously absent. She is barely mentioned, except as a "nonintrusive" promoter of family harmony. Why is she an afterthought now, and how does that coexist with the supposed firmness of his attachment to her?
3. The avoidance of his father is also striking. At one point in the second treatment, Jim describes he and his father as "getting along fantastically now" but that they rarely see each other, implying a significant limitation in his having worked through his oedipal issues vis-à-vis his father.
4. The depression of his brother is also noteworthy and speaks to possibly more profound family dysfunction than thought previously. That his brother is also "lost" does, I think, lend more weight to the thesis that there is a strong impairment of attachment in this family.
5. His use of alcohol and pot is striking: as a means of "filling" his core sense of emptiness, mitigating a possible depression and soothing an oral neediness.
6. Last, there is his lack of intimacy with a peer, male or female. This just doesn't make sense given his initial diagnosis or the course of his first treatment. It

does make considerably more sense, though, given the either/or quality of his Rorschach object-representations, the lack of fully human mutuality, the over-relatedness of his record, the hollowness of his fully human percepts, the great difficulties in modulating affect, and the awful, despairing, burnt, and malevolent quality of many of his responses.

We are left with a powerful dilemma. Had Jim never returned to treatment, we would have all been convinced by the depiction of the excellence of his initial outcome. My review of his Rorschach would have been rightfully seen as overly pathological. The status of Jim at the beginning of his second treatment, however, lends support to the notion that his underlying pain, despair, and primitiveness were being dealt with by the development of a false-self character, armoring what even his very worthy first treatment could not penetrate. I would like to believe that an initial focus on the preoedipal aspects of his object-representational paradigms might have shifted the nature of his treatment so that his core emptiness, dysphoria, and aloneness might have been more adequately addressed. The deprivations and impairments revealed at follow-up echo Winnicott's (1965a) depictions of patients whose false or "caretaker" self is insufficiently questioned in treatment, resulting in limited long-term gains in the capacity to feel fully real and alive.

Note

1 Copyright 2000, Academic Press. Reproduced with permission.

18
TWO CASE STUDIES OF CHILDREN WITH ADHD

Paper used: Tuber, S., Harris, B., Meehan, K., Reynoso, J., & Ueng-McHale, J. (2006). Rorschach configurations of children with ADHD. In *The Clinical Assessment of Children and Adolescents: A Practitioner's Guide.* Eds. S. Smith & L. Handler. New Jersey: Erlbaum, 451–468.[1]

As a follow-up to the paper I wrote with Meehan et al. on the regulatory difficulties of children with ADHD, the following paper goes beyond the original nomothetic assessment to the case studies of the protocols of two children with ADHD. In keeping with this section's focus, I have excised the nomothetic beginning of the paper below to focus exclusively on the case study material.

To best illustrate the thinking behind our approach and to demonstrate a way to use idiographic research to inform clinical practice, we will now present the RIM protocols of two of our ADHD participants. These cases provide an important complement to the empirical analysis in that they vividly illustrate how dynamic and context-dependent a child's responses can be, as opposed to a static and narrow view of ADHD children as having little access to human representations and internal resources across all settings.

Case 1: Terri

Terri, an eight-year-old African-American girl, was found to meet criteria for ADHD, Inattentive Type. We present Terri as an example of an ADHD child whose attention difficulties significantly impacted her ability to draw upon internal resources to organize her response to the Rorschach blots. Accordingly, her protocol is marked by mostly pure form responses, which are of varying quality.

TABLE 18.1 Terri's Entire Record

Determinant	Terri	Typical 8-year-old
R	14	15.9
M	0	1.3
FM	0	1.5
m	0	.4
FC+CF+C	0	1.7
FC'+CF'+C'	0	.9
Texture	4	.2
H+Hd+(H)+(Hd)	1	2.6
A+Ad+(A)+(Ad)	12	7.3
Lambda	2.5	1.37
X+%	29%	78%

Note: All Norms are derived from Ames et al. (1974).

Behaviorally, Terri was remarkably distracted throughout the two days of testing. She had a Full Scale IQ of 83 on the WASI, although the examiner noted that due to her distractibility during the administration of the test, this score did not likely represent her full potential. During the administration of the Rorschach she would continually climb under the table to pick at lint and fuzz on the carpet, or hang off of her chair to play with wires under the table. She did not spontaneously give responses to the Rorschach cards placed in front of her, but rather required a prompt almost every time. She also spun many of the cards on the table, sending them flying to the ground. Terri's entire record is shown in Table 18.1.

Terri's record contains fourteen responses, two fewer than a typical girl of her age (Ames et al., 1974). When one compares her record to that of a typical child her age, it quickly becomes apparent that hers is impoverished. With the notable exception of shading, Terri used no other determinants on any of her responses. While typical eight-year-olds do not tend to use a large number of determinants other than form, one can expect to see at least a minimal range of determinants in their responses.

In addition, subtle yet significant differences from a normative sample were noted in Terri's performance on the chromatic and achromatic cards (Table 18.2). On the five color cards, every one of her responses used only form, and all were of poor form quality. In contrast, on the five achromatic cards, more than half of her responses were of good form quality. Further, of the four responses using texture, the three responses that occurred on color cards were all of poor form quality. In contrast, the one texture response that occurred on an achromatic card was of good form quality. Thus it seems that while Terri has adequate ability to perceptually organize a response when presented with achromatic stimuli, she is unable to organize a good form level response in the face of color.

TABLE 18.2 Terri's Performance on Achromatic vs. Chromatic Cards

Determinant	Achromatic Cards	Chromatic Cards
R	6	8
M	0	0
FM	0	0
m	0	0
FC+CF+C	0	0
FC'+CF'+C'	0	0
Texture	1	3
H+Hd+(H)+(Hd)	1	0
A+Ad+(A)+(Ad)	4	8

Note: achromatic cards are I, IV, V, VI, & VII; chromatic cards are II, III, VIII, IX & X.

This difference suggests that despite the fact that Terri did not use color in her responses, the presence of the color nonetheless had a significant impact on her performance. It seems she expended so much "intrapsychic capital" attempting to be organized in the face of the color stimuli that she appeared like a much less integrated child in her responses. Indeed, Terri reacted to the cards with marked cognitive rigidity and inflexibility, in the manner of a child four or five years old (Leichtman, 1996). After expending a great deal of energy on the first few cards, Terri struggled to elaborate upon or explain her responses. A close examination of some of her responses (see Table 18.3 for Terri's Rorschach) will help to flesh out this dynamic.

On Card I she gave the responses of a "cat," an "elephant" and a "ghost." Thus she began with a well-formed object, a cat, but she was then drawn to the white space and provided a poor form quality response for which she could not account, an elephant. She then tried to organize the entire percept in a single response, but she was only able to provide a vague, global response of "the face, the face, the face," which illustrates her less developmentally appropriate, uninterested responsiveness.

On Card II, she appeared to experience color shock, exclaiming, "Ugh! What's that?" After struggling to organize her first two responses, "bat" and "snake," she provided a shading response (a thought disordered furry fish), which seemed to suggest a marked inner disruptiveness. It is important to note that even though color is not explicitly mentioned by her, and thus is not reflected in the scoring of this card, Terri appeared to have had a strong reaction to this stimulus.

When given Card VI, a card which often elicits shading responses, Terri initially asked whether she was finished, perhaps in recognition of the unpleasant affect the shading was stirring up in her. Nonetheless, she provided two responses, a "lion" and a "head," although it is not clear from the Inquiry whether or not the head was part of the lion. She was clearly drawn to the shading, as she made reference to a "lion rug," but then became angry with the examiner and yelled that the

TABLE 18.3 Terri's Rorschach

I.

1. A cat
[Anything else?]

2. An elephant
[Anything else?]

3. Mm, it look like a ghost
[Anything else or is that it?] (No response)

II.
Ewe! What's that?

4. (Rotates card 360 degrees) Oo, this looks like a cat. The other one was a bat. (She goes under the table. We have an exchange where I ask her to sit up in her seat. She picks at things on the rug. She gets up again, holding a Lego piece.)
[Anything else?]

5. A fish

6. A bat
[Is that it?]

7. A snake

III.
8. Tiger [Hm-hm. Is that it?] (Nods)

IV.
I don't know what's this. (Turns card around)
9. It's a pig, a piggy, a piggy, I don't know what's that. I don't want to make a sentence about this one.

1. [Where do you see a cat?] Right here (points to the middle) no; right here (points to right corner). These things, the, the ears.
[What makes it look like a cat?] The ears.
[Take your finger and show me where you see the cat.] (She taps the card on the ear.) [Only this part or the whole thing?] The whole thing.

2. [Where do you see the elephant?] The face.
[Can you use your finger and show me?] These, these. The white things.
[What makes it look like an elephant?] The white things.

3. [Where do you see the ghost?] The face.
[What makes it look like a ghost?] The face, the face, the ears.

4. [Where do you see a cat?] Right here. [Can you use your finger and trace it for me?] (unclear what she's pointing to) [Is it the whole part or...] The whole part.
[What makes it look like a cat?] (She doesn't answer) [What makes it look like a cat?] The whole face. (She's sitting with her face covered in her arms on the table.)

5. [Where do you see a fish?] The bat eyes. [Where do you see the fish?] (She points to the bottom.) [Just this part?] And this, the fur (points to black section). [The fur of the fish?] (She agrees.)

6. (She may not have responded to this inquiry or we got side-tracked. She had shown me the bat eyes earlier.)

7. [Where do you see the snake?] Here in the middle (points to the white space).
[What makes it look like a snake?] Because his face.
[Where do you see the face?] Right here (points).

8. [Where do you see the tiger?] (Points) The whole thing, the face, and the eyes, and these are the gorillas. These are the monkeys.

TABLE 18.3 (*Cont.*)

V.

10. A bat.
    [Anything else?] (No response)

10. The wings. [What makes it look like?] (No response.)
    [Additional response:]
    A sword. [Where?] This part, the line.

VI.

Are we done? Aw, I want to be done now.

11. A lion. [Anything else?] A head. [Is that part of the lion or a different thing?] (She doesn't respond and has gone under the table. She doesn't want to come out.)

11. [Where do you see the lion?] (points to top D) This top part, this part.
    [What makes it look like a lion?] Yes. And it looks like a lion coat, wait and a lion rug.
    [What makes it look like a lion coat or rug?] Because the, (rubs card), the fur. [Where do you see the head?] (Points to top D). [What makes it look like?] It looks like a fur coat. [What makes it look like a head?] I said a fur! A fur coat b/c it's furry and a rug b/c it ahs fur.

VII.

I don't know what this one is! (Shrugs) What are you writing? (She puts her face down in her arms on the table.)

VIII.

12. A lion, no, not, not, not a lion. A, a, a, cheaper, cheetah (V).

12. The mouth. [Where?] This, the re—no, this. [What makes it look like?] B/c it has spots. [Where are the spots?] Here. (points)

IX.

13. What is that? Oo, I know, this is a zebra. (sings zebra, zebra, zebra) [Anything else?] (No response)

13. It has stripes. [Where?] (She gestures vaguely toward the card.) Right here. [Can you touch the picture and show me?] I don't know where the eyes, right here. There's the eyes.
    [What makes it look like?] Because it has stripes and strips with whit stripes, too, and it got some hair on the back. [Where is the hair?] Right here (unclear where she's pointing). And it has a tail with some hair on the tail.

X.

14. What is that? There it, this way. (V) It's a gorilla.

14. This is the hair and it's black and it eats bananas. [What makes it look like a gorilla?] Because gorillas sometimes they get mad, and sometimes they get a mad face and they're black and they stink and they like bananas. [(The examiner is wearing black)]

"fur" and the "fug rug" make it look like a fur coat. While shading responses are relatively common on this card (she rejected Card IV, another common shading response card), this shading response provokes rage at the examiner, a disrupted move outside the frame of her test responses. Notably, she then rejected Card VII (another card which often elicits shading responses), and put her head down on the table. On the last four cards, she provided two more shading responses, both of which are of poor form level.

Clearly, Terri was both drawn to and overwhelmed by the shading of the cards. This conflict appears so central that it precluded her access to other determinants (i.e., movement or color), which are often reflective of the possible wealth of internal resources a child can bring to bear on this test. It seems as if she was experiencing so much inner confusion that she could not help but be preoccupied by this tension. On achromatic cards she was successfully able to screen out inner dysphoria, while on the chromatic cards this strategy was less successful. Unfortunately, this left her with minimal access to other internal resources. In the absence of further investigation, including but not limited to psychotherapy, it is difficult to assess whether Terri has access to an untapped store of resources upon which to draw.

Case 2: Henry

Henry, a seven-year-old boy of Caribbean descent, met criteria for ADHD, Combined type and was found to have a Full Scale IQ of 94. At the time of the referral, Henry was exhibiting disruptive behavior at school that included kissing girls against their will and looking up their skirts. Henry's mother noted that his teacher described him as "very active and impulsive." His mother also described a pattern of disruptive behavior at home, unsolicitedly stating that Henry was "always on the go."

With one notable exception, Henry's overall Rorschach record (see Table 18.4) does not differ dramatically from that of a typical seven-year-old. He matches or approximates norms on most determinants, with the notable exception of inanimate movement (m).

However, upon closer inspection, Henry's Rorschach record also reveals a bimodal way of viewing and interacting with the world, which is particularly highlighted by the ways in which he dealt with color and blackness (see Table 18.5).

Five of Henry's total of twenty-three responses occurred on the five black cards, all of which were whole responses. On the black cards, all of his responses used only pure form, but his form quality on these cards was quite good (X+%$_{black}$ = 0.83). He did not represent animate interaction in any way, and rejected one of the cards (VII) altogether. In sum, on these five achromatic cards he provided a bland, deadened and constricted record. Yet, on the five color cards, Henry responded like a different child. He gave eighteen responses, only two of which were whole responses. He provided very few pure form responses, and his form quality on these cards is significantly lower (X+%$_{color}$ = 0.33), compared with the achromatic cards.

Two Case Studies of Children With ADHD **217**

TABLE 18.4 Henry's Entire Record

Determinant	Henry	Typical 7-year-old
R	23	18.3
M	1	1.4
FM	2	2.0
m	8	0.8
H+Hd+(H)+(Hd)	1	2.6
A+Ad+(A)+(Ad)	7	7.6
FC+CF+C	4	2.9
FC'+CF'+C'	1	1.1
Texture	0	0.5

Note: All Norms are derived from Ames et al. (1974).

TABLE 18.5 Henry's Performance on Achromatic vs. Chromatic Cards

Determinant	Achromatic Cards	Chromatic Cards
R	5	18
M	1	0
FM	0	2
m	0	8
H+Hd+(H)+(Hd)	1	0
A+Ad+(A)+(Ad)	4	3
FC+CF+C	0	4
FC'+CF'+C'	0	1
Texture	0	0

Note: achromatic cards are I, IV, V, VI, & VIII; chromatic cards are II, III, VIII.

While Henry's responses to the achromatic cards were sparse, his responses to the color cards were quite full and alive. In fact, the total number of words he used on the first all-color card with which he was presented (VIII) surpassed the total number of words he used on the previous four cards combined (Cards IV–VI, Card VII was rejected). His responses to the color cards contained an enormous amount of movement, especially inanimate movement (m), and CF responses. Although he provided six form-dominated responses, the remaining twelve responses were all of vague form level, a less developmentally advanced type of response, or as Mayman (1970) writes, "(the) cheapest form level available."

A disparity between achromatic and chromatic cards was also noted with regard to content. With one exception, the responses to achromatic cards contained very ordinary content: two bats and a butterfly. There is one response of "a human, inside" and one rejection, but those seem tame when compared to the content on the color cards: explosions, fire, volcanoes, lava, fiery chaos, speed, motion and electricity.

Thus, Henry's presentation was quite different, depending upon the type of stimuli presented to him. It is only when one compares the chromatic and achromatic cards that the full picture of his Rorschach comes to light. Although Henry attempted to rely on a strategy of simplifying the stimulus by focusing excessively on form when presented with achromatic cards, the stimulation of the color cards seemed to be too great for him, leading to a "fiery chaos" of inanimate movement and vague forms. It should be noted that an assessment of children like Henry, without regard to this chromatic vs. achromatic dichotomy, would lump all his responses together, thus failing to depict his markedly different responses, depending on the degree of bold color he must wrestle with on the RIM.

Henry's RIM protocol is shown in Table 18.6.

TABLE 18.6 Henry's Rorschach

I.

1. A Butterfly. [Anything else?]	1. [What makes it look like a butterfly?] (points) This (a) and these things (b). [What makes those things look like a butterfly?] The eyes and the feelers. [Show the therapist feelers.] Not feelers, the decoration; these are the eyes, the little hands poking up, these are the decorations.
2. A bat, that's all. [Anything else?] No.	2. [What makes it look like bat?] It has these for the wings, and these things (b) up there, and this (a). [What makes these things look like a bat?] I don't know what that is but it looks like a bat with those. [That (a)?] The feet.

II.

3. Explosion.	3. [What makes it look like explosion?] (points to top and bottom D). [Explosion?] This happens, poom! (top D exploding) and this thing that's littler (bottom D) goes like that (motions lava coming out). This thing is from far distance you can see these, so from close distance it's big like that. [?] When this thing goes it's little from far distance (bottom D) but you can see this (top D) from close distance.
4. Volcano lava…I don't know any more.	4. [What makes it look like volcano lava?] (points to everything) [Volcano lava?] Because the volcano lava has this (bottom D and this thing breaks sometimes through that (top D) [?] This is the lava (the red under the black D) and this thing breaks (black D) and looks just like that (red coming out looks like top D), like you see its there and it's breaking on the side. [Breaking as if?] It has this (red) inside of it, and you can see its poking out, because you made it just like what I wanted. [?] Yeah, I know I was gonna see something like that.

TABLE 18.6 (*Cont.*)

III.

5. That one looks like a bug, cause look it has a bow, a bow on it, and these are the eyes, the feelers, and these things are the back of it.

5. [What makes it look like bug?] The eyes, the mouth, the back of it, that leads to the...foot, the feelers. How many more do he and the therapist have to do? Do he and the therapist have to do all of these, how about one more?

IV.

6. This one looks like a bat too, upside down.

6. Cause it has this...are the ears, the head, the little eyes, look the little eyes, the wing, and the legs upside down, and this is the bottom.

V.

7. Bat again.

7. It looks like a bat because of the legs, the ears, and the wings, and this is the little hands. Why do so many look like a bat?

VI.

8. I don't know what that looks like...a human being, inside.

8. Cause of the hands, the head, and...I don't know, this, the hand, the feet. [Human being inside?] Just this (center D). [What about it makes it look inside?] I don't know.

VII.

9. I don't know what that is. [Take you time, it's hard sometimes but I think you'll see something.] I don't see nothing...(15 sec) I don't see nothing. [Nothing?] No.

VIII.

10. A picture, cause of the colors, colors of a picture.

10. [What makes it look like picture?] The colors, and this little line, and that's it. [Lines?] These lines and the shape. [Show the therapist the shape] (points around perimeter) The shapes...this one looks like a cat, and this, I don't know what that looks like, but this looks like a spaceship lighting off the back of it going up, that's it. [Back of it going up?] Back of it, no, this is the spaceship, but the back has the fire, this is the fire. No, this whole thing is a spaceship, this is the front, this is the back, this is space animals, space cats, and this is the fire, this is the back of a thing, and this is the front. This is the missiles. [What makes it look like space cats?] No I just say space cats, they're not space cats, but I say it because I don't know what, I just put something there. [Going up?] The space things are climbing up the ship. [As if?] To...cause they're the enemies from the sky and he's gonna be brave and take out the missiles so they can shoot it. This is the missile. [What makes it look like fire?] That this goes down and this is smoke. [What makes it look like smoke?] This is the fire, this is the smoke going up, it's kinda grayish.

(*continued*)

TABLE 18.6 (*Cont.*)

IX.	
11. No. [Take you time, I know it's hard.] Dragonfly.	11. This is the speed that's pushing the air out. This is the fire that's behind it because he's going fast, cause he's going super fast, and this is the dragon in the middle, this is the wings. [Super fast as if?] It was a rocket. [What makes it look like fire?] Cause it's yellow, no orange. [Speed?] It's pushing the speed. [What makes it look like speed?] Cause you see how fast he's going? This is him, and this is where he's, the air is coming, this drops of water cause he's going fast and he's sweating, and this is the air cause, to show how fast he's going. [Sweating?] (points) [What makes it look like water?] It's little.
X.	
12. It's an electro-clip. [?] An electro-clip.	12. Cause it's got this (points to large D) and this is the clipper (top D). [What's an electro-clip?] You know when you put those electro-clips in the car (jumper cable clips)? Or if it's a toy one, you know Operation, the toy where you put the batteries in and then you pick up those little pieces? [Yes. Show the therapist again now.] This opens, and this you squeeze to go like this (imitates squeezing handles) and this whole thing is a clip, but leave this out (side D). This closes, this is the opening thing, and then this is the the thing that's like this (motions) and this has a line going across like that (center D) [?] So when it's apart, to keep it together, not to fall apart. And this things, this, looks like screws, and that's it. [Squeeze as if?] To, pretend this is what you are squeezing this, like if your taking a splinter out, that's sort of it.

On Card I, Henry began with the responses of "butterfly" and "bat," each a pure form response. However, when the examiner presented him with Card II, with the first hints of color, he responded with "explosion" and "volcano lava." When the examiner inquired about these responses, Henry provided a flood of color, unbound by form. Clearly Henry was overstimulated by this card and he reacted to it accordingly. Unable to find the words to describe his reaction, he turned to action language ("poom!"). His shift from an explosion to the slower-moving "lava" seemed to be an attempt on his part to slow down the speed with which he was experiencing the percepts (although the inanimate movement was clearly still present), and to retreat somewhat by invoking distance. Whatever anxiety and/or affect had been stimulated by the color in this card seemed to be breaking through, just like the lava; his language deteriorated, his capacity to self-modulate nearly vanished and he perseverated from the explosion to the lava. The experience of seeing the color rendered him passive (Schachtel, 1966/2001) in that he was unable to actively impose good form on the percept.

On Card III, Henry "recovered" by successfully avoiding the color stimuli, resulting in responses that were bland and simple. This suggests that on the RIM, just as in his everyday life, there may be moments when he can avoid affective dysregulation by screening out stimuli that threaten to overwhelm him. With the absence of bold color on the following four cards, Henry provided relatively sparse responses to this sequence, registering only 109 words on these four cards, including a rejection of Card VII. Thus, judging from the responses on the five achromatic cards, we are left with little sense of Henry's potential resources. He does not appear to be able to access achromatic color, movement, or shading, leaving the impression that his world is quite deadened. There is no mention of human connection or affect.

On Card VIII, Henry again seemed to become derailed by the vivid color in the stimulus. He provided the vague, formless response of "a picture," and when inquired about this, he again became overwhelmed by his associations. Although he initially attempted to employ the same strategy used on Card III, in which he avoided engaging color by providing a vague response (here, "a picture"), as the Inquiry progressed, his associations became more idiosyncratic. A popular response, the "cats," deteriorated into a vague, achromatic color-dominated response, with "smoke" and "fire coming out of a spaceship." Further, the benign cats became "space cats" that "take out the missiles so they can shoot it." This response illustrates his internal process quite well; although he has the internal resources to form an accurate percept (the commonly seen cats), he nevertheless became overstimulated by the color stimulus and then projected his feelings of attack onto the cats, so that his benign percept then became malevolent.

On Card IX, he provided the response of "dragonfly," which upon Inquiry is understood to be a thought-disordered, contamination response of a dragon and a fly co-existing in the same space on the blot. However, Henry finally achieved some integration of his two modes of response on Card X, which he saw as an "electro-clip," such as a jumper cable that one uses to charge a stalled car battery. On the Inquiry, he provided a vivid reflection of what he must do in the world to contain his affect and anxiety; he tries to screen out potentially overwhelming stimuli by clamping down his electro-clip "to keep it together, not to fall apart." This method of coping with overstimulation has been partially successful for Henry, but it also bespeaks the degree to which he must exert energy to hold this dysphoric stimulation and bodily discomfort at bay. Further, this strategy of screening out potentially overwhelming stimuli pinches off his access to internal resources in general and to human percepts in particular. In this case, an analysis of the sequential and chromatic/achromatic response patterns better allows one to understand Henry's difficulties in the context of unconscious conflict and defense against uncomfortable affect than a simple tallying of response categories.

Note

1 Copyright 2007, Taylor & Francis, Inc. Reproduced with permission.

19
BRIEFER VIGNETTES LINKING MOA SCALE SCORES TO CHILD TREATMENT

Primary paper: Tuber, S. (1989). Assessment of children's object representations with the Rorschach. *Bulletin of the Menninger Clinic,* 53, 432–441.[1]

The following paper links six children's MOA scores to vicissitudes in their treatment. These are all cases where I was the therapist and had received access to the patient's RIM protocols from their various testers. I put them here at the end of this section to highlight that the RIM and the MOA are not seen primarily as avenues for either nomothetic and/ or idiographic research, but rather are viewed as equally relevant to clinical practice. I am a strong advocate for using projective test material as a means of homing in on the central themes and organizational styles of children in treatment and am most fortunate to teach in a clinical milieu (the doctoral program in clinical psychology at the City College of New York) where this linkage of projective test assessment and ongoing long-term treatment is valued.

Psychological testing now comprises a number of methods for translating object relations theory into clinically useful and empirically tested concepts (Lerner, 1986). About 20 years ago, Mayman (1967) focused the psychological test literature on object-representations—the mental images we create that reflect early experiences with significant others—with his paper on an object-relational approach to psychological testing and to the Rorschach in particular. Beginning his article with a lucid depiction of the projective hypothesis underlying projective testing, Mayman linked the hypothesis to the patient's presentation of an inner representational world:

> When a person is asked to spend an hour immersing himself in a field of impressions where amorphousness prevails and where strange or even alien

forms may appear, he will set in motion a reparative process the aim of which is to replace formlessness with reminders of the palpably real world. He primes himself to recall, recapture, reconstitute his world as he knows it, with people, animals and things which fit most naturally into the ingrained expectancies around which he has learned to structure his phenomenal world ... An examination of Rorschach content from this point of view aims at answers to such questions as, What kind of world does each person recreate for himself in the ink-blot milieu? What kinds of animate and inanimate objects come most readily to mind? What manner of people and things is he prone to surround himself with?

(Mayman, 1967, p.17)

This viewpoint refocuses the projective hypothesis onto the world of interpersonal interaction. It states that what we have experienced in our early relationships with parents, siblings, and other family members becomes "metabolized" and forms the basis of our expectations of future encounters with other people. It also suggests that the study of the thematic content produced by the reparative process that Mayman described can help ascertain the nature of these metabolized experiences. Two of Mayman's students, Hatcher and Krohn (1980), have added to this point, helping define what is meant by object-representations and why it is important to assess them:

During development, especially the development of the ego by means of its relationship with others during the first five years of life, there develop a set of internal structures that reflect the individual's early experience of important others, structures that we may very roughly call mental images of people. These structures filter, select, and organize the experience of other people and the actions, thoughts, and feelings of the self. Thus an individual's experience of others will only be as differentiated or varied as are the internal representations with which he can match them up. He will perceive and encode only what he has the mental representational "language" to encode and will not perceive what he lacks the language to psychologically understand ... The basic object representations determine the limits of his experience of others.

(Hatcher and Krohn, 1980, pp. 229–300)

The Mutuality of Autonomy Scale

The Mutuality of Autonomy (MOA) scale (Urist, 1977) can be used with Rorschach testing to elucidate a child's inner template of object-representations. This method can provide a useful intergroup measure of children's interpersonal interactions and can also be used in the clinical assessment of individual children.

Diagnosis, Psychotherapy, and the Mutuality of Autonomy Scale

The heuristic value of the MOA in child research suggested that an assessment of its clinical utility for children in treatment was warranted. In the following six case examples, each child's clinical diagnosis and Rorschach MOA scores will be compared. In the first three examples, the object-relational paradigms each child presents will be apparent. The Rorschach MOA testing preceded treatment; therefore the redundancy between the vignettes and MOA data for the first three cases suggests the degree to which Rorschach MOA scores may correlate with later treatment experiences. The fourth case example is presented for cautionary purposes: The MOA scores for that child failed to provide significant understanding of the treatment process and emphasized the need to retain clinical judgment with use of the MOA scale.

Case Example 1

David was 8 years old and in residential treatment when he was tested. Four of his Rorschach responses were scoreable on the MOA scale. One response was "a human chest that's been stabbed twice" to the upper red areas of Card III (a score of 6). David's next scoreable response was "a face with oil oozing down to melt it" to the pink and center areas on Card IX (also a score of 6). His next scoreable response was "a mean face." When asked why it was "mean," he replied "Someone did something bad to him and he wants to get them back" (Card I, score of 5). David's last scoreable MOA response was "a tiger looking at himself in the water" (Card VII, score of 4).

For David, Rorschach interaction is usually perceived as malevolent, hurtful, and toxic. Deadly forces are an all-too-available inner experience. His history of horrific physical abuse from his mother, which occurred episodically throughout the first 4½ years of his life, makes his first three Rorschach responses easily understood. The following therapeutic vignette, 3 months into his twice-weekly treatment, deals with David's fourth response, a reflected tiger:

> David came to the session sullenly, angry over an incident on the playground in which he was kicked out of a game for harassing a peer. He didn't look at me. He walked over to the sandbox and looked out the window at the playground, haphazardly spilling sand out of the box. I was tempted to set a limit regarding the amount of sand thrown, but I noticed forlorn look in his eyes that stopped me momentarily. "It hurts when they feel so mean to you," I said. He said nothing, but turned and looked into the sandbox, letting the sand sift through his fingers. "Do this," he said, and I began to copy

> his movements, running my fingers through the sand. We did this silently together for a long time. He could begin to tell me in a much calmer tone what happened during the game.

In this vignette, David's fury was mixed with upset and isolation; he was forced to remove himself from one of the few activities—sports—in which he felt good about himself. It is significant that my comment about this hurt elicited a request that I copy his behavior—a reflecting, mirroring experience much like that of this "reflected tiger" Rorschach response. It was as if my empathy allowed him to respond with his highest mode of object relating, a desire for a parallel, mirroring validation of himself. Importantly, David could not go beyond that level of relating during that session. His ensuing depiction of the game was notably one-sided and was filled with expectations of malevolence much like his first three Rorschach responses described above. His best and his worst object-representations in this session were therefore paralleled in his Rorschach performance.

Case Example 2

Mary was almost 9 at the time of assessment. Her parents were in the midst of an acrimonious, even vicious, divorce, with continual cross-accusations of child neglect, adulterous affairs, and hiding the funds; a hotly contested custodial battle loomed on the horizon. However, both parents were able to describe responsive, caring parenting of the child during her first 4 years, with marked deterioration since then. Poor school performance, sadness, and distractibility were her presenting symptoms.

Mary had six MOA responses. Three responses were scored 1: "kids playing with each other" (Card I), "seals bouncing balls on their noses and passing them to each other" (Card II), and "two ladies chatting with each other" (Card VII). Her other three responses were scored 3: "two women holding up a dolly" (Card I), "two people holding on to big shoes" (Card III), and "two trees leaning on each other" (Card IV).

These responses revealed a youngster who had indeed internalized benign, autonomous, and mutual experiences of interpersonal relating. She was also preoccupied with relationships in which the need to "hold on" had become a major currency of interaction.

During her second session following assessment, Mary asked for a piece of paper and markers. She drew a rainbow with the last arc colored black. Hanging from the black band was a little girl, also in black, who hovered over a funnel-shaped black cloud. She then wrote the word "ouch" (spelled "awch") at the top of her drawing. She told me this was a little girl trying to hold on to the good part of her rainbow, but she slipped, said ouch, and was falling into a black hole. She later described the black hole as a "sad place."

Here both Mary's remarkable capacity to symbolize her experience and the meaning of "holding on" were strikingly portrayed, and again paralleled her Rorschach responses. The degree to which earlier positive representations had become "blackened" by the upheaval in her home and her desire to "hold on" to avoid sadness and loss were especially poignant.

Case Example 3

Ben was 6 when he was referred for psychological assessment. He had been deemed intellectually gifted in his first-grade school evaluation, but he was remarkably distracted and "lost in space." His mother reported that he was preoccupied with superhero figures and outer space creatures, yet both she and Ben's teacher noted his gentleness and compassion for peers, animals, and "unfortunate adults."

Ben's object-representation scores were notable for their juxtaposition of benign, autonomous percepts with savagely malevolent ones. Three of his five scoreable responses reflected high levels of mutuality and reciprocity. His first scoreable response was: "Three people dancing, two are in Russian hats on the side, and they are happily twirling a belly dancer in the middle who likes it too" (score of 1 on Card I). Next: "Two creatures slapping each other high fives after a good shot in a space ball game" (score of 1 on Card II). And then: "Two Indians having a conversation, sitting on two chairs" (score of 1 on Card VII). In contrast were these two responses, each scored 6: "A bag being torn apart by two people" (Card III) and "a person's face, all cut up and bloodied" (Card X).

In a play session several months into treatment, Ben was describing the heroic adventures of a superhero who fearlessly strove to do good things for others. Ben jumped violently when he heard a loud noise in the waiting room. He yelled, "Is something happening to my mom?" and went to take a look. Quieted by finding her unharmed, he returned to the playroom, but the play now shifted to the use of "Fisher Price" people. The boy figure was about to go to bed when Ben stopped and looked distractedly at the wall. "You've gone somewhere else?" I asked. He said nothing. I noted his worry that maybe his mother still wasn't safe. He then told me of his worry that the walls in the waiting room had crashed, crushing his mother. I asked him to tell me what else he had been thinking about. He sadly noted that not even a superhero could save her then. I spoke about how his wish to be a superhero was something he hoped would stop terribly dangerous things from happening. He corrected me by saying, "I try to be a superhero to stop my dangerous feelings from coming out. They're bound to hurt everyone, and I don't want them to."

Ben's attention difficulties in school were an understandable consequence of his creation of a benevolent superhero persona to ward off his malevolent fantasy. The depiction of his malevolent fantasies as unwanted feelings and his capacity to keep them separate from his gentle and altruistic behavior paralleled the dichotomy of benign versus malevolent object-representations in his Rorschach protocol. Also striking was how his adaptive responses on the Rorschach all involved foreign beings in some way (Russians, creatures, Indians, or belly dancers), while the malevolent responses were decidedly human. It appeared that only when distanced in this manner could such benign responses be kept safe and viable. This, in turn, may have paralleled Ben's need for perpetual niceness to others, for as long as he acted nice, aggressive fantasy was kept at bay.

Case Example 4

Martha was about 13 when she was referred to treatment by her school guidance counselor. Although problems in math were initially cited as the reason for Martha's referral, both her parents and her guidance counselor were actually concerned that Martha was too easily dominated and led by her peers, and that she was preoccupied with being popular while convinced that she was not. Martha's Rorschach protocol was noteworthy for its uniformity. She had 10 MOA responses, all of which similar examples of parallel activity in which two figures performed, oblivious to one another (score 2). During the testing, I had a passing feeling of wariness; I suspected that Martha was defending against a quality of response that was more boundary-compromised or even malevolent. I recommended once-weekly treatment to help Martha with her low self-esteem, thinking that more intensive treatment would be too burdensome to her capacity to safeguard her sense of cohesiveness. After four sessions of what I perceived as "supportive" discussions regarding the nature of her friendships and her upset over their pressured, cliquish quality, I received a call from Martha's mother. Martha had decided that she did not want to come to therapy anymore. During the phone conversation, her mother told me that Martha had not wanted her to tell me, but, although I was "nice," I asked too many "weird" questions; that is, I asked too much about what she and her friends were feeling, questions that made no sense to her. Martha refused to return for a closing session.

In Martha's case, I had assumed despite "gut" feelings to the contrary, that her capacity for parallel relatedness implied some degree of awareness or even acceptance of having feelings that were different and separate from others. In fact, her parallel Rorschach object-representations were not truly separate yet mutual representations; instead, her repetitive, bland depictions of interaction may have helped her ward off more dangerous representations of self and others.

Case Vignette 5

Samantha was an 8-year-old girl who, despite her "gifted" intellectual endowment, was reluctantly brought to treatment by her parents after not being promoted. She was described in school as constantly demanding and brassy with both teachers and peers, willing to do only the work she wished to do and refusing to follow class directions. Her parents initially focused on her great intellectual endowment and aesthetic sensibility. They did note with some apprehension her limited ability to be alone, which manifested itself both in her inordinate need to talk to them constantly throughout the day and in her great difficulty in falling asleep by herself at night.

Samantha had five scoreable MOA responses, all of them scored as either a 3 or 4: "two trees leaning together" on Card IV, "a lot of rocks about to tumble over" to Card VII, "a woman with a cape staring at herself in the mirror" to Card I, "a tug boat and its reflection in the ocean" to Card VI, and "a tiger looking at itself in a beautiful lake" to Card VIII.

These MOA responses all are striking in their lack of cohesion and autonomy. The preoccupation with reflection responses and the inability to "stand on one's own feet" speak to an inner vulnerability that gives her reflection responses a self-soothing quality, and her leaning, imbalanced responses a feeling of firmer neediness and fragility. The following vignette occurred 9 months into a twice weekly treatment.

> Samantha and I had been "playing school" for approximately 25 min. She was the teacher and I was the class, with the teacher giving very specific instructions that all the students needed to obey precisely. A small plastic stroller belonging to one of the toy figures had fallen on the floor near her foot earlier in the session, and she characteristically paid no attention to it. I soon heard a snap as she inadvertently stepped on the stroller, but she continued to play oblivious to the toy. I wondered aloud several minutes later about what that snapping noise was. She quickly and haughtedly said that she had noticed that broken stroller before and wondered aloud why didn't I fix things in the room. I spoke of how her telling me of my not fixing things was much safer than wondering about what might happen if she was the one who couldn't fix something. She then worriedly asked me if she would have to stop our "copying games" because she broke the toy. My addressing her fear that she might evoke my anger and hence my getting rid of her, led her to suggest, toward the end of the session, that perhaps the teacher would let the kids in the class "have time for themselves" some time soon.

Samantha's tottering, leaning, and reflection Rorschach responses depict the same fragile sense of self depicted in this therapy vignette. Her school performance and poor tolerance of being alone were overt behavioral manifestations of her "disorder of continuity" (Goldberg, 1990). The therapy vignette provides a parallel to both her MOA responses and her behavior at home and at school. Her shift to haughty critique following her being made aware of the broken toy flimsily disguised her great fear of dismissal and rejection. Speaking to her fear of being dismissed and reassuring her of our continuity led to her first, tentative "opening of the door" to a possible non-reflective, more autonomous interaction.

Case Vignette 6

Tom was a 7½-year-old youngster who came to treatment 6 months after witnessing the death of his 5-year-old sister. He and his sister were playing catch on the street in front of their house when a car turned the corner, went out of control, came up on the sidewalk, and fatally crushed his sister within 25 feet of Tom. Presenting symptoms were aggressiveness in school and provocative behavior with parents and friends (negativism and oppositional behavior).

Tom had four MOA scale responses, all of which were scored as a 6. The responses were: "a bat that crashed into a branch and the branch went right through it (the white open areas are where the branch went through)" to Card I; "a spider, he's got blood on his chest, he beat a monster up and got blood on him" to Card III; "a monster with those two things that grab, it's going to kill something" to Card V; and "a wolf smashed with its head sticking out of its skin, maybe something slit it open or a big boulder fell right on it and it got smashed" to Card VI.

Tom's exclusive focus on body damaging, attacking interaction and the striking congruence between his pierced, smashed percepts and his witnessing of his sister's death clearly suggest his still-acute re-experiencing of the traumatic event. Equally notable is the victim–victimizer dichotomy: the crushed, impaled, or mutilated perceptions alternating with equally aggressive interactions in which a murderous monster damages others. Two months into a three-times-per-week treatment, the following vignette occurred.

> With increasing delight at his performance, Tom was tracing the cover of a magazine that he had found in the waiting room. As it was nearing completion, he offered to give it to me and then decided to glue a separate sheet of paper underneath his drawing, to "give it more strength." The gluing went well until the two pieces of paper had to be stuck to one another. Three different times Tom tried to place the papers in perfect overlap with one another, and three times the fit was not exact, necessitating his pulling the papers apart. Suddenly a piece of his drawing tore slightly. He screamed, completely tore up the picture that he had so laboriously worked on, and yelled "It's all ruined. It's all ruined." He then immediately went over to a basket of small cars on a nearby shelf and began talking excitedly of his wish to be a race car driver and being able to "go 200 miles an hour without being touched."

In this vignette, the "proof" of Tom's prowess and particularly his capacity to strengthen and protect this prowess was damaged, ruining his "gift" to me and evoking the themes of damage and mutilation described in his MOA percepts. Interestingly, his response to the very minor damage to the drawing was to become the destroyer of the work and then the counterphobic race car driver – the understandable but striking counterbalance to being the helpless witness to a fatal car accident. His shift from identification with the damaged drawing to the untouchable racecar driver parallels his victim–victimizer MOA responses.

In keeping both with object relations theory and with the projective hypothesis underlying Rorschach testing, I have shown that Rorschach testing can be used to assess the quality of internalized object-representations and that those object-representations also need to be understood in the context of defense configurations, quality of thought organization, level of affect development, and other salient personality indices. Nevertheless, the usefulness of the MOA scale supports the time-honored axiom that enhanced diagnosis yields more informed treatment.

Note

1 Copyright 1989, Guilford Press. Reproduced with permission.

SECTION SIX
More Recent Research, Including Future Possibilities

20
ONGOING RESEARCH LINKING THE RORSCHACH TASK WITH CLINICAL WORK WITH CHILDREN

In recent years, I've gone back to nomothetic, empirical studies to further my thinking about the ways in which different methodologies may enhance our clinical and conceptual thinking. One avenue of research has been to attempt to extend the MOA scale to the TAT. My student and now colleague Katherine Eiges and I (2016) developed a manual for extending the MOA to the TAT and then conducted a study to begin to assess the reliaibility and validity of the new application of the measure. Three modifications to the MOA scale as used on the RIM were made:

1. For MOA scale point 4, the definition or stability of one character necessarily requires the other because it is merely an extension or reflection of the self. Some degree of fusion or lack of self–other differentiation is central. Characters are described as mirror-objects or are ascribed the exact same thoughts, feelings, and behaviors ... Individual experiences of the characters are merged in a way that diminishes their respective sense of individuality.
2. For scale points 5 and 6, we added themes of loss and abandonment, which reflect some degree of relational imbalance and distress, as another dimension to be used in the scoring.
3. Because the TAT is inherently about person(s) in interaction, a response that has no interactions at all is considered to be more concerning than a "no score" on the RIM. We thererefore added a scale point 8 to the MOA-TAT to be used for any response that was not scoreable on any of the other seven scale points.

Using these modifications, Eiges studied 47 children culled from a previously existing data set of children identified as at-risk for ADHD and/or language impairments with both the RIM (MOA) scale and the adapted version for the TAT (MOA-TAT). Pearson correlation analyses were used to examine the convergence between the MOA and MOA-TAT scales and she found preliminary support for the MOA-TAT scale as a reliable and valid measure of object representation. Inter-rater agreement for the MOA-TAT was excellent (ICC = .86), and significant convergence was revealed between the two scales. The MOA-TAT, however, evidenced a more adaptive object representation distribution and higher frequency of responses than the MOA scale. The finding that there were more plentiful MOA-TAT scores than RIM MOA scores makes intuitive sense given the inherently relational nature of the TAT cards, and with more data points to score, it makes sense to use the MOA-TAT scale in future work. The finding that the MOA-TAT scores were on the more adaptive end of the scale compared to the RIM is intriguing and also suggests further study.

A second student and now colleague of mine, Lily Thom (2016), followed up on Eiges' work with the MOA-TAT. Thom extended Eiges' work by assessing the degree of relationship between the MOA-TAT and Cramer's defense mechanism scale (Cramer & Kelly, 2004), an often-used TAT measure. Using the same data set as Eiges, she sought to provide further construct validity by assessing the degree to which more adaptive object relations would be correlated with more adaptive defense mechanisms. The findings showed several expected, significant relationships between level of defense and object relations that confirmed her study's hypotheses. Children who used the most mature defense of identification also showed more adaptive object relations. Use of denial, the most primitive defense on the Cramer measure, was negatively correlated with both maladaptive and adaptive object relations. Use of projection was most strongly correlated with the most disturbed object relations. The research constitutes a further, but still early stage of psychometric validation for the MOA as adapted for use with the TAT. The finding that it was projection and not denial that was associated with more disturbed object relations on the MOA-TAT is quite interesting to me. Because the TAT cards are in fact pictures with intrinsically morbid content, it may very well be that denial is a more adaptive means of coping with such adverse stimuli than projection may be. We can argue that in the face of such stimuli, negating its existence may be a more useful means of maintaining one's emotional equilibrium, whereas projection may keep the adverse feelings in play and cause more felt disruption.

A third student and now colleague, Juliana Martinez, took the study of the MOA-TAT (2016) in a fascinating direction. She reviewed the literature on a particular aspect of Latina culture in which Latinas are culturally expected to be "dutiful daughters," establishing strong attachments and adhering to the traditional values characterized by loyalty, cooperation, respect and interdependence within family members. Conventional Latina mother–daughter bonds, therefore, are expected to be exceptionally close. While healthy mother–daughter closeness can be a valuable source of support, closeness without differentiation from the mother may result in a lack of independence and poor interpersonal and personal growth. Attempting to assess the adaptiveness of such dutiful daughters, Martinez used the MOA-TAT measure and correlated it with self-report measures. In a sample of thirty college-aged Latinas, mother–daughter closeness was determined using the Mother–Adult Daughter Questionnaire (MAD) and the degree of dutifulness was established using the Latina Values Scale (LVS). Included in the LVS was a conflict scale, which measured the respondents' conflict with the traditional values they endorsed. Pearson correlation analyses were used to examine the relationships between the study variables. Participants with MOA scores reflecting more adaptive object relations also exhibited a greater degree of connection with their mothers as well as a lower degree of conflict with the traditional values they endorsed. Furthermore, a disproportionally high number of MOA Level 3 scores throughout the sample indicated a response style favoring a dependent relationship in which the maintenance of self is highly related to sustenance from another person. Given the highly adaptive nature of the sample, Martinez' study suggested that traditional values favoring interdependency over autonomy may be culturally mediated and should not be pathologized.

Future Research Possibilities

The useful findings regarding the construct validity and reliability of the MOA-TAT measure, coupled with the ongoing value of hundreds of studies using the MOA scale with the RIM, has been heartening personally, given the emphasis I have placed on the heuristic value of the study of object representations as an implicit measure of object relations in personality appraisal. The utility of these measures in both nomothetic and idiographic studies suggested a new direction that I have begun to explore, that of using object relations assessments at the start of treatment as a predictor variable in child psychotherapy.

The doctoral program in clinical psychology at City College where I've taught for over 30 years has its own clinic, The Psychological Center, where students provide psychodynamically informed psychotherapy on a once or twice weekly basis to a variety of patients typically under-represented in both treatment and research. A colleague of mine, Sasha Rudenstine, has, over the past three years, created a formidable psychotherapy outcome research project that follows child patients throughout their treatment. The laboratory component of the research project is called the INTERSECT Lab and I present below a brief description by Dr. Rudenstine of her project to provide a context for where my future research activities will take place.

The INTERSECT Lab is a clinical and epidemiological research program that examines the intersection of trajectories of well-being and the urban functioning poor. What are extraordinary events for many individuals are daily experiences in the lives of this population. And yet, while such stressors may become commonplace, they affect daily functioning and arguably long-term health outcomes. The INTERSECT Lab adopts a multi-level approach and ecological framework to understanding the cumulative effect of these chronic and yet quotidian experiences on well-being. We aim to examine and reassess frequently used terms such as trauma, health, family systems, and poverty to reflect the experiences that are relevant and specific to an urban marginalized population with the aim of promoting appropriate and targeted interventions and policies. In this vein, we are redefining "extraordinary" life course phenomena.

The INTERSECT Lab aims to examine three distinct dimensions of health as well as points of intersection:

1. Well-Being Among Marginalized Urban Populations

Using socioeconomic status and geographic location, we aim to determine what percent of the US population meets criteria for 'marginalized urban'. Additionally, we will identify those experiences that are unique to this population and which affect short- and long-term health outcomes. These explorations will inform interventions and policies that can improve health outcomes for marginalized urban populations.

2. Daily Stressors Over the Life Course

An abundance of research examines the long-term outcomes of trauma on well-being. However, less attention has been given to understanding the role of daily stressors on everyday functioning or long-term health. Within urban settings, such experiences are significantly more unique for marginalized populations. Our Lab explores the effect of such experiences on psychological health in a clinical care setting as well as at a population level.

3. Clinical Care: Access to, Utilization, and Long-Term Outcomes

Urban marginalized populations have access to disproportionally fewer mental health services and are less likely to receive care than non-Hispanic White Americans despite having similar rates of mental disorders. Similarly, due to the scarcity of resources, few urban community-based mental health clinics measure trajectories of clinical care or treatment outcomes. The INTERSECT Lab launched the Psychotherapy Evaluation and Clinical Effectiveness (PEACE)

Ongoing Research **239**

> and Child Health and Psychotherapy (CHAP) Programs to study (1) the individual-level factors that mediate treatment outcomes among patients of an urban community-based setting, (2) the effectiveness of psychodynamic individual therapy on a number of patient outcomes throughout the course of one's treatment, and (3) the role of stigma (individual and institutional) on the utilization and retention of psychological services among an urban marginalized population.

My future research will focus on the clinical care component of Rudenstine's research and, more specifically, the individual-level factors that influence outcome and the role of treatment in outcome. Each child entering our Psychological Center is given a number of self-report measures, their parents fill out a variety of measures and they are given the RIM and TAT. At six-month intervals over the course of treatment, caregivers self-report their levels of family stress, trauma incidence and changes in their child's behavior. Children provide self-reports on measures of self-esteem, anxiety, attention issues and traumatic incidents. Therapists report their goals for the child and how they are being met over time.

This omnibus study provides a potential wealth for linking projective test assessments with issues of psychotherapy outcome. Each of the three sets of assessments (patient, therapist and caregiver) can be intriguingly linked to the projective test assessments of the children.

For the caregiver, changes in how they assess their children's behavior over time can be linked to a baseline assessment of their child's object relations. Does improvement over time as measured by the caregiver correlate with better child object relations at intake? Is the RIM MOA measure more or less useful in these correlations than the MOA-TAT? Is there a relationship between familial stress and/or traumatic incidence and projective method performance? Do these measures of the caregivers show more robust correlations with object relational assessments at intake or at later points in the treatment? Are the relationships among the variables linear or curvilinear?

For the assessments by the children of their own functioning, how does a self-esteem measure link to projective-based assessments? Does self-awareness as measured by their acknowledgement of anxiety, sadness or attention issues correlate meaningfully with our implicit measures of object relations? What role does the child's explicit discussion of trauma have on their projective assessment? How do measures of the child's functioning at Time One on the projective-based measures link to both present-day and later self-reports?

And, last, for the therapist, what is the relationship between their assessment of the treatment process and the measures of object relations? Is the meeting of treatment goals related meaningfully to the quality of object relations assessed at the time treatment begins?

One final area that has yet to be put into place is whether we can establish annual testing of any child patients who stay in treatment for over one year. Much as Blatt et al. (1988) did in their study of adult patients over time from the Austen Riggs Center, the opportunity to look at and compare changes in treatment with changes in object representations on projective tests over time would be a major advance in validating the usefulness of object relational assessment.

Coda

I have been most fortunate to have had multiple opportunities across a variety of nomothetic and idiographic efforts to explore how the internalization of interactions with significant others creates a unique sense of self for all of us. It has been a passion of mine since early graduate school, and, of course, well before that into my early childhood in ways I didn't then have the words to think about. I am deeply indebted to my professorship at City College for providing me with the means to study these issues and to my colleagues and students over the years who have shared my passions in this arena. It has been extremely gratifying to have the opportunity to teach what I have learned about and from projective methods all these years. It has also been deeply meaningful for me to have had the chance to apply what I've learned from research, teaching and clinical practice in reciprocal, dialectic ways so that each domain has informed and continues to inform the other two. It has made me a better clinician, a better teacher and a better researcher, and through these interactions I have had the ultimate blessing: a professional life of utility and meaning.

REFERENCES

Aber, J. L., & Allen, J. P. (1987). Effects of maltreatment on young children's socioemotional development: An attachment theory perspective. *Developmental Psychology*, 23, 406–414.
Achenbach, T., & Edelbrock, C. (1983). *Manual for the Child Behavior Checklist and Revised Child Behavior Profile*. Burlington, VT: University of Vermont, Department of Psychiatry.
Ackerman, S. J., Clemence, A. J., Weatherill, R., & Hilsenroth, M. J. (1999). Use of the TAT in the assessment of DSM IV Cluster B personality disorders. *Journal of Personality Assessment*, 73, 422–448.
Ackerman, S. J., Hilsenroth, M. J., Clemence, A. J., Weatherill, R., & Fowler, J. C. (2000). The effects of social cognition and object representation on psychotherapy continuation. *Bulletin of the Menninger Clinic*, 64, 386–408.
Allison, J., & Blatt, S. (1964). The relationship of Rorschach whole responses to intelligence. *Journal of Projective Techniques*, 28, 255–260.
Allodi, F. (1980). The psychiatric effects in children and families of victims of political persecution and torture. *Danish Medical Bulletin* 27, 229–232.
American Psychiatric Association. (1980). *Diagnostic and Statistical Manual of Mental Disorders* (3rd ed.). Washington, DC: Author.
American Psychiatric Association. (1994). *Diagnostic and Statistical Manual of Mental Disorders* (4th ed.). Washington, DC: Author.
American Psychiatric Association. (2000). *Diagnostic and Statistical Manual of Mental Disorders* (4th ed., text rev.). Washington, DC: Author.
Ames, L. B., & Learned, J. (1946). Imaginary companions and related phenomena. *Journal of Genetic Psychology*, 69, 147–167.
Ames, L. B., Metraux, R., Rodell, J., & Walker, R. (1974). *Child Rorschach Responses* (rev. ed.). New York: Brunner/Mazel.
Amnesty International (1994). *Disappearances and Political Killings: Human Rights Crisis of the 1990s*. New York: Amnesty International.
Anastopolous, A. D., & Shelton, T. L. (2001). *Assessing Attention-Deficit/Hyperactivity Disorder*. Dordrecht, Netherlands: Kluwer Academic Publishers.

Angel, K. (1972). The role of the internal object and external object in object relations, separation anxiety, object constancy and symbiosis. *International Journal of Psychoanalysis*, 53, 541–546.

Anthony, E. J. (1974). The syndrome of the psychologically invulnerable child In E. J. Anthony & C. Koupernik (Eds.), *The Child in His Family: Children at Psychiatric Risk* (Vol. 3, pp. 529–545). New York: Wiley.

Anthony, E. J. (1987a). Children at high risk for psychosis growing up successfully. In E. J. Anthony & B. Cohler (Eds.), *The Invulnerable Child* (pp. 147–184). New York: Guilford Press.

Anthony, E. J. (1987b). Risk, vulnerability, and resilience: An overview. In E. J. Anthony & B. Cohler (Eds.), *The Invulnerable Child* (pp. 3–48). New York: Guilford Press.

Athey, G. I., Fleischer, J., & Coyne, L. (1980). Rorschach object representation as influenced by thought and affect organization. In J. S. Kwawer, H. D. Lerner, P. M. Lerner, & A. Sugarman (Eds.), *Borderline Phenomena and the Rorschach Test* (pp. 275–294). New York: International Universities Press.

Baideme, S. M., Kern, R. M., & Taffel-Cohen, S. (1979). The use of Adlerian family therapy in a case of school phobia. *Journal of Individual Psychology*, 35, 58–69.

Barends, A., Westen, D., Byers, S., Leigh, J., & Silbert, D. (1990). Assessing affecttone of relationship paradigms from TAT and interview data. *Psychological Assessment*, 2, 329–332.

Barkley, R. A. (1997). *ADHD and the Nature of Self-Control*. New York: Guilford Press.

Barkley, R. A. (2005). *Attention Deficit Hyperactivity Disorder: A Clinical Handbook* (3rd ed.). New York: Guilford Press.

Bartell, S. S., & Solanto, M. V. (1995). Usefulness of the Rorschach inkblot test in assessment of attention deficit hyperactivity disorder. *Perceptual and Motor Skills*, 80, 531–541.

Bassuk, E. L., & Rubin, L. (1987). Homeless children in America: A neglected population. *American Journal of Orthopsychiatry*, 57, 279–286.

Bauermeister, J. J., Shrout, P., Canino, G., Ramirez, R., Bravo, M., Alegria, M., et al. (2007). ADHD correlates, comorbidity, and impairment in community and treated samples of children and adolescents. *Journal of Abnormal Child Psychology*, 35, 883–898.

Baumgaertel, A., Wolraich, M. L., & Dietrich, M. (1995). Comparison of diagnostic criteria for attention deficit disorders in a German elementary school sample. *Journal of the American Academy of Child & Adolescent Psychiatry*, 34, 629–638.

Becker, D. (1995). The deficiency of the concept of post-traumatic stress disorder when dealing with victims of human rights violations. In R. J. Kleber, C. R. Figley, & P. R. Gersons, *Beyond Trauma: Cultural and Societal Dynamics* (pp. 99–110). New York: Plenum Press.

Becker, D., Castillo, M. I., Gómez, E., & Salamovich, S. (1987). Muerte y duelo. In E. Weinstein, E. Lira, & M. E. Rojas, *Trauma, Duelo y Reparación* (pp. 195–232). Santiago: Editorial Interamericana.

Becker, D., Castillo, M. I., Gómez, E., Kovalskys, J., & Lira, E. (1989). Subjectivity and politics: The psychotherapy of extreme traumatization in Chile. *International Journal of Mental Health*, 18, 80–97.

Becker, W. (1956). A genetic approach to the interpretation and evaluation of the process-reactive distinction in schizophrenia. *Journal of Abnormal Psychology*, 53, 229–236.

Beebe, B. (2005). Mother–infant research informs mother–infant treatment. *The Psychoanalytic Study of the Child*, 60(1), 7–46.

Beebe, B., & Lachmann, F. (1988). The contribution of mother-infant mutual influence to the origins of self and object representations. *Psychoanalytic Psychology*, 5, 305–337.

Bellak, L. (1986). *The TAT, CAT and SAT in Clinical Use* (4th ed.). New York: Grune & Stratton.

Bene, A. (1979). The question of narcissistic personality disorders: Selfpathology in children. *Bulletin of the Hampstead Clinic*, 2, 209–218.

Benedek, E. P. (1985). Children and psychic trauma: A brief review of contemporary thinking. In S. Eth & R. Pynoos (Eds.), *Post-Traumatic Stress Disorder in Children* (pp. 1–16). Washington, DC: American Psychiatric Press.

Benton, A. L. (1955). *The Revised Visual Retention Test: Clinical and Experimental Application*. New York: Psychological Corporation.

Beren, P. (Ed.). (1998). *Narcissistic Disorders in Children and Adolescents: Diagnosis and Treatment*. New York: Jason Aronson.

Berg, I., McGuire, R., & Whelan, E. (1973). The High Lands Dependency Questionnaire (HDQ): An administered version for use with the mothers of school children. *Journal of Child Psychology. Psychiatry and Allied Disciplines*, 14, 107–121.

Berg, I., Nichols, K., & Pritchard, C. (1969). School phobia: Its classification and relationship to dependency. *Journal of Child Psychology and Psychiatry*, 10, 123–141.

Berg, J. (1990). Differentiating ego functions of borderline and narcissistic personalities. *Journal of Personality Assessment*, 55, 537–548.

Biblow, E. (1973). Imaginative play and the control of aggression. In J. L. Singer (Ed.), *The Child's World of Make-Believe: Experimental Studies of Imaginative Play* (pp. 104–128). New York: Academic Press.

Biederman, J., Newcorn, J., & Sprich, S. (1991). Comorbidity of attention deficit hyperactivity disorder with conduct, depressive, anxiety, and other disorders. *American Journal of Psychiatry*, 148, 564–577.

Blatt, S. J. (1992). The differential effect of psychotherapy and psychoanalysis on anaclitic and introjective patients: The Menninger Psychotherapy Research Project revisited. *Journal of the American Psychoanalytic Association*, 40, 691–724.

Blatt, S. J., & Berman, W. H. (1984). A methodology for the use of the Rorschach in clinical research. *Journal of Personality Assessment*, 48, 226–239.

Blatt, S. J., & Feirstein, A. (1977). Cardiac response and personality organization. *Journal of Consulting and Clinical Psychology*, 45, 115–123.

Blatt, S. J., & Ford, R. (1994). *Therapeutic Change: An Object Relations Perspective*. New York: Plenum Press.

Blatt, S. J., & Lerner, H. (1983). The psychological assessment of object representation. *Journal of Personality Assessment*, 47, 7–28.

Blatt, S. J., & Ritzler, B. A. (1974). Thought disorder and boundary disturbances in psychosis. *Journal of Consulting and Clinical Psychology*, 42, 370–381.

Blatt, S. J., Brenneis, C. B., Schimek, J. G., & Glick, M. (1976a). A developmental analysis of the concept of the object on the Rorschach. Unpublished manual, Yale University School of Medicine. Department of Psychiatry, New Haven, CT.

Blatt, S. J., Brenneis, C. B., Schimek, J. G., & Glick, M. (1976b). Normal development and psychopathological impairment of the concept of the object on the Rorschach. *Journal of Abnormal Psychology*, 85, 364–373.

Blatt, S. J., Schimek, J. G., & Brenneis, C. B. (1980). The nature of the psychotic experience and its implications for the therapeutic process. In J. S. Strauss, M. Bowers, T. Downey, S. Fleck, S. Jackson, & I. Levine (Eds.), *The Psychotherapy of Schizophrenia* (pp. 101–114). New York: Plenum Press.

Blatt, S. J., Ford, R. Q., Berman, W., Cook, B., & Meyer, R. (1988). The assessment of change during the intensive treatment of borderline and schizophrenic young adults. *Psychoanalytic Psychology*, 5, 127–158.

Blatt, S., Tuber, S., & Auerbach, J. (1990). Representation of interpersonal interactions on the Rorschach and level of psychopathology. *Journal of Personality Assessment*, 54, 711–728.

Bleiberg, E. (1984). The question of narcissistic disorders in children. *Bulletin of the Menninger Clinic*, 48, 501–518.

Bleiberg, E. (1988). Developmental pathogenesis of narcissistic disorders in children. *Bulletin of the Menninger Clinic*, 52, 3–15.

Bleiberg, E. (1994). Normal and pathological narcissism in adolescence. *American Journal of Psychotherapy*, 48 (1), 30–51.

Bombel, G., Mihura, J., & Meyer, G. (2009). An examination of the construct validity of the Rorschach Mutuality of Autonomy Scale. *Journal of Personality Assessment*, 91(3), 227–237.

Bornstein, R. F. (2001). Clinical utility of the Rorschach Inkblot Method: Reframing the debate. *Journal of Personality Assessment*, 77, 39–47.

Bourling, K. A., & Collipp, P. J. (1969). Emotional responses of hospitalized children: Results of a pulse-monitor study. *Clinical Pediatrics*, 8, 641–646.

Bowlby, J. (1983). *Attachment and Loss* (Vol. 1, 2nd ed.). New York: Basic Books.

Bracken, P., Giller, J., & Summerfield, D. (1995). Psychological responses to war and atrocity: The limitations of current concepts. *Social Science and Medicine*, 40, 1073–1082.

Bresnahan, J. L., & Shapiro, M. M. (1966). A general equation and technique for the exact partitioning of chi-square contingency tables. *Psychological Bulletin*, 66(4), 252.

Bretherton, I. (1984). Representing the social world in symbolic play: Reality and fantasy. In I. Bretherton (Ed.), *Symbolic Play: The Development of Social Understanding* (pp. 1–39). New York: Academic Press.

Brown, L., Sherbenou, R. J., & Johnsen, S. (1990). *Test of Nonverbal Intelligence* (2nd ed.). Austin, TX: Pro-Ed.

Cass, L., & Thomas, E. (1979). *Childhood Pathology and Later Adjustment*. New York: Wiley.

Chomsky, N. (1968). *Language and Mind*. New York: Harcourt, Brace, Jovanovich.

Cicchetti, D., & Aber, J. L. (1986). Early precursors of later depression: An organizational perspective. In L. P. Lipsett (Ed.), *Advances in Infancy Research* (Vol. 3, pp. 172–194). Norwood, NJ: Ablex.

Cocking, R. R., Dana, J. M., & Dana, R. H. (1969). Six constructs to define Rorschach M: A response. *Journal of Projective Techniques and Personality Assessment*, 33, 322–323.

Cogan, R., & Porcerelli, J. H. (1996). Object relations in abusive partner relationships: An empirical investigation. *Journal of Personality Assessment*, 66, 106–115.

Cohen, J. (1988). *Statistical Power Analysis for the Behavioral Sciences* (2nd ed.). Hillsdale, NJ: Lawrence Erlbaum.

Cohen, J., & Cohler, B., Eds. (2000). *The Psychoanalytic Study of Lives Over Time*. New York: Academic Press.

Cohler, B. (1987). Adversity, resilience, and the study of lives. In E. J. Anthony & B. Cohler (Eds.), *The Invulnerable Child* (pp. 363–424). New York: Guilford Press.

Colarusso, C. (2000). A child analytic case report. In B. Cohler & J. Cohen (Eds.), *The Psychoanalytic Study of Lives Over Time* (pp. 49–65). New York: Academic Press

Coleman, L. L. (1950). Psychologic implications of tonsillectomy. *New York State Journal of Medicine*, 50, 1225–1228.

Commission on Human Rights, United Nations (1996). *Question of the Human Rights of All Persons Subjected to Any Form of Detention. Question of Enforced or Involuntary Disappearances.* Report of the Working Group on Enforced or Involuntary Disappearances. Item 8c of the provisional agenda. December 13.

Conners, C. K. (1999). Clinical use of rating scales in diagnosis and treatment of attention-deficit/hyperactivity disorder. *Pediatric Clinics of North America*, 46, 857–870.

Connolly, J. A., & Doyle, A. B. (1984). Relation of social fantasy play to social competence in preschoolers. *Developmental Psychology*, 20, 797–806.

Coolidge, J. C., Tessman, E., Waldfogel, S., & Willer, M. L. (1962). Patterns of aggression in school phobia. *Psychoanalytic Study of the Child*, 17, 319–333.

Cotugno, A. J. (1995). Personality attributes of attention deficit hyperactivity dis- order (ADHD) using the Rorschach inkblot test. *Journal of Clinical Psychology*, 51, 554–561.

Cramer, P., & Kelly, F. D. (2004). Defense mechanisms in adolescent conduct disorder and adjustment reaction. *The Journal of Nervous and Mental Disease*, 192(2), 139–145.

Dana, R. H. (1968). Six constructs to define Rorschach M. *Journal of Projective Techniques and Personality Assessment*, 32, 138–145.

Dansky, J. L. (1979). Cognitive consequences of sociodramatic play and exploration training for economically disadvantaged preschoolers. *Journal of Child Psychology and Psychiatry*, 20, 47–58.

Davenport, H. T., & Werry, J. S. (1970). The effect of general anesthesia, surgery and hospitalization upon the behavior of children. *American Journal of Orthopsychiatry*, 40, 806–824.

David, H., & Leach, W. W. (1957). The projective question: Further studies. *Journal of Projective Techniques*, 21, 3–9.

Davidson, S. (1960). School phobia as a manifestation of family disturbance: Its structure and treatment. *Journal of Child Psychology and Psychiatry*, 1, 270–287.

Dawes, A. (1990). Effects of political violence on children: A consideration of South African and related studies. *International Journal of Psychology*, 25, 13–31.

Deutsch, H. (1942). Some forms of emotional disturbance and their relation to schizophrenia. *Psychoanalytic Quarterly*, 11, 301–321.

Diamond, D., Kaslow, N., Coonerty, S., & Blatt, S. (1990). Changes in separation-individuation and intersubjectivity in long-term treatment. *Psychoanalytic Psychology*, 7, 363–397.

Diener, M. B., & Milich, R. (1997). Effects of positive feedback on the social interactions of boys with attention deficit hyperactivity disorder: A test of the self-protective hypothesis. *Journal of Clinical Child Psychology*, 26, 256–265.

Donahue, P., & Tuber, S. (1993). Rorschach adaptive fantasy images and coping in children under severe environmental stress. *Journal of Personality Assessment*, 60, 421–434.

Donahue, P., & Tuber, S. (1995). The impact of homelessness on children's levels of aspiration. *Bulletin of the Menninger Clinic*, 59, 249–255.

Drucker, J. (1975). Toddler play: Some comments on its function in the developmental process. *Psychoanalysis and Contemporary Science*, 4, 479–527.

Drucker, J. (1979). The affective context and psychodynamics of first symbolization. In N. Smith & M. Franklin (Eds.), *Symbolic Functioning in Childhood* (pp. 27–46). Hillsdale, NJ: Lawrence Erlbaum.

DuPaul, G. J., Power, T. J., & Anastopoulos, A. D. (1997). Teacher ratings of attention deficit hyperactivity disorder symptoms: Factor structure and normative data. *Psychological Assessment*, 9, 436–444.

DuPaul, G. J., Power, T. J., Anastopoulos, A. D., & Reid, R. (1998a). *ADHD Rating Scale–IV: Checklists, Norms and Clinical Interpretation*. New York: Guilford Press.

DuPaul, G. J., Power, T. J., McGoey, K. E., Ikeda, M. J., & Anastopoulos, A. D. (1998b). Reliability and validity of parent and teacher rating of attention deficit /hyperactivity disorder symptoms. *Journal of Psychoeducational Assessment*, 16, 55–68.

Edwards, J., Ruskin, N., & Turrini, P. (1991). *Separation and Individuation: Theory and Application.* New York: Gardner Press.
Egan, J., & Kernberg, P. (1984). Pathological narcissism in childhood. *Journal of the American Psychoanalytic Association,* 32, 39–63.
Eiges, K. (2016). *The Reciprocal Relationship Among Object Relations, Language, and Attention in a School-Aged Sample.* Unpublished doctoral dissertation.
Eisenberg, L. (1958). School phobia: A study in the communication of anxiety. *American Journal of Psychiatry,* 114, 712–715.
Elkan, B. M. (1969). Developmental differences in the manifest content of children's reported dreams. Unpublished doctoral dissertation, Columbia University, New York.
Emde, R. (1983). The prerepresentational self and its affective core. *The Psychoanalytic Study of the Child,* 38, 165–192.
Erikson, E. H. (1950). *Childhood and Society.* New York: Norton.
Escalona, S. (1968). *The Roots of Individuality.* Chicago, IL: Aldine.
Estes, H. R., Haylett, C. H., & Johnson, A. M. (1956). Separation anxiety. *American Journal of Psychotherapy,* 10, 682–695.
Exner, J. E. (1969). Rorschach responses as an index of narcissism. *Journal of Personality Assessment,* 33, 324–330.
Exner, J. E. (1986). Some Rorschach data comparing schizophrenics with borderline and schizotypal personality disorders. *Journal of Personality Assessment,* 50(3), 455–471.
Exner, J. E. (1993). *The Rorschach: A Comprehensive System.* Vol. 1 (3rd ed.). New York: Wiley.
Exner, J. E., & Weiner, I. B. (1982). *The Rorschach: A Comprehensive System.* Vol. 3. Assessment of children and adolescents. New York: Wiley.
Fairweather, G. W., Simon, R., Gebhard, M. E., Weingarten, E., Holland, J. L., Sanders, R., ... & Reahl, J. E. (1960). Relative effectiveness of psychotherapeutic programs: A multicriteria comparison of four programs for three different patient groups. *Psychological Monographs: General and Applied,* 74(5), 1.
Faraone, S. V. (2005). The scientific foundation for understanding attention-deficit/hyperactivity disorder as a valid psychiatric disorder. *European Child & Adolescent Psychiatry,* 14, 1–10.
Farina, J. J. (1987). El terrorismo de estado como fántasma. In Movimiento Solidario de Salud Mental (Ed.), *Terrorismo de Estado: Efectos Psicológicos en los Ninos* (pp. 153–159). Buenos Aires: Editorial Paidos.
Farris, M. A. (1988). Differential diagnosis of borderline and narcissistic personality disorders. In H. D. Lerner & P. M. Lerner (Eds.), *Primitive Mental States and the Rorschach* (pp. 299–337). Madison, CT: International Universities Press.
Fein, G. (1975). A transformational analysis of pretending. *Developmental Psychology,* 11, 291–296.
Flicek, M. (1992). Social status of boys with both academic problems and attention-deficit hyperactivity disorder. *Journal of Abnormal Child Psychology,* 20, 353–366.
Foulkes, D. (1982). *Children's Dreams: Longitudinal Studies.* New York: Wiley.
Fowler, A. (1978). Profile of a re-ed child. *Behavioral Disorders,* 3, 80–83.
Fox, J. (1956). The psychological significance of age patterns in the Rorschach records of children. In B. Klopfer (Ed.), *Developments in the Rorschach Technique* (pp. 88–103). Yonkers, NY: World Book.
Fraiberg, S. (1959). *The Magic Years.* New York: Scribner's.
Freed, E. X. (1965). Normative data on a self-administered projective question for children. *Journal of Projective Techniques,* 29, 3–6.

Freedenfeld, R., Ornduff, S., & Kelsey, R. M. (1995). Object relations and physical abuse: A TAT analysis. *Journal of Personality Assessment*, 64, 552–568.

Freud, A. (1952). The role of bodily illness in the mental life of children. *Psychoanalytic Study of the Child*, 7, 69–81.

Freyberg, J. T. (1973). Increasing the imaginative play of urban disadvantaged kindergarten children through systematic training. In J. L. Singer (Ed.), *The Child's World of Make-Believe: Experimental Studies of Imaginative Play* (pp. 129–154). New York: Academic Press.

Friedman, H. (1953). Perceptual regression in schizophrenia. An hypothesis suggested by the use of the Rorschach test. *Journal of Projective Techniques*, 17, 171–186.

Frieswyk, S., & Colson, D. (1980). Prognostic considerations in the hospital treatment of borderline states. In J. Kwawer, H. Lerner, A. Lerner, & A. Sugarman (Eds.), *Borderline Phenomena and the Rorschach Test* (pp. 229–256). New York: International Universities Press.

Gacono, C., Meloy, J., & Berg, J. (1992). Object relations, defensive operations and affective states in narcissistic, borderline and antisocial personality disorder. *Journal of Personality Assessment*, 59, 32–49.

Garmezy, N. (1983). Stressors of childhood. In N. Garmezy & M. Rutter (Eds.), *Stress, Coping, and Development in Children* (pp. 43–84). New York: McGraw-Hill.

Ghiaci, G., & Richardson, J. T. (1980). The effects of dramatic play upon cognitive structure and development. *The Journal of Genetic Psychology*, 136, 77–83.

Gilmore, K. (2000). A psychoanalytic perspective on attention-deficit/hyperactivity disorder. *Journal of the American Psychoanalytic Association*, 48(4), 1259–1293.

Gilmore, K. (2002). Diagnosis, dynamics, and development: Considerations in the psychoanalytic assessment of children with AD/HD. *Psychoanalytic Inquiry*, 22(3), 372–390.

Gittleman-Klein, R., & Klein, D. F. (1973). School phobia: Diagnostic considerations in the light of imipramine effects. *Journal of Nervous and Mental Disease*, 156, 199–215.

Gluckman, E., & Tuber, S. (1996). Object representations, interpersonal behavior and their relation to the dream reports of latency-aged girls. *Bulletin of the Menninger Clinic*, 60, 102–118.

Goddard, R., & Tuber, S. (1989). Boyhood separation anxiety disorder: Thought disorder and object relations psychopathology as manifested in Rorschach imagery. *Journal of Personality Assessment*, 53, 239–252.

Goldberg, A. (1990). Disorders of continuity. *Psychoanalytic Psychology*, 7, 13–28.

Goldberg, C. (1977). School phobia in adolescence. *Adolescence*, 12, 499–509.

Goldberg, E. H. (1989). Severity of depression and developmental levels of psychological functioning in 8–16-year-old girls. *American Journal of Orthopsychiatry*, 59(2), 167.

Goldfried, M. R., Stricker, G., & Weiner, I. B. (1971). *Rorschach Handbook of Clinical and Research Applications*. Englewood Cliffs, NJ: Prentice-Hall.

Goodman, L., & Kruskal, W. (1954). Measures of association for cross-classifications. *Journal of the American Statistical Association*, 49, 732–764.

Gordon, M., & Oshman, H. (1981). Rorschach indices of children classified as hyperactive. *Perceptual and Motor Skills*, 52, 703–707.

Gorney, J. E., & Weinstock, S. (1980). Borderline object relations, therapeutic impasse, and the Rorschach. *Borderline Phenomena and the Rorschach Test*, 167–187.

Graceffo, R. A., Mihura, J. L., & Meyer, G. J. (2014). A meta-analysis of an implicit measure of personality functioning: The Mutuality of Autonomy Scale. *Journal of Personality Assessment*, 96(6), 581–595.

Grayden, C. (1958). The relation between neurotic hypochondriasis and three personality variables: Feelings of being unloved, narcissism and guilt feelings. *Dissertation Abstracts International*, 18, 2209–2210.
Greenberg, J., & Mitchell, S. (1983). *Object Relations in Psychoanalytic Theory*. Cambridge, MA: Harvard University Press.
Griffiths, R. (1935). *A Study of Imagination in Childhood*. London: Kegan Paul.
Gronnerod, C. (2003). Temporal stability in the Rorschach method: A meta-analytic review. *Journal of Personality Assessment*, 80, 272–293.
Gronnerod, C. (2006). Reanalysis of the Gronnerod (2003). Rorschach temporal stability meta-analysis data set. *Journal of Personality Assessment*, 86, 222–225.
Gunderson, J., Ronningstam, E., & Smith, L. (1991). Narcissistic personality disorder: A review of data on DSMIIIR descriptions. *Journal of Personality Disorders*, 5 (2), 167–177.
Harder, D. (1979). The assessment of ambitiousnarcissistic character style with three projective tests. *Journal of Personality Assessment*, 43, 289–294.
Harder, D., & Ritzler, B. (1979). A comparison of Rorschach developmental level and form-level systems as indicators of psychosis. *Journal of Personality Assessment*, 43, 347–354.
Harder, D., Greenwald, D., Wechsler, S., & Ritzler, B. (1984). The Urist Rorschach mutuality of autonomy scale as an indicator of psychopathology. *Journal of Clinical Psychology*, 40, 1078–1082.
Harris, B., Reynoso, J., Meehan, K. B., Ueng-McHale, J., & Tuber, S. (2006). A child with ADHD: Convergences of Rorschach data and case material. *Journal of Infant, Child and Adolescent Psychotherapy*, 5, 499–517.
Harter, S. (1982). The Perceived Competence Scale for Children. *Child Development*, 53, 87–97.
Harter, S. (1985). *Manual for the Self-Perception Profile for Children (Revision of the Perceived Competence Scale for Children)*. University of Denver.
Harty, M., Cerney, M., Colson, D., Coyne, L., Frieswyk, S., Johnson, S. B., & Mortimer, R. (1981). Correlates of change and long-term outcome: An exploratory study of intensively treated hospital patients. *Bulletin of the Menninger Clinic*, 45(3), 209.
Hatcher, R. L., & Krohn, A. (1980). Level of object representation and capacity for intensive psychotherapy in neurotics and borderlines. In J. Kwawer, H. Lerner, P. Lerner, & A. Sugarman (Eds.), *Borderline Phenomena and the Rorschach Test* (pp. 299–320). New York: International Universities Press.
Heinicke, C. (1990). Toward generic principles of treating parents and children: Integrating psychotherapy with the schoolaged child and family intervention. *Journal of Consulting and Clinical Psychology*, 58, 713–719.
Hibbard, S., Hilsenroth, M., Hibbard, J., & Nash, M. (1995). A validity study of two projective object representations measures. *Psychological Assessment*, 7, 432–439.
Hickman, J. W. (1975). Manifest dream content and waking life variables in normal and disturbed boys. Doctoral dissertation, University of Texas at Austin, 1975. *Dissertation Abstracts International*, 36(02), 910B.
Hilsenroth, M. J., Hibbard, S. R., Nash, M. R., & Handler, L. (1993). A Rorschach study of narcissism, defense, and aggression in borderline, narcissistic and Cluster C personality disorders. *Journal of Personality Assessment*, 60, 346–361.
Hinshaw, S. P., March, J. S., Abikoff, H., Arnold, E., Cantwell, D. P., Conners, C. K., et al. (1997a). Comprehensive assessment of childhood attention-deficit hyperactivity disorder in the context of a multisite multimodal clinical trial. *Journal of Attention Disorders*, 1, 217–234.

Hinshaw, S. P., Zupan, B.A., & Simmel, C. (1997b). Peer status in boys with and without attention-deficit hyperactivity disorder: Predictions from overt and covert antisocial behavior, social isolation, and authoritative parenting beliefs. *Child Development*, 68, 880–896.
Hodgens, J. B., Cole, J., & Boldizar, J. (2000). Peer based differences among boys with ADHD. *Journal of Clinical Child Psychology*, 29, 443–452.
Hollingshead, A.B. (1957). *Two Factor Index of Social Position*. Unpublished manuscript.
Holt, R. R. (1968). *Manual for the Scoring of Primary Process Manifestations in Rorschach Responses* (10th ed.). New York: New York University, Research Center for Mental Health.
Huang-Pollock, C. L., Nigg, J. T., & Carr, T. H. (2005). Deficient attention is hard to find: Applying the perceptual load model of selective attention to attention deficit hyperactivity disorder subtypes. *Journal of Child Psychology and Psychiatry*, 46, 1211–1218.
Huang-Pollock, C. L., Nigg, J. T., & Halperin, J. M. (2006). Single dissociation findings of ADHD deficits in vigilance but not anterior or posterior attention systems. *Neuropsychology*, 20, 420–429.
Huesmann, L. R., Eron, L. D., Lefkowitz, M. M., & Walder, L. O. (1984). Stability of aggression over time and generations. *Developmental Psychology*, 20(6), 1120.
Hurlock, E. G., & Burstein, W. (1932). The imaginary playmate. *Journal of Genetic Psychology*, 41, 380–392.
Jacobson, E. (1964). *The Self and the Object World*. New York: International Universities Press.
Jain, R., Singh, B., Mohanty, S., & Kumar, R. (2005). SIS-I and Rorschach diagnostic indicators of attention deficit and hyperactivity disorder. *Journal of Projective Psychology & Mental Health*, 12, 141–152.
James, R. P. (1984). A correlational analysis between the Raven's matrices and WISC-R performance scales. *The Volta Review*, 86, 336–341.
Jensen, P. S., Shervette, R. E., Xenakis, S. N., & Richters, J. (1993). Anxiety and depressive disorders in attention deficit disorder with hyperactivity: New findings. *American Journal of Psychiatry*, 150, 1203–1209.
Jersild, A. T., Markey, F. V., & Jersild, C. L. (1933). *Children's Fears, Dreams, Wishes, Daydreams, Likes, Dislikes, Pleasant and Unpleasant Memories (Child Development Monographs No. 12)*. New York: Teachers College, Columbia University.
Jessner, L., Blom, G. E., & Waldfogel, S. (1952). Emotional implications of tonsillectomy and adenoidectomy on children. *Psychoanalytic Study of the Child*, 7, 126–169.
Kagan, J. (1966). Reflection–impulsivity: The generality and dynamics of conceptual tempo. *Journal of Abnormal Psychology*, 71, 17–24.
Kalter, N., & Marsden, G. (1970). Response productivity in Rorschach research. *Journal of Personality Assessment*, 34, 10–15.
Kaufman, A. (1979). *Intelligent Testing with the WISCR*. New York: Wiley.
Kaufman, J., Birmaher, B., Brent, D., Rao, U. M. A., Flynn, C., Moreci, P., ... & Ryan, N. (1997). Schedule for affective disorders and schizophrenia for school-age children-present and lifetime version (K-SADS-PL): Initial reliability and validity data. *Journal of the American Academy of Child & Adolescent Psychiatry*, 36(7), 980–988.
Kavanagh, G. (1985). Changes in object representations in psychoanalysis and psychoanalytic psychotherapy. *Bulletin of the Menninger Clinic*, 49, 546–564.
Kernberg, O. F. (1975). *Borderline Conditions and Pathological Narcissism*. New York: Jason Aronson.
Kernberg, O. F. (1976). *Object Relations Theory and Clinical Psychoanalysis*. New York: Aronson.

Kernberg, O. F. (1977). The structural diagnosis of borderline personality organization. In P. Horricollis (Ed.), *Borderline Personality Disorders* (pp. 87–122). New York: International Universities Press.

King, G. F. (1958). A theoretical and experimental consideration of the Rorschach human movement response. *Psychological Monographs*, 72 (5), 1–23.

Kinzie, J. D., Sack, W., Angell, R., Manson, S., & Rath, B. (1986). The psychiatric effects of massive trauma on Cambodian children: I. The children. *Journal of the Psychiatry*, 25, 370–376.

Klein, E. (1945). The reluctance to go to school. *The Psychoanalytic Study of Child*, 1, 263–279.

Klein, M. (1937). Love, guilt, and reparation. In *Love, Guilt, and Reparation and Other Works* (pp. 306–343). New York: Dell.

Klein, R. G. (1986). Questioning the clinical usefulness of projective psychological tests for children. *Developmental and Behavioral Pediatrics*, 7, 378–382.

Kliman, G. (1968). *Psychological Emergencies of Childhood*. New York: Grune & Stratton.

Klopfer, B., & Davidson, H. K. (1962). *The Rorschach Technique: An Introductory Manual*. New York: Harcourt Brace Jovanovich.

Klopfer, B., & Kelley, D. M. (1942). *The Rorschach Technique*. Oxford, UK: World Book.

Klopfer, B., Ainsworth, M., Klopfer, W.G., & Holt, R. (1954). *Developments in the Rorschach Technique: Volume I: Technique and Theory*. New York: Harcourt, Brace & World.

Kohut, H. (1968). The psychoanalytic treatment of narcissistic personality disorders: Outline of a systematic approach. In *The Psychoanalytic Study of the Child* (Vol. 23, pp. 86–113).

Kohut, H. (1971). *The Analysis of the Self: A Systematic Psychoanalytic Approach to the Treatment of Narcissistic Personality Disorders*. New York: International Universities Press.

Kohut, H. (1977). *The Restoration of the Self*. New York: International Universities Press.

Korchin, S. J., & Larson, D. G. (1977). Form perception and ego functioning. In M. Rickers-Ovsiankina (Ed.), *Rorschach Psychology* (pp. 159–187). Huntington, NY: Krieger.

Kordon, D., Edelman, L., Lagos, D. M., Nicoletti, E., & Bozzolo, R. C. (1988). *Psychological Effects of Political Repression*. Buenos Aires: Sudamericana-Planeta.

Krohn, A. S. (1972). Level of object-representation in the manifest dream and projective test: A construct validation study. Dissertation Abstracts International (University Microfilms No. 73–11, 182).

Krohn, A. S., & Mayman, M. (1974). Level of object representation in dreams and projective tests. *Bulletin of the Menninger Clinic*, 33, 445–466.

Krystal, H. (1988). *Integration and Self-Healing: Affect, Trauma, Alexithymia*. Hillsdale, NJ: The Analytic Press.

Lahey, B., Applegate, B., McBurnett, K., Biederman, J., Greenhill, L., Hynd, G., et al. (1994). DSM-IV field trials for attention deficit/hyperactivity disorder in children and adolescents. *American Journal of Psychiatry*, 151, 1673–1685.

Landau, S., & Moore, L. A. (1991). Social skill deficits in children with attention-deficit hyperactivity disorder. *School Psychology Review*, 20, 235–251.

Laurendeau, M., & Pinard, A. (1962). *Causal Thinking in the Child*. New York: International Universities Press.

Lazarus, A., Davidson, G. C., & Polefka, D. A. (1965). Classical and operant factors in the treatment of a school phobia. *Journal of Abnormal Psychology*, 70, 225–229.

Leary, T. (1957). *Interpersonal Diagnosis of Personality*. New York: Ronald Press.

Leichtman, M. (1996). *The Rorschach: A Developmental Perspective*. Hillsdale, NJ: Analytic Press.

Lerner, H. D. (1986). An object representation approach to Rorschach assessment. In M. Kissen (Ed.), *Assessing Object Relations Phenomena* (pp. 127–142). Madison, CT: International Universities Press.

Lerner, H. D., Sugarman, A., & Barbour, C. (1985). Patterns of ego boundary disturbance in neurotic, borderline, and schizophrenic patients. *Psychoanalytic Psychology*, 2, 47–66.

Lerner, P. M. (1990). Rorschach assessment of primitive defenses: A review. *Journal of Personality Assessment*, 54, 30–46.

Levenson, E. A. (1961). The treatment of school phobia in the young adult. *American Journal of Psychotherapy*, 15, 539–552.

Leventhal, T., & Sills, M. (1964). Self-image in school phobia. *American Journal of Orthopsychiatry*, 34, 685–695.

Levine, D., & Cohen, J. (1962). Symptoms and ego strength measures as predictors of the outcome of hospitalization in functional psychosis. *Journal of Consulting Psychology*, 26, 246–250.

Levitt, E., & Truumaa, A. (1972). *The Rorschach Technique with Children and Adolescents*. New York: Grune & Stratton.

Levy, D. M. (1945). Psychic trauma of operations in children. *American Journal of Diseases of Children*, 62, 716–729.

Lowe, M. (1975). Trends in the development of representational play in infants from 1–3 years: An observational study. *Journal of Child Psychology and Psychiatry*, 16, 33–47.

Lykes, M. B. (1994). Terror, silencing and children: International multidisciplinary collaboration with Guatemalan Maya communities. *Social Science & Medicine*, 38, 543–552.

Lyons, J. (1991). Strategies for assessing the potential for positive adjustment following trauma. *Journal of Traumatic Stress* 4, 93–111.

Maccoby, E. E., & Jacklin, C. N. (1980). Sex differences in aggression: A rejoinder and reprise. *Child Development*, 964–980.

Mack, L. T. (1975). Developmental differences in the manifest content of dreams of normal and disturbed children. Doctoral dissertation, Columbia University. Dissertation Abstracts International, 36(02), 915B.

Macksoud, M. (1992). Assessing war trauma in children: A case study of Lebanese children. *Journal of Refugee Studies*, 5 (1), 1–15.

Mahler, M., Pine, F., & Bergman, A. (1975). *The Psychological Birth of the Human Infant*. New York: Basic Books.

Manosevitz, M., Prentice, N. M., & Wilson, F. (1973). Individual and family correlates of imaginary companions in preschool children. *Developmental Psychology*, 8, 72–79.

Martin, A. W., & Wiechers, J. E. (1954). Raven's Colored Progressive Matrices and the Wechsler Intelligence Scale for Children. *Journal of Consulting Psychology*, 18, 143–144.

Martín-Baró, I. (1994). *Writings for a Liberation Psychology*. Cambridge, MA: Harvard University Press.

Martinez, J. (2016). *The Object Relations of the "Dutiful Daughter"*. Unpublished doctoral dissertation.

Mayman, M. (1960). *Rorschach Form Level Manual*. Unpublished manuscript, University of Michigan, Ann Arbor.

Mayman, M. (1962). *Rorschach Form Level Manual*. Unpublished Manuscript, The Menninger Foundation.

Mayman, M. (1967). Object representations and object relationships in Rorschach responses. *Journal of Personality Assessment*, 31, 17–24.

Mayman, M. (1968). Early memories and character structure. *Journal of Projective Techniques and Personality Assessment*, 32, 303–316.

Mayman, M. (1970). *Form Quality of Rorschach Responses*. Unpublished manuscript.

Mayman, M., & Ryan, E. (1972). Object relations and early memories. Unpublished manuscript.
McCune-Nicolich, L. (1981). Toward symbolic functioning: Structure of early pretend games and potential parallels with language. *Child Development*, 52, 785–797.
Mednick, S., & McNeil, T. (1968). Current methodology in research on the etiology of schizophrenia. *Psychological Bulletin*, 70, 681–693.
Meehan, K., Reynoso, J., Ueng-McHale, J., Harris, B., Wolfson, V., Gomes, H., & Tuber, S. (2009). Self-regulation and internal resources in school-aged children with ADHD. *Bulletin of the Menninger Clinic*, 72 (4) 237–261.
Mellsop, G. (1972). Psychiatric patients seen as children and adults. *Journal of Child Psychology and Psychiatry*, 13, 91–101.
Meyer, G., & Eblin, J. (2012). An overview of the Rorschach Performance Assessment System. *Psychological Injury and Law*, 5 (2), 107–121.
Meyer, G. J., Mihura, J. L., & Bruce, L. (2005). The interclinician reliability of Rorschach interpretation in four data sets. *Journal of Personality Assessment*, 84, 296–314.
Meyer, G. J., Hilsenroth, M. J., Baxter, D., Exner, J. E., Jr., Fowler, J. C., & Piers, B. C. (2002). An examination of interrater reliability for scoring the Rorschach comprehensive system in eight data sets. *Journal of Personality Assessment*, 78, 219–274.
Meyer, J., & Tuber, S. (1989). Intrapsychic and behavioral correlates to the phenomenon of imaginary companions in young children. *Psychoanalytic Psychology*, 6, 151–168.
Miller, D. (1972). School phobia: Diagnosis, emotional genesis and management. *New York State: Journal of Medicine*, 72, 1160–1165.
Miller, K. E. (1994). *Growing up in Exile: Mental Health and Meaning Making Among Indigenous Guatemalan Refugee Children in Chiapas, Mexico*. PhD dissertation. University of Michigan.
Miller, T. P. (1961). The child who refuses to attend school. *American Journal of Psychiatry*, 118, 398–404.
Modell, A. H. (1975). A narcissistic defense against affects and the illusion of selfsufficiency. *The International Journal of Psychoanalysis*, 56, 275–282.
Molnar, J. M. (1988). *Home Is Where the Heart Is: The Crisis of Homeless Children and Families in New York City*. New York: Bank Street College of Education.
Molnar, J. M., Rath, W. R., & Klein, T. P. (1990). Constantly compromised: The impact of homelessness on children. *Journal of Social Issues*, 46 (4), 109–124.
Moran, J. D., Sawyers, J. K., Fu, V. R., & Milgram, R. M. (1984). Predicting imaginative play in preschool children. *Gifted Child Quarterly*, 28 (2), 92–94.
Mordock, J. (1978). *Ego Impaired Children Grow up*. Rhinebeck, NY: Astor Home for Children.
Movimiento Solidario de Salud Mental. (1987). *Terrorismo de estado: efectos psicológicos en los ninos*. Buenos Aires: Editorial Paidos.
Munczek, D., & Tuber, S. (1998). Political repression and its psychological effects on Honduran children. *Social Science & Medicine*, 47, 1699–1713.
Munroe, J. P. (1894). Report at NEA meeting. *Pediatric Seminar*, 3, 182–184.
Murphy, L. B., & Moriarty, A. E. (1976). *Vulnerability, Coping and Growth: From Infancy to Adolescence*. New Haven, CT: Yale University Press.
Murray, H. (1943). *Thematic Apperception Test Manual*. Cambridge, MA: Harvard University Press.
Nagera, H. (1969). The imaginary companion: Its significance for ego development and conflict solution. *The Psychoanalytic Study of the Child*, 24, 165–196.

Neuman, E., Monreal, E., & Macchiavello, C. (1990). Violación de los derechos fundamentales: reparación individual y social. In H. Riquelme (Ed.), *Era de Nieblas: Derechos Humanos, Terrorismo de Estado y Salud Psicosocial en América Latina* (pp. 147–152). Caracas: Nueva Sociedad.

Nichols, S. L., & Waschbusch, D. A. (2004). A review of the validity of laboratory cognitive tasks used to assess symptoms of ADHD. *Child Psychiatry & Human Development*, 34, 297–315.

Nicolich, L. (1977). Beyond sensorimotor intelligence: Analysis of symbolic maturity through analysis of pretend play. *MerrillPalmer Quarterly*, 23, 89–99.

Nigg, J. T., Blaskey, L. G., & Stawicki, J. A. (2004). Evaluating the endophenotype model of ADHD neuropsychological deficit: Results for parents and siblings of children with ADHD combined and inattentive subtypes. *Journal of Abnormal Psychology*, 113, 614–625.

Nixon, E. (2001). The social competence of children with attention deficit hyperactivity disorder: A review of the literature. *Child & Adolescent Mental Health*, 6, 172–180.

Ornduff, S. R., & Kelsey, R. (1996). Object relations of sexually and physically abused female children: A TAT analysis. *Journal of Personality Assessment*, 66, 91–105.

Ornduff, S. R., Freedenfeld, R. N., Kelsey, R. M., & Critelli, J. W. (1994). Object relations of sexually abused female subjects: A TAT analysis. *Journal of Personality Assessment*, 63, 223–238.

Page, H. (1957). Studies in fantasy---daydreaming frequencies and Rorschach scoring categories. *Journal of Consulting Psychology*, 21, 111–114.

Parsons, M. (2000). The search for a goodenough self: From fragmentation toward cohesion in a young adult's second analysis. In J. Cohen & B. Cohler (Eds.), *The Psychoanalytic Study of Lives over Time* (pp. 95–124). New York: Academic Press.

Patrón, M. C., & Etchegoyhen, C. (1990). Memoria, dolor, olvido y castigo. In Instituto Latinoamericano de Salud Mental y Derechos Humanos, *Derechos Humanos: Todo Es Segu'n el Dolor con que Se Mira*, (pp. 77–94). Santiago, Chile: ILAS.

Pfiffner, L. J., Calzada, E., & McBurnett, K. (2000). Interventions to enhance social competence. *Child & Adolescent Psychiatric Clinics of North America*, 9, 689–709.

Phillips, A. (1988). *Winnicott*. Cambridge, MA: Harvard University Press.

Piaget, J. (1945). *Play, Dreams and Imitation in Childhood*. New York: Norton.

Pines, M. (1978). Invisible playmates. *Psychology Today*, September, 38–42.

Portelli, A. (1991). *The Death of Luigi Trastulli and Other Stories: Form and Meaning in Oral History*. Albany, NY: State University of New York Press.

Powers, S., & Barkan, J. H. (1986). Concurrent validity of the Standard Progressive Matrices for Hispanic and non-Hispanic seventh-grade students. *Psychology in the Schools*, 23, 333–336.

Poznanski, E. O. (1979). The hospitalized child. In S. I. Harrison (Ed.), *Basic Handbook of Child Psychiatry: Vol. 3. Therapeutic Interventions* (pp. 567–578). New York: Basic Books.

Pritchard, C., & Ward. R. I. (1974). The family dynamics of school phobics. *British Journal of Social Work*, 4, 61–94.

Psychological Corporation. (1999). *Wechsler Abbreviated Scale of Intelligence*. San Antonio, TX: Author.

Pynoos, R. S., & Eth, S. (1986). Witness to violence: The child interview. *Journal of the American Academy of Child Psychiatry*, 25, 306–319.

Pynoos, R. S., Steinberg, A. M., & Goenjian, A. (1996). Traumatic stress in childhood and adolescence: Recent developments and current controversies. In B. A. van der Kolk, A. C. McFarlane, & L. Weisaeth, *Traumatic Stress: The Effects of Overwhelming Experience on Mind, Body, and Society* (pp. 331–358). New York: Guilford Press.

Quay, H. C. (1997). Inhibition and attention deficit hyperactivity disorder. *Journal of Abnormal Child Psychology*, 25, 7–13.
Quirk, G. (1992). Symptoms that do not disappear. *Links Health and Development Report*, 9 (3), 4–5.
Quirk, G., & Casco, L. (1994). Stress disorders of families of the disappeared: A controlled study in Honduras. *Social Science and Medicine*, 39, 1675–1679.
Radin, N. (1974). Observed maternal behavior with four-year-old boys and girls in lower-class families. *Child Development*, 45, 1126–1131.
Radin, S. (1968). Psychotherapeutic considerations in school phobia. *Adolescence*, 3, 181–194.
Radin, S. (1972). Job phobia: School phobia revisited. *Comprehensive Psychiatry*, 13, 251–257.
Rafferty, Y., & Shinn, M. (1991). The impact of homelessness on children. *American Psychologist*, 46, 1170–1179.
Rapaport, D., Gill, M. M., & Schafer, R. (1968). *Diagnostic Psychological Testing* (rev. ed., R. R. Holt, Ed.). New York: International Universities Press.
Raven, J. C. (1977). *Manual for Raven's Progressive Matrices and Vocabulary Scales*. London: Lewis.
Reich, W. (1933). *Character Analysis*. London: Vision Press.
Rescorla, L., Parker, R., & Stolley, P. (1991). Ability, achievement and adjustment in homeless children. *American Journal of Orthopsychiatry*, 61, 210–220.
Rickers-Ovsiankina, M. (1977). *Rorschach Psychology*. Huntington, NY: Krieger.
Rinsley, D. (1980). The developmental etiology of borderline and narcissistic disorders. *Bulletin of the Menninger Clinic*, 44, 127–134.
Ritzler, B. A., Wyatt, D., Harder, D., & Kaskey, M. (1980). Psychotic patterns of the concept of the object on the Rorschach. *Journal of Abnormal Psychology*, 89, 46–55.
Rojas, E., & Mintzer, S. (1978). *The Use of the Animal Preference Test with Children*. Unpublished manuscript.
Rojas, E., & Tuber, S. (1991). The Animal Preference Test and its relationship to behavioral problems in young children. *Journal of Personality Assessment*, 57, 141–148.
Rorschach, H. (1942). *Psychodiagnostics* (P. Lemkau & B. Kronenberg, Trans.). New York: Grune & Stratton. (Original work published 1921.)
Ruff, H. A., & Rothbart, M. K. (1996). *Attention in Early Development: Themes and Variations*. New York: Oxford University Press.
Rutter, M. (1983). Stress, coping, and development: Some issues and some questions. In N. Garmezy & M. Rutter (Eds.), *Stress, Coping, and Development in Children* (pp. 1–41). New York: McGraw-Hill.
Ryan, R., Avery, R., & Grolnick, W. (1985). A Rorschach assessment of children's mutuality of autonomy. *Journal of Personality Assessment*, 49, 6–11.
Saltz, E., Dixon, D., & Johnson, J. (1977). Training disadvantaged preschoolers on various fantasy activities: Effects on cognitive functioning and impulse control. *Child Development*, 48, 367–380.
Sander, L. (1983). Polarity, paradox, and the organizing process of development. In J. Call, E. Galenson, & R. Tyson (Eds.), *Frontiers of Infant Psychiatry* (pp. 315–327). New York: Basic Books.
Sands, C. (1986). The regression of internal object representation in adolescent boys. Doctoral dissertation, Columbia University. *Dissertation Abstracts International*, 47(07), 3125 B.
Santostefano, S. (1978). *A Biodevelopmental Approach to Clinical Child Psychology: Cognitive Controls and Cognitive Control Therapy*. New York: Wiley.

Santostefano, S. (1988a). *Cognitive Control Battery Manual*. Los Angeles, CA: Western Psychological Services.
Santostefano, S. (1988b). Process and change in child therapy and development: The concept of metaphor. In D. Morrison (Ed.), *Imagination and Cognition in Childhood* (pp. 204–229). Amityville, NY: Baywood.
Santostefano, S., Rieder, C., & Berk, S. A. (1984). The structure of fantasied movement in suicidal children and adolescents. *Suicide and Life-Threatening Behavior*, 14(1), 3–16.
Sarnoff, C. (1976). *Latency*. New York: Aronson.
Saul, L. J. (1972). *Psychodynamically Based Psychotherapy*. New York: Science House.
Saunders, B., & Chambers, C. M. (1996). A review of the literature on attention-deficit hyperactivity disorder children: Peer interactions and collaborative learning. *Psychology in the Schools*, 33, 333–340.
Schachtel, E. (1966/2001). *Experiential Foundations of Rorschach's Text*. Hillsdale, NJ: The Analytic Press.
Schaeffer, C. E. (1969). Imaginary companions and creative adolescents. *Developmental Psychology*, 1, 747–749.
Schirmer, J. (1986). Chile: The loss of childhood. *Cultural Survival Quarterly* 10 (4), 40–42.
Schonbar, R. (1965). Differential dream recall frequency as a component of "life-style." *Journal of Consulting Psychology*, 29, 468–474.
Semel, E., Wiig, E. H., & Secord, W. A. (1995). *Clinical Evaluation of Language Fundamentals* (3rd ed.). San Antonio, TX: Psychological Corporation.
Semel, E., Wiig, E. H., & Secord, W. A. (2004). *Clinical Evaluation of Language Fundamentals* (4th ed.). San Antonio, TX: Psychological Corporation.
Shallice, T., & Plaut, D. (1992). From connectionism to neuropsychological syndromes. In J. Alegria, D. Holender, J. Junca de Morais, & M. Radeau (Eds.), *Analytic Approaches to Human Cognition* (pp. 239–258). Oxford, UK: North-Holland.
Shapiro, D. (1977). A perceptual understanding of color responses. In M. Rickers-Ovisankina (Ed.), *Rorschach Psychology* (pp. 251–301). Huntington, NY: Krieger.
Shmukler, D. (1983). Preschool imaginative play predisposition and its relationship to subsequent third grade assessment. *Imagination, Cognition, and Personality*, 2, 231–240.
Shrout, P. E., & Fleiss, J. L. (1979). Intraclass correlations: Uses in assessing rater reliability. *Psychological Bulletin*, 86, 420–428.
Shulman, D. G., McCarthy, E. C., & Ferguson, G. R. (1988). The projective assessment of narcissism: Development, reliability and validity of the NP. *Psychoanalytic Psychology*, 5, 285–297.
Siegel, S. (1956). *Non-Parametric Statistics*. New York: Harcourt.
Silverman, D. K. (1987). What are little girls made of? *Psychoanalytic Psychology*, 4(4), 315.
Singer, J. L. (1973). *The Child's World of Make-Believe: Experimental Studies in Imaginative Play*. New York: Academic Press.
Singer, J. L., & Herman, J. (1954). Motor and fantasy correlates of Rorschach human movement responses. *Journal of Consulting Psychology*, 18, 325–331.
Skipper, J. K., Jr., & Leonard, R. C. (1968). Children, stress, and hospitalization: A field experiment. *Journal of Health and Social Behavior*, 9, 275–287.
Skolnick, E. (1984). The changes in internal object representations and perception during the adolescence of females. Doctoral dissertation, Adelphi University. Dissertation Abstracts International, 44(12), 3957B.
Skynner, A. C. (1974). School phobia: A reappraisal. *British Journal of Medical Psychology*, 47, 1–16.

Slade, A. (1986). Symbolic play and separationindividuation: A naturalistic study. *Bulletin of the Menninger Clinic*, 50, 541–563.
Slade, A. (1987). Quality of attachment and early symbolic play. *Developmental Psychology*, 1, 78–85.
Slade, A. (2000). The development and organization of attachment: Implications for psychoanalysis. *Journal of the American Psychoanalytic Association*, 48, 1147–1174.
Smith, W. (1980). The Rorschach, the borderline patient and the psychotherapist. In J. Kwawer, P. Lerner, H. Lerner, & A. Sugarman (Eds.), *Borderline Phenomena and the Rorschach Test* (pp. 157–166). New York: International Universities Press.
Solnit, A. J. (1984). Preparing. *Psychoanalytic Psychology*, 1, 113–129.
Spear, W. E. (1978). The relationship of clinical diagnosis to structural and thematic aspects of manifest object representations in hospitalized borderline and schizophrenic patients. Doctoral dissertation, Columbia University. Dissertation Abstracts International, 39(10), 5089B.
Spear, W. E. (1980). The psychological assessment of structural and thematic object representations in borderline and schizophrenic patients. In J. S. Kwawer, H. D. Lerner, P. M. Lerner, & A. Sugarman (Eds.), *Borderline Phenomena and the Rorschach Test* (pp. 321–340). New York: International Universities Press.
Spear, W. E., & Sugarman, A. (1984). Dimensions of internalized object relations in borderline and schizophrenic patients. *Psychoanalytic Psychology*, 1, 113–129.
Sperling, M. (1967). School phobias: Classification, dynamics and treatment. *Psychoanalytic Study of the Child*, 22, 375–401.
Sperling, M. (1971). The diagnostic and prognostic significance of children's dreams and sleep. Paper presented at the annual meeting of the Psychoanalytic Association of New York, June 1971.
Sperling, O. E. (1954). An imaginary companion, representing a prestage of the superego. *The Psychoanalytic Study of the Child*, 9, 252–258.
Spiegel, D. (1988). Dissociation and hypnosis in post-traumatic stress disorders. *Journal of Traumatic Stress* 1, 17–33.
Spitz, R. A. (1945). Hospitalism: An inquiry into the genesis of psychiatric conditions in early childhood. *The Psychoanalytic Study of the Child*, 1(1), 53–74.
Stern, D. (1985). *The Interpersonal World of the Infant: A View from Psychoanalysis and Developmental Psychology*. New York: Basic Books.
Strauss, A. A., & Lehtinen, L. E. (1947). *Psychopathology and Education of the Brain-Injured Child*. New York: Grune & Stratton.
Strauss, J. C., & Harder, D. W. (1981). The Case Record Rating Scale: A method for rating symptom and social function data from case records. *Psychiatry Research*, 4, 333–345.
Strauss, J. C., Kokes, R. F., Ritzler, B. A., Harder, D. W., & Van Ord, A. (1978). Patterns of disorder in first admission psychiatric patients. *Journal of Nervous and Mental Disease*, 166, 611–615.
Stricker, O., & Healey, B. (1990). The projective assessment of object relations. *Psychological Assessment*, 2, 219–230.
Stubbe, D. E. (2000). Attention-deficit/hyperactivity disorder overview: Historical perspective, current controversies, and future directions. *Child & Adolescent Psychiatric Clinics of North America*, 9, 469–479.
Sugarman, A., & Kanner, K. (2000). The contribution of psychoanalytic theory to psychological testing. *Psychoanalytic Psychology*, 17, 3–23.

Summerfield, D. (1995). Addressing human response to war and atrocity: Major challenges in research and practices and the limitations of Western psychiatric models. In R. J. Kleber, C. R. Figley, & P. R. Gersons (Eds.), *Beyond Trauma: Cultural and Societal Dynamics* (pp. 17–29). New York: Plenum Press.
Svendsen, M. (1934). Children's imaginary companions. *Archives of Neurology and Psychiatry*, 12, 985–999.
Szyrynski, V. (1976). School phobia, its treatment and prevention. *Psychiatric Journal of the University of Ottawa*, 1, 165–170.
Tannock, R. (2000). Attention deficit disorders with anxiety disorders. In T. E. Brown (Ed.), *Attention-Deficit Disorders and Comorbidities in Children, Adolescents and Adults* (pp. 125–170). New York: American Psychiatric Press.
Taylor, C. W. (1988). Various approaches to and definitions of fantasy. In R. J. Sternberg (Ed.), *The Nature of Creativity* (pp. 99–121). Cambridge, UK: Cambridge University Press.
Terr, L. C. (1990). *Too Scared to Cry*. New York: Harper & Row.
Terr, L. C. (1991). Childhood traumas: An outline and overview. *American Journal of Psychiatry*, 148, 10–19.
Thom, L. (2016). *Object Relations in Children's Projective Testing*. Unpublished doctoral dissertation.
Thomas, T. (1987). A Rorschach investigation of borderline and attention deficit disorder children. Paper presented at the mid-winter meeting of the Society for Personality Assessment, San Francisco, March.
Tobier, K. (2000). The case of Lisa: From the baddest girl in the class to feeling sad and lonely: Reflections on the analysis of an 8-year-old girl. In J. Cohen & B. Cohler (Eds.), *The Psychoanalytic Study of Lives over Time* (pp. 67–94). New York: Academic Press.
Tower, R. B. (1983). Imagery: Its role in development. In A. Sheikh (Ed.), *Imagery: Current Theory and Research* (pp. 222–251). New York: Wiley.
Townsend, J. K. (1968). The relation between Rorschach signs of aggression and behavioral aggression in emotionally disturbed boys. *Journal of Projective Techniques and Personality Assessment*, 31, 3–21.
Tronick, E. (1989). Emotions and emotional communication in infants. *American Psychologist*, 44, 112–119.
Tuber, S. (1981). *Children's Rorschachs as Predictors of Their Later Adjustment*. Unpublished doctoral dissertation, University of Michigan.
Tuber, S. (1983). Children's Rorschach scores as predictors of later adjustment. *Journal of Consulting and Clinical Psychology*, 51, 379–385.
Tuber, S. (1988). An extension of the Mutuality of Autonomy Scale in the assessment of children's Rorschachs. In H. Lerner & P. Lerner (Eds.), *Primitive Mental States on the Rorschach* (pp. 655–664). New York: International Universities Press.
Tuber, S. (1989a). Assessment of children's object representations with the Rorschach. *Bulletin of the Menninger Clinic*, 53, 432–441.
Tuber, S. (1989b). Children's Rorschach object representations: Findings for a nonclinical sample. *Psychological Assessment*, 1, 146–149.
Tuber, S. (1992). Empirical and clinical assessments of children's object relations and object representations. *Journal of Personality Assessment*, 58, 179–197.
Tuber, S. (2000). Projective testing as a post-hoc predictor of change in psychoanalysis: The case of Jim. In J. Cohen & B. Cohler (Eds.), *The Psychoanalytic Study of Lives Over Time* (pp. 283–308). New York: Academic Press.

Tuber, S. (2004). Projective testing as a heuristic 'snapshot' of themes in child and adult psychoanalysis: The Case of Lisa. *Journal of Infant, Child and Adolescent Psychotherapy*, 3, 486–508.

Tuber, S. (2012). *Understanding Personality Through Projective Testing*. New York: Jason Aronson.

Tuber, S., Frank, M., & Santostefano, S. (1989). Children's anticipation of impending surgery. *Bulletin of the Menninger Clinic*, 53, 501–511.

Tuber, S., Harris, B., Meehan, K., Reynoso, J., & Ueng-McHale, J. (2006). Rorschach configurations of children with ADHD. In S. Smith & L. Handler (Eds.), *The Clinical Assessment of Children and Adolescents: A Practitioner's Guide* (pp. 451–468). Hillsdale, NJ: Lawrence Erlbaum.

Urist, J. (1977). The Rorschach test and the assessment of object relations. *Journal of Personality Assessment*, 41, 3–9.

Urist, J., & Shill, M. (1982). Validity of the Rorschach mutuality of autonomy scale: A replication using excerpted responses. *Journal of Personality Assessment*, 46, 450–454.

Vaal, J. J. (1973). Applying contingency contracting to a school phobic: A case study. *Journal of Behavioral Therapy and Experimental Psychiatry*, 4, 371–373.

Van Krevelen, D. A. (1955). The use of Pigem's test with children. *Journal of Projective Techniques*, 19, 292–300.

Viglione, D. J., & Hilsenroth, M. J. (2001). The Rorschach: Facts, fictions, and future. *Psychological Assessment*, 13, 452–471.

Vostrovsky, C. (1895). A study of imaginary companions. *Education*, 15, 393–398.

Waldron, S., Shrier, D., Stone, B., & Tobin, F. (1975). School phobia and other childhood neurosis: A systematic study of the children and their families. *American Journal of Psychiatry*, 132, 802–808.

Wallerstein, J. S. (1983). Children of divorce: Stress and developmental tasks. In N. Garmezy & M. Rutter (Eds.), *Stress, Coping, and Development in Children* (pp. 265–302). New York: McGraw-Hill.

Warner, S. (1987). Manifest dream analysis in contemporary practice. In M. L. Glucksman & S. L. Warner (Eds.), *Dreams in New Perspective: The Royal Road Revisited* (pp. 97–115). New York: Human Sciences Press.

Waschbusch, D. A., Pelham, W. E., Jr., & Jennings, J. R. (2002). Reactive aggression in boys with disruptive behavior disorders: Behavior, physiology, and affect. *Journal of Abnormal Child Psychology*, 30, 641–656.

Wechsler, D. (1974). *Wechsler Intelligence Scale for Children—Revised Manual*. New York: The Psychological Association.

Wechsler, D. (1991). *Manual for the Wechsler Intelligence Scale for Children-III*. New York: Psychological Corporation.

Weiland, H. (1966). Considerations on the development of symbiosis, symbiotic psychosis, and the nature of separation anxiety. *The International Journal of Psychoanalysis*, 47(1), 1.

Weinberger, G., Leventhal, T. S., & Beckman, G. (1973). The management of chronic school phobia through the use of consultation with school personnel. *Psychology in the Schools*, 10, 83–88.

Weine, S., Munczek, D., & Farley, M. (1995). Trauma research as intervention in human rights violations: Prostitution, disappearance, assassination, and genocide. 11th Annual Meeting of the International Society for Traumatic Stress Studies, Boston.

Weiner, I. B. (1995). Variable selection in Rorschach research. *Issues and Methods in Rorschach Research*, 73–98.

Weinstein, E., Lira, E., & Rojas, M. E., Eds. (1987). *Trauma, Duelo y Reparación*. Santiago: Editorial Interamericana.
Weise, K., & Tuber, S. (2004). The self and object representations of narcissistically disturbed children: An empirical investigation. *Psychoanalytic Psychology*, 21, 244–258.
Weissberg, P., & Springer, L. (1961). Environmental factors in creative function. *Archives of General Psychiatry*, 5, 534–564.
Werner, H. (1948). *Comparative Psychology of Mental Development* (rev. ed.). Chicago, IL: Follet.
Werner, H., & Kaplan, B. (1963). *Symbol Formation: An Organismic-Developmental Approach to Language and the Expression of Thought*. New York: Wiley.
Westen, D. (1991). Clinical assessment of object relations using the TAT. *Journal of Personality Assessment*, 56, 56–74.
Westen, D. (1995). *Social Cognition and Object Relations Scale: Qsort for Projective Stories (SCORSQ)*. Unpublished manuscript, Department of Psychiatry, The Cambridge Hospital and Harvard Medical School.
Westen, D., Lohr, N., Silk, K., Kerber, K., & Goodrich, S. (1985). *Object Relations and Social Cognition TAT Scoring Manual*. Ann Arbor: University of Michigan Press.
Westen, D., Lohr, N., Silk, K., Gold, L., & Kerber, K. (1990). Object relations and social cognition in borderlines, major depressives, and normals: A Thematic Apperception Test analysis. *Psychological Assessment*, 2, 355–364.
Westen, D., Ludolph, P., Block, J., Wixom, J., & Wiss, F. C. (1990). Developmental history and object relations in psychiatrically disturbed adolescent girls. *American Journal of Psychiatry*, 147, 1061–1068.
Westen, D., Ludolph, P., Lerner, H., Ruffins, S., & Wiss, F. C. (1990). Object relations in borderline adolescents. *Journal of the American Academy of Child and Adolescent Psychiatry*, 29, 338–348.
Westen, D., Klepser, J., Ruffins, S., Silverman, M., Lifton, N., & Boekamp, J. (1991). Object relations in childhood and adolescence: The development of working representations. *Journal of Consulting and Clinical Psychology*, 59, 400–409.
Westen, D., Ludolph, P., Misle, B., Ruffins, S., & Block, J. (1990). Physical and sexual abuse in adolescent girls with borderline personality disorder. *American Journal of Orthopsychiatry*, 60, 55–66.
Wilensky, H. (1959). Rorschach developmental level and social participation of chronic schizophrenics. *Journal of Personality Assessment*, 23, 87–92.
Wilson, A. (1985). Boundary disturbances in borderline and psychotic states. *Journal of Personality Assessment*, 49, 346–355.
Wilson, P. (1988). The psychoanalytic treatment of a boy dominated by omnipotent fantasies. *Journal of Child Psychotherapy*, 14, 13–31.
Winnicott, D. W. (1945). Primitive emotional development. *The International Journal of Psychoanalysis*, 26, 137.
Winnicott, D. W. (1958). Primary maternal preoccupation. In *Collected Papers* (pp. 300–305). New York: Basic. (Original work published 1956.)
Winnicott, D. W. (1960). The theory of the parent–infant relationship. *The International Journal of Psychoanalysis*, 41, 585.
Winnicott, D. W. (1965a). The capacity to be alone. In *The Maturational Processes and the Facilitating Environment* (pp. 29–36). London: Hogarth Press.
Winnicott, D. W. (1965b). Ego distortion in terms of true and false self. In *The Maturational Processes and the Facilitating Environment* (pp. 140–152). London: Hogarth Press.
Winnicott, D. W. (1965c). *The Maturational Processes and the Facilitating Environment: Studies in the Theory of Emotional Development*. London: Karnac Books.

Winnicott, D. W. (1971). *Maturational processes and the facilitating environment.* New York: International Universities Press.

Wolf, D., & Gardner, J. (1979). Style and sequence in early play. In N. Smith & M. Franklin (Eds.), *Symbolic Functioning in Childhood* (pp. 117–138). Hillsdale, NJ: Lawrence Erlbaum.

Wolraich, M. L., Hannah, J. N., & Pinnock, T. Y. (1996). Comparison of diagnostic criteria for attention-deficit hyperactivity disorder in a county-wide sample. *Journal of the American Academy of Child & Adolescent Psychiatry,* 35, 319–324.

Wolraich, M. L., Hannah, J. N., Baumgaertel, A., & Feurer, I. D. (1998). Examination of DSM-IV criteria for attention-deficit/hyperactivity disorder in county-wide sample. *Journal of Developmental and Behavioral Pediatrics,* 19, 162–168.

Zalecki, C. A., & Hinshaw, S. P. (2004). Overt and relational aggression in girls with attention deficit hyperactivity disorder. *Journal of Clinical Child & Adolescent Psychology,* 33, 125–137.

Zelnick, L., & Buchholz, E. (1990). The concept of mental representations in light of recent infant research. *Psychoanalytic Psychology,* 7, 29–58.

INDEX

Note: Tables are indicated by bold page references.

abnormality measures, of CBCL 55
Achenbach, T. 55, 56, 61–63, **62**, 68, 109–111, 115
achromatic determinants (D) score, in ADHD study 79, 88n3
achromatic vs. chromatic cards performance: for Henry ADHD case study 217, **217**; for Terri ADHD case study 212, **213**
actual experience phrase, of Escalona 5
adaptive fantasies: of homeless children, Rorschach assessments of 139–140; M+ scores on homeless children 141, 146–147, 148
ADHD see Attention Deficit Hyperactivity Disorder
adjusted scoring system, RIM, of Wilensky 132, 133
adolescent psychiatric population, MOA scale study 38; Bizarre-Disorganized factor for 41, 42; Bizarre-Retarded factor for 41, 42; case records rating for 39; clinical symptoms in case record of 41–42, 45–47, **46**, 49–50; confabulatory thinking and 43, **48**; contamination response and 43, **48**; discussion 49–51; fabulized combination response in 43, 44, **48**; Fairweather interpersonal communication scale 47, 50; independent clinical assessment 41–43; interpersonal behavior evaluation 42–43, 47; interrater reliability for 40–41; Menninger scales and 42, **46**; MOA scores and Concept of the Object scale correlation 44–45, **45**, 50; MOA scores and other Rorschach variables correlation **47**, 47–51, **48**; Neurosis factors for 41–42; psychological test variables for 43–44; Psychosis factors for 41; results 44–49; RIM and thought disorder estimate in 43, 44, 49; scales for 40–41; Strauss-Harder factor scales and 42, **46**, 50; subjects 40
adults: MOA scale reliability measure for 40; ORSD for 53; in personal interactions and MOA scores of inpatient 39; psychotic behaviors of annihilation anxiety 14; Rorschach MOA object representation scores for re-hospitalization predictors for 176; stranger anxiety and phobia orientation of 14–15
affective experiences, of self 10
aggression: autonomy compared to, in MOA scale 29; content scenes, in Lisa case study 179, 181–185, 190; gender-based differences in 36; hostility and, pathological SAD importance of 118; response, in APT study 67, **70**, 71
altruism 22–23

Ames, L. B. 111, 113–114
Andersen, Hans Christian 139
animal content (A) responses, in RIM 77
Animal Preference Test (APT) study 6; aggressive response in 67, **70**, 71; autonomous response in 67, **70**, 71; CBCL used with 68; discussion in 71–72; gender differences in 67–68; nurturance themes response in 67, **70**, 71; pleasure-beauty response in 67, **70**, 71; procedure for 68; reliability in 69; results in 69–71; SES and 68; subjects in 68; Van Krevelen first use of children for 66
annihilation anxiety 12, 18; adult psychotic behavior and 14; failure to thrive and 14; stranger anxiety compared to 14–15; in Z time 14
Anthony, E. J. 138, 139
antisocial personality disorder 92, 94
anxiety: annihilation 12–15, 19; castration 16–17, 21; existential 18; hierarchy, for children hospitalization trauma 156; separation 15–16, 20, 180; stranger 14–15; types, in object relations domain 10
APT *see* Animal Preference Test
assessments: of Patty 3–5; of symptoms 7; *see also specific assessments*
attachment: disrupted patterns of, for homeless children 140; types of 15–16
Attention Deficit Hyperactivity Disorder (ADHD) 73; CD comorbidity with 75; Combined type 216; diagnosis of 75; executive functions deficits and 76; Gilmore on ego capacities and 76; Inattentive Type 211; internalizing disorders of childhood comorbidity with 75–76; neuropsychological theories on 76; object relations of children with 75–88; ODD comorbidity with 75, 82, 84, **85**, 87; prevalence of 75; previous studies of 77; rating scale, of *DSM-IV* 80, 81; RIM used for assessment of 76–77; social consequences of 76
Attention Deficit Hyperactivity Disorder (ADHD) study: ADHD and comparison groups by gender and ethnicity 79, **79**; ADHD and comparison groups on Rorschach variables 83–84, **84**, 87–88; ADHD and ODD comorbidity 82, 84, **85**, 87; on ADHD child deficits 86; data analysis 82; discussion 85–88;

D scores and 79, 88n3; *DSM-IV* ADHD rating scale and 80, 81; EA score and 78–79, 85, 88n2; future research and 86–88; KSADS measure 81, 82, **83**; Mann-Whitney tests for 82; measures 81; minority ethnic groups sample in 77–78, 85; *M* responses in 78, 82, 85; procedure 81–82; results 82–85; RIM measure and 81–82; Rorschach use of color assessment 78, 86; TONI, WASI, CELF-3, and CELF-4 and 80; *see also* Henry ADHD case study; Terri ADHD case study
Auerbach, John 38
Austen Riggs Center, Rorschach and TAT protocols at 175–176
autonomous response, in APT study 67, **70**, 71
Axis I disorders: narcissistic pathology in children and 90–91, 93; *see also specific disorders*

baby: annihilation anxiety and 12–15; connection attempts by 13; crying and negative reinforcement paradigm 11, 13; failure to thrive 14; separation anxiety of 15–16; social smile of 12; stranger anxiety of 14–15; visual experience of 11; Winnicott on caregiver and 11, 107
Becker, D.: on rage in grieving process 162; Rorschach scoring system 132–133, 136
Bellak, L. 66, 97
Bender-Gestalt Test, for boys SAD study 120
benign versus malevolent object representations 228
Benton Visual Memory Test, in homeless children assessment 143
bereavement, in children 171
Blacky Picture Test, on narcissism 94–95
Blatt, Sid 38; thinking disturbance scale 121–122
Block Design subtest, of WISC-III 150
bonding, gender-based differences in readiness for 36
Bonferroni adjustment for multiple F tests 45–49
borderline personality disorder 29, 39, 40, 92, 94; adolescents, ORI treatment use for 176; narcissistic personality disorder compared to 95
Bowlby, J. 10

boys: aggression of 36; nonclinical population adaptive MOA scores of 34–35, **35**, 36; *see also* Separation Anxiety Disorder of boys

capacity to be alone, Winnicott on 20, 186
caregiver 239; baby crying negative reinforcement paradigm 11, 13; rapprochement and 15; Winnicott on baby and 11, 107
case examples: of MOA scale 225–231; for narcissistic pathology in children 90–91, 93
case records, clinical symptoms found in 41–42, 45–47, **46**, 49–50
case studies, projective methods use in 173
castration anxiety 16–17, 21
CAT *see* Children's Apperception Test
CBCL *see* Child Behavior Checklist
CBI *see* child behavior inventory
CD *see* conduct disorder
CELF-3 *see* Clinical Evaluation of Language Fundamentals – Third Edition
CELF-4 *see* Clinical Evaluation of Language Fundamentals – Fourth Edition
CHAP *see* Child Health and Psychotherapy Programs
character personality disorder 40
Child Behavior Checklist (CBCL), of Achenbach: ORSD study inclusion of 55, 56; preschoolers with imaginary companions study and 109–110, 111, 115; psychopathology measured by 56; social competence and abnormality measures of 55; subscales correlation with ORSD Scores 61, **62**, 62–63
child behavior inventory (CBI) 168
Child Health and Psychotherapy (CHAP) Programs 239
child inpatient population, MOA scale study 129; admitting diagnosis for 131; Becker weighted scoring system 132–133; on cognitive organizing capabilities 136; discussion 135–137; Fisher Exact Tests 132; gender-differences in 137; intergroup comparisons 135, **135**; interrater reliability in 133; IQ in 131; Klopfer method for Rorschach scoring 132–134; Mann-Whitney probability tests 132, 133; method 131–133; object relations scores 130, 133–134, **134**; psychiatric re-hospitalization criteria in 130, 136; results 133–135; Rorschach protocols scoring procedure 132; Rorschach scales in 132–133; thought organization measures 130

children: ADHD comorbidity with internalizing disorders of 75–76; bereavement in 171; depressive symptomatology, from political violence 164; dream material 53–55; emotional relationships to animals by 66–67; Heinicke on psychoanalysis of 176; object relations theory on long-term outcome for 6; political violence trauma of 163–164; resilient, fantasy adaptive use of 139–140; *see also* baby; homeless children; narcissistic pathology in children; preschoolers with imaginary companions; trauma in children

Children's Apperception Test (CAT): analysis of 177; as idiographic indicator of treatment themes 175–192; Lisa Card response and analysis 178–183, 188; protocol of Lisa 173

children undergoing surgery, Rorschach assessment of: discussion 159–160; Freud on 155; Mann-Whitney U test for 158, 159; method 157–158; MOA scale and 156–159, **159**; object-representational disruptions for 159–160; present procedure for 158; results 158–159; on Rorschach productivity 158–159; subjects for 157; WISC used for 157–158

children under political oppression, MOA responses study: ages and time since event/loss of **168**; committed psychology on 165–166; discussion 170–172; forcibly disappeared persons and 166, 167, 170, 171; Honduras and COADEH collaboration in 161–162; loss of parents and 162, 165, 170; measures for 168–169; methods 166–169; political assassinations and 166, 167, 170, 171; procedure for 168; PTSRC and CBI use in 168–169; results in 169–170; RIM used in 168; Rorschach MOA scale 169, **169**, 170; subjects in 166–167

City College of New York 79, 223, 237, 240
Clinical Evaluation of Language Fundamentals – Fourth Edition (CELF-4) 80

Clinical Evaluation of Language
   Fundamentals – Third Edition
   (CELF-3) 80
clinicians: dream material use by 53;
   intuitive capacities of 7; transference and
   184–185, 187, 191
COFADEH *see* Committee of Family
   Members of the Detained and
   Disappeared of Honduras
cognitive growth, of child 16
Cohen, Jonathan 193
Cohler, Bert 193
committed psychology, for children under
   political oppression 165–166
Committee of Family Members of the
   Detained and Disappeared of Honduras
   (COFADEH) 161–162, 166, 167, 168
Comprehensive System, of Exner 77
Concept of Dream Questionnaire, of
   Foulkes 57
Concept of the Object scale, MOA scale
   relations with 38, 44–45, **45**, 50
conduct disorder (CD), ADHD
   comorbidity with 75
confabulation responses 122
confabulatory thinking, in adolescent
   psychiatric population study 43, **48**
confounding variable of treatment, in
   ORSD study 64–65
consolidation of ego identity, of
   Kernberg 54
construct validity: of MOA-TAT 237;
   of RIM 6
contamination response, in adolescent
   psychiatric population study 43, **48**
Cramer, P. 236
creative competence 139

D *see* achromatic determinants score
defense mechanism scale, of Cramer 236
depression 40, 164
*Diagnostic and Statistical Manual of Mental
   Disorders, 3rd edition (DSM-III)*: MOA
   scores and psychopathology of 39;
   narcissistic personality disorder in 94; in
   ORSD study 56; on SAD 117, 120
*Diagnostic and Statistical Manual of Mental
   Disorders, 4th edition (DSM-IV)*: ADHD
   rating scale of 80, 81; on narcissistic
   pathology in children 90, 91–92, 96
Donahue, Paul 138, 144, 149
dreams: of children 53–55; human psyche
   and 53; material, clinicians use of 53; as
mental operation and organization 54;
   M scores and 141; recalled 55; samples,
   in sleep laboratory 64
*DSM-III see Diagnostic and Statistical Manual
   of Mental Disorders, 3rd edition*
*DSM-IV see Diagnostic and Statistical
   Manual of Mental Disorders, 4th edition*
dynamic context, of symptoms 7–8
dysphoric affect tone, in Lisa case study
   186, 187, 188, 190

EA *see* Experience Actual scores
Early Memories Test, on narcissistic
   personality disorder 95
Edelbrock, C. 109
effectance motivation, of White 21
ego capacities, ADHD and 76
ego identity, Kernberg's stages of 54
ego splitting 54
Eiges, Katherine 235–236
empathy 22–23
Erikson, E. H. 17
Escalona, S. 5
executive functions, ADHD deficits of 76
existential anxieties 18
Exner, J. E. 77
experience, of individual: human adaptation
   link to 6–7; from inside focus 7
Experience Actual (EA) scores 77; in
   ADHD study 78–79, 85, 88n2
external symptoms 7
extreme dependence, Winnicott, D. W.
   on 190

F+ *see* high form quality
fabulized combination response, in
   adolescent psychiatric population study
   43, 44, **48**
failure to thrive babies 14
Fairweather, G. W. 47, 50
fantasy: adaptive use of by resilient children
   139–140; Anthony on pseudo-resilience
   and 139; information organization
   and interpretation from 139–140;
   Santostefano on 139; Singer on 139;
   traumatic experiences of children
   and 139
fear of loss: of love 17, 22; of
   meaning 18, 22
Figure Drawings, for boys SAD study 120
Fisher Exact Test: in child inpatient
   population study 132; in ORSD study
   59, 59–60

Index

forcibly disappeared persons 166, 167, 170, 171
Foulkes, D. 54; Concept of Dream Questionnaire of 57; on dreams longitudinal research design 64
Freud, Anna 155
Friedman, H. 132, 133
Fruit Distraction Test, in homeless children assessment 143, 144–145, **145**, 147

gender and ethnicity, ADHD and comparison groups by 79, **79**
gender-based differences: in adaptive MOA scores 36; in aggression 36; in APT 67–68; in bonding readiness 36; in child inpatient population study 137; in interpersonal relatedness 36; in MOA scale for nonclinical population 32, 33, 34–35, **35**
gender identity disorder of childhood 120
Gilmore, K. 76
girls: nonclinical population adaptive MOA scores of 34–35, **35**, 36; ORSD study on 55–65
Gluckman, E. 52
Goddard, Rodger 117, 121
going towards/fear dichotomy, of Bowlby 10
good enough phrase, of Winnicott 5, 12, 20, 185

H *see* human content responses
hate addiction 163
Henry ADHD case study 216, 221–222; achromatic vs. chromatic cards performance 217, **217**; entire record **217**; RIM protocol **218–220**
heuristic power of object representations, individuality and 6
high form quality (F+), of RIM 143–144, **145**, **146**, 146–147
histrionic personality disorder 94
homeless children: impacts for 140, 149; Molnar on 140; variables for success of 138
homeless children, Rorschach assessments of 138; adaptive fantasies and 139–140; Benton Visual Memory Test used in 143; dependent variables 143–144; discussion 146–148; disrupted attachment patterns and 140; fantasy definition and 141; fantasy measurement by *M* score 140–141; F+ responses and 143–144,

145, **146**, 146–147; Fruit Distraction Test used in 143, 144–145, **145**, 147; hypotheses for 141–142; independent variables for 142–143; IQ and 143; on levels of functioning 141–142; Marble Board Test used in 143; method of 142–144; MOA scale and 144, 145, 146–147; *M* score and 143, 147–148; *M*+ scores on adaptive fantasy 141, 146–147, 148; procedure for 142; Raven's Colored Progressive Matrices and 143, 147; reliability in 144; results 144–146; subjects for 142; Teacher's Rating Scale: self-perception profile in 146, 148
homeless children study: Block Design subtest, of WISC-III on 150; conclusion 153–154; discussion and clinical implications 150–151; extended homelessness and 151–152; on extended shelter stays impact 149; level of aspiration in 150, 152–154; method 150; Raven's Colored Progressive Matrices used for 150; results 150; short-term homelessness and 152–153; subjects in 150; TAT stories used in 151–153
Honduras, political upheaval in: COFADEH study collaboration 161–162, 166, 167, 168; human rights situation in 164–165; U.S. counterinsurgency dollars in 165; U.S. military presence in 164
hospitalization, trauma to children from 155–156
human adaptation 6–7
human content (H) responses, in RIM 77
human movement (M) responses, in RIM 29, 50, 73, 77; ADHD children and 78, 82, 85; children imaginary companions and 115–116, 141; dreams and 141; for homeless children 140–141, 143, 147–148; TAT on creative story telling and 141
human rights situation, in Honduras 164–165

imaginary companions 188; case reports and vignettes approach on 104; children's features, for 106; as defensive phenomenon with functions 106; demographic data approach on 104; hypotheses for 107–108; loneliness and 105; maladaptive fantasy use for 105; Svendsen on 105; as symbolic play

aspect 106–107; *see also* preschoolers with imaginary companions
individuality: development 3; heuristic power of object representations and 6
infant *see* baby
infantile borderline patients 39
initiative versus guilt, of Erikson 17
inside focus, of experience 7
intellectual development, Piaget on 139
intelligence quotient (IQ): for boys SAD study 120–121; in child inpatient population study 131; homeless children and 143; MOA scores relationship with 33, 34, 35, **35**, 38; nonclinical population use, age comparison and 34, 35–36; in preschoolers with imaginary companions study 110, 111; WISC-R measurement of 32
internalization transition, separation anxiety and 20
internalizing symptoms 7
interpersonal communication scale, of Fairweather 47, 50
interpersonal interactions: cognitive structure and thematic content of 38; gender-based differences in 36; MOA scale on quality of 28; projective assessment techniques on 38
interrater reliability: for adolescent psychiatric population study 40–41; in child inpatient population study 133; for MOA scale 28; in nonclinical population use study 33; in ORSD study 58
INTERSECT Lab: caregiver and 239; children's self-report measures 239; on clinical care: access to, utilization, and long-term outcomes 238–239; on daily stressors over life course 238; therapist and 239–240; on well-being among marginalized urban populations 238
intuitive capacities, of clinicians 7
IQ *see* intelligence quotient

Jim RIM protocol 173, 193–197, **195–198**; content analysis of 200–202; during first treatment 207–208; MOA scale in 204, **205**, 206–207; quantitative analysis in 198–200; Rorschach sequence summary and treatment implications 203–204; Rorschach summary scores **199**; second treatment 208–210; summary of 207; WISC, TAT and 194

Kavanagh, G. 39
Kernberg, O. F.: ego identity stages of 54; on severely disturbed individuals 28
Klopfer, B. 110, 111, 120, 132–134, 194
Kohut, H. 28
Krohn, Alan 52, 53–54
KSADS *see* Schedule for Affective Disorders and Schizophrenia for School Aged Children

Latina Values Scale (LVS) 237
Laurendeau-Pinard Concept of Dream Questionnaire, in ORSD study 56, 57, 58, **59**, 59–60, 63
Levitt, E. 111, 113
Lisa case study: aggressive content scenes 179, 181–185, 190; capacity to be alone for 186; CAT at initial consultation process 177; CAT Card responses and analysis 178–183, 188; CAT summary and treatment implications 184–185; conclusion 191–193; depression and 186, 188; dysphoric affect tone 186, 187, 188, 190; extreme dependence 190; fantasies of replenishment 184; father sexual abuse 191; fearful and fearless, risky and self-protective behaviors 184; good enough self 189; loss of self 186; narratives process of 184; prominent oral hunger and neediness 184, 187, 188, 189, 190, 191; sadomasochism and 185, 186, 187, 189, 191; separation anxiety 184; symptomatology and early history 185–186; transference and 184–185, 187, 191; treatment at Time 1 185–188; treatment at Time 2 188–191
LVS *see* Latina Values Scale

M *see* human movement responses
MAD *see* Mother–Adult Daughter Questionnaire
maladaptive fantasy, imaginary companions use for 105
malevolence 225, 226
Mann-Whitney U Test 34; in ADHD study 82; boys SAD study and 121; on child inpatient population study 132, 133; in children undergoing surgery assessment 158, 159
Marble Board Test, in homeless children assessment 143
marginalized urban populations, INTERSECT Lab on 238

Martinez, Juliana 236–237
Mayman, Marty 19, 52, 194; on projective tests reparative process 27, 223–224
meaning-making process 8
Meehan, K. 211
Menninger Psychotherapy Project: interpersonal behavior scales and 42, 46; Kavanagh on 39; MOA scored and Rorschach protocols pre- and post-treatment 39; Object Representation Scale use 176
Meyer, Jodie 104
Minnesota MultiPhasic Inventory (MMPI) 6
Minnesota Scale of Paternal Occupation 110
minority ethnic groups, in ADHD study 77–78, 85
mirroring experience 226
MMPI see Minnesota MultiPhasic Inventory
MOA see Mutuality of Autonomy scale
MOA-TAT see Mutuality of Autonomy-Thematic Apperception Test
Molnar, J. M. 140
Mother–Adult Daughter Questionnaire (MAD) 237
"Motivation Reconsidered: the Concept of Competence" (White) 21
$M+$ scores, on homeless children adaptive fantasy 141, 146–147, 148
multivariate analysis of variance, of ORSD study **60**, 60–61
Munczek, Debra 161
Mutuality of Autonomy (MOA) scale 23, 176, 177, 224; aggression compared to autonomy in 29; case examples 225–231; on children undergoing surgery 156–159, **159**; clinical records ratings use with 39; Concept of the Object scale relations with 38, 44–45, **45**, 50; developmental/psychodynamic theory and 29, 31; diagnosis, psychotherapy and 225–231; in homeless children assessment 144, 145, 146–147; on interpersonal relatedness quality 28; interrater reliability for 28; Jim RIM protocol and 204, **205**, 206–207; Menninger Psychotherapy Project and 39; as ordinal index of adaptive and maladaptive object representations 31; reliability measure for adults, adolescents, and children 40; RIM modifications and 235; RIM toxic control and destruction of helpless victim 28; Rorschach testing and object-representations 224; scale points described 28; scores, in boys SAD study 122–123, **123**, **124**; on self–other representation and construction 27, 28, 38; studies distributions **30**; see also specific studies
Mutuality of Autonomy-Thematic Apperception Test (MOA-TAT): construct validity and reliability of 237; Eiges on 235–236; Martinez on 236–237; research on 235; Thom on 236

narcissism: assessment and modes of relating of 94–96; Blacky Picture Test on 94–95; checklists as assessment tools for 94–95; self-report questionnaires as assessment tools for 94–95; sentence completion test and RIM responses for 95
Narcissism-Projective (NP): use of in narcissistic personality disorders studies 95
narcissistic pathology in children: Axis I disorders and 90–91, 93; case example for 90–91, 93; characteristic object relationships in 92–94; *DSM-IV* and 90, 91–92, 96; features of 90, 91, 96; sense of self 92–94
narcissistic pathology in children and RIM study: conclusion 102–103; discussion 100–102; on identity instability 102; limitations in 102–103; materials for 97–98; method 96–99; procedure for 98–99; on relationships 101–102; reliability in 98, 99; results 99–100; SCORS use in 89, 96, 97–102; SES and 96; subjects in 96; TAT use in 89, 97–102, **99**
narcissistic personality disorder: borderline personality disorder compared to 95; in *DSM-III* 94; Early Memories Test on 95; empirical research on 94; NP studies use on 95; Rorschach for 95; TAT studies use on 95
narrative: converted from symptomatology 7, 8; symptoms meaning explained in 8
National Institute on Deafness and Other Communication Disorders (NIDCD) 79
negative object relations domain 7–12; annihilation anxiety and 12–15, 19; castration anxiety and 16–17; existential

anxieties 18; fear of loss of love and 17; fear of loss of meaning and 18; separation anxiety and 15–16; stranger anxiety and 14–15
neuropsychological theories, on ADHD 76
Neurosis factors, for adolescent psychiatric population 41–42
NIDCD *see* National Institute on Deafness and Other Communication Disorders
nomothetic assessment of inpatient progress and outcome 175–176
nonclinical population use, MOA scale study: age and IQ comparison 34, 35–36; benign parallel interaction 36; discussion 35–37; gender-based differences in 32, 33, 34–35, **35**; girls and boys adaptive MOA scores 34–35, **35**, 36; interrater reliability in 33; malevolent and adaptive scores balanced for 34, 36; method 32–33; MOA-*M* score for 33; results 33–35; RIM used in 33, **35**; subjects in 32–33; WISC-R used in 32, 33
nurturance themes response, in APT study 67, **70**, 71

object relations: of ADHD children 75–88; domain 8, 10; narcissistic pathology in children's characteristics 92–94; negative domain 7–18; positive domain 18–23; scores, in child inpatient population study 130, 133–134, **134**; studies on psychological conditions and 98
object relations assessment: of child populations under extreme duress 127; of preschoolers with imaginary companions 104–116, **112**, **114**; of SAD of boys 117–125, **122**, **123**, **124**
object-relations theory of personality: on conception of self–other in interactions 176, 193–194; early developmental failures and 97; long-term outcome and children 6; psychoanalysis focus on 38, 193–194; psychological testing translation of 223
Object Representation Inventory (ORI), borderline adolescents treatments and 176
object representations 159–160; benign versus malevolent 228; Hatcher and Krohn definition of 224; individuality and heuristic power of 6; pathology, of boys SAD study 125; Rorschach MOA scores, of re-hospitalization predictors for adults 176
object representations assessment measures 27–31; for boys SAD study 125; for narcissistic personality disorder 95
Object Representation Scale for Dreams (ORSD) study: CBCL inclusion in 55, 56; children's dream material use of 55; coding and interrater reliability in 58; confounding variable of treatment in 64–65; differentiation for clinical and nonclinical groups 60–61; differentiation for healthy and disturbed children 55; discussion 61–63; Fisher's Exact Test in **59**, 59–60; Laurendeau-Pinard Concept of Dream Questionnaire and 56, 57, 58, **59**, 59–60, 63; limitations of 64–65; measures of 56–57; multivariate analysis of variance of **60**, 60–61; ORSD Scores and CBCL subscales correlations in 61, **62**, 62–63; participants in 55–56; procedure 57–58; results of 59–60; scale description 53–54; void pathological scale point of 52–53; WISC-R used in 56–57
obsessive paranoid borderline patients 39
oppositional defiant disorder (ODD): ADHD comorbidity with 75, 82, 84, **85**, 87
ORI *see* Object Representation Inventory
ORSD *see* Object Representation Scale for Dreams

pathological SAD 117; aggression and hostility importance in 118; faulty character development and 119; self-cohesion disruptions 119
patient history, pervasive effects of symptoms linked to 9
Patty (client): assessment 3–5; neurological/developmental delay of 3
Peabody Picture Vocabulary Test – Revised (PPVT–R) 109, 110, 111
personality development: baby visual experience and 11; Winnicott on baby and caregiver 11, 107
personality disorders symptomatology 92; *see also specific disorders*
personality domains 7, 9
personality organizational chart 8, 9
pervasive effects, of symptoms 9
phobia orientation of adults, stranger anxiety and 14–15

Piaget, J. 139
pleasure-beauty response, in APT study 67, **70**, 71
pleasure principle, reality principle conflict with 17
political assassinations 166, 167, 170, 171
political violence: children's depressive symptomatology from 164; children's development regression and 164; continued persecution fear and 162, 166; effects on survivors 162–163; family member disappearance, impact from 163; grieving process and 162; hate addiction and 163; in Honduras 161–162; rage as intense emotion of 162–163; social denial of 162; stigmatization and social isolation from 162–163; temporal fragmentation from 163, 171–172; trauma in children 163–164
positive object relations domain: altruism in 22–23; competence and 21–22; curiosity and 21; empathy and 22–23; reflective functioning 22–23; trust deep experience 18–19
post-traumatic stress disorder (PTSD) 164; in children under political oppression study 171
post-traumatic stress reaction checklist (PTSRC), use of in children under political oppression study 168–169
PPVT–R *see* Peabody Picture Vocabulary Test – Revised
preschool children: castration anxiety of 16–17; guilt feelings of 17; reality and pleasure principle conflicts of 17
preschoolers with imaginary companions, object relations study 104–107; CBCL and 109–110, 111, 115; discussion 115–116; IQ scores and 110, 111; method 108–111; Minnesota Scale of Paternal Occupation on 110; MOA scale scores and 114, **114**; M responses and 115–116, 141; normative data comparison for 110–111, 115–116; PPVT–R for 109, 110, 111, 115; procedure for 109; results 111–114; Rorschach Test for 110, 111, **112**, 113–115; sample 108–109; subject recruitment for 109
projective assessment conceptual framework: in case studies 173; negative object relations domains 7–18; positive object relations domain 18–23

projective testing: on interactions, internalizations and affects 176; nomothetic assessment of inpatient progress and outcome 175–176; on object-relations theory self–other conceptions 176, 193–194; of ORI 176, 177; in psychiatric hospitals 175; reparative process in 27; symptoms pervasive effects and 9
pseudo-resilience, Anthony on fantasy and 139
psychiatric hospitals, projective testing in 175
psychoanalysis: of children, Heinicke on 176; object-relations theory focus of 38, 193–194
psychodynamic theory, psychological test data linked with 175
Psychological Center 237, 239
psychological development, self–other interactions and 38
psychological testing: in boys SAD study 120–121; data, psychodynamic theory linked with 175; object-relations theory of personality translation 223; shortly after hospital admission 175; variables, for adolescent psychiatric population study 43–44
psychopathology 3; CBCL measure of 56; MOA scale and *DSM-III* criteria 39; Rorschach and severe 49
Psychosis factors, for adolescent psychiatric population 41
psychotherapy, MOA scale and 225–231
psychotic behaviors 40; of adults, annihilation anxiety and 14
PTSD *see* post-traumatic stress disorder
PTSRC *see* post-traumatic stress reaction checklist

rage: in grieving process, Becker on 162; as political violence intense emotion 162–163; regarding unmet needs 181–182
rapprochement 15
Raven's Colored Progressive Matrices 143, 147, 150
reality principle, pleasure principle conflict with 17
recalled dreams 55
reflective functioning 22–23
reliability: of APT 69; in homeless children Rorschach assessment 144; measure

for adults, adolescents, and children MOA scale 40; of MOA-TAT 237; in narcissistic pathology in children study 98, 99; see also interrater reliability
reparative process, in projective testing 27
research: ADHD study future 86–88; empirical, on narcissistic personality disorder 94; Foulkes on dreams longitudinal design 64; on MOA-TAT 235; Rorschach task linking clinical work with children 235–240
resilient children 139–140
RIM see Rorschach Inkblot Method
Rojas, Evelyn Baez 66
Rorschach Inkblot Method (RIM) 23, 28, 33, **35**, 67, 73, 95, 214–215, 235; A and H responses in 77; ADHD assessment by 76–77; ADHD study and 81–82; ADHD use of color assessment 78, 86; at Austen Riggs Center 175–176; Becker scoring system 132–133, 136; benign versus malevolent object-representations in 228; for boys SAD study 120; Friedman scoring system 132, 133; Klopfer scoring method of 110, 111, 120, 132–134, 143, 194; meaningful construct validity of 6; for preschoolers with imaginary companions study 110, 111, **112**, 113–115; protocol, in Henry ADHD case study **218–220**; protocol, of Jim 173, 193–210, **195–198**; reparative process and 27; thought disorder estimate, in adolescent psychiatric population study 43, 44, 49; use of in children under political oppression study 168; variables, ADHD and comparison groups on 83–84, **84**, 87–88; Wilensky adjusted scoring system 132, 133; see also human movement responses; narcissistic pathology in children and RIM study; specific assessments
Rudenstine, Sasha 237–239
Ryan, R. 52

SAD see Separation Anxiety Disorder
sadomasochism, Lisa case study and 185, 186, 187, 189, 191
Santostefano, S. 139
Schedule for Affective Disorders and Schizophrenia for School Aged Children (KSADS) 81, 82, **83**
school phobia, SAD and 117, 118

SCORS see Social Cognition and Object Relations Scale
Self-Affect-Other, internalization of 10
self-other representation and construction: children's studies on 53; MOA scale scores on 27, 28, 38; in object-relations theory 176, 193–194; psychological development and 38; SAD and 119
self-perception profile, in homeless children assessment 146
sentence completion test, with RIM responses for narcissism 95
separation anxiety 180; of baby 15–16; cognitive growth and 15–16; internalization transition and 20; trust mitigation of 20
Separation Anxiety Disorder (SAD) 29; *DSM-III* on 117, 120; MOA on **30**; pathological 117–119; school phobia and 117, 118; self–other representation, construction and 119
Separation Anxiety Disorder (SAD) of boys, object relations study 117–119; discussion 123–125; *DSM-III* diagnosis and 120; IQ testing for 120–121; Mann-Whitney U Test and 121; methods 120–122; MOA scale scores in 122–123, **123**, **124**; object representations pathology of 125; psychological testing 120–121; results 122–123; Rorschach scoring procedure 121; thought disorder rating scale 121–122; thought disorder responses in 122, **122**, **123**, 124–125; WISC-R, Figure Drawings, Bender-Gestalt Test, and TAT, Rorschach testing for 120
separation-individuation theory 176
SES see socioeconomic status
Singer, J. L. 139
Social Cognition and Object Relations Scale (SCORS): subscales of 97, 98–99; use of in narcissistic pathology in children study 89, 96, 97–102
social competence measure, of CBCL 55
social consequences, of ADHD 76
social denial, of political violence 162
social smile, of baby 12
socioeconomic status (SES): APT and 68; narcissistic pathology in children study and 96
stigmatization and social isolation, from political violence 162–163
stranger anxiety 14–15, 19
Strauss-Harder factor scales 42, **46**, 47

Svendsen, M. 105
symbolic play aspect, imaginary companions as 106–107
symptomatology: children's depressive, from political violence 164; Lisa case study and 185–186; narrative converted from 7, 8; of personality disorders 92
symptoms: assessment of 7; clinical, in case records 41–42, 45–47, **46**, 49–50; dynamic context of 7; external and internalizing 7; human adaptation link to 7; narrative explanation of, in meaning-making process 8; pervasive effects of 9

TAT *see* Thematic Apperception Test
Teacher's Rating Scale: self-perception profile 146, 148
temporal fragmentation, from political violence 163, 171–172
Terri ADHD case study 211; achromatic vs. chromatic cards performance 212, **213**; entire record for **212**; Rorschach **214–215**
Test of Nonverbal Intelligence (TONI) 80
Thematic Apperception Test (TAT) 6, 23, 67; at Austen Riggs Center 175–176; for boys SAD study 120; in Jim RIM protocol assessment 194; M responses, creative story telling and 141; in narcissistic pathology study 89, 97–102, **99**; stories used, in homeless children study 151–153; use of in narcissistic personality disorders studies 95
therapist, INTERSECT Lab and 239–240
Thom, Lily 236
thought disorder: estimate, in adolescent psychiatric population 43, 44, 49; rating scale, in boys SAD study 121–122; responses, in boys SAD study 122, **122**, **123**, 124–125
thought organization measures, in child inpatient population study 130
transference, clinicians and 184–185, 187, 191
trauma in children: defense mechanisms personalities integration 163; developmental regression and 164; fantasy and 139; from hospitalization 155–156; political violence and 163–164; PTSD and 164

trust: deep experience of 18–19; separation anxiety mitigated by 20
Truumaa, A. 111, 113

United States (U.S.): counterinsurgency dollars in Honduras 165; Honduras military presence by 164
Urist, Jeffrey 31; MOA scale of 27, 36, 40, 49, 52, 130, 133

Van Krevelen, D. A. 66
Veterans Administration hospitals, projective testing in 175
visual experience, of baby 11
void pathological scale point, of ORSD study 52–53

Wechsler Abbreviated Scale of Intelligence (WASI) 80
Wechsler Intelligence Scale for Children (WISC): in Jim RIM protocol assessment 194; use of in children undergoing surgery assessment 157–158
Wechsler Intelligence Scale for Children-III (WISC-III), Block Design subtest of 150
Wechsler Intelligence Scale for Children – Revised (WISC-R) 131; for boys SAD study 120; use of in nonclinical population study 32, 33; use of in ORSD study 56–57
Weise, Karen 89
Westen, Drew 89, 96, 97–103
White, Robert W. 21; effectance motivation of 21
Wilensky, H. 132, 133
Winnicott, D. W.: on baby and caregiver unit 11, 107; on capacity to be alone 20, 186; on climax in ego-relatedness 187; on extreme dependence 190; good enough phrase of 5, 12, 20, 185; on X plus Y plus Z time 13–14, 18–19
WISC *see* Wechsler Intelligence Scale for Children
WISC-III *see* Wechsler Intelligence Scale for Children-III
WISC-R *see* Wechsler Intelligence Scale for Children – Revised

X plus Y plus Z time, of Winnicott 13–14, 18–19

Taylor & Francis eBooks

Helping you to choose the right eBooks for your Library

Add Routledge titles to your library's digital collection today. Taylor and Francis ebooks contains over 50,000 titles in the Humanities, Social Sciences, Behavioural Sciences, Built Environment and Law.

Choose from a range of subject packages or create your own!

Benefits for you
- Free MARC records
- COUNTER-compliant usage statistics
- Flexible purchase and pricing options
- All titles DRM-free.

REQUEST YOUR FREE INSTITUTIONAL TRIAL TODAY

Free Trials Available
We offer free trials to qualifying academic, corporate and government customers.

Benefits for your user
- Off-site, anytime access via Athens or referring URL
- Print or copy pages or chapters
- Full content search
- Bookmark, highlight and annotate text
- Access to thousands of pages of quality research at the click of a button.

eCollections – Choose from over 30 subject eCollections, including:

Archaeology	Language Learning
Architecture	Law
Asian Studies	Literature
Business & Management	Media & Communication
Classical Studies	Middle East Studies
Construction	Music
Creative & Media Arts	Philosophy
Criminology & Criminal Justice	Planning
Economics	Politics
Education	Psychology & Mental Health
Energy	Religion
Engineering	Security
English Language & Linguistics	Social Work
Environment & Sustainability	Sociology
Geography	Sport
Health Studies	Theatre & Performance
History	Tourism, Hospitality & Events

For more information, pricing enquiries or to order a free trial, please contact your local sales team:
www.tandfebooks.com/page/sales

The home of Routledge books

www.tandfebooks.com